Kartell- und Regulierungsrecht

herausgegeben von

Prof. Dr. Torsten Körber, LL.M. (Berkeley)
Prof. Dr. iur. Dr. rer. pol. Dres. h.c. Franz Jürgen Säcker
Prof. Dr. Matthias Schmidt-Preuß

Band 37

Torsten Körber

Regulierte Eisenbahnentgelte und Kartellrecht

Überlegungen zum Verhältnis von Kartell- und Regulierungsrecht nach Maßgabe der Urteile „CTL Logistics" (EuGH) und „Trassenentgelte" (BGH)

 Nomos

Onlineversion
Nomos eLibrary

Die Deutsche Nationalbibliothek verzeichnet diese Publikation in
der Deutschen Nationalbibliografie; detaillierte bibliografische
Daten sind im Internet über http://dnb.d-nb.de abrufbar.

ISBN 978-3-8487-6933-9 (Print)
ISBN 978-3-7489-1021-3 (ePDF)

1. Auflage 2020
© Nomos Verlagsgesellschaft, Baden-Baden 2020. Gedruckt in Deutschland. Alle Rechte,
auch die des Nachdrucks von Auszügen, der fotomechanischen Wiedergabe und der
Übersetzung, vorbehalten. Gedruckt auf alterungsbeständigem Papier.

Vorwort

Das Verhältnis der regulierungsbehördlichen zur zivilgerichtlichen Entgeltkontrolle hat Wissenschaft und Praxis schon sehr häufig beschäftigt. Es war und ist Gegenstand zahlreicher laufender Gerichtsverfahren. Diese Problematik stellt sich nicht nur im Verkehrssektor, sondern auch in anderen regulierten Wirtschaftsbereichen wie Telekommunikation und Energie. Lange Zeit galt es als ausgemacht, dass die Zivilgerichte über die Kompetenz verfügen, auch regulierte Entgelte einer Billigkeitskontrolle nach § 315 Abs. 3 BGB sowie einer Kontrolle am Maßstab des deutschen und europäischen Kartellrechts zu unterziehen. Das änderte sich jedenfalls für den Bereich des Eisenbahnverkehrs mit dem Urteil *CTL Logistics* vom 9. November 2017, in welchem der EuGH klarstellte, dass eine zivilgerichtliche Billigkeitskontrolle in Bezug auf Entgelte, welche dem Eisenbahnregulierungsrecht unterliegen, nicht unionsrechtskonform sei, weil sie das in der Regulierungsrichtlinie 2001/14/EG vorgesehene System der behördlichen Entgeltkontrolle störe und die (unbeschadet verwaltungsgerichtlicher Nachprüfung) alleinige Prüfkompetenz der BNetzA unterlaufe.

Schon die Vorgeschichte des Urteils unterstreicht, wie kontrovers die behandelten Fragen sind: Der BGH war viele Jahre lang davon ausgegangen, dass eine zivilgerichtliche Entgeltkontrolle (nach § 315 BGB wie nach Kartellrecht) „ohne vernünftigen Zweifel" mit dem EU-Regulierungsrecht vereinbar sei und hatte daher auch eine Vorlage an den EuGH unter Berufung auf die *acte clair*-Doktrin abgelehnt. Das BVerfG hatte dies 2015 anders gesehen und ein Vorabentscheidungsersuchen des BGH an den EuGH erzwungen, das 2016 erfolgt ist. Noch bevor der EuGH darüber entscheiden konnte, hatte der EuGH dann 2017 auf eine Vorlage des LG Berlin hin im Urteil *CTL Logistics* judiziert und damit zugleich die Auffassung des BGH verworfen. Der EuGH ist dabei nicht den Schlussanträgen des Generalanwalts gefolgt, der (wie der BGH) keinen Konflikt der zivilgerichtlichen Billigkeitskontrolle mit dem Richtlinienrecht gesehen hatte.

Auch nach dem *CTL Logistics*-Urteil sind viele Fragen offen. Die Vorlagefragen des LG Berlin hatten sich allein auf die zivilgerichtliche Billigkeitskontrolle nach dem BGB bezogen. Der EuGH hat daher nicht explizit zum Verhältnis von Regulierungsrecht und Kartellrecht judiziert. Daraus ergibt sich die Frage, ob eine Kontrolle von regulierungsbehördlich gebilligten bzw. genehmigten Eisenbahnentgelten durch die Zivilgerichte weiterhin möglich bleibt oder ob sich aus dem *CTL Logistics*-Urteil auch insoweit eine Sperrwirkung der Richtlinien und ein Vorrang der regulierungsbehördlichen Kontrolle ableiten lässt. Mehrere Landgerichte und das OLG Dresden hatten im zweiten Sinne judiziert und Klagen auf der Basis kartellrechtlicher Verbotsnormen und Anspruchsgrundlagen verworfen. Der BGH ist dem am 29. Oktober 2019 im Urteil *Trassenentgelte* entgegengetreten und hat die Auffassung geäußert, dass jedenfalls eine zivilgerichtliche Kontrolle am Maßstab des Art. 102 AEUV in Verbindung mit § 812 BGB oder § 33 GWB sogar dann „ohne vernünftigen Zweifel" möglich und zum Schutz der Rechte der Entgeltadressaten geboten sei, wenn dadurch das Funktionieren des Eisenbahnregulierungsrechts beeinträchtigt werde. Art. 102 AEUV gehe nämlich als Norm des EU-Primärrechts den EU-Eisenbahnrichtlinien vor.

Vor diesem Hintergrund hat die DB Netz AG ein Gutachten in Auftrag gegeben, um diese Fragen zu klären. Der vorliegende Band gibt dieses Gutachten in ungekürzter Fassung wieder. Das Gutachten wurde im Mai 2020 vorgelegt. Es bezieht sich allein auf das Verhältnis von Eisenbahnregulierungsrecht und Kartellrecht, insbesondere im Spannungsfeld der EuGH-Entscheidungen *CTL Logistics*, *Deutsche Telekom* und *Crehan/Courage*. Die nicht minder spannende Frage, ob sich die vom EuGH in *CTL Logistics* entwickelten Grundsätze auch auf andere regulierte Sektoren wie Telekommunikation und Energie übertragen lassen, war nicht Gegenstand des Untersuchungsauftrags und muss daher anderen Studien vorbehalten bleiben.

Torsten Körber, Köln im Juni 2020

Inhaltsverzeichnis

A. Ausgangspunkt

I. Problemstellung und Prüffragen der DB Netz AG vom 17.12.2019

Die DB Netz AG erhebt für die Nutzung ihrer Schienenwege ein Trassenentgelt. Dieses unterlag bereits nach dem Allgemeinen Eisenbahngesetz (AEG) alter Fassung und auch nach dem Eisenbahnregulierungsgesetz (ERegG) einem speziellen Regulierungsverfahren. Gegen die Billigung nach altem Recht bzw. die Genehmigung nach neuem Recht konnten und können Infrastrukturnutzer nach den spezialgesetzlichen Vorschriften Rechtsschutz vor der Regulierungsbehörde und anschließend vor den Verwaltungsgerichten in Anspruch nehmen.

Ungeachtet dessen haben in der Vergangenheit zahlreiche Infrastrukturnutzer einzelne Entgelte vor den Zivilgerichten angegriffen, und zwar ohne rechtskräftige Entscheidung durch die Regulierungsbehörde. Rechtlicher Anknüpfungspunkt war dabei zunächst – v.a. im Hinblick auf die Beweislastverteilung – die „Billigkeitskontrolle" nach § 315 BGB, aber auch das Kartellrecht. Nach zahlreichen Entscheidungen der Instanzgerichte, des Bundesgerichtshofs (BGH) und des Bundesverfassungsgerichts (BVerfG) hatte der Europäische Gerichtshof (EuGH) mit Urteil vom 09. 11. 2017 in der Rechtssache C-489/15 *CTL Logistics* entschieden, dass eine Prüfung regulierungsbehördlich nicht rechtskräftig widersprochener Entgelte nach einer nationalen Vorschrift wie § 315 BGB den Vorgaben der Richtlinie 2001/14/EG widerspricht. Im Einzelnen führte der EuGH aus, dass

- die Anwendung des Billigkeitsgrundsatzes durch die deutschen Gerichte im Widerspruch zu den in der Richtlinie 2001/14 festgelegten Grundsätzen stehe, insbesondere zum Grundsatz der Gleichbehandlung der Eisenbahnverkehrsunternehmen (Rn. 70 ff.)
- es Sache der Geschäftsführung des Infrastrukturbetreibers sei, die jeweiligen Entgelte zu bestimmen (Rn. 77 ff.)
- die materiellen Beurteilungskriterien auf der Grundlage von § 315 BGB entweder mit den in der Richtlinie 2001/14 vorgesehenen Beurteilungskriterien unvereinbar seien oder dass die Zivilgerichte andernfalls selbst die Vorschriften des Eisenbahnregulierungsrechts anwenden müssten; dies würde in die ausschließliche Zuständigkeit der Regulierungsstelle eingreifen (Rn. 84 ff.)

- unterschiedliche Einzelfallentscheidungen der Zivilgerichte ein diskriminierungsfreies Entgeltsystem in Frage stellen würden (Rn. 88 ff.)
- der verbindliche Charakter missachtet würde, den die Entscheidungen der Regulierungsstelle nach Art. 30 Abs. 5 Unterabs. 2 der Richtlinie 2001/14 hätten (Rn. 94 ff.)
- in Zivilverfahren eine gütliche Beilegung des Rechtsstreits nicht ausgeschlossen sei; dies impliziere, dass derartige Verhandlungen auch ohne Beteiligung der Regulierungsstelle stattfinden könnten, die nicht Partei eines solchen Verfahrens sei (Rn. 98 ff.).

Mit seinem jüngsten Urteil vom 21. 11. 2019 hat der EuGH seine Entscheidung vom 9. 11. 2017 in Sachen *CTL Logistics* bestätigt. Hier führt er in den Tz. 67 ff. aus:

> „Insoweit genügt die Feststellung, dass, wie der Gerichtshof bereits in einem vergleichbaren Kontext entschieden hat, mit der Anwendung von § 315 Abs. 3 BGB dadurch, dass ausschließlich darauf abgestellt wird, dass der individuelle Vertrag wirtschaftlich vernünftig ist, verkannt wird, dass nur dann gewährleistet werden kann, dass die Entgeltpolitik auf alle betroffenen Unternehmen gleich angewandt wird, wenn die Entgelte anhand einheitlicher Kriterien festgelegt werden (vgl. in diesem Sinne Urteil vom 9. November 2017, CTL Logistics, C-489/15, EU:C:2017:834, Rn. 74).
>
> Darüber hinaus finden, wie der Generalanwalt in Nr. 77 seiner Schlussanträge ausgeführt hat, andere „wesentliche" Gesichtspunkte des Verfahrens, das mit der Billigung der Flughafenentgelte abgeschlossen wurde, wie die Fragen der Willensbildung der unabhängigen Aufsichtsbehörde oder möglicher formaler Mängel, die bei der Formulierung des Inhalts der Billigung möglicherweise relevant waren, keinen Eingang in das zivilgerichtliche Verfahren.
>
> Eine Billigkeitskontrolle der Entgelte sowie gegebenenfalls eine Entscheidung nach billigem Ermessen gemäß § 315 Abs. 3 BGB sind schließlich nicht mit dem in Art. 3 der Richtlinie 2009/12 niedergelegten Verbot der Diskriminierung von Flughafennutzern vereinbar, zumal die Urteile der deutschen Zivilgerichte nur eine auf die Parteien des jeweiligen Rechtsstreits begrenzte Wirkung ausübten (vgl. entsprechend Urteil vom 9. November 2017, CTL Logistics, C-489/15, EU:C:2017:834, Rn. 83 und 94)."

Die zivilgerichtlichen Angriffe auf regulierungsbehördlich gebilligte Infrastrukturnutzungsentgelte waren neben § 315 BGB von Anfang an auch auf angebliche Verstöße gegen das deutsche und europäische Kartellrecht gestützt. Die gerügte Kartellrechtswidrigkeit der Entgelte spielte im Hinblick auf die „Erfolgsgeschichte" des § 315 BGB lange Zeit nur eine untergeordnete Rolle. Dies änderte sich nach der Entscheidung des EuGH vom 9. 11. 2017 und führte zuletzt zu einem Beschluss des Bundesgerichtshofs (BGH) vom 29. 10. 2019 – Az. KZR 39/19 –, der ein Urteil des OLG Dresden vom 17. 04. 2019 – Az. 4/18 Kart – aufhob und die Sache an das OLG Dresden zurückverwies. Bisher liegen die Entscheidungsgründe nicht vor. Nach der mündlichen Verhandlung scheint der BGH der Auffassung zu sein, dass regulierungsbehördlich gebilligte Entgelte ungeachtet der EuGH-Rechtsprechung zu § 315 BGB durch die Zivilgerichte im Hinblick auf das deutsche und/oder europäische Kartellrecht überprüft werden können.

Vor diesem Hintergrund stellen sich folgende Prüffragen:

1. Können vor dem dargestellten Hintergrund regulierungsbehördlich nicht rechtskräftig widersprochene Infrastrukturnutzungsentgelte im Einzelfall vor den Zivilgerichten am Maßstab des deutschen und/oder europäischen Kartellrechts geprüft werden?

2. In welchem Verhältnis steht die Entscheidung des EuGH vom 9. 11. 2017 in Sachen *CTL Logistics* zur Entscheidung des EuGH vom 14. 10. 2010 in der Rs. C-280/08 P in Sachen *Deutsche Telekom* (dort insb. Tz. 80)? Wie steht Art. 102 AEUV zu Art. 90 AEUV in Bezug auf Richtlinie 2014/104/EU und Richtlinie 2001/14/EG bzw. 2012/34/EU?

3. Spielt es für die Anwendbarkeit des europäischen Kartellrechts auf die Überprüfung regulierter Infrastrukturnutzungsentgelte eine Rolle, ob das Kartellrecht in Verfahren nationaler Wettbewerbsbehörden bzw. der Europäischen Kommission oder in nationalen Zivilprozessen angewendet wird? Ergibt sich ein weiterer Unterschied daraus, ob diese Zivilprozesse auf kartellrechtlichen Schadenersatz (nach §§ 33 ff. GWB in Umsetzung der Richtlinie 2014/104/EU) oder z. B. auf Rückzahlung gerichtet sind?

II. Struktur des Gutachtens

Nachfolgend sollen zunächst die Grenzen aufgezeigt werden, welche der EuGH der Anwendung nationalen Zivilrechts im Urteil *CTL Logistics* vom 9. November 2017 gesetzt und jüngst im Urteil *Deutsche Lufthansa* vom 21. November 2019 bestätigt hat (B).

Im Anschluss daran wird die Rezeption des *CTL Logistics*-Urteils durch die instanzgerichtliche Rechtsprechung, die Literatur und schließlich den BGH, insbesondere im Urteil *Trassenentgelte* vom 29. Oktober 2019, dessen Gründe mittlerweile vorliegen, aufgearbeitet (C).

Auf dieser Basis wird sodann auf die Frage eingegangen, ob die im *CTL Logistics*-Urteil entwickelten Grundsätze auch für eine kartellzivilgerichtliche Kontrolle von Infrastrukturnutzungsentgelten gelten oder ob ihre Anwendung, wie der BGH meint, auf eine Billigkeitskontrolle nach § 315 BGB beschränkt ist (D). Hierbei wird zunächst auf das Fehlen ausdrücklicher Abgrenzungsregelungen (I) sowie auf die Übertragbarkeit der *CTL Logistics*-Grundsätze auf das Kartellrecht im Allgemeinen nach ihrem Wortlaut (II) und nach ihrem Sinn und Zweck (III) eingegangen. Der Schwerpunkt liegt sodann bei der zentralen Frage nach Besonderheiten, die sich aus dem unionsprimärrechtlichen Charakter des Art. 102 AEUV und aus der Möglichkeit seiner privaten Durchsetzung für die kartellzivilgerichtliche Kontrolle regulierter Entgelte ergeben. Letztlich geht es dabei um das Verhältnis des *CTL Logistics*-Urteils des EuGH zu seinen Urteilen *Deutsche Telekom* und *Crehan/Courage* bzw. *Manfredi* (IV).

Auf dieser Basis werden schließlich die eingangs aufgeworfenen Fragen der DB Netz AG zusammenfassend beantwortet (E).

B. EuGH-Rechtsprechung zu Eisenbahnregulierung und zivilgerichtlicher Kontrolle

I. Vorabentscheidungsersuchen des LG Berlin (2015)

Ausgangspunkt des *CTL Logistics*-Verfahrens des EuGH war ein Vorabentscheidungsersuchen des LG Berlin. Dem Vorlagebeschluss vom 3. September 2015 lag ein Rechtsstreit über Ansprüche auf Erstattung von Stornierungs- und Änderungsentgelten im Zusammenhang mit der Nutzung der DB-Eisenbahninfrastruktur zugrunde. Das LG Berlin hat dem Gerichtshof folgende Fragen vorgelegt:

„1. Sind Regelungen des Europarechts, insbesondere Art. 30 Abs. 1 S. 1, Abs. 2, Abs. 3, Abs. 5 Uabs. 1, Abs. 6 RL 2001/14/EG dahingehend auszulegen, dass Rückforderungen von Fahrwegnutzungsentgelten, die zwischen einem Infrastrukturbetreiber und einem Antragsteller in einem Rahmenvertrag vereinbart oder bestimmt worden sind, ausgeschlossen sind, soweit diese nicht über die vor der nationalen Regulierungsstelle vorgesehenen Verfahren und die entsprechenden gerichtlichen Verfahren, die diese Entscheidungen der Regulierungsstelle nachgeprüft haben, geltend gemacht werden?

2. Sind Regelungen des Europarechts, insbesondere Art. 30 Abs. 1 S. 1, Abs. 2, Abs. 3, Abs. 5 Uabs. 1, Abs. 6 RL 2001/14/EG dahingehend auszulegen, dass Rückforderungen von Fahrwegnutzungsentgelten, die zwischen einem Infrastrukturbetreiber und einem Antragsteller in einem Rahmenvertrag vereinbart oder bestimmt worden sind, ausgeschlossen sind, wenn nicht zuvor die nationale Regulierungsstelle mit den strittigen Fahrwegnutzungsentgelten befasst worden ist?

3. Ist eine zivilgerichtliche Überprüfung der Billigkeit von Fahrwegnutzungsentgelten auf Grundlage einer nationalen zivilrechtlichen Norm, die es Gerichten erlaubt, bei einseitiger Leistungsbestimmung durch eine Partei diese auf die Billigkeit der Leistungsbestimmung hin zu kontrollieren und gegebenenfalls durch eigene Entscheidung nach billigem Ermessen zu treffen, mit den Vorgaben des Unionsrechts vereinbar, die den Infrastrukturbetreiber zur Einhaltung genereller Vorgaben für die Entgeltbemessung wie das Kostendeckungsgebot (Art. 6 Abs. 1 RL 2001/14/EG) oder die Berücksichtigung von Kriterien der Markttragfähigkeit (Art. 8 Abs. 1 RL 2001/14/EG) verpflichten?

4. Falls die Frage zu 3. bejaht wird: Muss das Zivilgericht bei seiner Er-messensausübung Maßstäbe der RL 2001/14/EG zur Fahrwegnutzungs-entgeltfestsetzung beachten, wenn ja, welche?
5. Ist die zivilgerichtliche Prüfung der Billigkeit von Entgelten auf Grund der in 3. genannten nationalen Norm mit dem Europarecht in-soweit vereinbar, als die Zivilgerichte in Abweichung von den allge-meinen Entgeltgrundsätzen und -höhen des Betreibers der Schienen-wege das Entgelt festlegen, obgleich der Betreiber der Schienenwege unionsrechtlich zur diskriminierungsfreien Gleichbehandlung aller Zugangsberechtigen verpflichtet ist (Art. 4 Abs. 5 RL 2001/14/EG)?
6. Ist die zivilgerichtliche Billigkeitsüberprüfung von Entgelten eines Infrastrukturbetreibers unter dem Gesichtspunkt mit dem Unions-recht vereinbar, dass das Unionsrecht von der Zuständigkeit der Regu-lierungsstelle ausgeht, Meinungsverschiedenheiten zwischen dem Be-treiber der Infrastruktur und den Zugangsberechtigten über die Fahr-wegnutzungsentgelte oder über die Höhe oder Struktur der Fahrweg-nutzungsentgelte, die der Zugangsberechtigte zu zahlen hat oder hät-te, zu entscheiden (Art. 30 Abs. 5 UAbs. 3 RL 2001/14/EG) und die Re-gulierungsstelle angesichts einer potenziellen Vielzahl von Streitigkei-ten vor unterschiedlichen Zivilgerichten die einheitliche Anwendung des Eisenbahnregulierungsrechts nicht mehr gewährleisten könnte (Art. 30 Abs. 3 RL 2001/14/EG)?
7. Ist es mit Unionsrecht, insb. Art. 4 Abs. 1 der RL 2001/14/EG verein-bar, wenn nationale Vorschriften eine ausschließlich einzelkostenba-sierte Berechnung sämtlicher Fahrwegnutzungsentgelte der Infrastruk-turbetreiber verlangen?"[1]

Mit Beschluss vom 7. Juni 2016 hat auch der BGH dem EuGH ein Vorab-entscheidungsersuchen im Zusammenhang mit der zivilrechtlichen Kon-trolle von Entgelten für die Stationsnutzung vorgelegt.[2] Dies geschah aller-dings erst, nachdem das BVerfG mit drei Beschlüssen vom 8. Oktober 2015 festgestellt hatte, dass mehrere Entscheidungen des BGH das Recht der DB Netz AG auf den gesetzlichen Richter aus Art. 101 Abs. 1 S. 2 GG verletzten.[3] Der BGH war rechtsirrtümlich der Auffassung gewesen, dass eine zivilrechtliche Kontrolle regulierter Entgelte im Eisenbahnbereich

---

1 LG Berlin, 3. 9. 2015, Az. 20 O 203/14, ECLI:ECLI:DE:LGBE:2015:0903.20O203. 14.0A, juris.
2 BGH, 7. 6. 2016, Az. KZR 12/15, ECLI:ECLI:DE:BGH:2016:070616BKZR12.15.0.
3 BVerfG, 8. 10. 2015, Az. 1 BvR 3509/13, ECLI:ECLI:DE:BVerfG:2015:rk20151008. 1bvr350913 und Az.1 BvR 1320/14, ECLI:ECLI:DE:BVerfG:2015:rk20151008.1b

eindeutig europarechtskonform sei *(acte clair)*. Er hatte daher eine Vorlage an den EuGH zunächst verweigert. Das Vorabentscheidungsersuchen des BGH wurde nach Verkündung des (der Auffassung des BGH widersprechenden) *CTL Logistics*-Urteils des EuGH vom 9. November 2017 seitens des BGH nicht mehr aufrechterhalten und die Rechtssache daher am 23. Januar 2018 im Register des EuGH gestrichen.[4]

II. Das Urteil CTL Logistics des EuGH (2017)

Der EuGH beantwortete die Vorlagefragen des LG Berlin in einer Weise, die keinen Zweifel daran lässt, dass eine eigenständige zivilrechtliche Kontrolle regulierter Eisenbahnentgelte nach § 315 BGB, um die es in dem Vorabentscheidungsverfahren allein ging, eindeutig *nicht* unionsrechtskonform ist[5] und widersprach damit zugleich der Auffassung des BGH, der bis zu dieser Entscheidung in ständiger Rechtsprechung das Gegenteil vertreten hatte.

Der EuGH macht zunächst die Ziele der Richtlinie 2001/14/EG und die zu deren Durchsetzung getroffenen verfahrensmäßigen Vorgaben deutlich. Als solche unterstreicht der EuGH die Sicherstellung eines nicht diskriminierenden Zugangs zu den Fahrwegen (Rn. 36), den Schutz des fairen Wettbewerbs (Rn. 37) und die Gewährleistung der Unabhängigkeit des Betreibers der Infrastruktur (Rn. 38), dem auch Anreize für die Optimierung der Nutzung der Fahrwege (Rn. 39) und für die Kostensenkung (Rn. 42) gegeben werden sollten und dem daher eine gewisse Flexibilität eingeräumt werden müsse (Rn. 40 f.). All dies, so der EuGH, erfordere die Einrichtung einer Regulierungsstelle, die über die Anwendung der unionsrechtlichen Regelungen wache und ungeachtet gerichtlicher Nachprüfung als Beschwerdestelle fungieren könne (Rn. 43).

Als „das zentrale Kriterium für die Berechnung und Erhebung der Wegeentgelte" stellt der EuGH unter Berufung auf Art. 4 Abs. 5 der Richtlinie und Erwägungsgrund 11 heraus, dass die Anwendung der Entgeltregulierung „zu gleichwertigen und nicht diskriminierenden Entgelten für unterschiedliche Eisenbahnunternehmen" führen müsse (Rn. 45 ff.). Dieses Diskriminierungsverbot sei das Gegenstück zu dem Spielraum, welche die

---

vr132014 und Az. 1 BvR 137/13, ECLI:DE:BVERFG:2015:RK20151008.1B-VR013713, juris.

4 EuGH, 23. 1. 2018, Rs. C-344/16, ECLI:EU:C:2018:116 – *Die Länderbahn*.

5 EuGH, 9. 11. 2017, Rs. C-489/15, EU:C:2017:834 – *CTL Logistics*.

Richtlinie dem Infrastrukturbetreiber – auch im Dienste der Verringerung der gesamtgesellschaftlich zu tragenden Kosten des Verkehrs – einräume (Rn. 51 ff.).

Nachfolgend betont der EuGH Funktion und Rolle der nach Art. 30 und Erwägungsgrund 46 der Richtlinie einzurichtenden nationalen Regulierungsstelle (Rn. 55 ff.). In diesem Kontext unterstreicht er, dass diese Regulierungsstelle (in Deutschland die BNetzA), obgleich sie auch als Beschwerdestelle fungiere, „nicht nur die im Einzelfall anwendbaren Entgelte zu beurteilen" habe. Sie habe „ferner dafür Sorge zu tragen, dass die Gesamtheit der Entgelte, d.h. die Entgeltregelung, mit der Richtlinie in Einklang" stehe (Rn. 57). „Die zentrale Überwachung durch die Regulierungsstelle, die dafür Sorge trägt, dass die Entgelte nicht diskriminierend sind", so der EuGH, „entspricht folglich dem Grundsatz, dass die zentrale Festlegung der Entgelte unter Beachtung des Diskriminierungsverbots vom Betreiber vorgenommen wird" (Rn. 58). Dies gewährleiste, dass die Entgelte den Vorschriften der Richtlinie entsprächen und nicht diskriminierend seien (Rn. 60). Daher seien „Verhandlungen zwischen Antragstellern und dem Betreiber der Infrastruktur über die Höhe von Wegeentgelten nur zulässig, sofern sie unter Aufsicht der Regulierungsstelle erfolgen, die einzugreifen hat, wenn bei den Verhandlungen ein Verstoß gegen die Bestimmungen der Richtlinie droht" (Rn. 60). Entscheidungen der Regulierungsstelle seien für alle Betroffenen verbindlich, wirkten also *erga omnes* (Rn. 61).

Vor diesem Hintergrund trifft der EuGH sieben Feststellungen:

1. *Erstens* sieht der EuGH eine auf den Einzelfall abstellende Billigkeitskontrolle im Widerspruch zum Diskriminierungsverbot der Richtlinie; dabei kritisiert der EuGH insbesondere den „eigenständigen Anwendungsbereich" des § 315 BGB, der Kriterien umfasse, die in der Richtlinie nicht vorgesehen seien (Rn. 70 ff.). Eine Billigkeitskontrolle nach § 315 BGB gefährde die Verwirklichung der Ziele der Richtlinie, „da in der genannten Rechtsprechung nämlich keine einheitlichen Kriterien anerkannt sind, sondern die Kriterien von Fall zu Fall je nach Vertragszweck und Interessen der Parteien des Rechtsstreits angewandt werden" (Rn. 73). § 315 BGB und die Richtlinie beruhten „auf verschiedenen Erwägungen, die bei der Anwendung auf ein und denselben Vertrag zu widersprüchlichen Ergebnissen führen könnten" (Rn. 75). Eine Kontrolle nach § 315 BGB stehe daher im Widerspruch zu den Grundsätzen der Richtlinie, insbesondere zum Gebot der Gleichbehandlung der Eisenbahnverkehrsunternehmen (Rn. 76).

2. *Zweitens* betont der EuGH, dass die Mitgliedstaaten in Umsetzung der Richtlinie einen Regulierungsrahmen zu schaffen hätten, welcher die Unabhängigkeit der Geschäftsführer des Betreibers der Eisenbahninfrastruktur wahre und dessen Spielraum schütze (Rn. 77 ff.). Die Regulierung solle Anreize zur Optimierung der Nutzung der Fahrwege geben (Rn. 80), was nicht gelingen könne, wenn ein Zivilgericht nach § 315 BGB das für ein einzelnes Eisenbahnverkehrsunternehmen geltende Entgelt nach billigem Ermessen bestimmen könne. Dies nämlich würde den Spielraum des Betreibers in einem nicht mit den Zielen der Richtlinie vereinbaren Maß einengen (Rn. 81).

3. *Drittens* sei eine zivilgerichtliche Prüfung nach § 315 BGB entweder mit den in Art. 4, 7 und 8 der Richtlinie vorgesehenen Beurteilungskriterien unvereinbar oder sie würde (falls die Anforderungen des § 315 BGB materiell denen der Richtlinie entsprächen) bedeuten, „dass die Zivilgerichte unmittelbar die Vorschriften des Eisenbahnregulierungsrechts anwenden und somit in die Zuständigkeiten der Regulierungsstelle eingreifen" (Rn. 84). Nach Maßgabe der Richtlinie würden die Entgelte aber vom Infrastrukturbetreiber, flankiert durch die Überwachung seitens der Regulierungsstelle, festgelegt (Rn. 85). Träte eine zivilgerichtliche Kontrolle hinzu, so würden die Vorschriften des Eisenbahnregulierungsrechts „nicht nur von der zuständigen Regulierungsstelle beurteilt und dann *ex post* von den mit Rechtsbehelfen gegen deren Entscheidungen befassten Gerichten überprüft, sondern auch durch jedes zuständige nationale Zivilgericht, das angerufen wird, angewandt und präzisiert. Dies verstößt gegen die der Regulierungsstelle durch Art. 30 der Richtlinie 2001/14 zuerkannte ausschließliche Zuständigkeit" (Rn. 86). Mehr noch: Die Uniformität der Kontrolle durch die zuständige Regulierungsstelle würde durch „verschiedene, unter Umständen nicht durch eine höchstrichterliche Rechtsprechung harmonisierte Entscheidungen unabhängiger Zivilgerichte unterlaufen, so dass in offenkundigem Widerspruch zu dem in Art. 30 der Richtlinie 2001/14 verfolgten Ziel zwei unkoordinierte Rechtswege nebeneinander bestünden" (Rn. 87).

4. *Viertens* hebt der EuGH die „praktisch unüberwindliche Schwierigkeit hervor, die verschiedenen Einzelfallentscheidungen der Zivilgerichte rasch in ein nicht diskriminierendes System zu integrieren, mag sich die Regulierungsstelle auch bemühen, auf diese Entscheidungen zu reagieren" (Rn. 88). Daher würde jedenfalls bis zu einer höchstrichterlichen Entscheidung eine Ungleichbehandlung drohen (Rn. 89). Die Regulierungsstelle müsste, um dies zu vermeiden, das Entgelt für alle

Eisenbahnverkehrsunternehmen entsprechend der zivilrechtlichen Entscheidung anpassen, obwohl die Richtlinie keine solche Verpflichtung vorsehe und dies im klaren Gegensatz zur Aufgabe der Regulierungsstelle nach Art. 30 Abs. 2 und 5 der Richtlinie stehe (Rn. 90 ff.). Schließlich widerspreche der von einer Billigkeitsentscheidung ausgehende Zwang, sich mit pauschalen, im Einzelfall festgelegten Billigkeitsentgelten auseinanderzusetzen auch der Unabhängigkeit des Betreibers der Infrastruktur (Rn. 93).

5. *Fünftens* würde durch zivilgerichtliche Entscheidungen der in Art. 30 Abs. 5 Unterabs. 2 der Richtlinie vorgesehene verbindliche Charakter der Entscheidungen der Regulierungsstelle für alle Beteiligten missachtet, zumal eine das Entgelt reduzierende zivilgerichtliche Entscheidung nur *inter partes* wirke und den Kläger gegenüber seinen Wettbewerbern begünstige; das Zivilgericht habe keine Möglichkeit, die Wirkung seiner Entscheidung auf weitere Infrastrukturnutzungsverträge oder sogar auf den gesamten Sektor auszudehnen (Rn. 94 f.). Dies würde, abgesehen von der daraus resultierenden Ungleichbehandlung, auch das Ziel gefährden, fairen Wettbewerb zu gewährleisten (Rn. 96). Eine Erstattung von Entgelten nach den Vorschriften des Zivilrechts komme daher nur in Betracht, „wenn die Unvereinbarkeit des Entgelts mit Regelung über den Zugang zur Eisenbahninfrastruktur zuvor von der Regulierungsstelle oder von einem Gericht, das die Entscheidung dieser Stelle überprüft hat, im Einklang mit den Vorschriften des nationalen Rechts festgestellt worden ist und der Anspruch auf Erstattung Gegenstand einer Klage vor den nationalen Zivilgerichten sein kann und nicht der in der genannten Regelung vorgesehenen Klage" (Rn. 97).

6. *Sechstens* komme vor dem Zivilgericht auch eine gütliche Streitbeilegung in Betracht, ohne dass die Regulierungsstelle beteiligt werden müsste. Dies sei nicht mit Art. 30 Abs. 3 S. 2 und 3 der Richtlinie vereinbar, wonach Verhandlungen der Parteien unter Aufsicht der Regulierungsstelle erfolgen müssten und diese einzugreifen habe, wenn ein Verstoß gegen die Richtlinie drohe (Rn. 98 f.).

7. *Siebtens* sei eine Korrektur der Entgelte in Anwendung des § 315 BGB auch nicht mit dem Ziel vereinbar, den Infrastrukturbetreibern einen Anreiz zur Optimierung ihrer Fahrwege zu geben. Der Umstand, dass § 315 BGB einen „eigenständigen Anwendungsbereich" habe, deute darauf hin, dass die Ziele der Richtlinie nicht berücksichtigt würden (Rn. 100). Aber auch wenn diese berücksichtigt würden, bestehe die Gefahr, dass eine im Einzelfall vorgenommene Ermäßigung einen An-

reiz auslöse, sich durch Zivilklagen Vorteile gegenüber den Wettbewerbern zu verschaffen (Rn. 101).

In der Summe folgerte der EuGH daraus, dass die Richtlinie 2001/14/EG, insbesondere deren Art. 4 Abs. 5 und deren Art. 30 Abs. 1, 3, 5 und 6, „der Anwendung einer nationalen Regelung wie der im Ausgangsverfahren fraglichen entgegenstehen, wonach die Wegeentgelte im Eisenbahnverkehr von den ordentlichen Gerichten im Einzelfall auf Billigkeit überprüft und gegebenenfalls unabhängig von der in Art. 30 der Richtlinie vorgesehenen Überwachung durch die Regulierungsstelle abgeändert werden können" (Rn. 103).

III. Das Urteil Deutsche Lufthansa des EuGH (2019)

Im Verfahren *Deutsche Lufthansa*, in dem es um den effektiven Rechtsschutz der Flughafennutzer im Zusammenhang mit der Festsetzung von Flughafenentgelten ging, hat der EuGH diesen Ansatz am 21. November 2019 bekräftigt.[6]

Die Besonderheit dieses Verfahrens lag darin, dass im deutschen LuftVG – anders als im Eisenbahnregulierungsrecht – kein verwaltungsgerichtliches Verfahren vorgesehen war (und ist), mittels dessen Flughafennutzer die Genehmigung der Flughafenentgeltordnung unmittelbar anfechten konnten. In Betracht kam lediglich eine mittelbare Überprüfung der Entgelte im Wege eines zivilgerichtlichen Verfahrens der Billigkeitskontrolle nach § 315 Abs. 3 BGB. Der EuGH unterstrich den unionsrechtlichen Effektivitätsgrundsatz (demzufolge das mitgliedstaatliche Recht die Ausübung der durch die Unionsrechtsordnung verliehenen Rechte nicht praktisch unmöglich machen oder übermäßig erschweren darf) und sah durch die Beschränkung auf eine bloße Privatklagemöglichkeit den Grundsatz effektiven Rechtsschutzes verletzt (Rn. 61 ff.).

Im Einzelnen hob der EuGH erneut die Notwendigkeit einer einheitlichen Anwendung der Kriterien der einschlägigen Richtlinie hervor, die durch eine zivilgerichtliche Kontrolle nicht gewährleistet sei. Dabei nahm der Gerichtshof explizit Bezug auf sein Urteil *CTL Logistics* und betonte, dass *einerseits* wesentliche Gesichtspunkte des Regulierungsverfahrens wie Fragen der unabhängigen Willensbildung der Aufsichtsbehörde oder mögliche formelle Mängel der Behördenentscheidung in ein zivilgerichtliches Verfahren keinen Eingang fänden (Rn. 67 f.). *Andererseits* sei eine zivilge-

---

6 EuGH, 21. 11. 2019, Rs. C-379/18, ECLI:EU:C:2019:1000 – *Deutsche Lufthansa*.

richtliche Billigkeitskontrolle angesichts ihrer nur zwischen den Streitparteien (*inter partes*) eintretenden Rechtswirkungen auch nicht mit dem Diskriminierungsverbot der dem LuftVG zugrunde liegenden Richtlinie vereinbar (Rn. 69):

> „Insoweit genügt die Feststellung, dass, wie der Gerichtshof bereits in einem vergleichbaren Kontext entschieden hat, mit der Anwendung von § 315 Abs. 3 BGB dadurch, dass ausschließlich darauf abgestellt wird, dass der individuelle Vertrag wirtschaftlich vernünftig ist, verkannt wird, dass nur dann gewährleistet werden kann, dass die Entgeltpolitik auf alle betroffenen Unternehmen gleich angewandt wird, wenn die Entgelte anhand einheitlicher Kriterien festgelegt werden (vgl. in diesem Sinne Urteil vom 9. November 2017, CTL Logistics, C-489/15, EU:C:2017:834, Rn. 74).
>
> Darüber hinaus finden, wie der Generalanwalt in Nr. 77 seiner Schlussanträge ausgeführt hat, andere „wesentliche" Gesichtspunkte des Verfahrens, das mit der Billigung der Flughafenentgelte abgeschlossen wurde, wie die Fragen der Willensbildung der unabhängigen Aufsichtsbehörde oder möglicher formaler Mängel, die bei der Formulierung des Inhalts der Billigung möglicherweise relevant waren, keinen Eingang in das zivilgerichtliche Verfahren.
>
> Eine Billigkeitskontrolle der Entgelte sowie gegebenenfalls eine Entscheidung nach billigem Ermessen gemäß § 315 Abs. 3 BGB sind schließlich nicht mit dem in Art. 3 der Richtlinie 2009/12 niedergelegten Verbot der Diskriminierung von Flughafennutzern vereinbar, zumal die Urteile der deutschen Zivilgerichte nur eine auf die Parteien des jeweiligen Rechtsstreits begrenzte Wirkung ausübten (vgl. entsprechend Urteil vom 9. November 2017, CTL Logistics, C-489/15, EU:C:2017:834, Rn. 83 und 94)."[7]

---

[7] EuGH, 21. 11. 2019, Rs. C-379/18, ECLI:EU:C:2019:1000 Rn. 67 ff. – *Deutsche Lufthansa.*

C. Rezeption des Urteils CTL Logistics

I. Instanzgerichtliche Rechtsprechung

Die in Deutschland nach dem *CTL Logistics*-Urteil des EuGH ergangene instanzgerichtliche Rechtsprechung spricht sich, soweit ersichtlich, einheitlich und explizit für eine Übertragbarkeit der Entscheidungsgrundsätze dieses EuGH-Urteils auf Kartellzivilprozesse aus.

Das LG Frankfurt am Main hat dazu am 9. Mai 2018 ausgeführt, dass die Erwägungen des EuGH aus dem *CTL Logistics*-Verfahren auch auf die zivilgerichtliche Geltendmachung kartellrechtlicher Ansprüche übertragbar seien. Insoweit könne für kartellrechtliche Zivilprozesse mit *inter partes*-Wirkung nichts anderes gelten als für solche, die auf eine Billigkeitskontrolle nach § 315 Abs. 3 BGB zielten, denn auch hier käme es bei Feststellung eines Verstoßes zu einer Entgeltreduzierung nur gegenüber einem (dem klagenden) Eisenbahnverkehrsunternehmen. Der EuGH habe aber deutlich hervorgehoben, dass eine Erstattung von Entgelten nur nach Feststellung der Unvereinbarkeit des Entgelts durch die zuständige Regulierungsstelle oder des zur Überprüfung der Entscheidungen dieser Stelle berufenen Verwaltungsgerichts in Betracht komme. Im Rahmen der kartellrechtlichen Entgeltkontrolle durch die Zivilgerichte dürften daher nur andere Kriterien zugrunde gelegt werden als die des Eisenbahnregulierungsrechts. Das sei aber vorliegend nicht der Fall, da es bei der kartellrechtlichen Prüfung letztlich um die Kontrolle der Preisbildung durch das Eisenbahninfrastrukturunternehmen gehe, der eisenbahnrechtliche Vorschriften zugrunde lägen und die von den Zivilgerichten gerade nicht im Einzelfall überprüft werden solle.[8]

Das LG Leipzig argumentierte in dem letztlich zur BGH-Entscheidung *Trassenentgelte* führenden Rechtsstreit in seinem Urteil vom 6. Juni 2018 in die gleiche Richtung. Das Urteil betont, die zivilgerichtliche Geltendmachung eines auf einer Verletzung des § 20 GWB a.F. basierenden Erstattungsanspruchs setze eine bestandskräftige Entscheidung der zuständigen Regulierungsbehörde oder eine rechtskräftige verwaltungsgerichtliche Entscheidung voraus, an der es im vorliegenden Fall fehle. Eine Diskrimine-

---

8 LG Frankfurt a. M., 9. 5. 2018, Az. 2-06 O 38/17, ECLI:DE:LGFFM:2018:0509.2. 06O38.17.00, Rn. 71 ff., juris m. zust. Anmerkung *Karolus*, EuR 2018, 477.

rung i.S.d. § 20 GWB a.F. könne nicht ohne Beachtung der eisenbahnrechtlichen Vorgaben festgestellt werden, doch schließe § 14f Abs. 1 S. 1 und 3 AEG a.F. die Anwendung eisenbahnrechtlicher Regelungen im Rahmen einer zivilgerichtlichen Einzelfallprüfung aus, weil diese der Regulierungsbehörde vorbehalten sei. Diese Regelung im AEG beruhe wiederum auf der Richtlinie 2001/14/EG, die nach der EuGH-Entscheidung *CTL Logistics* eine zivilgerichtliche Überprüfung regulierter Entgelte im Einzelfall ausschließe.[9] Dies gelte auch für kartellrechtliche Schadensersatzansprüche nach § 33 Abs. 3 GWB a.F. (jetzt § 33a GWB), denn ein Verstoß gegen §§ 19, 20 GWB und Art. 102 AEUV wäre nur bei Anwendung der eisenbahnrechtlichen Vorschriften feststellbar. Die Anwendung dieser Vorschriften durch die Zivilgerichte komme aber nicht in Betracht (Rn. 47).

Auch das LG Berlin hat sich diese Auffassung in einem Urteil vom 30. Oktober 2018 zu eigen gemacht. Das Urteil betont zunächst, dass sich durch das Inkrafttreten der Richtlinie 2012/34/EU anstelle der Richtlinie 2001/14/EG, welche dem *CTL Logistics*-Sachverhalt zugrunde lag, nichts geändert habe und dass die EuGH-Entscheidung unverändert Geltung beanspruche.[10] Es unterstreicht sodann das Erfordernis einer bestandskräftigen Entscheidung der zuständigen Regulierungsbehörde, deren Zuständigkeit nicht durch Zivilprozesse unterlaufen werden dürfe (Rn. 31 ff.). Dies gelte auch dann, wenn die BNetzA – im Vertrauen auf die frühere Rechtslage, die eine zivilgerichtliche Kontrolle für zulässig erachtete – Verstöße weniger konsequent verfolgt habe, weil der EuGH-Entscheidung nicht zu entnehmen sei, dass sie für die Vergangenheit nicht gelten solle (Rn. 37). Eine solche Beschränkung sei auch nicht sachgerecht, weil in einem Zivilprozess die Interessen der anderen Eisenbahnverkehrsunternehmen nicht berücksichtigt werden könnten, diese aber durch eine individuelle Absenkung der Entgelte belastet würden, weil letztlich ein bestimmtes Gesamtaufkommen erreicht werden müsse (Rn. 39). Nichts anderes gelte auch für Ansprüche, welche auf Kartellrecht basierten. Die Rechtsfolgen von Kartellverstößen ergäben sich (auch bei Anwendung des Art. 102 AEUV) aus dem nationalen Recht. Insoweit obliege den Mitgliedstaaten nur, sicherzustellen, dass die Rechte Einzelner unter Berücksichtigung des Missbrauchsverbots durchgesetzt würden. Dies könne aber auch im Rahmen der regulierungsbehördlichen Überprüfung auf der Basis des Eisenbahnregulie-

---

9   LG Leipzig, 6. 7. 2018, Az. 01 HK O 3364/14, ECLI:DE:LGLEIPZ:2018:0706.01 HKO3365.14.0A, Rn. 32 ff., juris.
10 LG Berlin, 30. 10. 2018, Az. 16 O 495/15 Kart, ECLI: DE: LGBE: 2018: 1030. 16O495.15KART.00, Rn. 30, juris mit zust. Anm. *Gerstner*, N&R 2019, 62 ff.

rungsrechts sichergestellt werden (Rn. 41 ff.). Zudem sei fraglich, ob überhaupt ein Kartellrechtsverstoß vorliege, weil das Eisenbahninfrastrukturunternehmen aufgrund der Entscheidung der BNetzA verpflichtet sei, von allen Betreibern ein bestimmtes Entgelt zu fordern (Rn. 44 f.). Art. 56 Abs. 2 der Richtlinie 2012/34/EU bestätige diese Auffassung, da danach nur die Befugnisse der Kartell*behörden* unberührt blieben. Eine zivilgerichtliche Durchsetzbarkeit sei damit nicht verbunden, sondern müsse vielmehr unterbleiben, um den Richtlinienvorgaben entsprechend, einheitliche, für alle Eisenbahnverkehrsunternehmen geltende Entgelte zu gewährleisten (Rn. 46).

Das OLG Dresden hat – als Vorinstanz der *Trassenentgelte*-Entscheidung des BGH – das Urteil des LG Leipzig mit Urteil vom 17. April 2019 unter Berufung auf die *CTL Logistics*-Entscheidung des EuGH bestätigt.[11] Das OLG betont in seinem Urteil, dass eine auf kartellrechtlichen Regelungen beruhende Korrektur im zivilgerichtlichen Verfahren, die ohne Beteiligung der Regulierungsstelle erfolge, neben der Gefahr paralleler unkoordinierter Rechtswege die Gefahr einer unionsrechtswidrigen Bevorzugung einzelner Eisenbahnverkehrsunternehmen begründen würde, welche die Richtlinie 2001/14/EG ausweislich der Prinzipien der Diskriminierungsfreiheit und der Gleichbehandlung der Eisenbahnverkehrsunternehmen gerade verhindern wolle. Zudem wären – wie bei einer Prüfung nach § 315 Abs. 3 BGB – auch bei einer kartellrechtlichen Prüfung „Kriterien zu berücksichtigen, die in der Richtlinie 2001/14/EG so nicht vorgesehen sind und im Einzelfall je nach Vertragszweck bzw. Fallkonstellation und Parteien auch unterschiedlich sein können". Eine derartige zivilgerichtliche Einzelfallprüfung könne nicht gewährleisten, dass die Trassenentgelte *erga omnes* anhand einheitlicher Kriterien festgesetzt und beurteilt würden (Rn. 45).

Eine zivilgerichtliche Aufhebung regulierungsbehördlich gebilligter Entgelte nur im Verhältnis zur Klägerin wäre nach Auffassung des OLG wertungswidersprüchlich. Daher komme auch eine zivilgerichtliche Kontrolle auf kartellrechtlicher Basis nicht in Betracht. Im Rahmen kartellrechtlicher Entgeltkontrollen durch die Zivilgerichte dürften nur andere Kriterien zugrunde gelegt werden als die des Eisenbahnregulierungsrechts, d.h. nicht die durch die Richtlinie 2001/14/EG und das deutsche Regulierungsrecht bereits berücksichtigten Grundsätze wie Diskriminierungsverbot, Gebot der Gleichbehandlung und Verbot des Ausnutzens einer markt-

---

11 OLG Dresden, 17. 4. 2019, Az. U 4/18 Kart, ECLI:DE:OLGDRES:2019:0417.U4. 18KART.0A, Rn. 44 ff.

beherrschenden Stellung (Rn. 46). Auf den Vorrang des Art. 102 AEUV vor dem Richtlinienrecht komme es nicht an, weil sich der EuGH nur mit den mitgliedstaatlichen Verfahrensregeln befasst habe und weil Art. 102 AEUV durch das Richtlinienrecht gerade konkretisiert und ausgeformt werde. Art. 102 AEUV sei zwar auf einseitige Verstöße anwendbar, doch komme für die Durchsetzung kein zivilgerichtliches Verfahren in Betracht, sofern nicht zuvor die zuständige Regulierungsbehörde bzw. das diese überprüfende Gericht einen Verstoß festgestellt hätten (Rn. 47).

Auch Ansprüche auf Schadensersatz wegen kartellrechtlicher Verstöße kämen nur in Betracht, soweit diese nicht der eisenbahnrechtlichen Regulierung unterlägen, weil die Überprüfung der Preisbildung anhand eisenbahnrechtlicher Vorschriften der zivilgerichtlichen Kontrolle im Einzelfall entzogen sei; ganz abgesehen davon, dass die BNetzA im vorliegenden Fall die Erhebung des umstrittenen Regionalfaktors im Wege eines öffentlich-rechtlichen Vertrages vom 30. Juli 2010 explizit akzeptiert habe (Rn. 48).

II. Monopolkommission

Die Monopolkommission hat sich in ihrem 7. Sektorgutachten Bahn (2019) ebenfalls kurz zum *CTL Logistics*-Urteil des EuGH geäußert, wirkt aber letztlich unsicher und unentschlossen. Sie äußert darin *einerseits* die Auffassung, den Zivilgerichten bleibe eine Überprüfung genehmigter Entgelte nach Art. 102 AEUV „unabhängig von den Vorgaben der Richtlinie 2012/34/EG" möglich,[12] *andererseits* betont sie auch, „eine solche Kontrolle liefe aber dem grundsätzlich legitimen Ziel des Richtliniengebers entgegen, die Kontrolle von Infrastrukturentgelten bei den Verwaltungsbehörden und -gerichten zu konzentrieren".[13]

---

[12] Monopolkommission, 7. Sektorgutachten Bahn, 6. 8. 2019, BT-Drucks. 1/12300, Tz. 178 und 182 im Einklang mit *Kühling*, der sich 2015 für die umfassende Zulässigkeit einer zivilgerichtlichen Kontrolle nach § 315 BGB und auch nach Art. 102 AEUV ausgesprochen hatte (s. *Kühling*, Eisenbahnentgeltregulierung jenseits AEG und EIBV, in: Ronellenfitsch/Eschweiler/Hörster, Aktuelle Probleme des Eisenbahnrechts, 2015, S. 73, 103) und heute stellvertretender Vorsitzender der Monopolkommission ist.

[13] Monopolkommission, 7. Sektorgutachten Bahn, 6. 8. 2019, BT-Drucks. 1/12300, Tz. 182.

III. Literatur

Die Rezeption der *CTL Logistics*-Entscheidung durch die deutschen Instanzgerichte hat in der Literatur Zuspruch, aber auch Kritik erfahren. Die Äußerungen in der Literatur stammen dabei ganz überwiegend von Prozessvertretern der einen oder anderen Seite in den laufenden Verfahren.

1. Argumente für eine Übertragbarkeit der CTL Logistics-Grundsätze

Als Argument gegen die Anwendbarkeit des Kartellrechts wird in der Literatur auf den Vorrang des Richtlinienrechts vor dem nationalen Kartellrecht hingewiesen.[14] Auch der Vorrang des Art. 102 AEUV ändere daran, soweit dessen Voraussetzungen überhaupt vorlägen, nichts, weil Art. 102 AEUV *einerseits* im Lichte der Richtlinie auszulegen sei und *andererseits* seine zivilgerichtliche Durchsetzung zu den gleichen Problemen führe wie eine Anwendung des nationalen Kartellrechts.[15] Der EuGH schränke mit seiner *CTL Logistics*-Entscheidung zudem nicht die Geltung des Art. 102 AEUV, sondern nur dessen *„private enforcement"* ein. Für Zivilklageverfahren fehle es auch an einem Rechtsschutzbedürfnis, weil die Eisenbahnverkehrsunternehmen nach § 66 Abs. 1 ERegG die Regulierungsbehörde anrufen könnten, die dann eine einheitlich für alle geltende Entscheidung herbeiführen könne.[16]

In der Sache führe eine zivilgerichtliche Einzelfallkorrektur richtlinienkonformer Entgelte auf der Basis des Kartellrechts zu Wertungswidersprüchen[17] sowie dazu, dass das vom EuGH hervorgehobene Richtlinienziel diskriminierungsfreier Entgelte durch effektive Ungleichbehandlung klagender und nicht klagender Eisenbahnverkehrsunternehmen vereitelt und die nach der Richtlinie bestehende alleinige Zuständigkeit der Regulierungsbehörde unterlaufen werde.[18] In diesem Kontext wird auch auf den

---

14 *Weitner*, EnWZ 2018, 73, 78.
15 *Weitner*, EnWZ 2018, 73, 78.
16 *Staebe*, EuZW 2019, 118, 121.
17 *Gerstner*, EuZW 2018, 74, 80; *ders.*, N&R 2019, 62, 63 f.; vgl. *Freise*, TranspR 2018, 425, 431.
18 *Weitner*, EnWZ 2018, 73, 78; *Staebe*, EuZW 2019, 118, 121; *Karolus*, EuR 2018, 477, 480 f.

rechtsstaatlichen Grundsatz verwiesen, Zuständigkeitsregelungen grundsätzlich so auszulegen, dass Doppelzuständigkeiten vermieden werden.[19]

Hinzu komme, dass zivilgerichtliche Entscheidungen zumeist nicht auf einer sinnvollen, umfassenden Prüfung der Entgelte, sondern auf der Beweislastverteilung beruhten[20] und dass die Rechtsprechung in Anwendung kartellrechtlicher Maßstäbe oftmals andere Kriterien als diejenigen des Regulierungsrechts heranziehe. Dabei halte sie teilweise an Kriterien fest, die sich regulierungsökonomisch bereits als unfruchtbar erwiesen hätten, wie z. B. die quasiregulatorische Rechtsprechung des BGH zu Stromentgelten zeige.[21] Zudem müsse der Gesetzgeber und nicht der BGH „Motor des Regulierungsrechts" bleiben.[22]

2. Argumente gegen eine Übertragbarkeit der CTL Logistics-Grundsätze

Von der Gegenauffassung wird darauf hingewiesen, dass sich der EuGH in seinem *CTL Logistics*-Urteil – anders als der Generalanwalt in seinen Schlussanträgen zu dieser Entscheidung und anders als der BGH in seinem Vorabentscheidungsersuchen von 2016 – nicht ausdrücklich zum Kartellrecht geäußert und insoweit mit *CTL Logistics* seine Rechtsprechung zum Kartellschadensersatz seit *Crehan/Courage* nicht revidiert habe.[23]

Gegen eine Heranziehung der *CTL Logistics*-Grundsätze auf eine kartellgerichtliche Entgeltkontrolle wird insbesondere der Vorrang des Art. 102 AEUV sowohl vor dem nationalen Recht als auch vor dem sekundären Richtlinienrecht ins Feld geführt.[24] Dies wird verbunden mit dem Hinweis auf das Fehlen von Regelungen, die eine Anwendung des Kartellrechts im Anwendungsbereich des Eisenbahnregulierungsrechts im Sinne einer Bereichsausnahme explizit ausschlössen.[25] Teilweise wird auch von der An-

---

19 *Ludwigs*, WuW 2008, 534, 549 mit Verweis auf OVG Münster, 13. 9. 1995, Az. 13 A 3687/94, LS 1 und, Rn. 15, juris = NVwZ 1995, 185 sowie BVerwG, 4. 7. 1986, Az. 4 C 31/84, Rn. 25 f., juris = BVerwGE 74, 315, 325.

20 *Weitner*, EnWZ 2018, 73, 77 (zu § 315 BGB).

21 *Fricke*, N&R 2018, 66, 72.

22 *Fricke*, N&R 2018, 66, 72.

23 *Bremer/Scheffczyk*, NZKart 2018, 121, 122; *Keding*, IR 2019, 90 92 f.; insoweit abweichend *Hauf/Baumgartner*, EuZW 2018, 1028, 1033, die zu Recht betonen, dass der EuGH in *CTL Logistics* überhaupt keinen Anlass hatte, sich zum Kartellrecht zu äußern.

24 *Bremer/Scheffczyk*, NZKart 2018, 121, 122 f.;

25 *Keding*, IR 2019, 90 93; *Bremer/Scheffczyk*, NZKart 2018, 121, 123; *Hauf/Baumgartner*, EuZW 2018, 1028, 1030 f.

wendbarkeit des Art. 102 AEUV neben dem Eisenbahnregulierungsrecht auf eine Anwendbarkeit des „weitgehend inhaltsgleichen" deutschen Kartellrechts geschlossen, das gleichsam „im Geleit des Europäischen Kartellrechts" fahre.[26]

Zudem sei Art. 56 Abs. 2 der neuen Richtlinie 2012/34/EU dahingehend zu verstehen, dass das Kartellrecht nicht durch diese Richtlinie verdrängt werde.[27] Die Richtlinie normiere keine kartellrechtlichen Vorgaben, sondern lasse das Kartellrecht unberührt.[28] Art. 56 Abs. 2 bestätige insoweit den „Dualismus von unterschiedlich ausgerichteten Entgeltkontrollen", wie auch der BGH und der Generalanwalt betont hätten.[29]

In der Tat hatte Generalanwalt *Mengozzi* in seinen Schlussanträgen ebenfalls die Ansicht geäußert, die alleinige Zuständigkeit der Regulierungsbehörde nach Art. 30 der Richtlinie 2001/14/EG schließe es nicht aus, dass eine außerhalb des Anwendungsbereichs der Richtlinie 2001/14/EG angesiedelte Kontrolle der Höhe der Entgelte sowohl auf behördlicher als auch auf gerichtlicher Ebene nach Maßgabe der Bestimmungen des Wettbewerbsrechts (oder auch des § 315 BGB) ausgeübt werden könne.[30] Der Generalanwalt hatte zum Beleg auf Art. 56 Abs. 2 verwiesen, der im Gegensatz zur Richtlinie 2001/14/EG ausdrücklich anerkenne, dass die Befugnisse der Regulierungsstelle die Befugnisse der nationalen Kartellbehörden unberührt ließen.[31]

Diese Auffassung wird in der Literatur weiter durch einen Hinweis auf die Zuständigkeit der nationalen Gerichte für die Anwendung der Art. 101 und 102 AEUV nach Art. 6 VO 1/2003 untermauert[32] und darauf hingewiesen, dass die Zivilgerichte zur Gewährleistung der vollen Wirksamkeit des Unionskartellrechts bzw. des effektiven Schutzes der subjektiven Rechte der Kartellbetroffenen nach der EuGH-Rechtsprechung in den Fällen *Crehan/Courage*,[33] *Manfredi*[34] und *Kone*[35] sowie auch nach „der nationalen

---

26 *Bremer/Scheffczyk*, NZKart 2018, 121, 123.

27 *Keding*, IR 2019, 90 92 f.

28 *Mietzsch/Uhlenhut/Keding*, IR 2018, 57, 61.

29 *Hauf/Baumgartner*, EuZW 2018, 1028, 1031.

30 GA *Mengozzi*, Schlussanträge vom 21. 11. 2016, Rs. 489/15, ECLI:EU:C:2016:901, Rn. 61.

31 GA *Mengozzi*, Schlussanträge vom 21. 11. 2016, Rs. 489/15, ECLI:EU:C:2016:901, Fn. 40.

32 *Hauf/Baumgartner*, EuZW 2018, 1028, 1030 und 1035.

33 EuGH, 20. 9. 2001, Rs. C-453/99, ECLI:EU:C:2001:465 – *Crehan/Courage*.

34 EuGH, 13. 7. 2006, Rs. C-295/04, ECLI:EU:C:2006:461 – *Manfredi*.

35 EuGH, 5. 6. 2014, Rs. C-557/12, ECLI:EU:C:2014:1317 – *Kone* (von *Hauf/Baumgartner*, EuZW 2018, 1028 durchgehend als „Krone"-Entscheidung bezeichnet).

Rechtsschutzgarantie des Art. 20 GG"[36] (gemeint ist vermutlich Art. 19 Abs. 4 GG) tätig würden bzw. bei Verneinung einer eigenständigen kartell-zivilgerichtlichen Kontrollmöglichkeit sogar eine „völlige Rechtsschutzlosigkeit" der Zugangsberichtigten drohe.[37] Insoweit bestehe im Anwendungsbereich des Art. 102 AEUV kein Umsetzungsspielraum der Mitgliedstaaten für eine Gewährleistung des Effektivitätsgrundsatzes und der Rechtsschutzgarantie durch andere als zivilgerichtliche Verfahren. Art. 102 AEUV sei „*self executing*".[38]

Art. 6 VO 1/2003 und die EuGH-Rechtsprechung machten in diesem Zusammenhang auch deutlich, dass eine zivilgerichtliche Entscheidung keine vorausgehende behördliche Entscheidung voraussetze.[39] Im Gegenteil zeige das Verfahren *Deutsche Telekom*,[40] dass sogar eine *ex ante*-Genehmigung eines Entgelts durch die zuständige Regulierungsbehörde einer kartellrechtlichen Kontrolle nach Art. 102 AEUV nicht entgegenstehe.[41] Die Regulierungsbehörde sei umgekehrt nicht befugt, Entgelte und Geschäftsbedingungen auf einen Missbrauch nach Art. 102 AEUV zu überprüfen[42] oder andere zivil- oder kartellrechtliche Normen heranzuziehen oder anzuwenden.[43]

Eine zivilgerichtliche Kontrolle führe auch deshalb zu keinem Eingriff in die Zuständigkeit der Regulierungsstelle, weil das Kartellrecht einen gegenüber dem Regulierungsrecht eigenständigen Anwendungsbereich habe, aber – anders als § 315 BGB – keinen eigenen Maßstab der Billigkeitskontrolle auf (rein) nationaler Ebene definiere, sondern einen einheitlichen, von marktbeherrschenden Unternehmen zu beachtenden Rechtsrahmen vorgebe, der vom Regelungsgehalt der Regulierungsrichtlinien abweiche.[44]

---

36 *Hauf/Baumgartner*, EuZW 2018, 1028, 1030 ff.; vgl. *Bremer/Scheffczyk*, NZKart 2018, 121, 123.

37 So *Hauf/Baumgartner*, EuZW 2020, 292, 293.

38 *Hauf/Baumgartner*, EuZW 2018, 1028, 1035; *dies.*, TranspR 2019, 69, 70.

39 *Hauf/Baumgartner*, EuZW 2018, 1028, 1032; *dies.*, TranspR 2019, 69, 71 mit Verweis auf EuGH, 10. 7. 2014, Rs. C-296/12 P, ECLI:EU:C:2014:2062, Rn. 135 – *Telefónica*.

40 EuGH, 14. 10. 2010, Rs. C-280/08 P, ECLI:EU:C:2010:603 – *Deutsche Telekom*.

41 *Hauf/Baumgartner*, EuZW 2018, 1028, 1030.

42 *Hauf/Baumgartner*, EuZW 2018, 1028, 1030; *dies.*, TranspR 2019, 69, 70.

43 *Hauf/Baumgartner*, EuZW 2018, 1028, 1031 mit Verweis auf BVerwG, 11. 11. 2015, Rs. 6 C 58.14, ECLI:DE:BVERWG:2015:111115U6C58.14.0, Rn. 50; s. auch *dies.*, EuZW 2018, 1028, 1034.

44 *Hauf/Baumgartner*, EuZW 2018, 1028, 1030.

Einige Autoren meinen, das Eisenbahnregulierungsrecht sei mit Blick auf unterschiedliche Schutzzwecke und Anwendungsvoraussetzungen keine *lex specialis* zum Kartellrecht, insbesondere setze die Anwendung des Kartellrechts eine marktbeherrschende Stellung voraus.[45] Andere sind der Auffassung, das Eisenbahnregulierungsrecht enthalte zwar für das Diskriminierungsverbot besondere Maßstäbe und sei insoweit *lex specialis*, nicht aber mit Blick auf die Preishöhenkontrolle.[46] Die Möglichkeit der zivilgerichtlichen Entgeltkontrolle im Wege eines „*private enforcement*" folge zudem aus den kartellrechtlichen Bindungen der Eisenbahninfrastrukturunternehmen.[47]

Dass die Geltendmachung jedes kartellrechtlichen Vorwurfs im Ergebnis zwangsläufig zu einer Einzelfallentscheidung (und damit zu einer Ungleichbehandlung gegenüber anderen Eisenbahnverkehrsunternehmen) führe, sei zwar richtig. Doch sei diese Ungleichbehandlung irrelevant, weil sonst der effektive Rechtsschutz der Betroffenen und das Kartellrecht ausgehöhlt würden, weil es keinen Anspruch auf eine „Gleichbehandlung im Unrecht" gebe[48] und weil Art. 102 AEUV normhierarchisch den Regulierungsrichtlinien vorgehe und daher Ungleichbehandlungen infolge der Anwendung des Unionskartellrechts und divergierender Entscheidungen verschiedener Zivilgerichte hingenommen werden müssten.[49]

IV. Rechtsprechung des Bundesgerichtshofs

1. Vorabentscheidungsersuchen an den EuGH (2016)

Bereits in seinem 2018 gestrichenen[50] Vorabentscheidungsersuchen vom 7. Juni 2016 hatte der BGH sich nachdrücklich dafür ausgesprochen, eine zivilgerichtliche Kontrolle sowohl nach § 315 Abs. 3 BGB als auch nach Maßgabe des nationalen und europäischen Kartellrechts weiter vollumfänglich neben der regulierungsbehördlichen Kontrolle von Eisenbahn-

---

45 *Hauf/Baumgartner*, TranspR 2019, 69, 70.
46 *Kühling*, Eisenbahnentgeltregulierung jenseits AEG und EIBV, in: Ronellenfitsch/Eschweiler/Hörster, Aktuelle Probleme des Eisenbahnrechts, 2015, S. 73, 103.
47 *Mietzsch/Uhlenhut/Keding*, IR 2018, 57, 61; *Hauf/Baumgartner*, EuZW 2018, 1028, 1031.
48 *Hauf/Baumgartner*, EuZW 2018, 1028, 1031 und 1034.
49 *Hauf/Baumgartner*, TranspR 2019, 69, 71.
50 S. EuGH, 23. 1. 2018, Rs. C-344/16, ECLI:EU:C:2018:116 – *Die Länderbahn*; dazu schon oben S. 16.

entgelten zuzulassen. In diesem Kontext wies der BGH auf die Parallelen zwischen der zivilgerichtlichen Durchsetzung von Ansprüchen nach § 315 BGB und nach dem Kartellrecht hin. Eine Kontrolle nach § 315 BGB fördere und sichere die Durchsetzung des Art. 102 AEUV. Die eisenbahnrechtlichen Entgeltvorschriften entbänden die Eisenbahninfrastrukturunternehmen nicht von ihrer Bindung an das Kartellrecht. Art. 56 Abs. 2 bestimme demgemäß ausdrücklich, dass die Befugnisse der Kartellbehörden unberührt blieben. Außerdem seien die gesetzlichen Aufgaben und Befugnisse der Regulierungsbehörden nicht so weit entwickelt, dass sie die Entgelte umfassend auf einen Missbrauch im kartellrechtlichen Sinne prüfen könnten. [51]

2. Beschluss Stationspreissystem (2019)

In seinem Beschluss *Stationspreissystem* vom 29. Januar 2019 hat der BGH erstmals Position zum *CTL Logistics*-Urteil des EuGH bezogen.[52] Der BGH gibt darin seine bisherige Rechtsprechung – nach welcher Vorschriften des BGB auch in Bezug auf Netzentgelte unmittelbar durch die Zivilgerichte angewendet werden konnten – in Bezug auf die Möglichkeit einer Billigkeitskontrolle nach § 315 BGB auf. Zugleich erkennt er *insoweit* die vom EuGH postulierte, vorrangige Entscheidungsbefugnis der BNetzA in Bezug auf Netzentgelte an und betont, es sei sachgerecht, die Verhandlung gemäß § 148 ZPO bis zur Entscheidung der BNetzA auszusetzen (Rn. 9 ff.).

In diesem Kontext unterstreicht der BGH ferner zu Recht, dass die deutschen Zivilgerichte zu einer unionsrechtskonformen und damit auch richtlinienkonformen Auslegung des nationalen Rechts verpflichtet seien. Er hebt die Bedeutung des Diskriminierungsverbots hervor und rekurriert dabei nicht nur auf eisenbahnrechtliche Regelungen, sondern auch auf das kartellrechtliche Diskriminierungsverbot (Rn. 21). Vor diesem Hintergrund könne, so der BGH, nicht ausgeschlossen werden (und werde vom EuGH auch nicht ausgeschlossen), dass am Ende ein zivilrechtlicher Rückzahlungsanspruch bestehe und geltend gemacht werden könne.[53] Dies set-

---

51 BGH, 7. 6. 2016, Az. KZR 12/15, ECLI:ECLI:DE:BGH:2016:070616BKZR12.15.0, Rn. 46 ff.

52 BGH, 29. 1. 2019, Az. KZR 12/15, ECLI:DE:BGH:2019:290119BKZR12.15.0 – *Stationspreissystem* = EuZW 2019. 348 m. zust. Anm. *Hauf/Baumgartner*.

53 BGH, a.a.O., Rn. 23 unter Verweis auf Rn. 97 der *CTL Logistics*-Entscheidung des EuGH.

ze allerdings eine Entscheidung der BNetzA voraus, die im vorliegenden Fall noch ausstehe und auch nicht offenkundig ausgeschlossen sei (Rn. 22 ff.).

Ob daneben auch kartellrechtliche Ansprüche bestehen und unmittelbar vor einem Zivilgericht geltend gemacht werden können, lässt der BGH in diesem Beschluss offen und betont lediglich, dass eine eisenbahnrechtliche Überprüfung der Infrastrukturnutzungsentgelte auf Verstöße gegen das Diskriminierungsverbot wertvolle Erkenntnisse über diskriminierungsfreie Entgeltgrundsätze erbringen könne, die auch einer etwa erforderlichen kartellrechtlichen Beurteilung förderlich seien (Rn. 31).

3. Urteil Trassenentgelte (2019)

Seine Auffassung zu der Frage, ob der Regulierung unterliegende Eisenbahnentgelte auch im Lichte des *CTL Logistics*-Urteils weiterhin ohne vorherige Entscheidung der BNetzA kartellzivilgerichtlich überprüft werden können, hat der BGH neun Monate später am 29. Oktober 2019 in seinem Urteil *Trassenentgelte* dargelegt.[54]

Der BGH geht in diesem Urteil nicht direkt darauf ein, ob die *CTL Logistics*-Entscheidung der kartellzivilgerichtlichen Kontrolle von Infrastrukturnutzungsentgelten auf der Basis des deutschen Kartellrechts, namentlich nach §§ 19, 20, 33 ff. GWB, entgegensteht. Allerdings betont er, die *CTL Logistics*-Entscheidung beziehe sich, wie der Antwort des EuGH „unzweifelhaft" zu entnehmen sei, „ausschließlich auf die zivilrechtliche Kontrolle von Wegeentgelten am Maßstab der individuellen vertraglichen Billigkeit im Sinne des § 315 Abs. 3 BGB".[55] Dadurch bringt der BGH zum Ausdruck, dass er sich durch *CTL Logistics* wohl nicht gehindert sieht, auch das deutsche Kartellrecht allein (§§ 33 ff., 19, 20 GWB) oder im Zusammenspiel mit Normen des BGB (z. B. in Verbindung mit § 812 BGB) weiter anzuwenden.

Der BGH konzentriert seine Argumentation gleichwohl ganz auf das unionsrechtliche Missbrauchsverbot des Art. 102 AEUV und dessen zivil-

---

54 BGH, 29. 10. 2019, Az. KZR 39/19, ECLI:DE:BGH:2019:291019UKZR39.19.0 – *Trassenentgelte* = EuZW 2020, 286 mit zust. Anm. *Hauf/Baumgartner*, ebenda, S. 292 ff. sowie *Bunte*, EWiR 2020, 253 f. und *Mietzsch/Uhlenhut*, IR 2020, 98.

55 BGH, a.a.O., Rn. 35; vgl. auch ebenda Rn. 27 ff., wo der BGH betont, dass Normen des nationalen Zivilrechts und nationalen Kartellrechts jedenfalls zur Effektuierung des Art. 102 AEUV weiter anwendbar seien.

gerichtliche Durchsetzung unter Berufung auf § 812 Abs. 1 S. 1, 1. Alt. BGB und § 33 Abs. 3 GWB a.F. (jetzt § 33a GWB). Ob die Voraussetzungen des Art. 102 AUEV im vorliegenden Fall erfüllt sind, prüft der BGH nicht, sondern unterstellt dies (zunächst[56]) für den Zweck seiner Analyse (Rn. 17). Mit Blick auf das Schutzziel der Norm betont er allerdings, dass Art. 102 AEUV nicht nur dem Schutz der Marktstruktur und des Wettbewerbs als solchem, sondern auch dem Schutz individueller Interessen diene sowie dass die Norm unmittelbar anwendbar sei und subjektive Rechte begründe, welche die Gerichte der Mitgliedstaaten zu wahren hätten (Rn. 19).[57]

Daran anschließend wendet sich der BGH der Frage zu, ob sich im Unionsrecht Vorschriften finden lassen, durch welche das Preissetzungsverhalten von Eisenbahninfrastrukturunternehmen einer Missbrauchskontrolle nach Art. 102 AEUV entzogen wird (Rn. 20 ff). Hierzu betont der BGH zunächst, dass das Primärrecht keine die Anwendung des Art. 102 AEUV ausschließende Regelung enthalte. Nach der *Asjes*-Entscheidung des EuGH[58] finde Art. 102 AEUV im Gegenteil grundsätzlich auch im Verkehrssektor Anwendung (Rn. 21). Ein Ausschluss der Anwendung des Art. 102 AEUV oder eine Verdrängung durch speziellere sekundärrechtliche Regelungen scheide schon aufgrund des Vorrangs des Unionsprimärrechts (hier also des Art. 102 AEUV) aus, und dessen ungeachtet seien auch der hier einschlägigen Richtlinie 2001/14/EG keine Vorschriften zu entnehmen, die einen solchen Ausschluss begründeten (Rn. 22).

Des Weiteren fehle es, so der BGH, auch nicht an einer zurechenbaren selbständigen Handlung des beklagten Eisenbahninfrastrukturunternehmens. Selbst der Umstand, dass eine staatliche Regulierung Anreize zu einem potentiell missbräuchlichen Verhalten gesetzt habe, immunisiere ein Unternehmen nach dem *Deutsche Telekom*-Urteil des EuGH[59] nicht gegenüber einer Anwendung des Art. 102 AEUV (Rn. 24). Die Beklagte sei daher Adressatin des Art. 102 AEUV, gerade weil ihr die Richtlinie 2001/14/EG einen gewissen Spielraum lasse (Rn. 25). Schließlich seien

---

56 In Rn. 52 und 53 gibt der BGH dem OLG Dresden dann allerdings doch einige Hinweise dazu, wie es seiner Ansicht nach bei der Anwendung des Art. 102 AEUV zu verfahren habe, dazu später.

57 Unter Verweis auf EuGH, 30. 1. 1974, Rs. 127/73, ECLI:EU:C:1974:6, Rn. 15/17 – *BRT/SABAM* sowie auf weitere Urteile und auf Erwägungsgründe 3 und 12 f. der Kartellschadensersatzrichtlinie 2014/104/EU.

58 EuGH, 30. 4. 1986, Rs. C-209/84, ECLI:EU:C:1986:188, Rn. 42 – *Asjes*.

59 EuGH, 14. 10. 2010, Rs. C-280/08 P, ECLI:EU:C:2010:603, Rn. 84 – *Deutsche Telekom*.

auch Vorschriften des nationalen Rechts von vornherein nicht geeignet, die Wegenutzungsentgelte einer Kontrolle nach Art. 102 AEUV zu entziehen (Rn. 26).

Art. 102 AEUV selbst enthält lediglich ein Verbot, nicht aber Rechtsfolgenanordnungen oder Anspruchsgrundlagen für einen Zivilprozess. Diese existieren auch sonst auf Unionsebene nicht, sondern sind dem nationalen Recht zu entnehmen. Vor diesem Hintergrund wendet sich der BGH anschließend der Frage zu, ob eine Anwendung von Normen des nationalen Zivilrechts, hier insbesondere der § 812 Abs. 1 S. 1, 1. Alt. BGB, § 134 BGB und § 33 Abs. 3 GWB a.f. durch Vorgaben des sektorspezifischen Regulierungsrechts ausgeschlossen ist (Rn. 27 ff.). Dies verneint der BGH und betont, dass diese Regelungen der Verwirklichung primärrechtlich verankerter subjektiver Rechte der Marktteilnehmer dienten, denen unmittelbare Geltung zukomme (Rn. 29). Die Mitgliedstaaten seien verpflichtet, die volle Wirksamkeit der Wettbewerbsregeln (Art. 101, 102 AEUV) zu gewährleisten. Diese wiederum setze nach der *Manfredi*-Entscheidung des EuGH[60] voraus, dass jedermann sich vor Gericht auf diese Normen berufen und Ersatz des Schadens verlangen könne, der ihm durch Verstöße gegen Art. 101 oder 102 AEUV entstehe. Nach Maßgabe des Effektivitätsgrundsatzes müssten die Mitgliedstaaten dafür Sorge tragen, dass die Ausübung der durch das Unionsrecht verliehenen Rechte nicht praktisch unmöglich gemacht oder übermäßig erschwert werde (Rn. 30).

Mit Blick auf das Verhältnis von Kartell- und Eisenbahnregulierungsrecht vertritt der BGH die Auffassung, dass privatrechtliche Ansprüche, die auf einer Verletzung des Art. 102 AEUV basieren, selbständig neben der sektorspezifischen Entgeltkontrolle stünden. Das Regulierungsrecht schränke die primärrechtlich begründeten subjektiven Rechte der klagenden Eisenbahnverkehrsunternehmen nicht ein, und ihm sei auch nicht zu entnehmen, dass Schadensersatz- und Erstattungsansprüche wegen missbräuchlicher Entgeltforderungen im Sinne des Art. 102 AEUV nur dann geltend gemacht werden könnten, wenn zuvor die Regulierungsbehörde die fehlende Übereinstimmung der Entgeltbestimmungen mit den Vorschriften des Eisenbahnregulierungsrechts festgestellt habe (Rn. 31). Mit Blick auf das deutsche Recht weist der BGH darauf hin, dass nach § 33 Abs. 1, Abs. 3 GWB a.f. die Zuerkennung eines Schadensersatzanspruchs durch ein Gericht keine Feststellung eines Kartellverstoßes durch eine Kartellbehörde voraussetze. Gleiches gelte für Ansprüche aus § 812 BGB. Sol-

---

60 EuGH, 13. 7. 2006, Rs. C-295/04, ECLI:EU:C:2006:461, Rn. 59 – *Manfredi*.

che Ansprüche seien auch nicht durch das Eisenbahnregulierungsrecht ausgeschlossen (Rn. 32).

Mit Blick auf das Unionsrecht nimmt der BGH sodann das *CTL Logistics*-Urteil ins Visier (Rn. 33 ff.). Diesem sei, so der BGH, schon nach seinem Wortlaut „unzweifelhaft" zu entnehmen, dass der EuGH sich „ausschließlich auf die zivilrechtliche Kontrolle von Wegeentgelten am Maßstab der individuellen vertraglichen Billigkeit im Sinne des § 315 Abs. 3 BGB" beziehe (Rn. 35). Das Verhältnis des kartellrechtlichen Missbrauchsverbots zum Regulierungsrecht werde aber anders als das Verhältnis des § 315 BGB zum Regulierungsrecht vom Vorrang des Primär- gegenüber dem Sekundärrecht bestimmt. Dies entspreche der Rechtsprechung des EuGH, wonach den Gerichten die Anwendung des Art. 102 AEUV nicht abgesprochen werden dürfe, weil dies bedeuten würde, dass den Unionsbürgern Rechte genommen würden, die ihnen aufgrund des AEUV selbst zustünden (Rn. 36).[61]

Der Grundsatz der unmittelbaren Anwendung des Art. 102 AEUV stehe auch dem Vorbehalt einer vorausgehenden regulierungsbehördlichen Verfügung entgegen, denn die „Verhängung von aus Art. 102 AEUV sich ergebenden Rechtspflichten" bedürfe nach der EuGH-Rechtsprechung gerade keiner vorherigen behördlichen Verbotsentscheidung (Rn. 37).[62] Zudem falle die Anwendung der Art. 101 und 102 AEUV nach Art. 6 der VO 1/2003 in die Zuständigkeit der einzelstaatlichen Gerichte. Die nationalen Gerichte seien zwar nach Art. 16 VO 1/2003 an Entscheidungen der EU-Kommission und nach Art. 9 der Richtlinie 2014/104/EU an bestandskräftige Entscheidungen der nationalen Wettbewerbsbehörden gebunden, doch gebe es keine vergleichbare Verpflichtung, die eine Bindung an Entscheidungen einer Regulierungsbehörde normiere. Im Gegenteil seien, „soweit die von der sektorspezifischen Regulierung eröffneten Handlungsspielräume eines marktbeherrschenden Infrastrukturunternehmens nicht hinreichend vom Wettbewerb kontrolliert werden, diese am primärrechtlichen Maßstab des Art. 102 AEUV zu messen" (Rn. 37).

Auch ein weitergehendes Regulierungsziel könnte nicht zur Einschränkung der Ansprüche der Schutzadressaten aus Art. 102 AEUV führen, weil

---

61 Unter Verweis auf EuGH, 30. 1. 1974, Rs. 127/73, ECLI:EU:C:1974:6, Rn. 15/17 – *BRT/SABAM* und EuGH, 10. 7. 1980, Rs. 37/79, ECLI:EU:C:1980:190, Rn. 13 – *Marty/Estée Lauder*.
62 Unter Verweis auf EuGH, 24. 10. 2018, Rs. C-595/17, ECLI: EU: C: 2018: 854, Rn. 35 – *Apple Sales International* und EuG, 22. 3. 2000, Rs. T-125/97, ECLI:EU:T: 2000:84, Rn. 80 – *Coca Cola*.

der Grundsatz der richtlinienkonformen Auslegung nicht als Grundlage für eine „Auslegung contra legem" dienen dürfe (Rn. 38).[63] Eine Richtlinie könne keine Einschränkungen von Rechten Dritter begründen, „da dies darauf hinausliefe, der Europäischen Union die Befugnis zuzuerkennen, mit unmittelbarer Wirkung zulasten Einzelner Verpflichtungen anzuordnen". Dies aber dürfe die Union außerhalb des Primärrechts nur dort, wo ihr die Befugnis zum Erlass von Verordnungen zugewiesen sei (Rn. 38).

Insofern sei ein durch Art. 47 der Grundrechtecharta verbriefter effektiver Schutz der dem Einzelnen durch Art. 102 AEUV eingeräumten Rechte nicht gewährleistet, „wenn die Eisenbahnverkehrsunternehmen bei der Durchsetzung ihrer Ansprüche verfahrensrechtliche Voraussetzungen beachten müssten, die weder im Zeitpunkt der Anspruchsentstehung noch zum Zeitpunkt der gerichtlichen Geltendmachung gesetzlich bestimmt und damit für die Berechtigten erkennbar waren" (Rn. 39). Damit meint der BGH wohl (wie in Zusammenschau mit Rn. 31 und 49 deutlich wird), dass es seiner Ansicht nach erforderlich gewesen wäre, Beschränkungen der Durchsetzung individueller zivilrechtlicher Ansprüche ausdrücklich im Regulierungsrecht zu normieren.

Dem Hinweis auf die durch eine zivilrechtliche Rechtsdurchsetzung drohende Ungleichbehandlung gegenüber anderen Eisenbahnverkehrsunternehmen und auf eine Verletzung des Grundsatzes der einheitlichen Wirkung der Regulierungsentscheidung, die der EuGH in *CTL Logistics* betont hatte, komme, so der BGH, „im Rahmen der Anwendung des Art. 102 AEUV keine maßgebliche Bedeutung zu", weil Art. 102 AEUV subjektive Rechte begründe, die unabhängig von der Richtlinie 2001/14/EG entstünden (was auch den wesentlichen Unterschied zu den von der BNetzA zu wahrenden Diskriminierungsverboten des Art. 4 Abs. 5 der Richtlinie ausmache) und die man nicht „dem Kollektiv der Zugangsberechtigten" unterordnen könne, ohne in Widerspruch zu Art. 102 AEUV zu geraten (Rn. 40).

Eine Relevanz der vom EuGH betonten ausschließlichen Zuständigkeit der BNetzA zur Überprüfung der Wegeentgelte auf der Grundlage der Richtlinie 2001/14/EG weist der BGH mit dem Hinweis zurück, eine solche ausschließliche Zuständigkeit bestehe nur im Anwendungsbereich die-

---

63 Unter Verweis auf EuGH, 20. 6. 2017, Rs. C-579/15, ECLI:EU:C:2017:503, Rn. 33 – *Poplawski* (wo der EuGH sich genaugenommen zu den Grenzen rahmenbeschlusskonformer Auslegung äußert).

ser Richtlinie, erstrecke sich aber – wie aus der EuGH-Rechtsprechung[64] und Art. 6 VO 1/2003 folge – nicht auf die Anwendung des Art. 102 AEUV (Rn. 41). Auch die Gefahr einer unzulässigen Einschränkung der durch die Richtlinie 2001/14/EG eröffneten und vom EuGH in *CTL Logistics* betonten Gestaltungsspielräume der Eisenbahninfrastrukturbetreiber durch eine zivilgerichtliche Durchsetzung des Art. 102 AEUV sieht der BGH nicht, da es gerade die zentrale Aufgabe des Missbrauchsverbots sei, die vom Wettbewerb nicht hinreichend kontrollierten Handlungsspielräume eines marktbeherrschenden Unternehmens der Kontrolle durch die Wettbewerbsbehörden und die Zivilgerichte zu unterwerfen (Rn. 42).

Anders als im Beschluss *Stationspreissystem* sieht der BGH vor diesem Hintergrund auch keinen Grund für eine Aussetzung des Verfahrens nach § 148 ZPO (Rn. 43 ff.). Der BGH ist – wie früher in Bezug auf die Anwendbarkeit des § 315 BGB – der Auffassung, die Anwendbarkeit des Kartellrechts durch die Zivilgerichte unterliege „keinen vernünftigen Zweifeln", so dass er vorliegend (erneut) keinen Anlass für ein Vorabentscheidungsersuchen an den EuGH sieht (Rn. 48).

Zwar könnten die Zivilgerichte, so der BGH, gegebenenfalls verpflichtet sein, den Ausgang eines anhängigen Regulierungsverfahrens abzuwarten, um bei der Anwendung des Art. 102 AEUV den Zwecken und Wirkungen sektorspezifischer Regulierung Rechnung zu tragen (Rn. 44).[65] Dies resultiere daraus, dass alle Träger öffentlicher Gewalt der Mitgliedstaaten (auch die Gerichte) nach Art. 4 Abs. 3 EUV verpflichtet seien, „alle zur Erfüllung der unionsrechtlichen Verpflichtungen geeigneten Maßnahmen allgemeiner oder besonderer Art zu treffen und von solchen Maßnahmen abzusehen, die geeignet sind, die Verwirklichung der Ziele des Vertrags zu gefährden" (Rn. 44).[66] Deshalb seien auch Feststellungen der Regulierungsbehörden in Anwendung regulierungsrechtlicher Regelungen bei Anwen-

---

64 Der BGH macht an dieser Stelle keine Quellenangaben, bezieht sich aber wohl auf seine Ausführungen bei Rn. 37 und damit vermutlich auf die Entscheidungen EuGH, 24. 10. 2018, Rs. C-595/17, ECLI:EU:C:2018:854, Rn. 35 – *Apple Sales International* und EuG, 22. 3. 2000, Rs. T-125/97, ECLI:EU:T:2000:84, Rn. 80 – *Coca Cola*.

65 Unter Verweis auf *Immenga/Mestmäcker*, in: Immenga/Mestmäcker, Wettbewerbsrecht, Band 1: EU, 6. Aufl. 2019, Einl EU A, Rn. 71.

66 BGH, a.a.O., berichtigte Urteilsfassung (im Original war an dieser Stelle von „Art. 5 EUV" die Rede) unter Verweis auf EuGH, 14. 12. 2000, Rs. 344/98, ECLI:EU:C:2000:689, Rn. 49 – *Masterfoods* (Bindung der Mitgliedstaaten an kartellrechtliche Entscheidungen der Kommission, jetzt normiert in Art. 16 VO 1/2003).

dung des Art. 102 AEUV zu berücksichtigen (Rn. 44). Das Berufungsgericht werde daher für seine Beurteilung, ob Ansprüche nach § 812 BGB oder § 33 GWB a.f. bestünden, die von der BNetzA am 5. März 2010 getroffene Entscheidung berücksichtigen, in welcher die Regulierungsbehörde einen Verstoß der Trassenpreise (genauer: der Regionalfaktoren) gegen das eisenbahnrechtliche Diskriminierungsverbot angenommen habe. Dass diese Entscheidung nie bestandskräftig geworden sei, stehe einer Berücksichtigung ebenso wenig entgegen, wie der später zwischen BNetzA und Eisenbahninfrastrukturbetreiber an Stelle der Entscheidung geschlossene öffentlich-rechtliche Vertrag, in dem die BNetzA die Regionalfaktoren im Gegensatz zu der Entscheidung vom 5. März 2010 akzeptiert hatte (Rn. 52).

Das Abwarten einer neuen Entscheidung der BNetzA hielt der BGH *allerdings* nicht für erforderlich, denn es sei im vorliegenden Fall nicht zu erwarten, dass die BNetzA „wenn überhaupt" in eine neue Sachprüfung eintreten werde, weil es ihr an einer Befugnis zur rückwirkenden Überprüfung von bereits gezahlten Wegeentgelten fehle (Rn. 45 ff.).[67] Ein Zuwarten sei den Klägern daher nicht zumutbar, weil anderenfalls die Ausübung ihrer durch das Unionsrecht verliehenen Rechte praktisch unmöglich gemacht oder zumindest übermäßig erschwert würde (Rn. 48).

Dreh- und Angelpunkt der Argumentation des BGH ist, kurzgefasst, die These, dass Art. 102 AEUV *erstens* Vorrang sowohl vor dem nationalen Recht als auch dem sekundären EU-Regulierungsrecht habe, dass Art. 102 AEUV *zweitens* einen vom Regulierungsrecht unabhängigen Anwendungsbereich habe und dass Art. 102 AEUV *drittens* ein ohne jedwede Vorbedingungen zivilgerichtlich durchsetzbares Recht auf Schadensersatz bei Kartellrechtsverstößen gewähre.

---

[67] Vgl. hierzu allerdings OVG Münster, 1. 3. 2019, Az. 13 B 1349/18, ECLI: DE: OVGNRW: 2019: 0301. 13B1349. 18.00, wo das OVG die Auffassung vertrat, die Rücknahme einer Genehmigung mit *ex tunc*-Wirkung sei unter den Voraussetzungen des § 48 VwVfG nicht grundsätzlich (auch nicht durch § 68 Abs. 3 ERegG) ausgeschlossen.

D. Reichweite und Grenzen kartellzivilgerichtlicher Kontrolle

I. Fehlen eindeutiger Regelungen zum Verhältnis von Eisenbahnrecht und Kartellrecht

Weder Eisenbahnregulierungsrecht noch Kartellrecht normieren eine klare Abgrenzung des Regulierungsrechts zu den kartellrechtlichen Missbrauchsverboten, wie sie für das deutsche Recht in § 111 EnWG und § 185 Abs. 3 GWB für das Verhältnis des EnWG zu den kartellrechtlichen Missbrauchsverboten des GWB (§§ 19, 20 und 29 GWB) getroffen wird.[68]

1. Nationales Recht

Nach § 9 Abs. 3 S. 1 BEVVG (früher: § 14b Abs. 2 S. 1 AEG) bleiben Aufgaben und Zuständigkeiten der Kartellbehörden nach dem GWB unberührt. Dies scheint im ersten Zugriff für eine parallele Anwendbarkeit von Eisenbahnregulierungsrecht und Kartellrecht zu sprechen, doch regelt diese Norm lediglich die institutionelle Abgrenzung der Behördenzuständigkeiten. Die Aufgaben und Zuständigkeiten der Kartell*behörden* bleiben danach unberührt, wenn und soweit das GWB anwendbar ist. Eine Aussage über die materiell-rechtliche Reichweite des GWB, also das „Ob" der Anwendbarkeit des deutschen Kartellrechts oder über gar dessen Durchsetzbarkeit durch die *Zivilgerichte*, wird dadurch nicht getroffen.[69]

Gleiches gilt für die Informationspflichten von Regulierungsbehörden, Eisenbahnaufsichtsbehörden und Kartellbehörden nach § 9 Abs. 3 S. 2 bis 4 BEVVG (früher: § 14b Abs. 2 S. 2 bis 4 AEG). Die Behörden sollen sich zwar nach S. 3 „gegenseitig über beabsichtigte Entscheidungen informieren, mit denen ein missbräuchliches oder diskriminierendes Verhalten von Eisenbahninfrastrukturunternehmen untersagt werden soll". Das bedeutet aber nicht, dass eine parallele Zuständigkeit in Bezug auf ein und

---

68 Einzig § 12 Abs. 7 AEG regelt (nach wie vor) eine Ausnahme von § 1 GWB, die im hier untersuchten Kontext aber irrelevant ist.

69 Vgl. *Bechtold*, GWB, 9. Aufl. 2018, § 19, Rn. 83; insoweit ebenso *Bremer/Höppner*, WuW 2009, 1271, 1272.

dasselbe Verhalten bestehen muss.[70] In erster Linie dürfte es darum gehen, sich über die Aktivitäten auf dem Laufenden zu halten, die zwar im jeweils eigenen Zuständigkeitsbereich liegen, aber Berührungspunkte zur Tätigkeit der anderen Behörden aufweisen, wie etwa die Vermietung von Gewerbeflächen in Bahnhofsgebäuden.[71] Auch diese Normen begründen mithin keine materielle Zuständigkeit. Sie normieren lediglich Mitteilungspflichten für den Fall, dass eine solche besteht.

Nichts anderes gilt für § 68 Abs. 1 S. 3 ERegG. Danach entscheidet die Regulierungsbehörde unabhängig von den Zuständigkeiten der Kartellbehörden von Amts wegen über geeignete Maßnahmen zur Verhütung von Diskriminierung und Marktverzerrung. Auch diese Regelung bezieht sich auf die institutionelle Abgrenzung der *Behörden*zuständigkeiten und trifft keine Entscheidung über das materielle Verhältnis von ERegG und GWB oder gar über die Befugnis der Zivilgerichtsbarkeit, unabhängig von der BNetzA in deren Zuständigkeitsbereich tätig zu werden.

Dass das nationale Recht nicht geeignet ist, Vorgaben zur Anwendung des Unionskartellrechts zu machen, versteht sich schon aus normhierarchischen[72] und kompetenziellen Gründen von selbst. Der nationale Gesetzgeber besitzt keine Befugnis, verbindliche Vorgaben zur Auslegung des Unionsrechts zu machen. Er würde durch eine solche Regelung auch gegen den Grundsatz der Unionstreue (Art. 4 Abs. 3 EUV) verstoßen.[73]

In der Summe ist festzuhalten, dass sich im nationalen Recht nach wie vor weder Regelungen finden, die eine parallele Anwendbarkeit von Eisenbahnregulierungsrecht und Kartellrecht anordnen, noch Regelungen, die eine solche Anwendbarkeit explizit ausschließen.[74]

---

70 Insoweit a.A. *Bremer/Höppner*, WuW 2009, 1271, 1272.

71 Vgl. *Ruge*, DVBl. 2005, 1405, 1407 f.; zur Zur Einordnung von Personenbahnhöfen vgl. allerdings auch jüngst EuGH, 10. 7. 2019, Rs. C-210/18, ECLI:EU:C:2019: 586 – *WESTbahn Management*.

72 Der Vorrang des Unionsrechts vor dem nationalen Recht wird vom EuGH in ständiger Rechtsprechung betont, vgl. schon EuGH, 13. 2. 1969, Rs. 14/68, ECLI: EU:C:1969:4, Rn. 6 – *Walt Wilhelm*. Diesen Grundsatz für das Verhältnis zum GG erstmals relativierend BVerfG, 5. 5. 2020, Az. 2 BvR 859/15, 2 BvR 980/16, 2 BvR 2006/15, 2 BvR 1651/15 – *EZB Staatsanleihekaufprogramm*.

73 So zu Recht OLG Düsseldorf, 17. 3. 2015, Az. VI-Kart 10/15 (V), ECLI: DE: OLGD:2017:0315.VI.KART10.15V.00, Rn. 362 ff. – *Rundholzvermarktung* zur offensichtlich unionsrechtswidrigen und daher unbeachtlichen Regelung des § 46 Abs. 2 BWaldG, mit welcher der deutsche Gesetzgeber verbindliche Vorgaben zur Anwendung der Art. 101 AEUV zu machen sucht.

74 Zu den überzeugenden historischen, systematischen und teleologischen Argumenten gegen eine parallele Kompetenz der Zivilgerichte, die hier nicht wieder-

2. Unionsrecht

a) Sekundärrecht

Auch die Richtlinie 2001/14/EG schweigt zum Verhältnis von Eisenbahnregulierungsrecht und Kartellrecht. Lediglich in Art. 9 Abs. 1 (Entgeltnachlässe), Art. 17 Abs. 2 (Rahmenverträge) und Art. 24 Abs. 2 (Besondere Fahrwege) findet sich der Hinweis, dass die betreffenden Regelungen „unbeschadet der Art. 81, 82 ... des Vertrags" (heute Art. 101, 102 AEUV) anzuwenden sind. Entsprechende Regelungen finden sich im aktuellen Recht in Art. 33 Abs. 1, Art. 42 Abs. 1 und Art. 49 Abs. 2 der Richtlinie 2012/34/EU.

Durch diese Normen wird allerdings nur deklaratorisch an die grundsätzliche Anwendbarkeit der Wettbewerbsregeln erinnert. Die grundsätzliche Anwendbarkeit der primärrechtlichen Wettbewerbsregeln (Art. 101 und 102 AEUV) muss weder durch eine sekundärrechtliche Regelung angeordnet werden, noch kann sie durch eine solche Regelung generell ausgeschlossen werden. Aus der Erwähnung der Art. 101 und 102 AEUV in einigen Richtlinienbestimmungen folgt daher weder, dass die Wettbewerbsregeln bei Anwendung der anderen Richtlinienbestimmungen unbeachtlich wären, noch dass Art. 101 und 102 AEUV in Bezug auf die Regelungsgegenstände, bei denen sie erwähnt werden, unabhängig vom regulierungsrechtlich vorgesehenen Verfahren auch vor den Zivilgerichten durchgesetzt werden könnten. Dies muss vielmehr durch Auslegung der Art. 101 und 102 AEUV im Kontext des Unionsrechts insgesamt ermittelt werden. Für die hier untersuchten Fragestellungen sind die zitierten Richtlinienbestimmungen daher unergiebig.

Gleiches gilt letztlich auch für Art. 56 Abs. 2 der Richtlinie 2012/34/EU, der keine Entsprechung in der Vorgängerregelung des Art. 30 der Richtlinie 2001/14/EG hat. Dieser normiert:

„Unbeschadet der Befugnisse der nationalen Wettbewerbsbehörden für die Sicherstellung des Wettbewerbs in den Schienenverkehrsmärkten ist die Regulierungsstelle berechtigt, die Wettbewerbssituation in den Schienenverkehrsmärkten zu überwachen".

---

holt werden sollen, s. *Bechtold/Linsmeier*, Gutachten „Zur Überprüfbarkeit von Eisenbahninfrastruktur-Nutzungsentgelten anhand §§ 19, 20 GWB und Art. 102 AEUV in zivilgerichtlichen Verfahren" vom 3. 3. 2010, S. 32 ff.

Der BGH hatte schon 2016 in seinem später zurückgezogenen Vorabent-scheidungsersuchen an den EuGH darauf hingewiesen, dass Art. 56 Abs. 2 ausdrücklich bestimme, dass die Befugnisse der Kartellbehörden unberührt blieben.[75] Auch Generalanwalt *Mengozzi* hat in seinen Schlussanträ-gen in der Rechtssache *CTL Logistics* die Auffassung vertreten, Art. 30 der Richtlinie 2001/14/EG schließe eine parallele Entgeltkontrolle durch Regu-lierungsbehörden und Zivilgerichte nicht aus. Er hatte insoweit zum Beleg auf Art. 56 Abs. 2 verwiesen, der „im Gegensatz zur Richtlinie 2001/14" ausdrücklich anerkenne, dass die Befugnisse der Regulierungsstelle die Be-fugnisse der nationalen Kartellbehörden unberührt ließen.[76] Indes ist der EuGH auf diesen Exkurs des Generalanwalts *erstens* nicht eingegangen. *Zweitens* kann man Art. 56 Abs. 2 schon seinem Wortlaut nach allenfalls eine Kompetenz der Kartell*behörden* nicht aber der Kartell*zivilgerichte* ent-nehmen,[77] und *drittens* hat Art. 56 schon ausweislich der Normüberschrift auch nicht die materiell-rechtliche Abgrenzung der Anwendungsbereiche von Kartell- und Eisenbahnregulierungsrecht zum Gegenstand, sondern re-gelt – ebenso wie § 9 Abs. 3 S. 1 BEVVG (früher: § 14b Abs. 2 S. 1 AEG) – lediglich die Abgrenzung der Behördenzuständigkeiten. Mit Inkrafttreten der Richtlinie 2012/34/EU haben sich mithin keine für die hier untersuch-ten Fragestellungen relevanten Änderungen ergeben.

Auch Art. 6 VO 1/2003 ist insoweit unergiebig. Danach sind zwar die „einzelstaatlichen Gerichte … für die Anwendung der Artikel 81 und 82 des Vertrages [heute Art. 101 und 102 AEUV] zuständig". Aus der generel-len Anwendungsbefugnis kann allerdings kein Recht abgeleitet werden, Art. 101 und 102 AEUV in jeder denkbaren Situation und ohne Rücksicht auf andere Regelungsgegenstände und Ziele des Unionsrechts anzuwen-den. Die Zivilgerichte sind z. B. unstreitig auch für die Anwendung des Zi-vilrechts (einschließlich des § 315 Abs. 3 BGB) „zuständig". Sie dürfen § 315 BGB aber nach Maßgabe des *CTL Logistics*-Urteils trotzdem nicht an-wenden, um regulierte Eisenbahnentgelte einer Billigkeitskontrolle zu un-terziehen, weil dies die Funktionsfähigkeit des Eisenbahnregulierungs-rechts infrage stellen würde. Art. 6 VO 1/2003 macht es insoweit allenfalls

---

75 BGH, 7. 6. 2016, Az. KZR 12/15, ECLI:ECLI:DE:BGH:2016:070616BKZR12.15.0, Rn. 47.

76 GA *Mengozzi*, Schlussanträge vom 21. 11. 2016, Rs. 489/15, ECLI:EU:C:2016:901, Fn. 40; ähnlich *Kühling*, Eisenbahnentgeltregulierung jenseits AEG und EIBV, in: Ronellenfitsch/Eschweiler/Hörster, Aktuelle Probleme des Eisenbahnrechts, 2015, S. 73, 102.

77 So zu Recht LG Berlin, 30. 10. 2018, Az. 16 O 495/15 Kart, ECLI:DE:LGBE:2018: 1030.16O495.15KART.00, Rn. 46.

möglich, dass behördliche Regulierung und zivilgerichtliche Kartellrechtsdurchsetzung (wie behördliche Regulierung und zivilgerichtliche Billigkeitskontrolle im Fall *CTL Logistics*) miteinander in Konflikt geraten, die Norm entscheidet diesen Konflikt aber nicht zugunsten des Kartellrechts oder der Kartellzivilgerichtsbarkeit.

Entsprechendes gilt für die Kartellschadensersatzrichtlinie 2014/104/EU. Diese betont in ihren Erwägungsgründen 2 und 13 zwar, dass die nationalen Gerichte zur unmittelbaren Anwendung der Wettbewerbsregeln (also der Art. 101 und 102 AEUV) befugt seien, ohne dass es der vorherigen Feststellung der Zuwiderhandlung durch eine „Wettbewerbsbehörde" bedürfe. Doch gilt dies eben nur für das Verhältnis zwischen *Wettbewerbs*behörden (also Kartellbehörden) und Gerichten. Eine Aussage zum Verhältnis von *Regulierungs*behörden und Zivilgerichten oder gar von materiellem Eisenbahnregulierungsrecht und Kartellrecht wird dadurch nicht getroffen.

In der Summe bleibt festzuhalten, dass das sekundäre Unionsrecht das Verhältnis von materiellem Eisenbahnregulierungsrecht und materiellem Kartellrecht ebenso wenig explizit regelt wie die Zuständigkeit der Zivilgerichte zur kartellrechtlichen Kontrolle von Eisenbahnentgelten, welche der Regulierung durch die BNetzA unterliegen. Aus dem Fehlen einer eindeutigen Abgrenzungsregelung im Sekundärrecht kann nicht auf eine parallele Anwendbarkeit des Kartellrechts durch die Zivilgerichte geschlossen werden. Diese Frage muss anhand einer Analyse der potentiell konfligierenden Normen beantwortet werden, wie es der EuGH in *CTL Logistics* in Bezug auf die – ebenfalls in den Richtlinien nicht explizit adressierte – Frage nach der Möglichkeit einer Billigkeitskontrolle nach § 315 BGB getan hat.

b) Primärrecht

Mit Blick auf die primärrechtlichen Regelungen im AEUV genügt an dieser Stelle der Hinweis, dass auch der AEUV keine explizite Regelung zum Verhältnis von Kartell- und Eisenbahnregulierungsrecht trifft. Weder beansprucht Art. 102 AEUV seinem Wortlaut nach eine unbeschränkte Anwendung durch die Zivilgerichte oder Vorrang vor dem Regulierungsrecht, noch normieren die verkehrsrechtlichen Regelungen in Art. 90 ff. AEUV eine kartellrechtliche Bereichsausnahme für den Verkehrssektor. Art. 101 und 102 AEUV sind daher, wie der EuGH in der *Asjes*-Entscheidung bestätigt hat, im Grundsatz auch im Verkehrssektor anwendbar.[78] Allerdings rechtfertigt das Fehlen eines ausdrücklich normierten kartellrechtlichen Ausnahmebereichs für sich genommen noch nicht den Umkehrschluss, dass die Wettbewerbsregeln auch im unionsrechtlich regulierten Bereich *erstens* ohne Rücksicht auf das Regulierungsrecht und *zweitens* gerade durch die Zivilgerichte angewendet werden könnten.[79] Durch die *Asjes*-Entscheidung wird ein Konflikt zwischen Eisenbahnverkehrsrecht und Kartellrecht ermöglicht, aber nicht bereits im Sinne eines unbedingten Vorrangs des Kartellrechts entschieden. Vor allem folgt daraus auch nicht, dass eine Kompetenz *gerade der nationalen Zivilgerichte* besteht, Art. 102 AEUV nach eigenen Vorstellungen anzuwenden, ohne dabei Rücksicht auf Ziele und Funktionsfähigkeit eines besonderen, unionsrechtlich vorgegebenen behördlichen Regulierungsregimes nehmen zu müssen, z. B. wenn ein Zivilgericht der Auffassung ist, das nationale Regulierungsrecht sei unzureichend oder die nationale Regulierungsbehörde werde ihrer Aufgabe nicht gerecht. Diese Frage ist vielmehr durch Auslegung der konkreten unionsrechtlichen Vorschriften zu klären, die nachfolgend unter Berücksichtigung der Entscheidung *CTL Logistics* und der übrigen EuGH-Rechtsprechung erfolgen soll, weil nur der EuGH nach Art. 267 AEUV letztverbindlich über die Auslegung des AEUV, des EU-Sekundärrechts und des Verhältnisses von Unionskartellrecht und Unionsregulierungsrecht zueinander entscheiden kann.

II. Wortlaut der CTL Logistics-Entscheidung

Der BGH ist der Auffassung, die *CTL Logistics*-Entscheidung des EuGH beziehe sich, „wie bereits der Antwort des Unionsgerichtshofs unzweifelhaft zu entnehmen ist – ausschließlich auf die zivilrechtliche Kontrolle von Wegeentgelten am Maßstab der individuellen vertraglichen Billigkeit im Sinne des § 315 Abs. 3 BGB".[80] Der EuGH hatte dem LG Berlin in der Tat geantwortet, dass die Richtlinie 2001/14/EG so auszulegen sei,

---

78 EuGH, 30. 4. 1986, Rs. C-209/84, ECLI:EU:C:1986:188, Rn. 42 – *Asjes*.
79 So aber *Keding*, IR 2019, 90 93; *Bremer/Scheffczyk*, NZKart 2018, 121, 123; *Hauf/ Baumgartner*, EuZW 2018, 1028, 1030 f.
80 BGH, a.a.O., Rn. 35. Vgl. auch, Rn. 27 ff., wo der BGH betont, dass Normen des nationalen Zivilrechts und Kartellrechts jedenfalls zur Effektuierung des Art. 102 AEUV weiter anwendbar seien.

„dass sie der Anwendung einer nationalen Regelung wie der im Ausgangsverfahren fraglichen entgegenstehen, wonach die Wegeentgelte im Eisenbahnverkehr von den ordentlichen Gerichten im Einzelfall auf Billigkeit überprüft und gegebenenfalls unabhängig von der in Art. 30 der Richtlinie 2001/14 in der durch die Richtlinie 2004/49 geänderten Fassung vorgesehenen Überwachung durch die Regulierungsstelle abgeändert werden können".[81]

Dies folgte allerdings schlicht daraus, dass das den EuGH um eine Vorabentscheidung ersuchende LG Berlin nur nach der Vereinbarkeit der Richtlinie mit einer zivilgerichtlichen Billigkeitskontrolle nach § 315 BGB gefragt hatte. Die Frage, ob auch eine zivilgerichtliche Kontrolle anhand kartellrechtlicher Vorschriften möglich ist, war überhaupt nicht Gegenstand des Verfahrens.[82]

Anders als der Generalanwalt, der ein umfassendes Rechtsgutachten erstellt und daher bisweilen auch in Exkursen auf Rechtsfragen eingeht, die über das Vorabentscheidungsersuchen hinausreichen, beschränkt sich der EuGH – seiner Aufgabe nach Art. 267 AEUV entsprechend – auf die Beantwortung der ihm vorgelegten Fragen zur Auslegung des Unionsrechts.[83] Dass sich der EuGH – anders als Generalanwalt *Mengozzi* in seinen Schlussanträgen zu *CTL Logistics* und der BGH in seinem Vorabentscheidungsersuchen von 2016 – nicht ausdrücklich zum Kartellrecht geäußert hat, kann daher entgegen einigen Stimmen in der Literatur[84] nicht als Argument gegen eine Übertragbarkeit der *CTL Logistics*-Grundsätze auf eine kartellzivilgerichtliche Entgeltkontrolle herangezogen werden. Für den EuGH bestand dafür angesichts der ihm vorgelegten Fragen schlicht kein Anlass, ganz abgesehen davon, dass auch der Generalanwalt[85] und der BGH[86] das Kartellrecht eher beiläufig erwähnt haben.

Das Vorabentscheidungsersuchen des BGH von 2016 lässt sich sogar für eine Übertragbarkeit der *CTL Logistics*-Grundsätze auf eine kartellzivilgerichtliche Kontrolle fruchtbar machen, denn darin hatte der BGH (noch in dem Glauben, sowohl die Anwendung des § 315 BGB als auch des Kartellrechts durch die Zivilgerichte sei mit dem Unionsrecht vereinbar) selbst

---

81 EuGH, 9. 11. 2017, Rs. C-489/15, EU:C:2017:834, Tenor – *CTL Logistics.*
82 S. Wiedergabe der Vorlagefragen oben auf S. 15.
83 So auch zu Recht *Hauf/Baumgartner*, EuZW 2018, 1029, 1033.
84 *Bremer/Scheffczyk*, NZKart 2018, 121, 122 (mit Bezug auf die *Crehan/Courage*-Entscheidung des EuGH); *Keding*, IR 2019, 90 92 f.
85 S. oben S. 29.
86 S. oben S. 31.

auf die Parallelitäten zwischen der zivilgerichtlichen Durchsetzung von Ansprüchen nach § 315 BGB und nach dem Kartellrecht hingewiesen.[87]

Für eine Gleichbehandlung aller Privatklagen mit Blick auf die *CTL Logistics*-Grundsätze sprechen auch die Beschlüsse des BVerfG vom 8. Oktober 2015, durch welche der BGH letztlich zu seinem Vorabentscheidungsersuchen von 2016 veranlasst wurde. Dort heißt es:

> „Soweit von Seiten der im Ausgangsverfahren beteiligten Eisenbahnverkehrsunternehmen die Entscheidungserheblichkeit eines Vorabentscheidungsverfahrens mit der Begründung verneint wird, dass die Zivilgerichte die Beschwerdeführerin über den kartellrechtlichen Schadensersatz nach § 823 Abs. 2 BGB, § 33 GWB ohnehin zur Rückzahlung hätten verurteilen beziehungsweise eine Nachforderung hätten abweisen müssen, erstrecken sich die seitens der Beschwerdeführerin vorgebrachten Bedenken hinsichtlich des Vorrangs des unionsrechtlichen Richtlinienrechts gegenüber dem nationalen Recht, ohne dass es auf deren abschließende Überzeugungskraft ankommt, auch auf eine Anwendung von § 823 Abs. 2 BGB, § 33 GWB".[88]

In der Summe lässt sich allein aus dem Wortlaut des EuGH-Urteils *CTL Logistics* keine eindeutige Antwort auf die Frage ableiten, ob die darin entwickelten Grundsätze auch für die kartellzivilgerichtliche Kontrolle regulierter Entgelte gelten. Der EuGH spricht diesen Aspekt ganz einfach nicht an, lässt die Frage also formell betrachtet offen.

Es ist daher erforderlich, zu untersuchen, ob die vom EuGH vorgebrachten Argumente in der Sache auf eine zivilgerichtliche Kontrolle am Maßstab des Kartellrechts übertragbar sind. Dies soll nachfolgend in zwei Schritten geschehen. Zunächst wird der Frage nachgespürt, ob sich die zivilgerichtliche Durchsetzung des Kartellrechts bereits an sich so grundlegend von derjenigen des § 315 BGB unterscheidet, dass eine Übertragung der *CTL Logistics*-Grundsätze ausscheidet oder ob eine solche im Gegenteil

---

87 BGH, 7. 6. 2016, Az. KZR 12/15, ECLI:ECLI:DE:BGH:2016:070616BKZR12.15.0, Rn. 46 ff.; vgl. auch *Kühling*, Eisenbahnentgeltregulierung jenseits AEG und EIBV, in: Ronellenfitsch/Eschweiler/Hörster, Aktuelle Probleme des Eisenbahnrechts, 2015, S. 73, 102 ff., der betont, für die Anwendung des § 315 BGB und des Kartellrechts müsse das Gleiche gelten, damit allerdings (wie der BGH im Vorlagebeschluss) rechtsirrig meint, beide wären parallel zum Regulierungsrecht durch die Zivilgerichte anwendbar.

88 BVerfG, 8. 10. 2015, Az. 1 BvR 3509/13, ECLI: ECLI: DE: BVerfG: 2015: rk20151008.1bvr350913, Rn. 21 und Az.1 BvR 1320/14, ECLI:ECLI:DE:BVerfG: 2015:rk20151008.1bvr132014, Rn. 21, juris.

– unbeschadet eventueller Besonderheiten des Unionskartellrechts – geboten erscheint (III). Nachfolgend werden sodann die Besonderheiten des Unionskartellrechts, insbesondere die Frage nach dem Vorrang des Art. 102 AEUV bzw. seiner privatrechtlichen Durchsetzung vor dem Eisenbahnregulierungsrecht betrachtet (IV).

III. Übertragbarkeit der CTL Logistics-Grundsätze auf die Kartellzivilgerichtsbarkeit

Im Zentrum des *CTL Logistics*-Urteils steht in materieller Hinsicht das eisenbahnrechtliche Diskriminierungsverbot – bzw. genauer: das Gebot der diskriminierungsfreien Gleichbehandlung aller Eisenbahnverkehrsunternehmen nach Maßgabe der Beurteilungskriterien der Richtlinie 2001/14/EG, insbesondere des Art. 4 Abs. 5 (Rn. 45 ff.). Dieses Gebot wird institutionell durch die Unabhängigkeit des Infrastrukturbetreibers bei der Entgeltbestimmung unter zentraler Überwachung durch die zuständige Regulierungsstelle (unbeschadet verwaltungsgerichtlicher Nachprüfung) nach Art. 30 der Richtlinie abgesichert (Rn. 55 ff.).

Auf der Basis dieser beiden Grundprinzipien hat der EuGH die oben wiedergegebenen sieben Feststellungen getroffen, aus denen die Unvereinbarkeit einer zivilgerichtlichen Billigkeitskontrolle mit dem Richtlinienrecht folgt[89] und die nachfolgend in strukturierter Form auf ihre Anwendbarkeit auf die zivilgerichtliche Kontrolle am Maßstab des Kartellrechts hin untersucht werden.

1. Konflikt mit dem Diskriminierungsverbot und eigenständiger Anwendungsbereich

Das Verhältnis der materiellen Regelungsanliegen der Eisenbahnregulierungsrichtlinien (insbesondere des eisenbahnrechtlichen Diskriminierungsverbots) zu Privatklageverfahren kommt in den Feststellungen 1, 4 und 7 des EuGH zum Ausdruck.[90]

---

89 Siehe im Einzelnen oben S. 18 ff.
90 EuGH, 9. 11. 2017, Rs. C-489/15, EU:C:2017:834 Rn. 70 ff. – *CTL Logistics*; siehe auch oben S. 18 ff.

a) Diskriminierungsverbot und Wettbewerbsverzerrung

Der EuGH betont den Widerspruch einer auf den Einzelfall abstellenden zivilgerichtlichen Billigkeitskontrolle zum Diskriminierungsverbot des Richtlinienrechts (Rn. 70). Er hebt dazu die „praktisch unüberwindliche Schwierigkeit" hervor, die verschiedenen, nur *inter partes* wirkenden Einzelfallentscheidungen der Zivilgerichte rasch in ein nicht diskriminierendes System zu integrieren, möge sich die Regulierungsstelle auch bemühen, auf diese Entscheidungen zu reagieren. Daraus würde, so der EuGH, jedenfalls bis zu einer höchstrichterlichen Entscheidung eine Ungleichbehandlung der Eisenbahnverkehrsunternehmen drohen (Rn. 88), die dem oder den Klägern einen Wettbewerbsvorteil verschaffe (Rn. 95 f.) und andere dazu anreize, sich durch Zivilklagen (statt z. B. durch Steigerung ihrer Effizienz) Vorteile gegenüber den Wettbewerbern zu verschaffen (Rn. 101).

Es ist unstreitig, dass die Gefahr einer Ungleichbehandlung der Kläger und der anderen Eisenbahnverkehrsunternehmen unabhängig davon besteht, ob der materielle Prüfmaßstab dem allgemeinen Zivilrecht oder dem Kartellrecht entnommen wird – und auch unabhängig davon, ob es sich dabei um Erstattungsansprüche oder (ein mutmaßlich überhöhtes Entgelt kompensierende) Schadensersatzansprüche handelt. Eine zivilgerichtliche Entscheidung in einem Verfahren auf Rückzahlung von Entgelten oder Schadensersatz wirkt unabhängig von der materiellen Anspruchsgrundlage nur *inter partes* und führt daher, wie auch der BGH einräumt, notwendig zu einer Ungleichbehandlung in Bezug auf das Entgelt. Ein Zivilprozess unterliegt anders als ein Behördenverfahren zudem nicht der Amtsermittlung, sondern der Disposition der Parteien. Außerhalb des Wettbewerbsschutzes liegende Regulierungsanliegen werden dagegen im Kartellzivilprozess typischerweise ebenso wenig berücksichtigt wie die Interessen der anderen Eisenbahnverkehrsunternehmen, obwohl diese letztlich möglicherweise durch eine individuelle Absenkung der Entgelte belastet würden, weil am Ende ein bestimmtes Gesamtaufkommen erreicht werden muss.[91]

Schließlich entscheidet im Zivilverfahren nicht immer die gleiche zentrale Instanz wie im behördlichen Regulierungsverfahren, sondern eine Vielzahl von Zivilgerichten (nebst unterschiedlicher Berufungsgerichte) mit unterschiedlichen Auffassungen sowie unterschiedlicher kartellrechtli-

---

91 So zu Recht LG Berlin, 30. 10. 2018, Az. 16 O 495/15 Kart, ECLI:DE:LGBE:2018:
1030.16O495.15KART.00, Rn. 39.

cher und (wenn überhaupt) eisenbahnregulierungsrechtlicher Sachkunde, so dass jahrelange Uneinheitlichkeit und Rechtsunsicherheit drohen würden. Diese Uneinheitlichkeit würde sogar nach einer höchstrichterlichen Entscheidung weiterbestehen, da die Höhe der Entgelte auch danach im Wesentlichen von den tatrichterlichen Feststellungen sowie davon abhängen würde, ob ein Eisenbahnverkehrsunternehmen gegen die Entgelte zivilrechtlich vorgeht oder nicht. Dass dadurch auch Wettbewerbsverzerrungen zwischen verschiedenen Eisenbahnverkehrsunternehmen entstehen würden, liegt ebenfalls auf der Hand.

Weder der BGH[92] noch die seine Auffassung unterstützenden Literaturstimmen[93] stellen vor diesem Hintergrund infrage, dass eine zivilgerichtliche Kontrolle von Eisenbahnentgelten zu einer Ungleichbehandlung führt. Sie halten eine solche Ungleichbehandlung lediglich für irrelevant, weil eine Anwendung des Kartellrechts ihrer Auffassung nach durch Art. 102 AEUV geboten ist und das Unionsprimärrecht damit das richtlinienrechtliche Gleichbehandlungsgebot überspielt. Darauf wird noch in Abschnitt IV zurückzukommen sein.

b) Eigenständige, vom Regulierungsrecht abweichende Kriterien

Den Hinweis auf einen Konflikt mit dem richtlinienrechtlichen Diskriminierungsverbot flankiert der EuGH durch eine Kritik am „eigenständigen Anwendungsbereich" des § 315 BGB, der *einerseits* Kriterien umfasse, die in der Richtlinie nicht vorgesehen seien (Rn. 71, 100), *andererseits* aber auch dazu führen könne, dass die Richtlinienziele, namentlich das Ziel, den Betreibern einen Anreiz zur Optimierung ihrer Fahrwege zu geben, nicht hinreichend berücksichtigt würden (Rn. 101 f.).

Dass auch die Maßstäbe von Regulierungs- und Kartellrecht nicht deckungsgleich sind, ist im Grundsatz ebenfalls unstreitig.[94] Der BGH hat schon in seinem Vorabentscheidungsersuchen von 2016 die inhaltliche Eigenständigkeit nicht nur des § 315 BGB, sondern auch des Kartellrechts ex-

---

92 Vgl. BGH, 29. 10. 2019, Az. KZR 39/19, ECLI: DE: BGH: 2019: 291019UKZR39. 19.0, Rn. 40 – *Trassenentgelte.*
93 Vgl. etwa *Hauf/Baumgartner*, EuZW 2018, 1028, 1031 und 1034.
94 Vgl. OLG Dresden, 17. 4. 2019, Az. U 4/18 Kart, ECLI:DE:OLGDRES:2019:0417. U4.18KART.0A, Rn. 45.

plizit betont und daraus sogar ein Argument für die parallele Anwendbarkeit zivilrechtlicher Maßstäbe abgeleitet.[95]

Dabei dürften mögliche Konfliktfelder in aller Regel gerade nicht mit Blick auf das Diskriminierungsverbot und den Wettbewerbsschutz bestehen (die Kartell- und Regulierungsrecht gleichermaßen verfolgen), sondern eher dadurch auftreten, dass die eine oder andere Materie falsch angewendet wird oder dass das Regulierungsrecht über das Kartellrecht hinausgehende, außerwettbewerbliche Ziele verfolgt. Konflikte zwischen Kartell- und Regulierungsrecht dürften auch deshalb in tendenziell geringerem Maße auftreten als solche zwischen Regulierungsrecht und § 315 BGB, weil das Kartellrecht dem nationalen Zivilrichter einen weniger großen Spielraum lässt als die Billigkeitsnorm § 315 BGB und weil für das Kartellrecht in der Tat in stärkerem Maße (und insbesondere auch auf Unionsebene) einheitliche Maßstäbe existieren.[96]

Allerdings sind die kartellrechtlichen Maßstäbe *einerseits* nur generalklauselartig formuliert und auch durch die Praxis weniger ausdifferenziert als die regulierungsrechtlichen Vorgaben, *andererseits* sind sie mit den Vorgaben des Regulierungsrechts, wie oben beschrieben, nicht notwendig völlig deckungsgleich. Das Kartellrecht ist *erstens* enger auf den Schutz allein des Wettbewerbs fokussiert, ohne notwendig die sonstigen Regulierungsziele zu berücksichtigen.

Zweitens unterliegt auch der Wettbewerbsschutz im regulierten Bereich (z. B. weil die Regulierung der Marktöffnung angesichts früherer Staatsmonopole dient) besonderen Anforderungen und wird daher durch das Regulierungsrecht an die Besonderheiten des regulierten Sektors angepasst. In diesem Kontext betont der EuGH in *CTL Logistics* z. B. auch die Wechselbeziehung zwischen dem besonderen, für die Funktionsfähigkeit des eisenbahnrechtlichen Entgeltsystems erforderlichen Spielraum des Infrastrukturbetreibers und dem sein „Gegenstück" bildenden eisenbahnregulierungsrechtlichen Diskriminierungsverbot.[97]

Drittens ist die Durchsetzung des Kartellrechts im Zivilprozess offener für die Berücksichtigung individueller Belange der Streitparteien; dies wird auch und gerade im Falle privater Klagen deutlich, die auf eine individuelle Erstattung von Entgelten bzw. auf Kartellschadensersatz gerichtet

---

95 BGH, 7. 6. 2016, Az. KZR 12/15, ECLI:ECLI:DE:BGH:2016:070616BKZR12.15.0, Rn. 46 ff.; ebenso *Hauf/Baumgartner*, EuZW 2018, 1028, 1030; *Hauf/Baumgartner*, TranspR 2019, 69, 70.
96 Vgl. *Hauf/Baumgartner*, EuZW 2018, 1028, 1030.
97 EuGH, 9. 11. 2017, Rs. C-489/15, EU:C:2017:834 Rn. 51 – *CTL Logistics*.

sind. Die private Kartellrechtsdurchsetzung mag das öffentliche Interesse an der Durchsetzung des Kartellrechts fördern, aber sie erfolgt primär (wenn nicht sogar allein) zur Verfolgung individueller Interessen und insoweit aus eigennützigen Motiven der Kläger.[98]

Viertens unterliegt das Kartellrecht einer eigenständigen, richterrechtlich getriebenen Entwicklung, die nicht notwendig parallel oder auch nur konform zu der vom Gesetzgeber vorangetriebenen Entwicklung des Regulierungsrechts verläuft. In der Literatur wird beispielhaft darauf hingewiesen, dass der BGH im Energierecht teilweise an Kriterien festhalte, die sich regulierungsökonomisch bereits als unfruchtbar erwiesen hätten, und dass der BGH bisweilen dazu neige, sich als „Motor des Regulierungsrechts" zu verstehen, obwohl er nur deren „Mechaniker" sei, während die Rolle des Motors dem Gesetzgeber zukomme.[99]

c) Ergebnis

In der Summe ist damit festzustellen, dass die Gefahr einer Ungleichbehandlung klagender und nicht klagender Eisenbahnverkehrsunternehmen, aber auch zwischen bei verschiedenen Gerichten klagenden Eisenbahnverkehrsunternehmen, bei einer auf kartellrechtlichen Normen basierenden zivilgerichtlichen Kontrolle ebenso besteht wie bei einer zivilgerichtlichen Billigkeitskontrolle nach § 315 BGB und dass auch Wertungswidersprüche zwischen dem von der BNetzA angewendeten Eisenbahnregulierungsrecht und dem durch eine Vielzahl von Zivilgerichten interpretierten und angewendeten Kartellrecht drohen.[100] Die in *CTL Logistics* getroffenen Feststellungen des EuGH zum Konflikt einer zivilgerichtlichen Einzelfallkontrolle mit dem eisenbahnrechtlichen Diskriminierungsverbot und mit den anderen materiellen Beurteilungskriterien der Richtlinien gelten daher für die

---

98 Vgl. in diesem Kontext *Bornkamm/Tolkmitt*, in: Langen/Bunte, Kartellrecht, Band 1, 13. Aufl. 2018 Vor § 33 GWB, Rn. 3, die zu Recht darauf hinweisen, dass in der Vergangenheit mehrfach zu beobachten gewesen sei, „dass sich Kartellzivilverfahren von großer Tragweite unmittelbar vor der Entscheidung des BGH erledigten – ganz offensichtlich, weil eine Seite die mit den Entscheidungen verbundene Klärung der Rechtslage vermeiden wollte".

99 So zu Recht *Fricke*, N&R 2018, 66, 72.

100 So zu Recht schon OLG Dresden, 17. 4. 2019, Az. U 4/18 Kart, ECLI:DE:OLGD-RES: 2019: 0417.U4. 18KART. 0A, Rn. 46; *Gerstner*, EuZW 2018, 74, 80; *ders.*, N&R 2019, 62, 63 f.; *Weitner*, EnWZ 2018, 73, 78; *Staebe*, EuZW 2019, 118, 121; *Karolus*, EuR 2018, 477, 480 f.

Kontrolle am Maßstab des Kartellrechts ebenso wie für eine zivilgerichtliche Billigkeitskontrolle.

2. Konflikt mit der zentralen Überwachung durch die zuständige Regulierungsstelle

Nach Maßgabe des Eisenbahnregulierungsrechts ist es Aufgabe der Regulierungsstelle (in Deutschland der BNetzA) bzw. des für deren Kontrolle zuständigen gerichtlichen Instanzenzugs (in Deutschland der Verwaltungsgerichtsbarkeit) dafür zu sorgen, dass die Eisenbahnentgelte vom Infrastrukturbetreiber nach den Vorgaben der Richtlinie und des sie umsetzenden nationalen Rechts bestimmt werden und dass insbesondere das eisenbahnrechtliche Diskriminierungsverbot gewahrt bleibt. Diese institutionelle Absicherung des Regulierungsverfahrens und damit auch des materiellen Diskriminierungsverbots findet ihren Ausdruck in Feststellungen 2 bis 6 des EuGH im *CTL Logistics*-Urteil.[101]

a) Unabhängigkeit des Infrastrukturbetreibers

Der EuGH betont in diesem Kontext, dass die Mitgliedstaaten einen Regulierungsrahmen zu schaffen hätten, der die Unabhängigkeit der Geschäftsführer des Betreibers der Eisenbahninfrastruktur wahre und dessen Spielraum schütze, um Anreize zur Optimierung der Nutzung der Fahrwege zu geben. Dies könne nicht gelingen, wenn ein Zivilgericht nach § 315 BGB das für ein einzelnes Verkehrsunternehmen geltende Entgelt nach billigem Ermessen bestimmen könne, weil der Betreiber dadurch gezwungen werde, sich mit pauschalen, im Einzelfall festgelegten Billigkeitsentgelten auseinanderzusetzen (Rn. 77 ff., 93).

Es ist unstreitig (und wie der EuGH betont hat, für Eisenbahnwesen und Eisenbahnregulierung funktionsnotwendig), dass der Infrastrukturbetreiber nach Maßgabe des Regulierungsrechts die Entgelte mit einer gewissen Unabhängigkeit und daher auch mit einem gewissen Spielraum festlegen darf. Im Anwendungsbereich des Kartellrechts wird diese Unabhängigkeit vom BGH allerdings als Argument für eine kartellzivilgerichtliche Kontrolle herangezogen, weil sie zeige, dass ein unternehmerischer Ent-

---

101 EuGH, 9. 11. 2017, Rs. C-489/15, EU:C:2017:834 Rn. 77 ff. – *CTL Logistics*; siehe auch oben S. 18 ff.

scheidungsspielraum bestehe, ohne den eine Kontrolle am Maßstab des Kartellrechts schon tatbestandlich ausscheide.[102]

Im Ausgangspunkt ist richtig, dass eine kartellrechtliche Kontrolle schon tatbestandlich nicht in Betracht kommt, wenn ein Unternehmen über keinen eigenen Entscheidungsspielraum verfügt, sondern lediglich gesetzlichen oder behördlichen Vorgaben folgt.[103] Das Kartellrecht dient einer Kontrolle unternehmerischer Entscheidungen und findet daher keine Anwendung, wo es effektiv an solchen Entscheidungen fehlt, weil ein Unternehmen lediglich staatliche Befehle ausführt. In einem solchen Fall käme allenfalls ein Vertragsverletzungsverfahren gegen den Mitgliedstaat in Betracht, der ein unionskartellrechtswidriges Verhalten anordnet. In diesem Kontext ist relevant, dass ein Entscheidungsspielraum der Eisenbahninfrastrukturbetreiber in Bezug auf die Entgeltbemessung grundsätzlich nur bis zur Notifizierung durch die Regulierungsbehörde besteht. Hat die Regulierungsbehörde das Entgelt nach altem Recht (AEG) gebilligt oder nach neuem Recht (ERegG) genehmigt, existiert für den Eisenbahninfrastrukturbetreiber kein Entscheidungsspielraum mehr. Vielmehr ist dieser verpflichtet, die behördlich gebilligten bzw. genehmigten Entgelte zu erheben. Die Allgemeinverbindlichkeit der diesbezüglichen Regulierungsentscheidung folgt, wie der EuGH in *CTL Logistics* betont hat, aus den Vorgaben des Richtlinienrechts.[104]

Richtig ist auch, dass ein Unternehmen, das über einen Spielraum verfügt, diesen nicht kartellrechtswidrig missbrauchen darf.[105] Die These, dass daraus zwingend die Möglichkeit einer von der behördlichen Regulierung unabhängigen *zivilgerichtlichen* Kontrolle dieses Verhaltens folgen muss,[106] schießt gleichwohl über das Ziel hinaus. *Einerseits* ist es in institutionell-prozessualer Hinsicht, wie der EuGH in ständiger Rechtsprechung betont hat, mangels einer einschlägigen Unionsregelung „Sache des innerstaatlichen Rechts der einzelnen Mitgliedstaaten, die zuständigen Gerichte zu

---

102 BGH, 29. 10. 2019, Az. KZR 39/19, ECLI:DE:BGH:2019:291019UKZR39.19.0, Rn. 25 – *Trassenentgelte*.

103 Vgl. auch LG Berlin, 30. 10. 2018, Az. 16 O 495/15 Kart, ECLI:DE:LGBE:2018: 1030.16O495.15KART.00, Rn. 44 f.

104 EuGH, 9. 11. 2017, Rs. C-489/15, EU:C:2017:834 Rn. 61 und 94 – *CTL Logistics* unter Verweis auf Art. 30 Abs. 5 UAbs. 2 Richtlinie 2001/14/EG.

105 Vgl. etwa *Kühling*, Eisenbahnentgeltregulierung jenseits AEG und EIBV, in: Ronellenfitsch/Eschweiler/Hörster, Aktuelle Probleme des Eisenbahnrechts, 2015, S. 73, 104.

106 So *Mietzsch/Uhlenhut/Keding*, IR 2018, 57, 61; *Hauf/Baumgartner*, EuZW 2018, 1028, 1031.

bestimmen und die Verfahrensmodalitäten für Klagen zu regeln".[107] *Andererseits* wäre jedenfalls eine Kontrolle am Maßstab des nationalen Kartellrechts grundsätzlich ebenso wie eine zivilgerichtliche Billigkeitskontrolle an die Vorgaben der Regulierungsrichtlinien gebunden. Sie wäre daher – unbeschadet eventueller Besonderheiten des Unionskartellrechts – unionsrechtswidrig, wenn und soweit sie den Spielraum der Geschäftsführung des Infrastrukturbetreibers in einem Maße einschränkt, das den Richtlinienvorgaben widerspricht.[108] Aber auch eine Kontrolle am Maßstab des Unionskartellrecht kann nicht ohne Rücksicht auf das Unionsregulierungsrecht erfolgen, weil beide Materien in einer Wechselbeziehung stehen und sich gegenseitig beeinflussen.[109]

In der Sache ist ein inhaltlicher Konflikt in Bezug auf den Spielraum des Infrastrukturbetreibers bei Anwendung kartellrechtlicher Maßstäbe weniger wahrscheinlich als bei einer allgemeinen zivilrechtlichen Billigkeitskontrolle nach § 315 BGB, *erstens*, weil Kartellrecht und Regulierungsrecht danach streben, Diskriminierungen und Wettbewerbsverzerrungen zu vermeiden, *zweitens*, weil der kartellrechtliche Missbrauchsmaßstab deutlich strenger ist als der Billigkeitsmaßstab des § 315 BGB, und *drittens*, weil die Beweislast für den Missbrauch in Kartellzivilverfahren beim Kläger liegt.

Diese Aspekte schließen es aber nicht aus, dass jedenfalls eine *zivilgerichtliche* Kontrolle am Maßstab des Kartellrechts ebenso mit den Richtlinienvorgaben in Konflikt geraten kann wie eine zivilgerichtliche Billigkeitskontrolle. Dies folgt (ähnlich wie bei einer Kontrolle am Maßstab des § 315 BGB) wiederum aus der relativen Vagheit der sektorübergreifend formulierten und anwendbaren kartellrechtlichen Maßstäbe, vor allem aber daraus, dass die Entscheidungsfindung nicht auf eine kompetente Regulierungsbehörde zentralisiert, sondern auf eine Vielzahl von Instanzgerichten verstreut ist.

---

107 Z. B. EuGH, 20. 9. 2001, Rs. C-453/99, ECLI:EU:C:2001:465, Rn. 29 – *Crehan/Courage*. Dazu noch ausführlich Abschnitt IV.

108 Angesichts des Vorrangs des EU-Richtlinienrechts vor dem nationalen Recht (vgl. dazu etwa *Weitner*, EnWZ 2018, 73, 78) wäre es sogar denkbar, dass eine Richtlinie Vorgaben macht, die den Unternehmen einen größeren Spielraum einräumen, als dies das nationale Recht tut (insbesondere dort, wo das nationale Kartellrecht in Ausübung des den Mitgliedstaaten insoweit zustehenden Spielraums nach Art. 3 Abs. 2 S. 2 VO 1/2003 strenger ist als das Unionskartellrecht, in Deutschland z. B. in Bezug auf § 20 GWB). Es ist allerdings nicht ersichtlich, dass die Maßstäbe der Eisenbahnrichtlinien und des Kartellrechts sich insoweit in relevanter Weise unterscheiden.

109 Dazu noch ausführlich Abschnitt IV.

Statt sich in *einem* einheitlichen Verfahren mit *einer* zuständigen Regulierungsstelle über die Grenzen des eigenen Spielraums auseinanderzusetzen und die Entscheidungen der Regulierungsstelle ggf. durch *einen* verwaltungsgerichtlichen Instanzenzug kontrollieren zu lassen, d.h. anstelle eines einheitlichen Verfahrens, an dessen Ende ein *inter omnes* geltender und für alle verbindlicher Maßstab steht, würde sich der Infrastrukturbetreiber nicht nur potenziell einer Vielzahl von zivilgerichtlichen Verfahren ausgesetzt sehen, sondern müsste auch deren möglicherweise voneinander abweichende oder sich sogar widersprechende Entscheidungen in sein Entgeltsystem integrieren sowie zur Vermeidung von Diskriminierungen und um seine Kosten zu decken, dann auch die Entgelte gegenüber den anderen Eisenbahnverkehrsunternehmen (möglicherweise sogar rückwirkend) ständig anpassen.

Einem solchen Vorgehen des Eisenbahninfrastrukturbetreibers steht bereits entgegen, dass er seine Entgelte mit Blick auf seine Bindung an die regulierungsbehördlich gebilligten bzw. genehmigten Entgelte gar nicht ständig und nur mit Rücksicht auf zivilgerichtliche Entscheidungen anpassen *darf*, da die notifizierten Entgelte zunächst wirksam bleiben und es offen ist, ob neue mit Rücksicht auf Urteile von Zivilgerichten angepasste Entgelte überhaupt von der Regulierungsbehörde gebilligt bzw. genehmigt werden. Und selbst wenn ihm eine solche Anpassung im konkreten Fall gestattet würde, erschiene es zweifelhaft, ob es ihm überhaupt gelingen könnte, die zivilgerichtlichen Urteile miteinander und mit den weiterhin geltenden regulierungsrechtlichen Vorgaben in Einklang zu bringen. Daher hat der EuGH genau diesen Zwang, sich mit pauschalen, im Einzelfall von Zivilgerichten festgelegten Entgelten auseinanderzusetzen, in der *CTL Logistics*-Entscheidung zu Recht *bereits an sich* als Beeinträchtigung der von den Richtlinien dem Infrastrukturbetreiber gewährten und von den Mitgliedstaaten geforderten Unabhängigkeit des Eisenbahninfrastrukturbetreibers bewertet. Dort heißt es:

„Außerdem beruht das Vorbringen, durch eine solche Vorgehensweise werde eine nicht diskriminierende Behandlung der Eisenbahnunternehmen gewährleistet, auf der Annahme, dass sich die Regulierungsstelle darauf zu beschränken habe, auf Einzelfallentscheidungen zu reagieren, die von den Zivilgerichten bereits gemäß § 315 BGB getroffen wurden. Eine solche Annahme steht aber in klarem Gegensatz zu der Aufgabe, die der Regulierungsstelle durch Art. 30 Abs. 2 und 5 der Richtlinie 2001/14 übertragen wird.

Schließlich würde diese Annahme die Unabhängigkeit der Betreiber der Eisenbahninfrastruktur beeinträchtigen. Sie wären gezwungen, sich als Reaktion auf eine Entscheidung eines Zivilgerichts mit pauschalen, nach einer Einzelfallprüfung festgesetzten „Billigkeitsentgelten" auseinanderzusetzen. Dies stünde in Widerspruch zu der ihnen durch die Richtlinie 2001/14 übertragenen Aufgabe".[110]

b) Ausschließliche Zuständigkeit der Regulierungsstelle

Im institutionellen Kontext betont der EuGH dementsprechend weiter, durch nur *inter partes* wirkende zivilgerichtliche Entscheidungen werde (nicht nur im Verhältnis zu den Unternehmen, sondern auch zur Regulierungsstelle) der nach Art. 30 Abs. 5 UAbs. 2 der Richtlinie 2001/14/EG vorgesehene verbindliche Charakter der Entscheidungen der zuständigen Regulierungsstelle für alle Beteiligten missachtet (Rn. 94). Und selbst wenn das Zivilgericht die Beurteilungskriterien des Richtlinienrechts respektiere, würde dies bedeuten, dass jedes angerufene nationale Zivilgericht unmittelbar die Vorschriften des Eisenbahnregulierungsrechts anwenden und auslegen und somit in die Zuständigkeiten der Regulierungsstelle eingreifen könnte. Dies verstoße gegen die ausschließliche Zuständigkeit der Regulierungsstelle (Rn. 84 ff.). Gleiches gelte im Fall gütlicher Streitbeilegung vor dem Zivilgericht, an der die Regulierungsstelle nicht beteiligt werden müsse. Dies sei nicht mit Art. 30 Abs. 3 S. 2 und 3 der Richtlinie 2001/14/EG vereinbar, wonach Verhandlungen der Parteien unter Aufsicht der Regulierungsstelle erfolgen müssten und die Regulierungsstelle einzugreifen habe, wenn ein Verstoß gegen die Richtlinie drohe (Rn. 98 f.). Eine Erstattung von Entgelten nach den Vorschriften des Zivilrechts komme daher nur in Betracht, „wenn die Unvereinbarkeit des Entgelts mit Regelung über den Zugang zur Eisenbahninfrastruktur zuvor von der Regulierungsstelle oder von einem Gericht, das die Entscheidung dieser Stelle überprüft hat, im Einklang mit den Vorschriften des nationalen Rechts festgestellt worden ist und der Anspruch auf Erstattung Gegenstand einer Klage vor den nationalen Zivilgerichten sein kann und nicht der in der genannten Regelung vorgesehenen Klage" (Rn. 97).

Der EuGH hat damit in *CTL Logistics* unmissverständlich zum Ausdruck gebracht, dass er von der (unbeschadet verwaltungsgerichtlicher Nachprüfung) alleinigen Zuständigkeit der Regulierungsstelle für die Anwendung der regulierungsrechtlichen Vorschriften und für die Kontrolle der in den Anwendungsbereich der Richtlinie fallenden Entgelte ausgeht. In

---

110 EuGH, 9. 11. 2017, Rs. C-489/15, EU:C:2017:834, Rn. 92 f. – *CTL Logistics*.

Deutschland ist danach allein die BNetzA zuständig, deren Entscheidungen aufgrund der diesbezüglichen (unstreitig unionsrechtskonformen) Entscheidung des deutschen Gesetzgebers der Nachprüfung durch die Verwaltungsgerichtsbarkeit (und nicht auch der Zivilgerichte) unterliegen.

Mit der Herausarbeitung dieses klaren Zuständigkeitsgefüges widerspricht der EuGH *einerseits* ausdrücklich Generalanwalt *Mengozzi*, der aus Erwägungsgrund 46 zur Richtlinie 2001/14/EG, nach welcher die Regulierungsstelle „ungeachtet der gerichtlichen Nachprüfung als Beschwerdestelle" fungiert, die Möglichkeit einer parallelen zivilgerichtlichen Kontrolle abgeleitet hatte.[111] Der EuGH betont demgegenüber explizit, dass die gerichtliche Überprüfung der Entscheidungen der BNetzA in Deutschland allein den Verwaltungsgerichten obliege.[112] *Andererseits* hat der EuGH klare Vorgaben für die Geltendmachung zivilrechtlicher Ansprüche gemacht. Er hat insoweit unterstrichen, dass eine zivilprozessuale Geltendmachung von Ansprüchen aufgrund rechtswidriger Entgelte *einerseits* voraussetzt, dass die Erstattung nach dem nationalen Recht überhaupt Gegenstand einer Klage vor einem Zivilgericht sein kann (also keiner anderen Stelle zugewiesen ist) – das ist in Deutschland der Fall – und dass *andererseits* auch in diesem Fall einem auf Erstattung von Entgelten gerichteten Zivilprozess zwecks Wahrung der alleinigen Zuständigkeit der Regulierungsstelle (und der Verwaltungsgerichtsbarkeit), aber auch zur Wahrung der Allgemeinverbindlichkeit der Regulierungsverfügungen eine bestandskräftige Feststellung der Unvereinbarkeit des Entgelts mit den regulierungsrechtlichen Vorgaben durch *diese* Stelle (also die BNetzA oder der diese kontrollierenden Verwaltungsgerichtsbarkeit) vorausgehen muss,[113] mit anderen Worten: der EuGH betont, dass zivilgerichtliche Verfahren in Bezug auf der Regulierung unterliegende Eisenbahnentgelte nur als nachfolgende Verfahren, nicht aber als davon unabhängige *Stand alone*-Verfahren in Betracht kommen.

Diese Argumentation gilt augenscheinlich nicht nur für eine zivilgerichtliche Kontrolle auf der Basis des § 315 BGB, sondern für *jedwede* zivilgerichtliche Kontrolle, auch eine solche auf der Basis kartellrechtlicher Vorschriften, weil eine parallele zivilgerichtliche Kontrolle – unabhängig von der Anspruchsgrundlage und auch unabhängig davon, ob der Anspruch als Erstattungsanspruch oder Schadensersatzanspruch geltend ge-

---

111 GA *Mengozzi*, Schlussanträge vom 21. 11. 2016, Rs. 489/15, ECLI:EU:C:2016:901, Rn. 61.
112 EuGH, 9. 11. 2017, Rs. C-489/15, EU:C:2017:834, Rn. 87 – *CTL Logistics*.
113 EuGH, 9. 11. 2017, Rs. C-489/15, EU:C:2017:834, Rn. 97 – *CTL Logistics*.

macht wird – das durch die Richtlinie vorgegebene regulierungsrechtliche Zuständigkeitsgefüge unterlaufen würde.

Eine von einer vorausgehenden Entscheidung der Regulierungsstelle unabhängige, eigenständige zivilgerichtliche Kontrolle auf der Basis des nationalen Kartellrechts kommt daher – wie die deutschen Instanzgerichte zu Recht einmütig betont haben – nur in Betracht, sofern es sich um nicht vom Eisenbahnregulierungsrecht erfasste Aspekte handelt und andere Kriterien angewendet werden. Dies wäre aber vorliegend mit Blick auf die Trassenentgelte nicht der Fall, da es bei der kartellrechtlichen Überprüfung dieser Entgelte letztlich um die Kontrolle der Preisbildung durch das Eisenbahninfrastrukturunternehmen geht, der eisenbahnrechtliche Vorschriften zugrunde liegen und die von den Zivilgerichten gerade nicht im Einzelfall überprüft werden sollen.[114]

Nichts anderes gilt schließlich auch mit Blick auf die in kartellzivilgerichtlichen Verfahren bestehende Möglichkeit einer gütlichen Streitbeilegung im Wege eines Vergleichs. Zwar kann, worauf Generalanwalt *Mengozzi* in seinen Schlussanträgen hingewiesen hat,[115] die Regulierungsstelle an Zivilverfahren beteiligt werden. Obgleich der BGH eine solche Beteiligung der BNetzA noch 2007 abgelehnt hat,[116] ist sie nunmehr sogar in § 76 ERegG i.V.m. § 90 GWB gesetzlich vorgesehen. Doch würde eine bloße *Beteiligung* nicht den vom EuGH in *CTL Logistics* herausgearbeiteten Richtlinienvorgaben genügen, denn nach Art. 30 Abs. 3 S. 2 der Richtlinie 2001/14/EG sind Verhandlungen zwischen den Parteien nur unter *Aufsicht* der Regulierungsstelle zulässig, während die Verhandlungen im Zivilprozess zwar unter Aufsicht des Gerichts erfolgen, letztlich aber der Parteidisposition unterliegen, ohne dass die BNetzA, wie es die Richtlinie vorschreibt, einen Vergleich verhindern könnte, der nicht den Richtlinienvorgaben entspricht. Der EuGH hat daher auch insoweit der Auffassung von Generalanwalt *Mengozzi*, der eine bloße Beteiligung der Regulierungsstelle

---

114 So schon LG Frankfurt a. M., 9. 5. 2018, Az. 2-06 O 38/17, ECLI:DE:LGFFM: 2018:0509.2.06O38.17.00, Rn.71 ff., juris; m. zust. Anmerkung *Karolus*, EuR 2018, 477; ebenso LG Leipzig, 6. 7. 2018, Az.. 01 HK O 3364/14, ECLI:DE: LGLEIPZ: 2018:0706.01HKO3365.14.0A, Rn. 32 ff., 47, juris; OLG Dresden, 17. 4. 2019, Az. U 4/18 Kart, ECLI: DE: OLGDRES: 2019: 0417.U4. 18KART. 0A, Rn. 48.

115 GA *Mengozzi*, Schlussanträge vom 21. 11. 2016, Rs. 489/15, ECLI:EU:C:2016: 901, Rn. 65.

116 BGH, 10. 12. 2007, Az. KZR 14/07, NJW 2008, 1165 – *Eisenbahntrassennutzung*.

am Privatklageverfahren für ausreichend erachtet hatte,[117] zu Recht eine klare Absage erteilt. Das ist richtig, zumal die Kläger im Zivilkartellprozess (verständlicherweise) in aller Regel weder die Interessen anderer Eisenbahnverkehrsunternehmen noch öffentliche Interessen verfolgen, sondern allein im eigenen, individuellen Interesse agieren (und aus diesem Grunde zugleich auch den gerichtlichen Erkenntnis- und Steuerungsmöglichkeiten Grenzen setzen).[118]

c) Vermeidung unkoordinierter Rechtswege

Schließlich betont der EuGH in *CTL Logistics*, eine eigenständige zivilgerichtliche Kontrolle regulierter Entgelte könne die Uniformität der Kontrolle durch die zuständige Regulierungsstelle durch verschiedene, unter Umständen nicht durch eine höchstrichterliche Rechtsprechung harmonisierte Entscheidungen unabhängiger Zivilgerichte unterlaufen, und es bestünden – in offenkundigem Widerspruch zu dem in Art. 30 der Richtlinie 2001/14/EG verfolgten Ziel – zwei unkoordinierte Rechtswege nebeneinander (Rn. 87). Ein Zivilgericht habe zudem keine Möglichkeit, die Wirkung seiner Entscheidung auf weitere Infrastrukturnutzungsverträge oder sogar auf den gesamten Sektor auszudehnen (Rn. 94 f.). Die Regulierungsstelle müsste also, um eine Ungleichbehandlung bis zur höchstrichterlichen Entscheidung zu vermeiden, das Entgelt für alle Eisenbahnverkehrsunternehmen entsprechend der zivilrechtlichen Entscheidung anpassen, obwohl die Richtlinie eine solche Verpflichtung nicht vorsehe und eine solche Anpassungspflicht auch im klaren Gegensatz zur Aufgabe der Regulierungsstelle nach Art. 30 Abs. 2 und 5 der Richtlinie stehe (Rn. 89 ff.).
In diesem Argumentationsstrang verbindet der EuGH materielle und institutionelle Argumente und macht deutlich, dass eine Zuständigkeitskonzentration bei *einer* Regulierungsstelle (in Deutschland bei der BNetzA) und auf *einen* zur Überprüfung ihrer Entscheidungen berufenen Instanzenzug (in Deutschland die Verwaltungsgerichtsbarkeit) Voraussetzung für die Verwirklichung des eisenbahnrechtlichen Diskriminierungsverbots bei gleichzeitiger Gewährleistung einer Entgeltregulierung nach den übrigen Richtlinienvorgaben ist. Dass zivilgerichtliche Urteile nur *inter partes* wirken und nicht geeignet sind, aus sich heraus eine *erga omnes*-Wirkung

---

117 GA *Mengozzi*, Schlussanträge vom 21. 11. 2016, Rs. 489/15, ECLI: EU: C: 2016: 901, Rn. 65.
118 Vgl. dazu bereits oben bei und in Fn. 98.

im Sinne einer Gleichbehandlung aller Eisenbahnverkehrsunternehmen zu erreichen, wie dies das Eisenbahnregulierungsrecht zwingend vorschreibt, ist unstreitig und gilt unabhängig von den angewendeten zivilrechtrechtlichen Rechtsgrundlagen gleichermaßen für eine Billigkeitskontrolle nach § 315 BGB wie für eine Kontrolle an kartellrechtlichen Maßstäben.[119]

Generalanwalt *Mengozzi* hatte in diesem Kontext darauf hingewiesen, dass sich andere Eisenbahnverkehrsunternehmen nach einem Urteil, durch welches ein reguliertes Entgelt zivilgerichtlich korrigiert wurde, an die Regulierungsstelle wenden könnten, um eine *erga omnes* wirkende Entscheidung herbeizuführen.[120] Der Gerichtshof hat auch diese Auffassung zu Recht zurückgewiesen. Die Regulierungsstelle, die nach den Richtlinienvorgaben die alleinige Befugnis zur Kontrolle der regulierten Entgelte haben soll, würde dadurch gezwungen, entweder eine Ungleichbehandlung klagender und nicht klagender Eisenbahnverkehrsunternehmen hinzunehmen (und damit gegen das zentrale materielle Regelungsanliegen der Richtlinie zu verstoßen) oder sich der Entscheidung verschiedener Zivilgerichte unterzuordnen und ihre Entscheidungen immer wieder (möglicherweise sogar rückwirkend) deren – unter Umständen einander (z. B. hinsichtlich des Ob und der Höhe der Rückerstattungs- oder Schadensersatzansprüche) widersprechenden – Vorgaben anzupassen.

An die Stelle einer verlässlichen, einheitlichen, diskriminierungsfreien und in sich konsistenten Regulierung, welche nicht nur Anreize für die Zukunft setzt, sondern vor allem auch allen beteiligten Unternehmen die erforderliche Planungssicherheit gibt, würde ein hochvolatiles System dezentraler Ersatzregulierung durch die Zivilgerichte treten, das zudem regelmäßig nur (oder jedenfalls primär) das individuelle Verhältnis zwischen den Streitparteien und nicht die Gesamtheit der Entgelte im Auge hätte. Die BNetzA würde in diesem System zur ausführenden Stelle zivilgerichtlicher Entscheidungen degradiert. Das würde, wie der EuGH ausgeführt hat, im klaren Gegensatz zur Aufgabe der Regulierungsstelle nach Art. 30 Abs. 2 und 5 der Richtlinie stehen. Das im Regulierungsrecht vorgesehene Kompetenzgefüge würde dadurch auf den Kopf gestellt, denn dieses sieht genau umgekehrt vor, dass die Regulierungsstelle allgemeinverbindliche Entscheidungen über die Entgelte trifft, an welche die Zivilgerichte gebun-

---

119 So schon LG Frankfurt a. M., 9. 5. 2018, Az. 2-06 O 38/17, ECLI:DE:LGFFM: 2018:0509.2.06O38.17.00,Rn. 71 ff., juris.

120 GA *Mengozzi*, Schlussanträge vom 21. 11. 2016, Rs. 489/15, ECLI:EU:C:2016: 901, Rn. 77 ff.

den sind und zu deren Effektuierung die Zivilgerichte (z. B. bei Feststellung ihrer Rechtswidrigkeit durch die Regulierungsstelle) beitragen können, indem sie über daran anknüpfende zivilrechtliche Ansprüche entscheiden. Dies gilt unabhängig von der materiellen zivilrechtlichen Rechtsgrundlage.

Hinzu kommt, dass eine Situation eintreten kann, in der verschiedene, nicht durch eine höchstrichterliche Rechtsprechung harmonisierte Entscheidungen unabhängiger erst- oder zweitinstanzlicher Zivilgerichte ergehen. In diesem Fall wäre die BNetzA nicht nur gezwungen, ihre Entscheidungen fortwährend und gegebenenfalls auch rückwirkend zu revidieren, sondern möglicherweise auch vor der unmöglichen Aufgabe stehen, sich widersprechende zivilgerichtliche Entscheidungen zu berücksichtigen. Und selbst wenn eine höchstrichterliche Rechtsprechung des BGH gefunden wäre, wäre weder sichergestellt, dass diese dem Richtlinienrecht hinreichend Rechnung trägt (im Gegenteil geht der BGH ja selbst davon aus, insoweit einen vom Richtlinienrecht unabhängigen Spielraum zu besitzen), noch wäre bei einem unkoordinierten Nebeneinander zweier Rechtswege (Zivil- und Verwaltungsgerichtsbarkeit) sichergestellt, dass die Rechtsprechung des BGH mit derjenigen des letztinstanzlich für die Überprüfung der Entscheidungen der BNetzA zuständigen Bundesverwaltungsgerichts übereinstimmt oder damit in Einklang gebracht werden kann.[121] Die vom EuGH und ihm folgend von den deutschen Instanzgerichten betonte Gefahr eines unkoordinierten Nebeneinander verschiedener Rechtswege und eines Unterlaufens der Zuständigkeit der Regulierungsstelle würde mithin nicht minder bestehen, wenn man statt der zivilrechtlichen Billigkeitskontrolle eine solche am Maßstab des Kartellrechts zulassen würde.[122]

---

121 Den von GA *Mengozzi* in seinen Schlussanträgen vom 21. 11. 2016 (Rs. 489/15, ECLI:EU:C:2016:901, Rn. 64) aufgegriffenen Gedanken einer Harmonisierung durch den Gemeinsamen Senat der obersten Gerichtshöfe (BGH und BVerwG) hat der EuGH zu Recht nicht weiterverfolgt, da eine solche zwar theoretisch denkbar ist, aber in der Praxis nicht nur so gut wie nie erfolgt, sondern auch voraussetzen würde, dass der Instanzenzug sowohl in der Zivilgerichtsbarkeit als auch der Verwaltungsgerichtsbarkeit bis zum jeweiligen Höchstgericht ausgeschöpft wird, was praxisfern erscheint, dazu eingehend und überzeugend *Freise*, TranspR 2018, 425, 430.

122 S. LG Leipzig, 6. 7. 2018, Az. 01 HK O 3364/14, ECLI:DE:LGLEIPZ:2018:0706. 01HKO3365.14.0A, Rn. 32 ff., juris; LG Berlin, 30. 10. 2018, Az. 16 O 495/15 Kart, ECLI:DE:LGBE:2018:1030.16O495.15KART.00, Rn. 31 f.; OLG Dresden, 17. 4. 2019, Az. U 4/18 Kart, ECLI:DE:OLGDRES:2019:0417.U4.18KART.0A,

d) Fazit

In der Summe ist festzustellen, dass auch die institutionellen Einwände gegen eine zivilgerichtliche Billigkeitskontrolle, welche der EuGH in *CTL Logistics* angeführt hat, unabhängig von den materiellen Rechtsgrundlagen gelten, die einem Privatklageverfahren zugrunde liegen. Sie finden auf eine zivilgerichtliche Kontrolle am Maßstab des Kartellrechts (z. B. nach Maßgabe der §§ 19, 20, 33 GWB) oder aufgrund anderer zivilrechtlicher Normen (etwa §§ 134, 812 oder 823 BGB) genauso Anwendung wie auf die vom EuGH in *CTL Logistics* explizit adressierte Kontrolle am Maßstab des § 315 Abs. 3 BGB.

3. Ergebnis

Zur Frage nach der Übertragbarkeit der *CTL Logistics*-Grundsätze auf kartellzivilgerichtliche Verfahren kann festgehalten werden, dass die Bedenken, welche der EuGH gegenüber einer zivilgerichtlichen Billigkeitskontrolle von der Regulierung unterliegenden Eisenbahnentgelten geäußert hat, jeder eigenständigen zivilgerichtlichen Kontrolle, einschließlich einer solchen am Maßstab des Kartellrechts, entgegenstehen. Eine kartellzivilgerichtliche Kontrolle würde ebenso wie eine zivilgerichtliche Billigkeitskontrolle den Kernanliegen der Regulierungsrichtlinien sowohl in materieller Hinsicht (Diskriminierungsverbot) als auch in institutioneller Hinsicht (einheitliche Kontrolle durch die zuständige Regulierungsstelle) widersprechen und ist daher nicht mit den zentralen Bestimmungen der Eisenbahnregulierungsrichtlinien und deren praktischer Wirksamkeit vereinbar.

Dies gilt nicht nur für die Richtlinie 2001/14/EG, welche unmittelbarer Gegenstand der EuGH-Entscheidung *CTL Logistics* war, sondern auch für die aktuelle Richtlinie 2012/34/EU, die insoweit keine wesentlichen Änderungen im Vergleich zur Vorgängerregelung enthält.[123] Insbesondere gebietet auch Art. 56 Abs. 2 Richtlinie 2012/34/EU keine abweichende Bewertung, da diese Norm (abgesehen davon dass sie schon ihrem Wortlaut

---

Rn. 45; ebenso *Weitner*, EnWZ 2018, 73, 78; *Staebe*, EuZW 2019, 118, 121; *Karolus*, EuR 2018, 477, 480 f.

123 So zu Recht schon LG Berlin, 30. 10. 2018, Az. 16 O 495/15 Kart, ECLI:DE:LG-BE:2018:1030.16O495.15KART.00, Rn. 30 mit zust. Anm. *Gerstner*, N&R 2019, 62 ff.

nach nur die Zuständigkeit der Kartell*behörden* adressiert) keine Kompetenzen begründet, sondern sie voraussetzt.[124]

Eine zivilgerichtliche Kontrolle am Maßstab des Kartellrechts ist – abgesehen von zivilgerichtlichen Rückerstattungsklagen, die auf eine bestandskräftige Entscheidung der BNetzA oder ein rechtskräftiges verwaltungsgerichtliches Urteil folgen – ebenso richtlinienwidrig und damit (unbeschadet von sogleich in Abschnitt IV adressierten Besonderheiten des Unionskartellrechts) unionsrechtswidrig wie eine solche am Maßstab des BGB.

IV. Vorrang des Art. 102 AEUV und seiner privaten Durchsetzung?

Nachfolgend wird untersucht, ob sich aus der unmittelbaren Geltung und Anwendbarkeit des Art. 102 AEUV und seiner Bewehrung mit privaten Schadensersatzansprüchen eine von der soeben getroffenen Auslegung der *CTL Logistics*-Entscheidung abweichende Bewertung ergibt.

Dreh- und Angelpunkt der Argumentation des BGH für eine – im Gegensatz zur Billigkeitskontrolle nach § 315 Abs. 3 BGB – fortbestehende, von der regulierungsbehördlichen Kontrolle weitgehend unabhängige Befugnis der nationalen Zivilgerichte zur Kontrolle regulierter Eisenbahnentgelte nach Maßgabe des Kartellrechts ist, wie oben ausgeführt wurde, seine Interpretation des Art. 102 AEUV. Im Einzelnen: dass Art. 102 AEUV *erstens* als unmittelbar geltende Norm des Unionsprimärrechts Vorrang sowohl vor dem nationalen Recht als auch dem sekundärrechtlichen EU-Regulierungsrecht habe, dass Art. 102 AEUV *zweitens* einen vom Regulierungsrecht unabhängigen Anwendungsbereich habe und dass Art. 102 AEUV *drittens* ein ohne jedwede Vorbedingungen zivilgerichtlich durchsetzbares Recht auf Schadensersatz bei Kartellrechtsverstößen gewähre.

1. Unmittelbare Geltung und Anwendbarkeit des Art. 102 AEUV

Der dieser Argumentation zugrunde liegende Ausgangspunkt des BGH ist korrekt. Unstreitig ist *erstens*, dass es sich bei Art. 102 AEUV um unmittelbar geltendes EU-Primärrecht handelt, *zweitens*, dass die Norm grundsätzlich auch im Verkehrssektor Anwendung findet[125] und *drittens*, dass auch die nationalen Gerichte im Grundsatz befugt sind, Art. 102 AEUV unmit-

---

124 S. dazu oben S. 43 f.
125 Dazu bereits oben S. 45.

telbar anzuwenden. Die diesbezügliche ständige Rechtsprechung des EuGH hat auch in Art. 6 VO 1/2003 Niederschlag gefunden, welcher die grundsätzliche Zuständigkeit der nationalen Gerichte zur Anwendung der Wettbewerbsregeln normiert. Dementsprechend hatte der EuGH z. B. bereits 1974 im Urteil *BRT/SABAM* zu Art. 85 und 86 EWGV (heute Art. 101 und 102 AEUV) betont:

> „Die Zuständigkeit dieser Gerichte zur Anwendung des Gemeinschaftsrechts, insbesondere in Streitsachen dieser Art, ergibt sich aus der unmittelbaren Geltung dieses Rechts. Da die in den Artikeln 85 Absatz 1 und 86 enthaltenen Verbote ihrer Natur nach geeignet sind, in den Beziehungen zwischen einzelnen unmittelbare Wirkungen zu erzeugen, lassen sie unmittelbar in deren Person Rechte entstehen, welche die Gerichte der Mitgliedstaaten zu wahren haben. Diesen Gerichten die Zuständigkeit hierzu unter Berufung auf den bereits zitierten Artikel 9 abzusprechen, würde bedeuten, daß den einzelnen Rechte genommen würden, die ihnen aufgrund des Vertrages selbst zustehen".[126]

Wie ebenfalls schon aus dieser Entscheidung deutlich wird, bedarf eine Anwendung des Kartellrechts durch ein einzelstaatliches Gericht auch keiner vorhergehenden Entscheidung der EU-Kommission.[127] Dies gilt, wie der EuGH 1980 im Urteil *Marty/Estée Lauder* weiter ausgeführt hat, sogar dann, wenn die Kommission bereits ein Verfahren eingeleitet hat. Das innerstaatliche Gericht könne, so der EuGH, in diesem Fall „aber seine Entscheidung aussetzen, bis die Kommission ihr Verfahren abgeschlossen hat, wenn ihm dies aus Gründen der Rechtssicherheit geboten erscheint".[128] Im Urteil *Apple Sales International* betonte der EuGH 2018, dass auch die Geltendmachung von Schadensersatz aufgrund eines Verstoßes gegen

---

126 EuGH, 30. 1. 1974, Rs. 127/73, ECLI:EU:C:1974:6, Rn. 15/17 – *BRT/SABAM*. Der in dem Zitat angesprochene Art. 9 VO 1/62 normierte die Kompetenz der Kommission und der nationalen Kartellbehörden zur Durchsetzung der Art. 85, 86 EWGV (heute Art. 101, 102 AEUV), ohne die Gerichte zu erwähnen.
127 Ebenso in jüngerer Zeit EuG, 22. 3. 2000, Rs. T-125/97, ECLI:EU:T:2000:84, Rn. 80 – *Coca Cola*.
128 EuGH, 10. 7. 1980, Rs. 37/79, ECLI:EU:C:1980:190, Rn. 13 f. – *Marty/Estée Lauder*; s. auch EuGH, 14. 12. 2000, Rs. 344/98, ECLI:EU:C:2000:689, Rn. 47 – *Masterfoods*.

Art. 102 AEUV keine vorausgehende Entscheidung einer nationalen oder europäischen Wettbewerbsbehörde voraussetze.[129]

Der BGH folgert aus dieser Rechtsprechung sowie aus Art. 6 VO 1/2003 in seinem Urteil *Trassenentgelte*, der Grundsatz der unmittelbaren Anwendung des Art. 102 AEUV stehe „auch einem Vorbehalt entgegen, nach dem kartellzivilrechtliche Ansprüche nur dann durchgesetzt werden können, wenn die Regulierungsbehörde zuvor einen Verstoß festgestellt hat".[130]

Das erscheint auf den ersten Blick einleuchtend, ist aber – wie schon oben in Bezug auf Art. 6 VO 1/2003 ausgeführt wurde – zu kurz gesprungen, denn der EuGH befasst sich in keiner der zitierten Entscheidungen mit dem Verhältnis von Kartell- und Regulierungsrecht, sondern lediglich mit dem kartellrechtsinternen Verhältnis von *Kartell*behörden und *Kartell*zivilgerichtsbarkeit. Innerhalb des kartellrechtlichen Koordinatensystems haben EuGH und Unionsgesetzgeber eine Entscheidung zugunsten einer parallelen Durchsetzung durch Behörden und Gerichte getroffen, durch welche die Durchsetzung des Kartellrechts und der sich daraus ergebenden individuellen Rechte beschleunigt wird. Für das Kartellrecht hat die Union damit zugleich die Gefahr einer (zunächst) uneinheitlichen Kartellrechtsanwendung durch eine Vielzahl mehr oder minder kompetenter nationaler Zivilgerichte akzeptiert. Dies wird im Anwendungsbereich des Kartellrechts durch die Bindung der nationalen Gerichte an vorausgehende Entscheidungen der Kommission (Art. 16 VO 1/2003) und nationaler Wettbewerbsbehörden (Art. 9 Richtlinie 2014/104/EU) und in Deutschland auch durch die Zuständigkeit der Zivilgerichtsbarkeit sowohl für Privatklagen als auch für die Kontrolle kartellbehördlicher Entscheidungen ein Stück weit kompensiert und auf diese Weise eine gewisse Vereinheitlichung und Kohärenz der Kartellrechtsanwendung herbeigeführt.

Entgegen dem BGH lässt sich dieser Ansatz aber nicht ohne Weiteres auf das Verhältnis von Kartell- und Regulierungsrecht bzw. von Kartellzivilgerichtsbarkeit und Regulierungsbehörden übertragen, weil insoweit – wie oben auf der Basis des Urteils *CTL Logistics* ausgeführt wurde – Konflikte der zivilgerichtlichen Kontrolle sowohl mit den Zielen des materiellen Regulierungsrechts (z. B. Diskriminierungsverbot, Setzung von Anreizen zur Optimierung der Fahrwegenutzung, Kostensenkung, Investitions-

---

129 EuGH, 24. 10. 2018, Rs. C-595/17, ECLI:EU:C:2018:854, Rn. 35 – *Apple Sales International*.

130 BGH, 29. 10. 2019, Az. KZR 39/19, ECLI:DE:BGH:2019:291019UKZR39.19.0, Rn. 37 – *Trassenentgelte*; ebenso *Hauf/Baumgartner*, EuZW 2018, 1028, 1032; *dies.*, TranspR 2019, 69, 71.

anreize, Investitionssicherheit) als auch mit der zur institutionell-prozes-sualen Absicherung dieser Ziele normierten alleinigen Zuständigkeit der Regulierungsbehörde (unter Kontrolle der Verwaltungsgerichtsbarkeit) auftreten würden. Diese Konflikte existieren „kartellrechtsintern" nicht, und man kann sie auch nicht einfach pauschal mit dem Hinweis auf den Vorrang des Art. 102 AEUV als Norm des Unionsprimärrechts beiseite wi-schen, weil die Eisenbahnregulierungsrichtlinien ebenfalls primärrechtlich in Art. 90, 91 AEUV verankert sind.

Nichts anderes gilt mit Blick auf die *Telefónica*-Entscheidung des EuGH. Darin hatte der EuGH 2014 zwar angemerkt, dass ein Einschreiten der EU-Kommission nach Art. 102 AEUV keine vorherige Überprüfung bestimm-ter Maßnahmen durch die spanische Telekommunikationsbehörde CMT voraussetze.[131] Doch folgt aus dieser Entscheidung (abgesehen davon, dass sie den Telekommunikationssektor und nicht den Eisenbahnsektor be-trifft) gerade nicht, dass auch *jedes nationale Zivilgericht* Art. 102 AEUV un-abhängig von den Regulierungsbehörden und ohne Rücksicht auf die Vor-gaben des Regulierungsrechts anwenden darf.[132] Gegenstand dieser Ent-scheidung ist die uneingeschränkte Durchsetzbarkeit des Art. 102 AEUV *durch die EU-Kommission*. Anders als bei einer zivilgerichtlichen Kontrolle besteht bei einer Anwendung des Art. 102 AEUV durch die EU-Kommissi-on weder die Gefahr einer Vielzahl von unter Umständen voneinander ab-weichenden und dem Regulierungsrecht (mangels Kompetenz zu dessen Anwendung) nicht Rechnung tragenden Gerichtsentscheidungen (es gibt zahllose nationale Zivilgerichte, aber nur eine EU-Kommission), noch wer-den dadurch mehrere unkoordinierte Rechtswege eröffnet. Im Gegenteil werden Entscheidungen der EU-Kommission durch den EuGH und damit durch die für die letztverbindliche Auslegung des Unionsrechts zuständige Instanz überprüft, was Rechtseinheit und Rechtssicherheit in der ganzen EU nicht abträglich, sondern im Gegenteil förderlich ist.

Über die Frage, ob auch die nationalen Zivilgerichte im Anwendungsbe-reich des Eisenbahnregulierungsrechts unabhängig von einer Entschei-dung der zuständigen nationalen Regulierungsbehörde (wenn schon nicht das nationale Kartellrecht, so doch wenigstens) Art. 102 AEUV anwenden dürfen, hat der EuGH bisher nicht entschieden. Um sie zu beantworten, ist eine eingehende Analyse der unionsrechtlichen Regelungen zum Kar-tell- und Eisenbahnregulierungsrecht erforderlich.

---

131 EuGH, 10. 7. 2014, Rs. C-296/12 P, ECLI:EU:C:2014:2062, Rn. 135 – *Telefónica*.
132 A.A. *Hauf/Baumgartner*, TranspR 2019, 69, 71.

2. Verhältnis des Art. 102 AEUV zum Regulierungsrecht

a) Bindungswirkung im Verhältnis von EU-Kommission, nationalen Behörden und nationalen Gerichten

aa) Unabhängigkeit der Kommission von Entscheidungen nationaler Stellen

Die EU-Kommission kann Art. 101 und 102 AEUV nicht nur nach Maßgabe der oben zitierten *Telefónica*-Entscheidung ohne vorausgehende Entscheidung einer Regulierungsbehörde anwenden. Sie ist, wie das Urteil *Deutsche Telekom* des EuGH zeigt, sogar befugt, Bußgelder wegen Verletzung des Art. 101 oder 102 AEUV gegen Unternehmen zu verhängen, deren Entgeltfestsetzung zuvor von einer nationalen Regulierungsbehörde akzeptiert wurde. In dem diesem Urteil zugrunde liegenden Sachverhalt, der wiederum im Telekommunikationssektor spielte, hatte die EU-Kommission ein Bußgeld wegen Verletzung des Art. 82 EG (heute Art. 102 AEUV) durch eine Preis-Kosten-Schere gegen die Deutsche Telekom AG verhängt, obwohl deren Vorleistungsentgelte sich in dem durch die Regulierungsbehörde (damals RegTP, heute BNetzA) genehmigten Rahmen bewegten.[133] Der EuGH betont in diesem Urteil, dass die RegTP durch Missachtung des Art. 82 EG in Verbindung mit Art. 10 EG (heute Art. 102 AEUV i.V.m. Art. 4 Abs. 3 EUV) möglicherweise gegen das Unionskartellrecht verstoßen habe,[134] doch entbinde dies die Deutsche Telekom AG nicht von ihrer eigenen Bindung an Art. 82 EG, solange die Verfügung der RegTP den Kartellrechtsverstoß zwar veranlasst oder erleichtert habe, dem Unternehmen aber Raum für eine Anpassung der Entgelte lasse[135] oder es diesem möglich war, eine Änderung der Entgeltgenehmigung zu beantragen[136] und auf diese Weise einen Verstoß gegen Art. 102 AEUV zu vermeiden.

Daran anknüpfend betont der BGH im Urteil *Trassenentgelte* (im Ausgangspunkt wiederum korrekt), selbst die *ex ante*-Genehmigung eines Entgelts durch eine nationale Regulierungsbehörde immunisiere ein Unternehmen, soweit dieses über einen eigenen Spielraum verfüge, nicht gegen

---

133 EuGH, 14. 10. 2010, Rs. C-280/08 P, ECLI:EU:C:2010:603, Rn. 80 ff. – *Deutsche Telekom*.
134 EuGH, a.a.O., Rn. 91.
135 EuGH, a.a.O., Rn. 80 ff.
136 EuGH, a.a.O., Rn. 86.

eine Anwendung des Art. 102 AEUV.[137] Allerdings fehlt bei dieser Argumentation des BGH wiederum der Hinweis darauf, dass auch bei der Entscheidung *Deutsche Telekom* nur die Frage nach einer Anwendbarkeit des Art. 102 AEUV *durch die EU-Kommission* infrage stand. Aus den bereits im Zusammenhang mit der *Telefónica*-Entscheidung des EuGH beschriebenen Gründen, kann daraus nicht ohne Weiteres gefolgert werden, dass die gleiche Befugnis auch jedem nationalen Zivilgericht zusteht. In der Sache folgt aus beiden EuGH-Entscheidungen nur, dass fehlende oder fehlerhafte Entscheidungen nationaler Regulierungsbehörden einer Anwendung des Art. 102 AEUV *durch die EU-Kommission* nicht entgegenstehen. Dass die EU-Kommission auch nicht an die Auslegung der Wettbewerbsregeln durch nationale Gerichte gebunden ist, hatte der EuGH bereits im Jahr 2000 in seiner *Masterfoods*-Entscheidung festgestellt.[138]

bb) Bindung nationaler Gerichte an Entscheidungen der Kartellbehörden

Eigentlicher Gegenstand der *Masterfoods*-Entscheidung des EuGH war die Frage, ob umgekehrt nationale Gerichte an Entscheidungen der EU-Kommission gebunden sind. Dies hat der EuGH bejaht und betont, dass die nationale Gerichtsbarkeit keine Entscheidung treffen dürfe, die einer vorausgehenden Entscheidung der Kommission auf dem Gebiet des Kartellrechts zuwiderliefen.[139] Diese Bindung hat ihre primärrechtliche Grundlage in Art. 101 und 102 AEUV in Verbindung mit dem Loyalitätsgebot des Art. 4 Abs. 3 EUV. Letzterer lautet:

> „Nach dem Grundsatz der loyalen Zusammenarbeit achten und unterstützen sich die Union und die Mitgliedstaaten gegenseitig bei der Erfüllung der Aufgaben, die sich aus den Verträgen ergeben.
> Die Mitgliedstaaten ergreifen alle geeigneten Maßnahmen allgemeiner oder besonderer Art zur Erfüllung der Verpflichtungen, die sich aus den Verträgen oder den Handlungen der Organe der Union ergeben.
> Die Mitgliedstaaten unterstützen die Union bei der Erfüllung ihrer Aufgabe und unterlassen alle Maßnahmen, die die Verwirklichung der Ziele der Union gefährden könnten".

---

137 BGH, 29. 10. 2019, Az. KZR 39/19, ECLI:DE:BGH:2019:291019UKZR39.19.0, Rn. 24 f. – *Trassenentgelte*; *Hauf/Baumgartner*, EuZW 2018, 1028, 1030.
138 EuGH, 14. 12. 2000, Rs. 344/98, ECLI:EU:C:2000:689, Rn. 48 – *Masterfoods*.
139 EuGH, 14. 12. 2000, Rs. 344/98, ECLI:EU:C:2000:689, Rn. 49 – *Masterfoods*.

Der EuGH betont in diesem Kontext, die sich aus Art. 4 Abs. 3 EUV „für die Mitgliedstaaten ergebende Verpflichtung, alle zur Erfüllung der gemeinschaftsrechtlichen Verpflichtungen geeigneten Maßnahmen allgemeiner oder besonderer Art zu treffen und von solchen Maßnahmen abzusehen, die geeignet sind, die Verwirklichung der Ziele des Vertrages zu gefährden"; dies binde „alle Träger öffentlicher Gewalt in den Mitgliedstaaten, also im Rahmen ihrer Zuständigkeiten auch die Gerichte".[140] Der Grundsatz der *Masterfoods*-Entscheidung wurde in Art. 16 VO 1/2003 verrechtlicht, der eine Bindung nationaler Stellen an Entscheidungen der EU-Kommission normiert.

Die Bindung der nationalen Gerichte an Entscheidungen der Kommission ist durch Art. 9 der EU-Kartellschadensersatzrichtlinie 2014/104/EU um eine Bindung an Entscheidungen der nationalen EU-Wettbewerbsbehörden erweitert worden.[141] Erwägungsgrund 34 zu dieser Richtlinie weist darauf hin, eine solche Bindung werde im Interesse der Rechtssicherheit, zur Vermeidung von Widersprüchen bei der Anwendung des Art. 101 und 102 AEUV, zur Erhöhung der Wirksamkeit und Effizienz von Schadensersatzklagen und zur Förderung des Funktionierens des Binnenmarktes etabliert.

cc) Bindung nationaler Gerichte an Entscheidungen der
    Regulierungsbehörden

Hinsichtlich der sich anschließenden Frage nach einer Bindung nationaler Zivilgerichte an bestandskräftige Entscheidungen der zuständigen Regulierungsbehörden, wie sie der EuGH in der *CTL Logistics*-Entscheidung in Bezug auf die Feststellung der Unvereinbarkeit von Entgelten mit den Vorga-

---

140 EuGH, 14. 12. 2000, Rs. 344/98, ECLI:EU:C:2000:689, Rn. 49 – *Masterfoods*.
141 Darauf weist auch BGH, 29. 10. 2019, Az. KZR 39/19, ECLI: DE: BGH: 2019: 291019UKZR39. 19.0, Rn. 37 – *Trassenentgelte* hin. Art. 9 Abs. 1 gebietet, dass durch eine bestandskräftige Entscheidung festgestellte Wettbewerbsverstöße als unwiderlegbar festgestellt gelten, wenn sie von einer zuständigen Behörde desselben Mitgliedstaates getroffen wurden, während Entscheidungen von Behörden anderer Mitgliedstaaten nach Art. 9 Abs. 2 „zumindest als Anscheinsbeweis vorgelegt" werden können. In Deutschland wurde in § 33b GWB von dieser Differenzierungsmöglichkeit kein Gebraucht gemacht, so dass eine Bindung der Gerichte auch an bestandskräftige EU-ausländische Behördenentscheidungen besteht.

ben des Regulierungsrechts angenommen hat,[142] fällt das Votum des BGH im Urteil *Trassenentgelte* weniger eindeutig aus: Zunächst betont der BGH, es gebe *keine* der Bindung an kartellbehördliche Entscheidungen vergleichbare Verpflichtung, welche eine Bindung der Zivilgerichte an Entscheidungen einer Regulierungsbehörde normiere. Im Gegenteil seien, „soweit die von der sektorspezifischen Regulierung eröffneten Handlungsspielräume eines marktbeherrschenden Infrastrukturunternehmens nicht hinreichend vom Wettbewerb kontrolliert werden, diese am primärrechtlichen Maßstab des Art. 102 AEUV zu messen".[143] Später stellt er dann allerdings unter Bezugnahme auf die Urteile *CTL Logistics* und *Masterfoods* des EuGH klar, die Zivilgerichte könnten „gegebenenfalls" verpflichtet sein, den Ausgang eines anhängigen Regulierungsverfahrens abzuwarten, um bei der Anwendung des Art. 102 AEUV den Zwecken und Wirkungen sektorspezifischer Regulierung Rechnung zu tragen, weil alle Träger öffentlicher Gewalt der Mitgliedstaaten (auch die Gerichte) nach Art. 4 Abs. 3 EUV verpflichtet seien, „alle zur Erfüllung der unionsrechtlichen Verpflichtungen geeigneten Maßnahmen allgemeiner oder besonderer Art zu treffen und von solchen Maßnahmen abzusehen, die geeignet sind, die Verwirklichung der Ziele des Vertrags zu gefährden", weshalb auch Feststellungen der Regulierungsbehörden in Anwendung regulierungsrechtlicher Regelungen bei Anwendung des Art. 102 AEUV zu berücksichtigen seien.[144]

Diese Bindung wird in Bezug auf nach dem ERegG genehmigte Entgelte auch durch §§ 33 Abs. 2 und 45 Abs. 2 ERegG unterstrichen. Diese Normen verbieten es den Infrastrukturbetreibern, von den genehmigten Entgelten abweichende Entgelte zu verlangen. Eine entsprechende Bindung bestand auch nach altem Recht in Bezug auf unwidersprochene Entgelte, die nach § 21 Abs. 6 und 7 EiBV gegenüber allen Zugangsberechtigten innerhalb einer Netzfahrplanperiode in gleicher Weise zu berechnen und zu erheben waren. §§ 33 Abs. 2 und 45 Abs. 2 ERegG legen ferner fest, dass genehmigte Entgelte als „billig" i.S.d. § 315 BGB gelten. Der Gesetzgeber wollte damit den Vorgaben der *CTL Logistics*-Rechtsprechung Rechnung tragen. Ausweislich der Materialien zum ERegG ist daher bei „genehmig-

---

142 EuGH, 9. 11. 2017, Rs. C-489/15, EU:C:2017:834, Rn. 97 – *CTL Logistics*.
143 BGH, 29. 10. 2019, Az. KZR 39/19, ECLI:DE:BGH:2019:291019UKZR39.19.0, Rn. 37 – *Trassenentgelte*.
144 BGH, a.a.O., Rn. 44. Einen Grund für eine Aussetzung nach § 148 ZPO sieht der BGH darin aber nicht und gibt zur Begründung an, es sei nicht zu erwarten, dass die BNetzA (zeitnah) eine solche Entscheidung treffen werde (a.a.O., Rn. 45 ff.).

ten Entgelten ... nur der Weg zu den Verwaltungsgerichten eröffnet. Damit ist effektiver Rechtsschutz gewährleistet".[145]

Werden die Zivilgerichte in einem nachfolgenden Verfahren tätig, sind sie an die Entscheidungen der Regulierungsbehörden nicht nur „gegebenenfalls", sondern definitiv ebenso gebunden wie an die Entscheidungen der Kartellbehörden. Dies folgt zwar nicht aus Art. 9 der EU-Schadensersatz-Richtlinie 2014/104/EU oder dessen Umsetzung in § 33b GWB, aber aus den Eisenbahnrichtlinien in der verbindlichen Auslegung durch den EuGH im Urteil *CTL Logistics*, weil danach eine Erstattung von Entgelten nach den Vorschriften des Zivilrechts nur in Betracht kommt, „wenn die Unvereinbarkeit des Entgelts mit Regelung über den Zugang zur Eisenbahninfrastruktur zuvor von der Regulierungsstelle oder von einem Gericht, das die Entscheidung dieser Stelle überprüft hat, im Einklang mit den Vorschriften des nationalen Rechts festgestellt worden ist".[146]

Dabei erscheint selbstverständlich, dass eine Bindungswirkung nur von bestandskräftigen oder zumindest wirksamen Entscheidungen der Regulierungsbehörde ausgehen kann. Es ist daher aus rechtsstaatlicher Sicht schwer nachvollziehbar, dass der BGH dies im Urteil *Trassenentgelte* anders gesehen und eine Bindung an die Entscheidung der BNetzA vom 5. März 2010 angenommen hat, obwohl diese nie bestandskräftig geworden ist, sondern im Gegenteil nach einem dagegen gerichteten Widerspruch durch einen inhaltlich gegensätzlichen öffentlich-rechtlichen Vertrag ersetzt und damit gegenstandslos wurde, während die in diesem wirksamen Vertrag zum Ausdruck kommende neue Position der BNetzA nach Auffassung des BGH unbeachtlich sein soll.[147] Gibt es zu einer Rechtsfrage zwei sich inhaltlich widersprechende Entscheidungen der zuständigen Regulierungsstelle, von denen die eine unwirksam und die andere wirksam ist, so kann sich das Gericht nicht einfach die unwirksame „aussuchen" und sich daran gebunden halten, auch wenn diese ihm inhaltlich besser gefällt.

dd) Bindung der Regulierungsbehörden an Art. 102 AEUV

Wenn in diesem Kontext in der Literatur gegen eine Bindung der Gerichte an regulierungsbehördliche Entscheidungen angeführt wird, die BNetzA

---

145 Gegenäußerung der BReg, BT-Drucks. 18/8334, S. 315.
146 EuGH, 9. 11. 2017, Rs. C-489/15, EU:C:2017:834, Rn. 97 – *CTL Logistics*.
147 BGH, 29. 10. 2019, Az. KZR 39/19, ECLI:DE:BGH:2019:291019UKZR39.19.0, Rn. 52 – *Trassenentgelte*.

sei nicht befugt, Entgelte und Geschäftsbedingungen auf einen Missbrauch nach Art. 102 AEUV zu überprüfen[148] oder andere zivil- oder kartellrechtliche Normen heranzuziehen oder anzuwenden,[149] so ist das mindestens missverständlich. Richtig ist, dass die Regulierungsbehörden nicht unmittelbar Privatrecht anwenden und durchsetzen, also z. B. nicht ohne besondere Befugnisnorm eine AGB-Kontrolle nach § 307 BGB vornehmen, dürfen.[150] Sie dürfen auch nicht in Konkurrenz zu den Kartellbehörden eigenständig kartellrechtliche Vorschriften durchsetzen. Das ist grundsätzlich Sache der Kartellbehörden und -gerichte. Ebenso selbstverständlich sind die Regulierungsbehörden aber wie jede staatliche Stelle über Art. 4 Abs. 3 EUV an die Wettbewerbsregeln des AEUV gebunden und müssen deren Einhaltung *bei Anwendung des Regulierungsrechts*, d.h. innerhalb des ihnen zugewiesenen Zuständigkeitsbereichs, sicherstellen.[151] Dies gilt umso mehr als auch das Eisenbahnregulierungsrecht der Verhinderung von Diskriminierungen und dem Wettbewerbsschutz dient.

b) Vorrang des Art. 102 AEUV oder wechselseitige Beeinflussung von Kartell- und Regulierungsrecht?

Art. 102 AEUV bindet also Gesetzgeber, Behörden und Gerichte und beeinflusst insoweit auch die Ausgestaltung und Anwendung des Regulierungsrechts. Es ist vor diesem Hintergrund im Ausgangspunkt korrekt, wenn der BGH den Vorrang des Primär- gegenüber dem Sekundärrecht betont.[152] Allerdings ist Art. 102 AEUV generalklauselartig formuliert und macht nur vergleichsweise generelle Vorgaben. Das hat den Vorteil, dass Art. 102 AEUV im Grundsatz auf alle Wirtschaftssektoren angewendet werden kann und dass die Kartellbehörden und -gerichte über eine hohe Flexibilität verfügen, um sich den stetig wechselnden Herausforderungen der ökonomischen Realität zu stellen.

---

148 *Hauf/Baumgartner*, EuZW 2018, 1028, 1030; *dies.*, TranspR 2019, 69, 70.

149 *Hauf/Baumgartner*, EuZW 2018, 1028, 1031 mit Verweis auf BVerwG, 11. 11. 2015, Az. 6 C 58.14, ECLI:DE:BVERWG:2015:111115U6C58.14.0, Rn. 50; s. auch *dies.*, EuZW 2018, 1028, 1034.

150 Darauf bezieht sich BVerwG, 11. 11. 2015, Az.. 6 C 58.14, ECLI:DE:BVERWG:2015:111115U6C58.14.0, Rn. 50.

151 Insoweit abweichend Monopolkommission, 7. Sektorgutachten Bahn, 6. 8. 2019, BT-Drucks. 1)/12300, Tz. 177.

152 BGH, 29. 10. 2019, Az. KZR 39/19, ECLI:DE:BGH:2019:291019UKZR39.19.0, Rn. 22 und 36 – *Trassenentgelte*.

Es gibt allerdings Sektoren, in denen der Schutz oder die Ermöglichung des Wettbewerbs besondere Anforderungen stellen oder in denen durch Regulierung weitere, über den Wettbewerbsschutz hinausreichende Unionsziele verfolgt werden. Für diese Sektoren werden besondere regulierungsrechtliche Regelungen geschaffen, deren Anwendungsbereiche sich mit denjenigen der allgemein gefassten Wettbewerbsregeln überschneiden. *Mestmäcker und Schweitzer* betonen:

> „Aus den faktisch fortbestehenden beherrschenden Stellungen der früheren Staatsmonopole und der Netzstruktur der betroffenen Märkte folgten Hindernisse für die Entwicklung von Wettbewerb, die durch das nachträglich eingreifende Missbrauchsverbot in Art. 102 AEUV (damals Art. 82 EG) nicht überwunden werden konnten. Die Entwicklung eines leistungsfähigen Wettbewerbs kann deshalb Regulierungen erfordern, die den Zugang zu den Vorleistungen des Marktbeherrschers gewährleisten, die für den Zugang der Konkurrenten zum Endverbraucher notwendig sind. Diese *ex ante*-Kontrolle kann auch die Festsetzung der Entgelte notwendig machen. Dies hat im Unionsrecht dazu geführt, dass die Wettbewerbsregeln, deren Geltung nicht in Frage steht, durch sektorspezifische Regulierungen ergänzt und teilweise modifiziert werden".[153]

Zu diesen einer besonderen Regulierung unterliegenden Sektoren zählt auch der Eisenbahnsektor. Sowohl Art. 102 AEUV als auch die Eisenbahnrichtlinien 2001/14/EG und 2012/34/EU verfolgen (nach Normtext und Erwägungsgründen) das Ziel, Diskriminierungen und Wettbewerbsverfälschungen entgegenzuwirken. Dabei setzen nicht nur die Wettbewerbsregeln der Art. 101, 102 AEUV der Ausgestaltung und Anwendung des Regulierungsrechts äußere Grenzen, sondern sie werden auch umkehrt inhaltlich durch das Regulierungsrecht konkretisiert und ausgeformt. Das Sekundärrecht kann dem letztlich zur verbindlichen Auslegung der Art. 101 und 102 AEUV berufenen EuGH nicht verbindlich vorschreiben, wie *dieser* die Wettbewerbsregeln auszulegen hat, gleichwohl beeinflusst das Richtlinienrecht – wie im Anwendungsbereich der Grundfreiheiten, wo der EuGH im harmonisierten Bereich sogar auf eine Anwendung der Grundfreiheiten verzichtet, sofern die betreffende Richtlinie nicht evident

---

153 *Mestmäcker/Schweitzer*, Europäisches Wettbewerbsrecht, 3. Aufl. 2014, § 1 Rn. 67.

gegen das Primärrecht verstößt[154] – die Auslegung der Wettbewerbsregeln.[155]

Der BGH betont in diesem Zusammenhang in seinem Urteil *Trassententgelte*, das Verhältnis von Missbrauchsverbot zu sektorspezifischer Entgeltkontrolle werde – anders als das Verhältnis sektorspezifischer Entgeltkontrolle zu zivilrechtlicher Billigkeitskontrolle – vom Vorrang des Primär- gegenüber dem Sekundärrecht bestimmt[156] und beruft sich zum Beleg auf die EuGH-Entscheidung *Ahmed Saeed*.[157] An der vom BGH angegebenen Fundstelle bei Rn. 45 behandelt der EuGH diesen Aspekt allerdings gar nicht, sondern betont lediglich, dass es – wenn die Kommission nicht zur Durchsetzung des Art. 102 AEUV (damals Art. 86 EWGV) tätig werde – Sache der nationalen Verwaltungsbehörden und Gerichte sei, die Wettbewerbsregeln in Anwendung des nationalen Rechts durchzusetzen. Kurz davor in Rn. 43 führt der EuGH demgegenüber mit Blick auf die Kriterien für die Feststellung eines Verstoßes gegen Art. 86 EWGV (Art. 102 AEUV) aus:

„Für die Beurteilung der Frage, ob der Tarif in diesem Sinn überhöht oder übermäßig niedrig ist, lassen sich aus der Richtlinie 87/601, die die von den Luftverkehrsbehörden bei der Genehmigung von Tarifen einzuhaltenden Grundsätze festlegt, bestimmte Auslegungskriterien ableiten".

Mit anderen Worten: Der EuGH zieht zur Konkretisierung der Verbotsreichweite des Art. 102 AEUV im Luftverkehrsbereich die Bestimmungen der einschlägigen Regulierungsrichtlinie heran und entnimmt dieser die Maßstäbe für die Konkretisierung des Missbrauchsmaßstabs des Art. 102 AEUV. Das ist auch sachgerecht, denn das Regulierungsrecht schafft einen Rahmen, der nicht nur die Anforderungen an den Wettbewerbsschutz in dem betreffenden Sektor ausgestaltet, sondern ihn dabei auch mit den anderen Regulierungszielen zu versöhnen sucht und damit einen Ausgleich der Interessen sowohl der Allgemeinheit als auch der Marktteilnehmer, im Eisenbahnrecht also insbesondere von Infrastrukturbetreibern und Ver-

---

154 Vgl. etwa EuGH, 30. 11. 1983, Rs. 227, 82, ECLI:EU:C:1983:354, Rn. 35 – *Van Bennekom*; zum Wechselspiel von Grundfreiheiten und Sekundärrecht eingehend *Körber*, Grundfreiheiten und Privatrecht, 1994, S. 89 ff.

155 BGH, 29. 10. 2019, Az. KZR 39/19, ECLI:DE:BGH:2019:291019UKZR39.19.0, Rn. 36 – *Trassenentgelte*.

156 BGH, 29. 10. 2019, Az. KZR 39/19, ECLI:DE:BGH:2019:291019UKZR39.19.0, Rn. 36 – *Trassenentgelte*.

157 EuGH, 11. 4. 1986, Rs. 66/86, ECLI:EU:C:1989:140, Rn. 45 – *Ahmed Saeed*.

kehrsunternehmen, anstrebt. So muss die Regulierungsstelle insbesondere – wie der EuGH in *CTL Logistics* betont hat – nicht nur die im Einzelfall angewendeten Entgelte und ihre Angemessenheit im bilateralen Verhältnis, sondern eine Vereinbarkeit der Gesamtheit der Entgelte, also der Entgeltregelung insgesamt mit den Vorgaben des Regulierungsrechts sicherstellen,[158] durch welche ein bestimmtes, kostendeckendes Gesamtaufkommen ermöglicht wird. *Immenga* und *Mestmäcker* führen in einer vom BGH in Rn. 44 des Urteils *Trassenentgelte* zitierten Passage dementsprechend aus:

> „Hier ist es unstreitig, dass die Maßnahmen der Regulierung zugleich den Erfordernissen des auf den betroffenen Märkten möglichen Wettbewerbs Rechnung tragen müssen. Das entsprechende gilt jedoch auch für die Anwendung der Wettbewerbsregeln in regulierten Bereichen. Die dem Unionsrecht entsprechende Regulierung setzt sich gegenüber den Wettbewerbsregeln durch, soweit sie die Handlungsfreiheit der betroffenen Unternehmen einschränkt. Soweit Raum für Wettbewerb bleibt, sind die Wettbewerbsregeln anwendbar. Zwecke und Wirkungen der Regulierung sind bei der Anwendung der Wettbewerbsregeln zu berücksichtigen".[159]

Daraus folgt: Das in Art. 101 und 102 AEUV normierte Unionskartellrecht bleibt in materieller Hinsicht *einerseits* auch auf regulierte Unternehmen und auch durch die Zivilgerichte uneingeschränkt anwendbar, soweit es um Verhaltensweisen *außerhalb des regulierten Bereichs* geht.[160]

Andererseits dürften Konflikte zwischen Kartell- und Regulierungsrecht aber auch *innerhalb des regulierten Bereichs* die Ausnahme sein. In aller Regel lassen sie sich dadurch vermeiden, dass nicht nur die Richtlinien im Lichte der Wettbewerbsregeln, sondern auch umgekehrt – wie im Fall *Ahmed Saeed* – die Wettbewerbsregeln im Lichte der Regulierungsrichtlinien ausgelegt werden. Dies gilt ebenso, wenn sich Zielkonflikte daraus ergeben, dass die Richtlinien nicht allein auf den Schutz des Wettbewerbs fokussiert sind, sondern zusätzlich anderen Regelungsanliegen (z. B. der Op-

---

158 EuGH, 9. 11. 2017, Rs. C-489/15, EU:C:2017:834, Rn. 57 – *CTL Logistics*.
159 *Immenga/Mestmäcker*, in: Immenga/Mestmäcker, Wettbewerbsrecht, Band 1: EU, 6. Aufl. 2019, Einl EU A, Rn. 71.
160 Das dürfte auch gemeint sein, wenn das LG Frankfurt, a. M., 9. 5. 2018, Az. 2-06 O 38/17, ECLI:DE:LGFFM:2018:0509.2.06O38.17.00, Rn. 71 ff., juris und das OLG Dresden, 17. 4. 2019, Az. U 4/18 Kart, ECLI:DE:OLGDRES:2019:0417.U4. 18KART.0A, Rn. 46 betonen, im Rahmen der kartellrechtlichen Entgeltkontrolle dürften nur „andere Kriterien" als diejenigen des Regulierungsrechts zugrunde gelegt werden.

timierung der Verkehrswege) dienen. Die durch den Unionsgesetzgeber getroffene Strukturentscheidung kann in diesem Fall auch Einfluss auf den dem Infrastrukturbetreiber nach dem Richtlinienrecht eingeräumten Spielraum haben und dadurch den Maßstab beeinflussen, mittels dessen dieser an Art. 102 AEUV gemessen wird.

Unionskartellrecht und Unionsregulierungsrecht stehen also keineswegs in einem simplen Verhältnis der Über- und Unterordnung zueinander. Das Primärrecht der Union besteht nicht nur aus Art. 101 und 102 AEUV und ist auch nicht allein auf den Schutz des Wettbewerbs gerichtet. Der AEUV verfolgt ebenso eine Reihe anderer Zielsetzungen. Nach Art. 90 AEUV gebietet er die Verfolgung der Ziele der Verträge im Rahmen einer gemeinsamen Verkehrspolitik und ermächtigt Parlament und Rat zu diesem Zweck in Art. 91 AEUV, alle dazu zweckdienlichen Regeln aufzustellen. Davon hat der Unionsgesetzgeber u.a. in Gestalt der Richtlinien 2001/14/EG und 2012/34/EU Gebrauch gemacht. Diese Richtlinien sind mithin Ausformungen primärrechtlicher Vorgaben. Sie beeinflussen in ihrem Anwendungsbereich (wie die Richtlinie 87/801 im Fall *Ahmed Saeed*) die Auslegung des Art. 102 AEUV und können daher nicht einfach unter Hinweis auf den primärrechtlichen Charakter des Art. 102 AEUV beiseite gewischt werden. Vielmehr ist danach zu fragen, wie eine praktische Konkordanz zwischen Unionskartell- und Unionsregulierungsrecht, die beide im Primärrecht verankert sind, hergestellt werden kann, um die Widerspruchsfreiheit der Unionsrechtsordnung sicher zu stellen und den *Zielen des AEUV in ihrer Gesamtheit volle und praktische Wirksamkeit* zu verschaffen.

In dieser Vorgehensweise kommen nicht nur richterliche Zurückhaltung und Respekt gegenüber der Rechtssetzungsbefugnis und dem Gestaltungsspielraum des Gesetzgebers zum Ausdruck. Sie ist auch Ausdruck des Bestrebens, verschiedene Unionsziele miteinander in praktische Konkordanz zu bringen.

c) Konsequenzen der wechselseitigen Beeinflussung für die Rechtsdurchsetzung

Für einen solchen Ausgleich spielt nicht nur das „Ob" und „Wie", sondern auch das „Wer" eine erhebliche Rolle. Praktische Konkordanz zwischen Kartell- und Regulierungsrecht muss nicht nur hinsichtlich der materiellen Ziele und Maßstäbe hergestellt werden, sondern auch hinsichtlich der institutionell-prozessualen Effektuierung dieser Ziele im Rahmen ihrer

Durchsetzung durch Behörden und Gerichte. In diesem Kontext ist relevant, dass der Unionsgesetzgeber in Bezug auf die Durchsetzung des Kartellrechts und des Eisenbahnregulierungsrechts voneinander abweichende Wege gewählt hat.

aa) Durchsetzung des Kartellrechts

Hinsichtlich des Kartellrechts hat sich der Unionsgesetzgeber für eine parallele Durchsetzung der Art. 101 und 102 AEUV durch EU-Kommission, nationale Behörden und nationale Gerichte entschieden (Art. 4 bis 6 VO 1/2003).[161] Gerichtsentscheidungen auf diesem Rechtsgebiet setzen keine vorausgehende Behördenentscheidung voraus. Doch sind die Gerichte nach Art. 16 VO 1/2003, wenn solche Entscheidungen ergangen sind, an Entscheidungen der EU-Kommission und nach Maßgabe des Art. 9 Richtlinie 2014/104/EU auch an bestandskräftige Entscheidungen mitgliedstaatlicher Kartellbehörden gebunden, während umgekehrt eine Bindung der Kommission an Entscheidungen nationaler Stellen ausscheidet und das letzte Wort über die Auslegung der Art. 101 und 102 AEUV nach Art. 267 AEUV ohnehin der EuGH hat.

bb) Durchsetzung des Eisenbahnregulierungsrechts

Für das Eisenbahnregulierungsrecht hat der Unionsgesetzgeber eine andere Grundsatzentscheidung getroffen. Er hat die Entgeltregulierung im Anwendungsbereich der betreffenden Richtlinien allein in die Hände der zuständigen Regulierungsstelle und der zu deren Kontrolle berufenen Gerichtsbarkeit (in Deutschland also von BNetzA und Verwaltungsgerichtsbarkeit) gelegt (Art. 30 Richtline 2001/14/EG bzw. Art. 56 Richtlinie 2012/34/EU). Er hat dadurch, wie der EuGH in *CTL Logistics* deutlich gemacht hat, zugleich zivilrechtliche Erstattungs- oder Schadensersatzansprüche in Bezug auf Entgelte, die in den Anwendungsbereich dieser Regelungen fallen, unter den Vorbehalt einer bestandskräftigen regulierungsbehördlichen Entscheidung gestellt, welche die Rechtswidrigkeit dieser Entgelte feststellt. Hintergrund dieses vom Kartellrecht abweichenden Durchsetzungsregimes sind insbesondere die spezifischen Regulierungsziele, die nur durch eine Konzentration der Entscheidungsbefugnisse und des

---

161 Dazu bereits oben S. 67.

Rechtswegs erreicht werden können sowie die gegenüber der Anwendung des Kartellrechts nochmals deutlich gesteigerte Komplexität der Anwendung des Regulierungsrechts, bei welcher die zuständige Regulierungsbehörde die wirtschaftlichen Verhältnisse des betreffenden Sektors und das Entgeltsystem insgesamt im Auge haben muss und sich nicht nur auf einen von individuellen Interessen geprägten Parteivortrag stützen kann.

cc) Durchsetzung des Kartellrechts im Anwendungsbereich des Eisenbahnregulierungsrechts?

Treffen beide Regelungsmaterien samt ihrer unterschiedlichen Durchsetzungsregime aufeinander, so gilt Folgendes:

(1) EU-Kommission

Die EU-Kommission ist nach Art. 4 VO 1/2003 zur Durchsetzung der Art. 101 und 102 AEUV befugt. Sie ist dabei nach der EuGH-Rechtsprechung, wie oben ausgeführt wurde, nicht an Entscheidungen nationaler Behörden oder Gerichte gebunden, sondern unterliegt nur der Kontrolle durch den Europäischen Gerichtshof. Sie kann Art. 101 und 102 AEUV daher auch im Anwendungsbereich des Eisenbahnregulierungsrechts unabhängig davon, ob eine regulierungsbehördliche Entscheidung vorliegt oder nicht und ohne an Entscheidungen mitgliedstaatlicher Stellen oder Gerichte gebunden zu sein, unmittelbar gegenüber Unternehmen anwenden oder auch ein Vertragsverletzungsverfahren gegen den betreffenden Mitgliedstaat einleiten, wenn sie Art. 102 AEUV durch eine staatliche Stelle eines Mitgliedstaates verletzt sieht. An die Entscheidungen der Kommission sind (soweit sie nicht vom EuGH aufgehoben werden) auch die mitgliedstaatlichen Behörden und Gerichte gebunden. Es droht insoweit weder eine materiell uneinheitliche Rechtsanwendung noch eine Rechtswegspaltung. Der vom EuGH in *CTL Logistics* beschriebene Konflikt zwischen Eisenbahnrecht und Zivilrecht bzw. Kartellrecht scheidet aus.

(2) Wettbewerbsbehörden der Mitgliedstaaten, insbesondere Bundeskartellamt

Nach Art. 5 VO 1/2003 sind neben der Kommission (auch parallel zu dieser) ferner die Wettbewerbsbehörden der Mitgliedstaaten für die Durchsetzung der VO 1/2003 zuständig. Die nationalen Wettbewerbsbehörden sind dabei nach Art. 16 VO 1/2003 an Entscheidungen der Kommission gebunden. Nach dem derzeitigen § 50 GWB sind sowohl das BKartA als auch die Landeskartellbehörden zur Durchsetzung der Art. 101 und 102 AEUV befugt. Dies soll allerdings in Umsetzung der ECN+-Richtlinie 2019/1/EU mit der 10. GWB-Novelle dahingehend geändert werden, dass in Zukunft (vermutlich ab 1. Januar 2021) allein das BKartA dafür zuständig sein wird.[162] Hinsichtlich der Frage nach einer Zuständigkeit des BKartA neben der BNetzA im regulierten Bereich, ist die Rechtslage nicht eindeutig.

Auf der einen Seite betont Erwägungsgrund 9 zur Richtlinie 2012/34/EU explizit:

> „Entscheidungen der Regulierungsstelle sind für alle davon Betroffenen verbindlich und unterliegen keiner Kontrolle durch eine andere Verwaltungsinstanz".

Dementsprechend streitet auch der allgemeine rechtsstaatliche Grundsatz, Zuständigkeitsregelungen grundsätzlich so auszulegen, dass Doppelzuständigkeiten vermieden werden,[163] gegen die Annahme einer parallelen Zuständigkeit von BKartA und BNetzA in Bezug auf regulierte Entgelte. Das BVerwG hat dazu ausgeführt, bei einem Konflikt zweier Zuständigkeitsregelungen gelte:

> „Die in einer solchen Situation für die Entscheidung über die Einhaltung dieser Vorschrift zuständige Behörde ist durch Auslegung der jeweiligen fachgesetzlichen Zuständigkeitsregelungen nach dem Gesichtspunkt zu bestimmen, zu welchem in die originäre Zuständigkeit der jeweiligen Behörden fallenden Regelungsgegenstand der stärkere Bezug besteht, ...
> Die gebotene Bestimmtheit der gesetzlichen Zuständigkeitsordnung schließt es aus, daß verschiedene Behörden zur verbindlichen Regelung einer Frage nebeneinander zuständig sind. Einander widerspre-

---

162 S. Referentenentwurf zum „GWB-Digitalisierungsgesetz" vom 24. 1. 2020, S. 103 (abrufbar unter https://t1p.de/cwdr).
163 *Ludwigs*, WuW 2008, 534, 549.

chende Regelungen eines Einzelfalls mit dem Anspruch der Verbindlichkeit könnten sonst nämlich nur durch die Bindung der anderen Behörde an die Entscheidung der erstbefaßten Behörde vermieden werden; das würde einen vom Gesetz nicht gewollten Zufallsfaktor in die Zuständigkeitsordnung hineintragen".[164]

Und das OVG Münster hat betont:

„Eine Zuständigkeitenverordnung ist unter dem Gesichtspunkt des rechtsstaatlichen Gebots klarer und fester Kompetenzabgrenzungen und Zuständigkeitsabgrenzungen auszulegen. Das Rechtsstaatprinzip gebietet, Kompetenz nur einer Behörde einzuräumen und Doppelbeauftragungen zu vermeiden".[165]

Mit Blick auf die Kontrolle von Eisenbahnentgelten liegt es nahe, dass die dazu in erster Linie berufene BNetzA einen „stärkeren Bezug" aufweist als das BKartA.

Auf der anderen Seite ist nach Art. 56 Abs. 2 Richtlinie 2012/34/EU die Regulierungsstelle (in Deutschland also die BNetzA), „[u]nbeschadet der Befugnisse der nationalen Wettbewerbsbehörde für die Sicherstellung des Wettbewerbs in den Schienenverkehrsmärkten berechtigt, die Wettbewerbssituation in den Schienenverkehrsmärkten zu überwachen". Diese Norm regelt zwar – ebenso wie § 9 Abs. 3 S. 1 BEVVG (früher: § 14b Abs. 2 S. 1 AEG) – lediglich die institutionelle Abgrenzung der Behördenzuständigkeiten, so dass aus ihr keine Rückschlüsse auf die Anwendbarkeit des materiellen Kartellrechts oder gar auf eine Zuständigkeit der Zivilgerichte gezogen werden können.[166] Es liegt daher nahe, sie in der Weise zu interpretieren, dass jede Behörde (nur) in dem ihr zugewiesenen Bereich zuständig bleibt, ohne dass diese sich überschneiden müssten. Die Regelung lässt aber ggf. auch als Argument für eine Zuständigkeit des BKartA neben der BNetzA jedenfalls in Fällen heranziehen, in denen das BKartA die Entgeltentscheidung der BNetzA nicht direkt überprüft, aber die Anwendung des Kartellrechts durch das BKartA auf den der BNetzA zugewiesenen Zuständigkeitsbereich „ausstrahlt".[167]

---

164 BVerwG, 4. 7. 1986, Az. 4 C 31/84, Rn. 25 f., juris = BVerwGE 74, 315, 325.
165 OVG Münster, 13. 9. 1995, Az. 13 A 3687/94, LS 1 und Rn. 15, juris = NVwZ 1995, 185.
166 Dazu oben S. 43.
167 Ein solcher Fall könnte z. B. in dem sogleich beschriebenen (dem *Deutsche Telekom*-Urteil des EuGH zugrunde liegenden) Fall einer Preis-Kosten-Schere zwischen regulierten Vorleistungsentgelten und Endkundenentgelten auftreten.

Mit Blick auf das materielle Recht liegt es insoweit nahe, dass das Eisenbahnregulierungsrecht jedenfalls in Bezug auf die Diskriminierungskontrolle im Verhältnis zum nationalen Kartellrecht *lex specialis* ist.[168] Entsprechendes gilt grundsätzlich auch für die Kontrolle von Preishöhenmissbräuchen. Einer Kontrolle von nach dem ERegG genehmigten Entgelten dürfte in diesem Kontext auch die Wertung der §§ 33 Abs. 2 und 45 Abs. 2 ERegG entgegenstehen. Danach gilt das von der BNetzA genehmigte Entgelt als billiges Entgelt im Sinne des § 315 BGB. Der Billigkeitsmaßstab des § 315 BGB ist aber anerkanntermaßen milder als der kartellrechtliche Missbrauchsmaßstab, der ein über die bloße Unbilligkeit hinausreichendes besonderes „Unwerturteil" beinhaltet.[169] Nicht jedes unbillige Entgelt ist daher auch missbräuchlich, aber jedes im Sinne des Kartellrechts missbräuchliche Entgelt ist zugleich unbillig i.S.d. § 315 BGB.[170] Wenn die regulierten Eisenbahnentgelte nach der gesetzlichen Vorgabe der §§ 33 Abs. 3 und 45 Abs. 2 ERegG noch nicht einmal „unbillig" i.S.d. § 315 BGB sind, können sie mithin erst recht nicht „missbräuchlich" i.S.d. § 19 GWB sein. Eine andere Sichtweise würde, auch wenn der Gesetzgeber das Kartellrecht bei Schaffung dieser Normen vermutlich nicht im Auge hatte, in Konflikt mit dem Grundsatz der Einheit der Rechtsordnung geraten und wertungswidersprüchlich erscheinen.

Eine Anwendung des Art. 102 AEUV durch das BKartA kann allein durch Regelungen des deutschen Regulierungsrechts allerdings nicht ausgeschlossen werden, weil – wie oben ausgeführt wurde – das deutsche Recht keine verbindlichen Vorgaben zur Auslegung des EU-Rechts machen darf.[171] Das BKartA geht dementsprechend wohl davon aus, jedenfalls zu einer Preiskontrolle nach Art. 102 AEUV neben der BNetzA befugt zu sein, weil die BNetzA keine vollumfängliche Preishöhenkontrolle vornehme. Aus der Genehmigung von Trassenpreisen folge z. B. nicht, dass diese nicht im Zusammenspiel mit nicht regulierten Endkundenpreisen zu Preis-Kosten-Scheren führen könnten. Würde das BKartA allerdings solche Preis-Kosten-Scheren (ähnlich wie die Kommission im Fall *Deutsche Telekom*) am Maßstab des Art. 102 AEUV prüfen und dadurch effektiv zugleich

---

168 So auch *Kühling*, Eisenbahnentgeltregulierung jenseits AEG und EIBV, in: Ronellenfitsch/Eschweiler/Hörster, Aktuelle Probleme des Eisenbahnrechts, 2015, S. 73, 104 f.

169 Z. B. BGH, 15. 5. 2012, Az. KVR 51/11, NJW 2012, 3243, Rn. 26 – *Wasserpreise Calw.*

170 S. BGH, 29. 4. 2008, Az. KZR 2/07, NJW 2008, 2172, Rn. 15 – *Erdgassondervertrag.*

171 S. oben S. 42.

ein von der BNetzA genehmigtes Entgelt monieren, so würde dies entgegen Erwägungsgrund 9 zur Richtlinie 2012/34/EU effektiv eine „Kontrolle durch eine andere Verwaltungsinstanz" bewirken und – wie die zivilgerichtliche Kontrolle im Fall *CTL Logistics* – dazu führen, dass die nach dieser Entscheidung aus den Eisenbahnrichtlinien resultierende alleinige Kontrollkompetenz der BNetzA relativiert würde. Mit Blick darauf, dass die Entscheidung des BKartA nach §§ 63 Abs. 4 S. 1, 74 GWB der zivilgerichtlichen Kontrolle durch das OLG Düsseldorf und letztlich durch den BGH unterliegt, würde jedenfalls in Deutschland zudem das Problem zweier unkoordinierter Rechtswege auftreten, und auch mit Blick auf mögliche Vergleiche käme der BNetzA nicht die von den Regulierungsrichtlinien geforderte Kontrollbefugnis, sondern allenfalls eine beratende Funktion zu.

Im Ergebnis wären die aus einer Kontrolle durch BNetzA und BKartA drohenden Verwerfungen zwischen Kartell- und Regulierungsrecht immerhin deutlich geringer als im Falle einer zivilgerichtlichen Kontrolle, weil das BKartA ähnlich wie die EU-Kommission (und im Gegensatz zu einer potentiellen Vielzahl von Zivilgerichten erster und zweiter Instanz) als zentrale weitere Kontrollstelle agieren würde. Das BKartA würde auch keine individuellen Ansprüche einzelner Eisenbahnverkehrsunternehmen durchsetzen, sondern die Entgelte von Amts wegen überprüfen und sich dabei nach aller Erfahrung mit der BNetzA ins Benehmen setzen. Es würde mithin keine völlige Disruption des in den Eisenbahnrichtlinien vorgesehenen Systems nichtdiskriminierender und zentraler Entgeltbestimmung und Kontrolle drohen wie im Falle einer zivilgerichtlichen Entgeltkontrolle.

In der Summe könnten die seitens des EuGH in der Entscheidung *CTL Logistics* gegenüber der zivilgerichtlichen Billigkeitskontrolle regulierter Entgelte erhobenen *institutionellen Bedenken* mithin auch einer Kontrolle regulierter Entgelte durch das BKartA entgegengehalten werden, wobei aber immerhin „nur" eine Doppelkontrolle der Entgelte durch zwei kompetente, miteinander im Dialog stehende Behörden und keine unkoordinierte Vielfachkontrolle drohen würde. Dementsprechend wiegen auch die *materiellen Bedenken* weniger schwer, weil die Gefahr einer materiellen Ungleichbehandlung der Eisenbahnverkehrsunternehmen, jedenfalls bei einer Konzentration der Zuständigkeit zur Durchsetzung der Art. 101 und 102 AEUV beim BKartA (wie sie § 50 GWB-RefE im Verhältnis zu den Landeskartellbehörden vorsieht), weitgehend entschärft wäre. Strebt man nach einer Herstellung praktischer Konkordanz von Kartell- und Regulierungsrecht, spricht daher jedenfalls mehr für eine sich überschneidende

Zuständigkeit von BNetzA und BKartA als für eine neben die regulierungsbehördliche Kontrolle tretende Zuständigkeit der Zivilgerichte. Eine sich überschneidende Zuständigkeit könnte in der Weise konturiert sein, dass das BKartA zwar nicht bereits von der BNetzA kontrollierte und gebilligte oder genehmigte Entgelte als solche zusätzlichen Kontrollen unterziehen darf, dass es aber in bestimmten Sonderfällen, in denen diese Entgelte in Zusammenschau mit anderen, nicht regulierten Entgelten kartellrechtliche Probleme aufwerfen – wie dem oben beschriebenen Fall der Preis-Kosten-Schere – befugt bleibt, diese Entgelte mittelbar nach Maßgabe des Art. 102 AEUV zu kontrollieren. Letztlich ist diese Frage aber auch im Lichte der *CTL Logistics*-Entscheidung des EuGH als offen anzusehen. Für die Praxis sinnvoll und mit dem Unionsrecht am besten vereinbar wäre daher eine Behördenkooperation in der Weise, dass das BKartA sich, wenn es Bedenken (z. B. wegen einer Preis-Kosten-Schere) hat und deren kartellrechtliche Adressierung zu einer Korrektur regulierter Entgelte führen würde, an die BNetzA wendet, sich mit dieser ins Benehmen setzt und es dann der BNetzA überlässt, eine Korrektur ihrer Entgeltentscheidung unter Berücksichtigung der kartellrechtlichen Bedenken vorzunehmen.

(3) Gerichte der Mitgliedstaaten

Nach Art. 6 VO 1/2003 sind auch die Gerichte der Mitgliedstaaten (einschließlich der Zivilgerichte) zur Anwendung der Art. 101 und 102 AEUV befugt. Wie oben festgestellt wurde, setzt diese Befugnis innerhalb des kartellrechtlichen Koordinatensystems keine vorausgehende Entscheidung einer Kartellbehörde voraus. Damit ist jedoch noch nicht entschieden, dass die Zivilgerichte Art. 102 AEUV auch anwenden dürfen, um der Regulierung unterliegende Eisenbahnentgelte zu kontrollieren. Durch die grundsätzliche Befugnis der Zivilgerichte zur Anwendung der Wettbewerbsregeln wird der hier beschriebene Konflikt mit dem Regulierungsrecht, wie bereits ausgeführt wurde, zwar möglich gemacht, aber noch nicht im Sinne des Kartellrechts entschieden. Schließlich sind die mitgliedstaatlichen Gerichte – wie auch der BGH bestätigt hat – nach Art. 4 Abs. 3 AEUV nicht nur an das Unions*kartellrecht* gebunden, sondern vielmehr dazu verpflichtet, „alle zur Erfüllung der unionsrechtlichen Verpflichtungen geeigneten Maßnahmen allgemeiner oder besonderer Art zu treffen und von solchen Maßnahmen abzusehen, die geeignet sind, die Verwirklichung der

Ziele des Vertrags zu gefährden".[172] Zu diesen Zielen gehören auch die Ziele der auf der Basis von Art. 90, 91 AEUV erlassenen Eisenbahnrichtlinien.

Die Gerichte der Mitgliedstaaten sind bei Anwendung des Kartellrechts daher nicht nur an Entscheidungen der Kartellbehörden, sondern auch an Entscheidungen der Regulierungsbehörden gebunden. Das nationale Zivilgericht darf die Entscheidung der Regulierungsbehörde, wie oben festgestellt wurde, weder selbst am Maßstab des Regulierungsrechts überprüfen (das fällt in die Zuständigkeit der Verwaltungsgerichtsbarkeit) noch kann es in Anwendung anderer (z. B. kartellrechtlicher) Maßstäbe eine auf der Grundlage des Eisenbahnregulierungsrechts getroffene Entgeltgenehmigung für den Einzelfall außer Kraft setzen, ohne sich nach Maßgabe der Entscheidung *CTL Logistics* des EuGH in Widerspruch zum Richtlinienrecht zu setzen, weil dies – unstreitig – eine Ungleichbehandlung der Verkehrsunternehmen zur Folge haben und in die alleinige Kompetenz der BNetzA eingreifen würde. Die Bundesregierung hat im Rahmen der Umsetzung der Richtlinie 2012/34/EU in das ERegG den Einwand des Bundesrates, eine zivilgerichtliche Billigkeitskontrolle müsse möglich bleiben, zurückgewiesen und dazu explizit betont: „Bei genehmigten Entgelten ist nur der Weg zu den Verwaltungsgerichten eröffnet. Damit ist effektiver Rechtsschutz gewährleistet".[173]

Entsprechendes gilt, wenn eine bestandskräftige Entscheidung der Regulierungsbehörde fehlt. Die sich in diesem Kontext stellende Frage, ob ein Zivilgericht allein nach kartellrechtlichen Maßstäben entscheiden darf, ob es neben dem Kartellrecht auch die regulierungsrechtlichen Vorgaben anwenden muss bzw. überhaupt anwenden darf oder ob es eine Entscheidung der Regulierungsbehörde abwarten und das Verfahren bis dahin nach § 148 ZPO aussetzen muss, hat der EuGH in der *CTL Logistics*-Entscheidung zwar nicht ausdrücklich, aber doch der Sache nach im Sinne der dritten Variante entschieden: Die Kontrolle regulierter Entgelte obliegt danach (unbeschadet der verwaltungsgerichtlichen Überprüfung ihrer Entscheidungen) allein der BNetzA. Zivilgerichte dürften regulierungsrechtliche Regelungen deshalb nicht anwenden und dadurch der Entscheidung der allein zuständigen Regulierungsstelle vorgreifen. Die zivilgerichtliche

---

172 BGH, 29. 10. 2019, Az. KZR 39/19, ECLI:DE:BGH:2019:291019UKZR39.19.0, Rn. 44 – *Trassenentgelte* unter Zitierung von EuGH, 14. 12. 2000, Rs. 344/98, ECLI:EU:C:2000:689, Rn. 49 – *Masterfoods*.

173 Gegenäußerung der Bundesregierung vom 4. 5. 2016, BT-Drucks. 18/8334, S. 315.

Geltendmachung von Erstattungs- oder Schadensersatzansprüchen auf der Basis privatrechtlicher Anspruchsgrundlagen einschließlich des Kartellrechts kommt folglich, soweit sie auf eine Korrektur der Entgelthöhe abzielt, erst nach bestandskräftiger Feststellung der Rechtswidrigkeit der Entgelte durch die BNetzA in Betracht. Bis eine solche vorliegt, ist eine Aussetzung nach § 148 ZPO geboten.

Mit Inkrafttreten und Umsetzung der Richtlinie 2012/34/EU hat sich daran im Grundsatz nichts geändert. Im Gegenteil: Nach deutschem Recht unterliegen Entgelte seit Umsetzung dieser Richtlinie im ERegG sogar einer formellen Genehmigungspflicht. Es ist den Infrastrukturbetreibern durch §§ 33 Abs. 2 und 45 Abs. 2 ERegG verboten, von den genehmigten Entgelten abweichende Entgelte zu verlangen,[174] und diese Normen bestimmen zugleich, dass genehmigte Entgelte als „billig" i.S.d. § 315 BGB gelten und damit effektiv der zivilgerichtlichen Kontrolle entzogen sind.

3. Bedeutung und Grenzen der privaten Durchsetzung des Art. 102 AEUV

Eine zivilgerichtliche Kompetenz zu einer – von einer Entscheidung der BNetzA unabhängigen und diese abändernden – Entscheidung am Maßstab des Art. 102 AEUV würde vor dem beschriebenen Hintergrund allenfalls dann bestehen, wenn das nach dem Urteil *CTL Logistics* aus den Eisenbahnrichtlinien resultierende *Verbot* der eigenständigen zivilgerichtlichen Entgeltkontrolle durch ein aus Art. 102 AEUV folgendes *Gebot* einer eigenständigen zivilgerichtlichen Entgeltkontrolle überspielt würde. Nachfolgend ist daher zu untersuchen, wie weit das Gebot zur privatrechtlichen Effektuierung des Art. 102 AEUV reicht, ob es *erstens* tatsächlich – wie der BGH meint – gegenüber dem aus dem Regulierungsrecht folgenden Verbot einer solchen Kontrolle Vorrang beanspruchen kann, ob *zweitens* umgekehrt – wie im Fall *CTL Logistics* – Ziele und Funktionsfähigkeit des Regulierungsrechts Vorrang vor dem Individualschutz haben, oder ob es

---

174 Vgl. zum früheren Recht § 21 Abs. 6 und 7 EiBV. Im Falle einer solchen Bindung an die Entscheidung der BNetzA besitzen die Infrastrukturbetreiber grds. nicht mehr den für die Anwendung des Art. 102 AEUV tatbestandlich vorausgesetzten Handlungsspielraum, weil sie gegen mitgliedstaatliches, auf einer Richtlinie basierendes Recht verstoßen würden, wenn sie ein anderes Entgelt fordern würden. Nach Maßgabe der Entscheidung *Deutsche Telekom* ist dies aber möglicherweise noch nicht ausreichend, solange es ihnen möglich ist, eine Änderung der gebilligten bzw. genehmigten Entgelte zu beantragen, s. EuGH, 14. 10. 2010, Rs. C-280/08 P, ECLI:EU:C:2010:603, Rn. 86 – *Deutsche Telekom*.

einen *dritten* Weg gibt, welcher dem Ziel der vollen Wirksamkeit des Unionsrechts insgesamt besser gerecht wird, indem praktische Konkordanz zwischen den – jeweils für sich betrachtet – berechtigten Anliegen von Kartell- und Regulierungsrecht hergestellt wird.

a) EuGH-Rechtsprechung zum Kartellschadensersatz

Die Durchsetzung der Art. 101 und 102 AEUV war lange Zeit eine Domäne der Kartellbehörden. Einer privaten Rechtsdurchsetzung durch Klagen vor den Zivilgerichten wurde eine untergeordnete Bedeutung beigemessen, ohne dass man darin ein Problem für die praktische Wirksamkeit der Wettbewerbsregeln sah. Dies änderte sich 2001 mit dem grundlegenden Urteil *Crehan/Courage* des EuGH. Gegenstand dieses Verfahrens war die Klage eines Kartellmitglieds auf Ersatz von durch ein Kartell auf dem Gebiet des Brauereiwesens erlittenen Schäden. Insoweit stellte sich dem Court of Appeal (England & Wales) insbesondere die Frage, ob ein Grundsatz des nationalen Zivilrechts mit dem Unionsrecht vereinbar sei, nach dem sich niemand auf seine eigenen rechtswidrigen Handlungen berufen kann, um Schadensersatz zu erlangen („*unclean hands*"-Einwand).

Der EuGH betont auf das Vorabentscheidungsersuchen des englischen Gerichts zunächst in Bekräftigung der oben zitierten *BRT/SABAM*-Rechtsprechung,[175] dass Art. 101 und 102 AEUV in den Beziehungen zwischen Einzelnen unmittelbare Rechtswirkungen erzeugten und unmittelbar in deren Person Rechte entstehen ließen, welche die Gerichte der Mitgliedstaaten zu wahren hätten.[176] Dann setzt er mit Blick auf die zivilgerichtliche Durchsetzung der Wettbewerbsregeln hinzu:

> „25. Was die Befugnis angeht, Ersatz des Schadens zu verlangen, der durch einen Vertrag, der den Wettbewerb beschränken oder verfälschen kann, oder ein entsprechendes Verhalten verursacht worden ist, so müssen die nationalen Gerichte, die im Rahmen ihrer Zuständigkeit das Gemeinschaftsrecht anzuwenden haben, die volle Wirkung von dessen Bestimmungen gewährleisten und die Rechte schützen, die das Gemeinschaftsrecht dem Einzelnen verleiht [...]

---

175 EuGH, 30. 1. 1974, Rs. 127/73, ECLI:EU:C:1974:6, Rn. 15/17 – *BRT/SABAM* (s. Zitat oben in Fn. 57).
176 EuGH, 20. 9. 2001, Rs. C-453/99, ECLI:EU:C:2001:465, Rn. 23 – *Crehan/Courage*.

26. Die volle Wirksamkeit des Artikels 85 EG-Vertrag und insbesondere die praktische Wirksamkeit des in Artikel 85 Absatz 1 ausgesprochenen Verbots wären beeinträchtigt, wenn nicht jedermann Ersatz des Schadens verlangen könnte, der ihm durch einen Vertrag, der den Wettbewerb beschränken oder verfälschen kann, oder durch ein entsprechendes Verhalten entstanden ist.

27. Ein solcher Schadensersatzanspruch erhöht nämlich die Durchsetzungskraft der gemeinschaftlichen Wettbewerbsregeln und ist geeignet, von - oft verschleierten - Vereinbarungen oder Verhaltensweisen abzuhalten, die den Wettbewerb beschränken oder verfälschen können. Aus dieser Sicht können Schadensersatzklagen vor den nationalen Gerichten wesentlich zur Aufrechterhaltung eines wirksamen Wettbewerbs in der Gemeinschaft beitragen.

28. Daher darf nicht von vornherein ausgeschlossen werden, dass eine solche Klage von einer Partei eines gegen die Wettbewerbsregeln verstoßenden Vertrages erhoben wird.

29. Mangels einer einschlägigen Gemeinschaftsregelung ist es jedoch Sache des innerstaatlichen Rechts der einzelnen Mitgliedstaaten, die zuständigen Gerichte zu bestimmen und die Verfahrensmodalitäten für Klagen zu regeln, die den Schutz der dem Bürger aus der unmittelbaren Wirkung des Gemeinschaftsrechts erwachsenden Rechte gewährleisten sollen, sofern diese Modalitäten nicht weniger günstig ausgestaltet sind als die entsprechender innerstaatlicher Klagen (Äquivalenzgrundsatz) und die Ausübung der durch die Gemeinschaftsrechtsordnung verliehenen Rechte nicht praktisch unmöglich machen oder übermäßig erschweren (Effektivitätsgrundsatz) [...]

30. Hierzu hat der Gerichtshof bereits entschieden, dass das Gemeinschaftsrecht die innerstaatlichen Gerichte nicht daran hindert, dafür Sorge tragen, dass der Schutz der gemeinschaft[s]rechtlich gewährleisteten Rechte nicht zu einer ungerechtfertigten Bereicherung der Anspruchsberechtigten führt [...]

31. Ebenso wenig verbietet das Gemeinschaftsrecht, sofern die Grundsätze der Äquivalenz und der Effektivität beachtet werden [...], dass das innerstaatliche Recht einer Partei, die eine erhebliche Verantwortung für die Wettbewerbsverzerrung trägt, das Recht verwehrt, von ihrem Vertragspartner Schadensersatz zu verlangen. [...]".[177]

---

[177] EuGH, 20. 9. 2001, Rs. C-453/99, ECLI: EU: C: 2001: 465, Rn. 25 ff. – *Crehan/ Courage*.

Der EuGH hat diese Grundsätze 2006 im Urteil *Manfredi* bekräftigt, dem ein Kartell im Bereich der Versicherungswirtschaft zugrunde lag. Der Gerichtshof unterstreicht in diesem Urteil, dass jeder (einschließlich der Versicherungsnehmer und Verbraucher) Ersatz des ihm durch ein Kartell entstandenen Schadens verlangen könne, wenn zwischen diesem Schaden und dem Kartell oder kartellrechtswidrigen Verhalten ein ursächlicher Zusammenhang bestehe.[178] In diesem Fall stellte sich insbesondere die Frage, ob Art. 101 AEUV einer nationalen Vorschrift entgegensteht, „wonach Dritte eine Schadensersatzklage wegen Verstoßes gegen die gemeinschaftlichen und nationalen Wettbewerbsvorschriften bei einem anderen Gericht erheben müssen als dem, das gewöhnlich für solche Klagen bei gleichem Streitwert zuständig ist, was zu erheblich höheren Verfahrenskosten und einer erheblich längeren Verfahrensdauer führt".[179]

In seiner Antwort betonte der EuGH unter Berufung auf den Äquivalenzgrundsatz und den Effektivitätsgrundsatz,

> „dass es in Ermangelung einer einschlägigen Gemeinschaftsregelung Aufgabe des innerstaatlichen Rechts eines jeden Mitgliedstaats ist, die Gerichte zu bestimmen, die für Schadensersatzklagen wegen Verstoßes gegen die Wettbewerbsvorschriften der Gemeinschaft zuständig sind, und die Einzelheiten der entsprechenden Verfahren festzulegen, wobei die betreffenden Vorschriften nicht weniger günstig ausgestaltet sein dürfen als die für Schadensersatzklagen wegen Verstoßes gegen nationale Wettbewerbsvorschriften und die Geltendmachung des Anspruchs auf Ersatz des durch ein nach Artikel 81 EG verbotenes Kartell oder Verhalten entstandenen Schadens nicht praktisch unmöglich machen oder übermäßig erschweren dürfen".[180]

b) Kartellschadensersatzrichtlinie 2014/104/EU

Der Unionsgesetzgeber hat diese Rechtsprechungsgrundsätze in der Kartellschadensersatzrichtlinie 2014/104/EU normiert und dadurch die prakti-

---

178 EuGH, 13. 7. 2006, Rs. C-295/04, ECLI:EU:C:2006:461, Rn. 58 ff. – *Manfredi*.
179 EuGH, 13. 7. 2006, Rs. C-295/04, ECLI:EU:C:2006:461, Rn. 65 – *Manfredi*.
180 EuGH, 13. 7. 2006, Rs. C-295/04, ECLI:EU:C:2006:461, Rn. 72 – *Manfredi*; ebenso in jüngerer Zeit auch z. B. EuGH, 5. 6. 2014, Rs. C-557/12, ECLI:EU:C:2014: 1317, Rn. 21 ff. – *Kone*.

sche Rolle der privaten Durchsetzung des Kartellrechts weiter gestärkt.[181] Erwägungsgrund 3 zu dieser Richtlinie bekräftigt den Anspruch von Kartellgeschädigten auf Schadensersatz. Erwägungsgrund 4 verpflichtet die Mitgliedstaaten zur Schaffung von Verfahrensvorschriften, welche die Geltendmachung dieses Anspruchs ermöglichen. Erwägungsgrund 11 unterstreicht in diesem Kontext den Äquivalenzgrundsatz und den Effektivitätsgrundsatz. Erwägungsgrund 13 betont, dass das Recht auf Schadensersatz unabhängig von der vorherigen Feststellung einer Zuwiderhandlung durch eine Wettbewerbsbehörde bestehe.

Der Unionsgesetzgeber hat in den Erwägungsgründen aber auch anerkannt, dass die private Rechtsdurchsetzung nicht für sich steht, sondern neben (und möglichst Hand in Hand mit) der behördlichen Rechtsdurchsetzung erfolgt. Erwägungsgrund 5 betont, dass Schadensersatzklagen neben der einvernehmlichen Streitbeilegung und der behördlichen Kartellrechtsdurchsetzung nur eines unter mehreren Elementen der Rechtsdurchsetzung seien. Erwägungsgrund 6 unterstreicht, dass private und behördliche Rechtsdurchsetzung zusammenwirken müssten, was es erforderlich mache, die Koordinierung zwischen ihnen kohärent zu regeln. Erwägungsgrund 24 hebt hervor, die Richtlinie lasse das Recht der Gerichte unberührt, nach nationalem Recht oder Unionsrecht das Interesse an einer wirksamen öffentlichen Durchsetzung des Wettbewerbsrechts zu berücksichtigen. Dies wird in Erwägungsgrund 26 insbesondere im Sinne der Möglichkeit einer Beschränkung der Offenlegung von Beweismitteln betont, die zwar dem Erfolg von Schadensersatzklagen dienlich wäre, aber die Funktionsfähigkeit der Kronzeugenprogramme und damit insbesondere der behördlichen Rechtsdurchsetzung behindern würde.

c) Folgerungen des BGH im Urteil Trassenentgelte

Der BGH betont vor dem Hintergrund der zitierten EuGH-Rechtsprechung und der Kartellschadensersatzrichtlinie (im Ausgangspunkt wiederum korrekt), die Gewährleistung der vollen Wirksamkeit der Wettbewerbsregeln (Art. 101, 102 AEUV) setze nach der *Manfredi*-Entscheidung des EuGH voraus, dass jedermann sich vor Gericht auf diese Normen beru-

---

181 In Deutschland wurde die Möglichkeit privater Kartellrechtsdurchsetzung im Lichte der EuGH-Rechtsprechung bereits mit der 7. GWB-Novelle 2005 deutlich erweitert und die Kartellschadensersatzrichtlinie dann mit der 9. GWB-Novelle 2017 in §§ 33 ff. GWB umgesetzt.

fen und Ersatz des Schadens verlangen könne, der ihm durch Verstöße gegen die Wettbewerbsregeln entstehe.[182] Dann schießt er allerdings erneut über das Ziel hinaus, indem er nicht nur (zu Recht) unterstreicht, die Vorschriften des deutschen Zivilrechts, insbesondere § 812 Abs. S. 1, 1. Alt. BGB, § 134 BGB und § 33 Abs. 3 GWB a. F., dienten der Verwirklichung dieser im Primärrecht verankerten Rechte, sondern aus der EuGH-Rechtsprechung weitergehend auch folgert, dass ihre Anwendung nicht durch Vorgaben sektorspezifischer Regulierung ausgeschlossen sei (Rn. 27 ff.) und keine regulierungsbehördliche Entscheidung voraussetze (Rn. 31 f.).

Der BGH meint, seine Auffassung entspreche der EuGH-Rechtsprechung, wonach den Gerichten die Anwendung des Art. 102 AEUV nicht abgesprochen werden dürfe, weil dies bedeuten würde, dass den Unionsbürgern Rechte genommen würden, die ihnen aufgrund des AEUV selbst zustünden (Rn. 36).[183] Auch ein weitergehendes Regulierungsziel könne nicht zur Einschränkung der Ansprüche der Schutzadressaten des Art. 102 AEUV führen, weil der Grundsatz richtlinienkonformen Auslegung nicht als Grundlage für eine Auslegung *contra legem* dienen dürfe (Rn. 38).[184] Eine Richtlinie könne keine Einschränkungen von Rechten Dritter begründen, „da dies darauf hinausliefe, der Europäischen Union die Befugnis zuzuerkennen, mit unmittelbarer Wirkung zulasten Einzelner Verpflichtungen anzuordnen". Dies aber dürfe die Union außerhalb des Primärrechts nur dort, wo ihre die Befugnis zum Erlass von Verordnungen zugewiesen sei (Rn. 38). Zudem sei auch ein effektiver Schutz der dem Einzelnen durch Art. 102 AEUV eingeräumten Rechte nicht gewährleistet, „wenn die Eisenbahnverkehrsunternehmen bei der Durchsetzung ihrer Ansprüche verfahrensrechtliche Voraussetzungen beachten müssten, die weder im Zeitpunkt der Anspruchsentstehung noch zum Zeitpunkt der gerichtlichen Geltendmachung gesetzlich bestimmt und damit für die Berechtigten erkennbar waren" (Rn. 39).

Dem Hinweis auf eine durch die zivilgerichtliche Rechtsdurchsetzung drohende Ungleichbehandlung gegenüber anderen Eisenbahnverkehrsunternehmen und auf eine Verletzung des Grundsatzes der einheitlichen

---

182 Unter Verweis auf EuGH, 13. 7. 2006, Rs. C-295/04, ECLI: EU: C: 2006: 461, Rn. 59 – *Manfredi*.

183 Unter Verweis auf EuGH, 30. 1. 1974, Rs. 127/73, ECLI:EU:C:1974:6, Rn. 15/17 – *BRT/SABAM* und EuGH, 10. 7. 1980, Rs. 37/79, ECLI:EU:C:1980:190, Rn. 13 – *Marty/Estée Lauder*; ebenso *Hauf/Baumgartner*, EuZW 2018, 1028, 1030 ff.; *dies.*, TranspR 2019, 69, 71; *Bremer/Scheffczyk*, NZKart 2018, 121, 123.

184 Unter Verweis auf EuGH, 14. 12. 2000, Rs. 344/98, ECLI:EU:C:2000:689, Rn. 47 – *Masterfoods*.

Wirkung der Regulierungsentscheidung, die der EuGH in *CTL Logistics* kritisiert hatte, komme, so der BGH, „im Rahmen der Anwendung des Art. 102 AEUV keine maßgebliche Bedeutung zu", weil Art. 102 AEUV subjektive Rechte begründe, die unabhängig von der Richtlinie 2001/14/EG entstünden und die man nicht „dem Kollektiv der Zugangsberechtigten" unterordnen könne, ohne in Widerspruch zu Art. 102 AEUV zu geraten (Rn. 40).

d) Regulierungsbehördliche Durchsetzung des Eisenbahnrechts vs. private Kartellrechtsdurchsetzung?

Die Argumentation des BGH geht in ihrer Essenz von einem absoluten Vorrang des Art. 102 AEUV gegenüber dem Regulierungsrecht aus und will sogar die evidente Vereitelung der Regulierungsziele hinnehmen, um die volle Wirksamkeit des Art. 102 AEUV durchzusetzen, wobei der Schwerpunkt der Argumentation des BGH nicht auf dem Schutz des Wettbewerbs als Institution, sondern auf dem effektiven Schutz der sich aus Art. 102 AEUV ableitenden subjektiven Rechte der durch einen Kartellrechtsverstoß Geschädigten liegt.

aa) Institutioneller Schutz des Wettbewerbs vs. Regulierungsrecht?

Die private Durchsetzung der Art. 101 und 102 AEUV leistet unbestreitbar einen wichtigen Beitrag für den Schutz des Wettbewerbs als Institution, welcher auch in der Entscheidung *Crehan/Courage* das zentrale Anliegen der Art. 101 und 102 AEUV bleibt. Die private Kartellrechtsdurchsetzung steht insoweit nicht allein, sondern flankiert vielmehr – wie auch die oben zitierten Erwägungsgründe zur Kartellschadensersatzrichtlinie 2014/104/EU deutlich machen – die behördliche Kartellrechtsdurchsetzung. Die BGH-Richter *Bornkamm* und *Tolkmitt* betonen in diesem Kontext sogar zu Recht, es sei

> „nicht zu leugnen, dass der vom **Beibringungsgrundsatz** geprägte Zivilprozess **dem Verwaltungsverfahren strukturell unterlegen** ist, in dem die KartB den Sachverhalt von Amts wegen mithilfe der ihr zu Gebote stehenden Ermittlungsbefugnisse umfassend aufklärt [...] Ein weiterer struktureller Nachteil des Zivilprozesses kommt hinzu: Der **Zivilprozess unterliegt der Parteidisposition.** Er ist darauf gerichtet, den Konflikt zwischen zwei Parteien zu lösen. [...] Andererseits ist die

zivilrechtliche Durchsetzung des KartR i.S.e. **flankierenden Maßnahme** unerlässlich, [...]". [185]

Dabei können schon innerhalb des kartellrechtlichen Durchsetzungsregimes Konflikte zwischen privater und behördlicher Rechtsdurchsetzung auftreten, die eine Interessenabwägung erforderlich machen. Dies gilt insbesondere dann, wenn eine zu starke Betonung des Schutzes subjektiver Rechte die behördliche Rechtsdurchsetzung beeinträchtigen und dadurch „unter dem Strich" den Schutz des Wettbewerbs als Institution beeinträchtigen würde. Einen solchen Fall beschreibt z. B. der Konflikt zwischen den Informationsinteressen der Kartellgeschädigten und dem öffentlichen Interesse am Funktionieren behördlicher Kronzeugenprogramme. Die BGH-Richter *Bornkamm* und *Tolkmitt* fassen die Zielsetzung der Kartellschadensersatzrichtlinie 2014/104/EU im Spannungsfeld von privater und behördlicher Rechtsdurchsetzung prägnant und trefflich zusammen:

> „Der Unionsgesetzgeber sieht darin im Anschluss an die Rspr. des EuGH eine zwingend notwendige Stärkung der Durchsetzung der Wettbewerbsregeln insgesamt und als zweite Säule neben der behördlichen Durchsetzung einen wesentlichen Beitrag zur Aufrechterhaltung wirksamen Wettbewerbs (Erwägungsgrund 11). Gleichzeitig zielte er darauf ab, mögliche limitierende Wechselwirkungen zwischen privater und öffentlicher Durchsetzung im Hinblick auf Kronzeugenprogramme und Vergleichsverfahren zugunsten des **relativen Vorrangs der öffentlichen Durchsetzung** zu begrenzen (Erwägungsgrund 26), was aus primärrechtlicher Perspektive nicht unbestritten ist".[186]

Wenn der EuGH in seinen grundlegenden Entscheidungen *Crehan/Courage* und *Manfredi* und in der nachfolgenden Rechtsprechung betont, die volle und insbesondere praktische Wirksamkeit der Wettbewerbsregeln wäre *beeinträchtigt*, wenn nicht jedermann Ersatz von Kartellschäden verlangen könnte,[187] so ist dies nicht im Sinne eines absoluten Verbots jedweder Beeinträchtigung der privaten Rechtsdurchsetzung („koste es, was es wolle") zu verstehen. Die Forderung „voller" Wirksamkeit ist kein Gebot

---

185 *Bornkamm/Tolkmitt*, in: Langen/Bunte, Kartellrecht, Band 1, 13. Aufl. 2018 Vor § 33 GWB, Rn. 1 ff. (Hervorhebung im Original).
186 *Bornkamm/Tolkmitt*, in: Langen/Bunte, Kartellrecht, Band 1, 13. Aufl. 2018 Vor § 33 GWB, Rn. 15 (Hervorhebung im Original).
187 Ständige Rechtsprechung seit EuGH, 20. 9. 2001, Rs. C-453/99, ECLI: EU: C: 2001:465, Rn 26 – *Crehan/Courage*.

einer Durchsetzung des Kartellrechts gegenüber anderen Unionszielen „zu 100%", sondern weist lediglich darauf hin, dass eine Beeinträchtigung der vollen und praktischen Wirksamkeit der Wettbewerbsregeln nicht ohne sachlich gerechtfertigten Grund erfolgen darf.

Die Möglichkeit zur Geltendmachung privater Kartellschadensersatzansprüche ist nach der EuGH-Rechtsprechung dementsprechend auch nicht vollkommen unverzichtbar für die praktische Wirksamkeit des Art. 102 AEUV. Sie „erhöht", wie der EuGH explizit weiter ausführt, lediglich die Durchsetzungskraft der Wettbewerbsregeln und kann wesentlich zur Aufrechterhaltung eines wirksamen Wettbewerbs in der Union „beitragen".[188] Dementsprechend hat der EuGH in *Crehan/Courage* auch lediglich betont, es dürfe durch das nationale Recht „nicht von vornherein ausgeschlossen" werden, dass eine Klage auf Schadensersatz erhoben werden könne.[189] Er hat einen solchen Ausschluss aus legitimen Erwägungen des mitgliedstaatlichen Rechts (wie der *„unclean hands"*-Einrede im Fall *Crehan/Courage*) aber explizit für zulässig erachtet, solange das nationale Recht und seine Durchsetzung dem Äquivalenzgrundsatz und dem Effektivitätsgrundsatz genügen.[190] Ist dies der Fall, so ist, wie der EuGH in *Manfredi* betont hat, auch der Schutz individueller Rechte vor einem anderen nationalen Gericht als dem üblicherweise für solche Ansprüche zuständigen mit dem Unionsrecht vereinbar.[191]

Ausweislich des Urteils *Trassenentgelte* ist der BGH der Auffassung, dass eine Abwägung zwischen dem Ziel der Ermöglichung privater Rechtsdurchsetzung und weitergehenden Regulierungszielen von EU-Richtlinien von vornherein ausgeschlossen sei, weil dadurch *erstens* in individuelle, aus Art. 102 AEUV abgeleitete Rechte eingegriffen werde und dies *zweitens* zu einer „richtlinienkonformen Auslegung contra legem" (d.h. im Widerspruch zu Art. 102 AEUV, so wie ihn der BGH versteht) führen würde und *drittens* darauf hinausliefe, „der Europäischen Union die Befugnis zuzuer-

---

188 Ständige Rechtsprechung seit EuGH, 20. 9. 2001, Rs. C-453/99, ECLI: EU: C: 2001:465, Rn. 27 – *Crehan/Courage*.

189 EuGH, 20. 9. 2001, Rs. C-453/99, ECLI:EU:C:2001:465, Rn. 28 – *Crehan/Courage*.

190 EuGH, 20. 9. 2001, Rs. C-453/99, ECLI: EU: C: 2001: 465, Rn. 29 ff. – *Crehan/Courage*.

191 EuGH, 13. 7. 2006, Rs. C-295/04, ECLI:EU:C:2006:461, Rn. 65 und 72 – *Manfredi*.

kennen, mit unmittelbarer Wirkung zu Lasten einzelner Verpflichtungen anzuordnen".[192]

Abgesehen davon, dass es Aufgabe des EuGH und nicht des BGH wäre, über die Primärrechtswidrigkeit einer Eisenbahnrichtlinie zu entscheiden, basiert diese Ansicht auf einem Missverständnis der Reichweite des Gebots „voller Wirksamkeit", welches der BGH im Gegensatz zum EuGH nicht als relatives, sondern als absolutes Gebot deutet. Die Ausführungen des BGH vermögen auch deshalb nicht zu überzeugen, weil es – wenn schon die Mitgliedstaaten nach der EuGH-Rechtsprechung die private Durchsetzung des Unionskartellrechts aus legitimen Gründen beschränken dürfen – dem Unionsgesetzgeber selbstverständlich erst recht zusteht, Regelungen zu treffen, durch welche die eine private Durchsetzung des Art. 102 AEUV unter Beachtung des Effektivitätsgrundsatzes zugunsten anderer, primärrechtlich legitimierter Ziele eingeschränkt wird. Dies zeigt übrigens auch die Schadensersatzrichtlinie 2014/1004/EU, welche – wie *Bornkamm* und *Tolkmitt* in dem oben wiedergegebenen Zitat zu Recht betonen – der privaten Rechtsdurchsetzung durch Schadensersatzklagen im Kontext der Privilegierung von Kronzeugen zugunsten des relativen Vorrangs der öffentlichen Rechtsdurchsetzung Grenzen setzt. Eine Abwägung unterschiedlicher Unionsziele und der zu ihrer Effektuierung dienenden Regelungen des Unionsrechts und des nationalen Rechts kann selbstverständlich nicht nur innerhalb des Kartellrechts, sondern auch und erst recht im Verhältnis zu anderen primärrechtlich anerkannten Regelungsmaterien und Unionszielen erfolgen, also auch im Verhältnis zu der in Art. 90, 91 AEUV adressierten Regulierung im Verkehrsbereich.

Die vom BGH im Urteil *Trassenentgelte* zum Beleg für seine Auffassung angeführten EuGH-Urteile betreffen dann auch eine ganz andere Frage. Aus ihnen geht hervor, dass eine EU-Richtlinie, die nicht oder falsch umgesetzt wurde, keine unmittelbaren Rechtswirkungen zwischen Privaten entfaltet.[193] Vorliegend ist weder eine falsche oder fehlende Umsetzung der Richtlinie 2001/14/EG (oder der Richtlinie 2012/34/EU) durch den deutschen Gesetzgeber ersichtlich, noch geht es überhaupt um die Frage der unmittelbaren Drittwirkung von Richtlinien im laufenden Zivilpro-

---

192 So BGH, 29. 10. 2019, Az. KZR 39/19, ECLI: DE: BGH: 2019: 291019UKZR39.
19.0, Rn. 38 – *Trassenentgelte.*
193 EuGH, 7. 8. 2018, Rs. C-122/17, ECLI: EU: C: 2018: 631, Rn. 40, 42 – *Smith*;
EuGH, 28. 2. 1986, Rs. 152/84, ECLI: EU: C: 1986: 84, Rn. 48 – *Marshall* sowie
EuGH, 20. 6. 2017, Rs. C-579/15, ECLI: EU: C: 2017: 503, Rn. 33 – *Poplawski* (zu
den Grenzen rahmenbeschlusskonformer Auslegung).

zess, sondern – wie im Verfahren *CTL Logistics* – um die vorgelagerte Frage, ob eine zivilgerichtliche Kontrolle regulierter Entgelte überhaupt zulässig ist, wenn dadurch die Funktionsfähigkeit des öffentlichen Eisenbahnregulierungsrechts infrage gestellt wird. Dabei geht es nicht um eine „richtlinienkonforme Auslegung contra legem", sondern um die Herstellung praktischer Konkordanz zwischen gleichwertigen Unionszielen, welche den berechtigten Regelungsanliegen des Kartellrechts in angemessenem Umfang Rechnung trägt, ohne die berechtigten Regelungsanliegen des Regulierungsrechts zu negieren.

bb) Schutz subjektiver Rechte vs. Regulierungsrecht?

Erst recht unzutreffend ist es, wenn in der Literatur behauptet wird, es bestehe im Anwendungsbereich des Art. 102 AEUV kein Umsetzungsspielraum der Mitgliedstaaten für eine Gewährleistung des Effektivitätsgrundsatzes und der Rechtsschutzgarantie durch andere Verfahren als durch ein *„private enforcement"*.[194] Im Gegenteil betont der EuGH sogar in ständiger Rechtsprechung zu genau dieser Frage ausdrücklich, dass die verfahrensmäßige Effektuierung der aus Art. 102 AEUV resultierenden subjektiven Rechte in Ermangelung einer unionsrechtlichen Regelung „Sache der Mitgliedstaaten" sei, die insoweit in den durch den Äquivalenzgrundsatz und den Effektivitätsgrundsatz gesetzten Grenzen über einen Gestaltungsspielraum verfügten.

Eine private Rechtsdurchsetzung vor den Zivilgerichten ist angesichts der oben beschriebenen strukturellen Defizite privater gegenüber der behördlichen Kartellrechtsdurchsetzung nicht nur für den institutionellen Schutz des Wettbewerbs weder der einzige noch der beste Weg. Entsprechendes kann auch für den Schutz individueller Rechte gelten. Dies hat der EuGH jüngst in seiner Entscheidung *Deutsche Lufthansa* zum Luftverkehrssektor unterstrichen. In dem der Entscheidung zugrunde liegenden Sachverhalt stellte sich das Problem, dass für die Überprüfung regulierungsbehördlicher Entscheidungen in Deutschland nur der Zivilrechtsweg, aber kein verwaltungsgerichtliches Verfahren eröffnet war. Der EuGH sah gerade durch die Beschränkung auf eine bloße Privatklagemöglichkeit den Grundsatz effektiven Rechtsschutzes verletzt.[195]

---

194 *Hauf/Baumgartner*, EuZW 2018, 1028, 1035.
195 EuGH, 21. 11. 2019, Rs. C-379/18, ECLI:EU:C:2019:1000, Rn. 61 ff. – *Deutsche Lufthansa;*, s. oben S. 21.

Umgekehrt hält der deutsche Gesetzgeber in Bezug auf nach dem ER-egG genehmigte Entgelte im Eisenbahnsektor den Verwaltungsrechtsweg für ausreichend, um einen effektiven Rechtsschutz zu gewährleisten. Die Bundesregierung hat im Rahmen der Umsetzung der Richtlinie 2012/34/EU in das ERegG den Einwand des Bundesrates, eine zivilgerichtliche Billigkeitskontrolle müsse möglich bleiben, zurückgewiesen und dazu explizit betont:

> „Bei genehmigten Entgelten ist nur der Weg zu den Verwaltungsgerichten eröffnet. Damit ist effektiver Rechtsschutz gewährleistet".[196]

Dementsprechend wurde dadurch, dass §§ 33 Abs. 2 und 45 Abs. 2 ERegG eine „Billigkeit" genehmigter Entgelte i.S.d. § 315 BGB explizit gesetzlich normieren, eine zivilgerichtliche Kontrolle solcher Entgelte nach § 315 BGB ausgeschlossen. Da es, wie oben ausgeführt, einen Wertungswiderspruch bedeuten würde, ein „billiges" Entgelt als „missbräuchlich" i.S.d. §§ 19, 20 GWB anzusehen, obwohl der Missbrauchsmaßstab strenger ist als der Billigkeitsmaßstab, führt dies mit Blick auf die Einheit der Rechtsordnung und das Ziel, Wertungswidersprüche zu vermeiden, dazu, dass effektiv auch eine Kontrolle am Maßstab des deutschen Kartellrechts ausgeschlossen ist.

Die Genese des ERegG macht zugleich deutlich, dass auch der deutsche Gesetzgeber in dieser Frage offensichtlich nicht die Position des BGH teilt, ein kartellzivilgerichtlicher Rechtsschutz sei unverzichtbar, um der Rechtsschutzgarantie des Art. 47 GRCh (und des Art. 19 Abs. 4 GG) Genüge zu tun. Der nationale Gesetzgeber kann zwar nicht festlegen, wie Art. 102 AEUV auszulegen ist, doch ist es – wie der EuGH in *Crehan/Courage* und ständiger Rechtsprechung gerade in Bezug auf das Kartellschadensersatzrecht betont hat – mangels einer einschlägigen Unionsregelung

> „Sache des innerstaatlichen Rechts der einzelnen Mitgliedstaaten, die zuständigen Gerichte zu bestimmen und die Verfahrensmodalitäten für Klagen zu regeln, die den Schutz der dem Bürger aus der unmittelbaren Wirkung des Gemeinschaftsrechts erwachsenden Rechte gewährleisten sollen, sofern diese Modalitäten nicht weniger günstig ausgestaltet sind als die entsprechender innerstaatlicher Klagen (Äquivalenzgrundsatz) und die Ausübung der durch die Gemeinschaftsrechts-

---

196 Gegenäußerung der BReg, BT-Drucks. 18/8334, S. 315.

ordnung verliehenen Rechte nicht praktisch unmöglich machen oder übermäßig erschweren (Effektivitätsgrundsatz)".[197]

Vor diesem Hintergrund geht es letztlich um die Frage, ob eine Beschränkung der zivilgerichtlichen Entgeltkontrolle nach dem Muster der *CTL Logistics*-Entscheidung den Äquivalenzgrundsatz und/oder den Effektivitätsgrundsatz verletzt. Da nicht ersichtlich ist, dass die Durchsetzung des Unionskartellrechts in irgendeiner Weise weniger günstig ausgestaltet ist als die Durchsetzung des deutschen Kartellrechts, scheidet ein Verstoß gegen den Äquivalenzgrundsatz offensichtlich aus.

Der in Art. 197 AEUV primärrechtlich verankerte Effektivitätsgrundsatz wäre nach der vom EuGH in ständiger Rechtsprechung wiederholten Definition nur dann verletzt, wenn die nationalen Zuständigkeits- und Verfahrensregeln die Ausübung der durch die Unionsrechtsordnung verliehenen Rechte „praktisch unmöglich machen oder übermäßig erschweren".[198] Man spricht deshalb auch vom „Vereitelungsgrundsatz".[199] Dieser Grundsatz schließt es, wie oben gezeigt wurde, nicht aus, dass die Geltendmachung eines Rechts unter bestimmte Bedingungen gestellt wird. Er ist erst dann verletzt, „wenn sich eine nationale Lösung im Vergleich mit den anderen mitgliedstaatlichen Rechtsordnungen als „extrem" oder sonstwie besonders problematisch erweist, oder wenn das nationale Recht zu besonderen Wettbewerbsverzerrungen führt".[200]

Der BGH ist insoweit der Auffassung, ein effektiver gerichtlicher Schutz der durch Art. 102 AEUV eingeräumten individuellen Rechte wäre nicht gewährleistet, „wenn die Eisenbahnverkehrsunternehmen bei der Durchsetzung ihrer Ansprüche verfahrensrechtliche Voraussetzungen beachten müssten, die weder im Zeitpunkt der Anspruchsentstehung noch zum Zeitpunkt der gerichtlichen Geltendmachung gesetzlich bestimmt und damit für die Berechtigten erkennbar waren".[201] Damit dürfte der BGH meinen, dass es seiner Ansicht nach erforderlich gewesen wäre, Beschränkungen der Durchsetzung individueller zivilrechtlicher Ansprüche ausdrück-

---

197 EuGH, 20. 9. 2001, Rs. C-453/99, ECLI:EU:C:2001:465, Rn. 29 – *Crehan/Courage.*

198 EuGH, 20. 9. 2001, Rs. C-453/99, ECLI:EU:C:2001:465, Rn. 29 – *Crehan/Courage.*

199 Grabitz/Hilf/Nettesheim-*Classen*, Das Recht der Europäischen Union, 68. EL Oktober 2019, Art. 197 AEUV Rn. 23.

200 Grabitz/Hilf/Nettesheim-*Classen*, Das Recht der Europäischen Union, 68. EL Oktober 2019, Art. 197 AEUV Rn. 26.

201 BGH, 29. 10. 2019, Az. KZR 39/19, ECLI:DE:BGH:2019:291019UKZR39.19.0, Rn. 39 – *Trassenentgelte.*

lich im Regulierungsrecht zu normieren. Das überzeugt aus einer Vielzahl von Gründen nicht.

Erstens hat sich der EuGH in *CTL Logistics* dadurch, dass weder der Unionsgesetzgeber in Richtlinie 2001/14/EG noch der deutsche Gesetzgeber bei deren Umsetzung in das AEG a.F. eine zivilrechtliche Billigkeitskontrolle ausdrücklich ausgeschlossen hatte, daran gehindert gesehen, einen solchen Ausschluss gleichwohl im Wege der Auslegung aus der Richtlinie abzuleiten.

Zweitens wäre es auch vollkommen unüblich, gesetzlich zu normieren, welche Rechtsmittel *nicht* zur Verfügung stehen. Üblich ist es vielmehr, zu regeln, welche Rechtsmittel zur Verfügung stehen, und dies hat der deutsche Gesetzgeber getan. Die Eisenbahnverkehrsunternehmen hatten bzw. haben die Möglichkeit, ein Tätigwerden der Regulierungsbehörde nach § 14b oder § 14f AEG a.F. (bzw. heute nach § 66 Abs. 1 ERegG) zu beantragen und, falls die BNetzA ein Einschreiten ablehnt,[202] notfalls mittels einer verwaltungsgerichtlichen Verpflichtungsklage dagegen vorzugehen, also zunächst den Verwaltungsrechtsweg zu beschreiten. Wenn in der Literatur behauptet wird, ohne eine eigenständige zivilkartellgerichtliche Kontrolle drohe den Eisenbahnverkehrsunternehmen „völlige Rechtsschutzlosigkeit",[203] ist das vor diesem Hintergrund schlichtweg unzutreffend.

Drittens hat der EuGH in *CTL Logistics* ausdrücklich klargestellt, dass auch eine Geltendmachung zivilrechtlicher Ansprüche nicht „von vornherein ausgeschlossen" ist, sondern lediglich eine vorausgehende bestandskräftige Entscheidung der zuständigen Regulierungsbehörde verlangt. Den Eisenbahnverkehrsunternehmen stand und steht frei, sich nach einem bei der BNetzA bzw. vor den Verwaltungsgerichten erfolgreichen Abhilfeersuchen an die Zivilgerichte zu wenden, um eine Kompensation für überhöhte Entgeltzahlungen geltend zu machen. Auf diese Weise wird dann auch das hinsichtlich des Schutzes subjektiver Rechte von Art. 102 AEUV angestrebte Ziel erreicht. Der EuGH hat in *CTL Logistics* insoweit lediglich unterstrichen, dass ein vom BGH rechtsirrtümlich für möglich gehaltener zweiter, unkoordinierter Rechtsweg nicht mit dem auf Art. 90, 91 AEUV basierenden Eisenbahnregulierungsrecht vereinbar ist. Der „Umweg" über das nach *CTL Logistics* zur Wahrung der praktischen Wirksamkeit des Regulierungsrechts zwingend erforderliche und daher unionsrechtlich gebotene „Vorverfahren" erschwert zwar die Geltendmachung von zivilrechtli-

---

202 Vgl. etwa BNetzA, Beschluss vom 11. 10. 2019, Az. BK-10-18-0038_E.
203 So *Hauf/Baumgartner*, EuZW 2020, 292, 293.

chen Rückzahlungs- oder Schadensersatzansprüchen, aber er vereitelt sie nicht.

Falls die Eisenbahnverkehrsunternehmen es versäumt haben, die ihnen zur Verfügung stehenden Rechtsmittel rechtzeitig geltend zu machen, haben sie sich dies schließlich *viertens* selbst zuzuschreiben. Dass die Versäumung formeller Klageerhebungsfristen der Zulässigkeit eines Rechtsmittels oder eine materielle Verjährung der Durchsetzbarkeit des Anspruchs entgegenstehen, steht nicht in Konflikt mit dem Effektivitätsgrundsatz, weil solche Begrenzungen auch durch Unionsrecht und die Rechtsordnungen aller Mitgliedstaaten im Grundsatz anerkannt sind und z. B. auch für die Erhebung von Klagen vor dem EuGH gelten.[204]

Gegen die Annahme einer „übermäßigen" Erschwerung (und dadurch Verletzung) des Effektivitätsgrundsatzes spricht *sechstens* auch, dass durch das vom EuGH in *CTL Logistics* beschriebene gestufte Verfahren sowohl eine effektive Durchsetzung von Erstattungs- und Entschädigungsansprüchen als auch die das Funktionieren des Eisenbahnregulierungsrechts sichergestellt und damit die praktische Wirksamkeit des Unionsrechts insgesamt (d.h. von Kartellrecht und Regulierungsrecht) „unter dem Strich" am besten gefördert wird.

Die subjektiven Rechte einzelner Verkehrsunternehmen werden auf diese Weise *siebtens* auch nicht, wie der BGH meint, „dem Kollektiv der Zugangsberechtigten" (deren regulierungsrechtlicher Anspruch auf Gleichbehandlung mittelbar durch einen Ausschluss einer zivilgerichtlichen Kontrolle gewahrt bleibt) untergeordnet und dadurch verletzt.[205] Das regulierungsrechtliche Diskriminierungsverbot dient nicht in erster Linie dem Interessenausgleich zwischen Privatrechtssubjekten, welchen der BGH aus einer rein privatrechtlichen Perspektive in den Mittelpunkt rückt, sondern auch und vor allem der Sicherung der Funktionsfähigkeit des öffentlich-rechtlichen Regulierungsregimes und der dadurch ermöglichten Öffnung des Eisenbahnwesens für den Wettbewerb. Durch die Begrenzung der zivilgerichtlichen Durchsetzung von Erstattungs- und Schadensersatzansprüchen auf nachfolgende Verfahren wird praktische Konkordanz zwischen dem individuellen Interesse an einer Durchsetzung privatrechtlicher An-

---

204 Zu den Klagefristen vgl. etwa Art. 50 der Verfahrensordnung des EuGH; zur Verjährung von Kartellschadensersatzansprüchen s. z. B. EuGH, 13. 7. 2006, Rs. C-295/04, ECLI:EU:C:2006:461, Rn. 77 ff. – *Manfredi* und Art. 10 der Kartellschadensersatzrichtlinie 2014/104/EU.

205 BGH, 29. 10. 2019, Az. KZR 39/19, ECLI:DE:BGH:2019:291019UKZR39.19.0, Rn. 40 – *Trassenentgelte*.

sprüche vor den Zivilgerichten und der im öffentlichen Interesse liegenden kohärenten und wirksamen Regulierung des Eisenbahnsektors durch die BNetzA erreicht. Der vom BGH favorisierte Ansatz würde demgegenüber, wie dieser selbst einräumt, zu einer Ungleichbehandlung der Eisenbahnverkehrsunternehmen führen und dadurch sowie durch Aushebelung der im Eisenbahnregulierungsrecht vorgesehenen Zuständigkeitsverteilung dessen Funktionsfähigkeit nachhaltig beeinträchtigen, wenn nicht sogar aufheben.

4. Ergebnis

Das durch die *CTL Logistics*-Entscheidung vorgesehene System des Rechtsschutzes von Eisenbahnverkehrsunternehmen weicht vom „innerkartellrechtlichen" Rechtsschutzsystem insoweit ab, als eine zivilgerichtliche Kompensation überhöhter Entgelte eine bestandskräftige Entscheidung der BNetzA (bzw. eine rechtskräftige verwaltungsgerichtliche Entscheidung) voraussetzt, mit welcher die Rechtswidrigkeit der Entgelte festgestellt worden ist.

Dieses Verfahren ist für die Eisenbahnverkehrsunternehmen aufwendiger als die Möglichkeit, Erstattungs- oder Schadensersatzansprüche unmittelbar und ohne Rücksicht auf die Funktionsfähigkeit des Eisenbahnregulierungsrechts vor jedem Zivilgericht geltend machen zu können. Doch wird die Geltendmachung der zivilrechtlichen Ansprüche dadurch weder unter Verletzung des Effektivitätsgrundsatzes vereitelt, noch die volle und praktische Wirksamkeit des Art. 102 AEUV in unionsrechtswidriger Weise beeinträchtigt.

Die richtlinienkonforme Auslegung der Vorschriften des deutschen Privat- und Verfahrensrechts nach Maßgabe der Entscheidung *CTL Logistics* schränkt auch weder den durch Art. 102 AEUV angestrebten Schutz des Wettbewerbs als Institution noch den Schutz der subjektiven Rechte der Adressaten überhöhter Entgelte in einer Weise ein, die mit dem Unionsrecht oder den Rechtsschutzgarantien des Art. 47 GRCh bzw. Art. 19 Abs. 4 GG unvereinbar wäre.

Der vom BGH in der Entscheidung *Trassenentgelte* konstruierte Konflikt zwischen den Eisenbahnregulierungsrichtlinien und Art. 102 AEUV existiert bei genauerer Betrachtung nicht in der vom BGH angenommenen Schärfe und eine richtlinienkonforme Auslegung der Normen des deutschen Rechts würde daher auch nicht „*contra legem*" erfolgen, wie der BGH zu Unrecht annimmt. Im Gegenteil wird gerade durch Respektierung der

CTL Logistics-Grundsätze die „für das ordnungsgemäße Funktionieren der Union entscheidende effektive Durchführung des Unionsrechts durch die Mitgliedstaaten" (Art. 197 AEUV) ermöglicht und dem Effektivitätsgrundsatz Genüge getan, ohne dass ein Konflikt mit der EuGH-Rechtsprechung zum Kartellschadensersatz oder mit der Kartellschadensersatzrichtlinie auftritt. Diese nämlich sind offen für einen vermittelnden Ansatz, der eine Einschränkung der privaten Rechtsdurchsetzung zulässt, um berechtigen anderen Regelungsanliegen, einschließlich der Funktionsfähigkeit der behördlichen Durchsetzung des Kartellrechts oder des Regulierungsrechts, angemessen Rechnung zu tragen.

Im Ergebnis steht mithin auch Art. 102 AEUV einer richtlinienkonformen Auslegung des deutschen Rechts nach Maßgabe der *CTL Logistics*-Grundsätze nicht entgegen. Eine diese Grundsätze missachtende, von den Entscheidungen der BNetzA und vom Regulierungsrecht losgelöste Anwendung des Art. 102 AEUV durch deutsche Zivilgerichte würde dagegen im Widerspruch zu den Vorgaben des Unionsrechts stehen und das Loyalitätsgebot des Art. 4 Abs. 3 EUV verletzen, dass es allen staatlichen Stellen (auch den Zivilgerichten) gebietet, die Einheit der Unionsrechtsordnung zu wahren und, wo nötig, in verhältnismäßiger Weise praktische Konkordanz zwischen verschiedenen Unionsregelungen und Unionszielen herzustellen, um auf diese Weise die volle und praktische Wirksamkeit nicht nur des Kartellrechts, sondern des AEUV und des Unionsrechts insgesamt sicherzustellen.

E. Gesamtergebnis

1. Können vor dem dargestellten Hintergrund regulierungsbehördlich nicht rechtskräftig widersprochene Infrastrukturnutzungsentgelte im Einzelfall vor den Zivilgerichten am Maßstab des deutschen und/oder europäischen Kartellrechts geprüft werden?

Die im Urteil *CTL Logistics* entwickelten Grundsätze zum Verhältnis zwischen regulierungsbehördlicher Kontrolle von Eisenbahnentgelten und zivilgerichtlicher Einzelfallkontrolle gelten für *jede* zivilgerichtliche Kontrolle unabhängig von den dieser Kontrolle zugrunde liegenden materiellen Anspruchsgrundlagen. Auch eine nicht mit dem Regulierungsrecht koordinierte zivilkartellgerichtliche Kontrolle ist danach im Anwendungsbereich der Regulierungsrichtlinien unionsrechtswidrig. Klagen auf Erstattung von Infrastrukturentgelten oder auf Schadensersatz wegen überhöhter Entgelte setzen danach eine bestandskräftige Entscheidung der BNetzA (bzw. eine rechtskräftige Entscheidung der Verwaltungsgerichtsbarkeit) voraus, mit welcher die Rechtswidrigkeit der betreffenden Entgelte festgestellt wurde.

Eine zivilgerichtliche Kontrolle am Maßstab des deutschen Kartellrechts scheidet schon deshalb aus, weil sie – ebenso wie eine Kontrolle am Maßstab des BGB – offensichtlich den Richtlinienvorgaben widerspricht. Aber auch eine eigenständige zivilgerichtliche Kontrolle von der Regulierung unterliegenden Eisenbahnentgelten am Maßstab des Art. 102 AEUV kommt nicht in Betracht. Eine solche ist weder zur Effektuierung des Art. 102 AEUV zwingend erforderlich, noch beeinträchtigt sie in unzulässiger Weise die Rechtsschutzinteressen der Entgeltadressaten, weil diese *einerseits* zunächst den Verwaltungsrechtsweg beschreiten können und *andererseits* bei einer zu ihren Gunsten ergehenden Entscheidung die Möglichkeit haben, im Wege eines zivilgerichtlichen Rückerstattungsprozesses eine Erstattung zu fordern. Dadurch wird die Geltendmachung von Ersatzansprüchen zwar im Vergleich zu einer unmittelbaren, eigenständigen Privatklage erschwert, aber nicht unter Verletzung des Effektivitätsgrundsatzes vereitelt. Eine Anwendung der *CTL Logistics*-Grundsätze auf die Kartellzivilgerichtsbarkeit steht daher auch nicht im Widerspruch zur EuGH-Rechtsprechung zum Kartellschadensersatz seit *Crehan/Courage* und zur Kartellschadensersatzrichtlinie.

2. In welchem Verhältnis steht die Entscheidung des EuGH vom 9. 11. 2017 in Sachen *CTL Logistics* zur Entscheidung des EuGH vom 14. 10. 2010 in der Rs. C-280/08P in Sachen *Deutsche Telekom* (dort insb. Tz. 80)? Wie steht Art. 102 AEUV zu Art. 90 AEUV in Bezug auf Richtlinie 2014/104/EU und Richtlinie 2001/14/EG bzw. 2012/34/EU?

Kartellrecht und Eisenbahnregulierungsrecht sind primärrechtlich in Art. 101 und 102 AEUV bzw. Art. 90 und 91 AEUV verankert. Die Ziele dieser primärrechtlichen Normen müssen ebenso wie diejenigen der darauf basierenden Richtlinien in praktische Konkordanz gebracht werden, um die Einheit der Unionsrechtsordnung zu wahren und eine optimale Verwirklichung der Ziele des AEUV insgesamt zu gewährleisten. Auch die Entscheidungen *Deutsche Telekom* und *CTL Logistics* lassen sich auf dieser Basis in Einklang bringen.

Die Entscheidung *Deutsche Telekom* betrifft das Verhältnis zwischen Regulierungsverfügungen nationaler Behörden und der Anwendung des Unionskartellrechts durch die EU-Kommission. Der EuGH hat darin im Kern festgestellt, dass eine (fehlerhafte) Entgeltgenehmigung durch eine nationale Behörde *die EU-Kommission* nicht daran hindert, das Unionskartellrecht gegen das der Regulierung unterliegende Unternehmen durchzusetzen, sofern die Regulierungsentscheidung diesem Unternehmen einen hinreichenden Entscheidungsspielraum lässt. Dies gilt auch für den Anwendungsbereich des Eisenbahnregulierungsrechts.

Die Entscheidung *CTL Logistics* betrifft demgegenüber die Frage, ob der Regulierung durch die BNetzA unterliegende Entgelte zusätzlich einer nicht damit koordinierten, eigenständigen zivilgerichtlichen Kontrolle unterliegen. Dies hat der EuGH verneint, weil dadurch die Funktionsfähigkeit des Eisenbahnregulierungsrechts beeinträchtigt würde. Dies gilt auch für eine zivilgerichtliche Kontrolle am Maßstab des Kartellrechts. Der Wunsch nach einer Förderung der Kartellrechtsdurchsetzung durch Privatklagen muss in diesem Fall ein stückweit hinter dem Ziel der Erhaltung der Funktionsfähigkeit des Eisenbahnregulierungsrechts zurückstehen. Dem Schutz der subjektiven Rechte der Eisenbahnverkehrsunternehmen ist in diesem Fall durch eine auf eine bestandskräftige Behördenentscheidung folgende und darauf aufbauende Privatklagemöglichkeit hinreichend Genüge getan.

3. Spielt es für die Anwendbarkeit des europäischen Kartellrechts auf die Überprüfung regulierter Infrastrukturnutzungsentgelte eine Rolle, ob das Kartellrecht in Verfahren nationaler Wettbewerbsbehörden bzw. der Europäischen Kommission oder in nationalen Zivilprozessen angewendet wird? Ergibt sich ein weiterer Unterschied daraus, ob diese Zivilprozesse auf kartellrechtlichen Schadenersatz (nach §§ 33 ff. GWB in Umsetzung der Richtlinie 2014/104/EU) oder z. B. auf Rückzahlung gerichtet sind?

Eine Kontrolle am Maßstab des Art. 102 AEUV durch die EU-Kommission ist auch im regulierten Bereich unabhängig davon möglich, ob bzw. wie die BNetzA entschieden hat. Die EU-Kommission wird dabei nicht nur Art. 102 AEUV, sondern auch Eisenbahnrichtlinien gebührend Rechnung tragen.

Eine Kontrolle von regulierten Entgelten durch das BKartA am Maßstab des Art. 102 AEUV würde der vom EuGH in der Entscheidung *CTL Logistics* postulierten alleinigen Kontrollkompetenz der BNetzA widersprechen, auch wenn er sowohl in institutioneller als auch materieller Hinsicht deutlich weniger Probleme aufwirft als eine Kontrolle durch beliebige Zivilgerichte. Ob bzw. in welchem Umfang das BKartA im Schnittfeld zum regulierten Bereich neben der BNetzA tätig werden darf, erscheint insoweit offen. Der praktisch sinnvollste Weg wäre eine Behördenkooperation, bei welcher es letztlich der BNetzA überlassen bleibt, kartellrechtlichen Bedenken des BKartA durch eine Korrektur ihrer Entgeltentscheidung zu berücksichtigen.

Eine eigenständige zivilgerichtliche Einzelfallkontrolle regulierter Eisenbahnentgelte scheidet demgegenüber nach Maßgabe der *CTL Logistics*-Entscheidung eindeutig aus. Dies gilt auch für die zivilgerichtliche Durchsetzung des Art. 102 AEUV. Es macht dabei keinen Unterschied, ob eine Privatklage auf Kartellschadensersatz nach §§ 33 ff. GWB oder Rückzahlung (etwa aus § 812 BGB) gerichtet ist, soweit die Klage letztlich darauf gerichtet ist, in Anwendung kartellrechtlicher Maßstäbe Entgelte zu korrigieren, deren Kontrolle nach den Eisenbahnrichtlinien und den sie umsetzenden Regelungen des deutschen Regulierungsrechts allein der BNetzA überantwortet ist.

Anhang: Eisenbahnrechtliche Gesetzestexte

A. Außer Kraft getretene Regelungen

I. Richtlinie 2001/14/EG

Artikel 4 Festsetzung, Berechnung und Erhebung von Entgelten

(1) Die Mitgliedstaaten schaffen eine Entgeltrahmenregelung, wobei die Unabhängigkeit der Geschäftsführung gemäß Artikel 4 der Richtlinie 91/440/EWG zu wahren ist.

Vorbehaltlich der genannten Bedingung der Unabhängigkeit der Geschäftsführung legen die Mitgliedstaaten auch einzelne Entgeltregeln fest oder delegieren diese Befugnisse an den Betreiber der Infrastruktur. Die Berechnung des Wegeentgeltes und die Erhebung dieses Entgelts nimmt der Betreiber der Infrastruktur vor.

(2) Ist der Betreiber der Infrastruktur rechtlich, organisatorisch oder in seinen Entscheidungen nicht von Eisenbahnunternehmen unabhängig, so werden die in diesem Kapitel dargelegten Aufgaben - außer der Erhebung von Entgelten - von einer entgelterhebenden Stelle wahrgenommen, die rechtlich, organisatorisch und in ihren Entscheidungen von Eisenbahnunternehmen unabhängig ist.

(3) Die Betreiber der Infrastruktur arbeiten im Interesse einer effizienten Durchführung von Eisenbahnverkehrsdiensten, die mehrere Schienennetze berühren, zusammen. Sie müssen insbesondere bestrebt sein, die bestmögliche Wettbewerbsfähigkeit des grenzüberschreitenden Schienengüterverkehrs zu gewährleisten und die effiziente Nutzung des Transeuropäischen Schienengüternetzes sicherzustellen. Sie können die dafür erforderlichen geeigneten gemeinsamen Einrichtungen schaffen. Für die Zusammenarbeit und die gemeinsamen Einrichtungen gelten die Bestimmungen dieser Richtlinie.

(4) Außer im Fall besonderer Maßnahmen gemäß Artikel 8 Absatz 2 tragen die Betreiber der Infrastruktur dafür Sorge, dass die Entgeltregelung in ihrem gesamten Netz auf denselben Grundsätzen beruht.

(5) Die Betreiber der Infrastruktur tragen dafür Sorge, dass die Anwendung der Entgeltregelung zu gleichwertigen und nichtdiskriminierenden Entgelten für unterschiedliche Eisenbahnunternehmen führen, die Dienste gleichwertiger Art in ähnlichen Teilen des Markts erbringen und dass

die tatsächlich erhobenen Entgelte den in den Schienennetz-Nutzungsbedingungen vorgesehenen Regeln entsprechen.

(6) Betreiber der Infrastruktur und entgelterhebende Stellen wahren das Geschäftsgeheimnis hinsichtlich der ihnen von Antragstellern gemachten Angaben.

Artikel 30 Regulierungsstelle

(1) Unbeschadet des Artikels 21 Absatz 6 richten die Mitgliedstaaten eine Regulierungsstelle ein. Diese Stelle, bei der es sich um das für Verkehrsfragen zuständige Ministerium oder eine andere Behörde handeln kann, ist organisatorisch, bei ihren Finanzierungsbeschlüssen, rechtlich und in ihrer Entscheidungsfindung von Betreibern der Infrastruktur, entgelterhebenden Stellen, Zuweisungsstellen und Antragstellern unabhängig. Für die Tätigkeit der Regulierungsstelle gelten die Grundsätze dieses Artikels; Rechtsbehelfs- und Regulierungsfunktionen können gesonderten Stellen übertragen werden.

(2) Ist ein Antragsteller der Auffassung, ungerecht behandelt, diskriminiert oder auf andere Weise in seinen Rechten verletzt worden zu sein, so kann er die Regulierungsstelle befassen, und zwar insbesondere mit Entscheidungen des Betreibers der Infrastruktur oder gegebenenfalls des Eisenbahnunternehmens betreffend

a) die Schienennetz-Nutzungsbedingungen,

b) die darin enthaltenen Kriterien,

c) das Zuweisungsverfahren und dessen Ergebnis,

d) die Entgeltregelung,

e) die Höhe oder Struktur der Wegeentgelte, die er zu zahlen hat oder hätte,

f) die Sicherheitsbescheinigung sowie die Durchsetzung und Überwachung der Sicherheitsnormen und -regeln.

(3) Die Regulierungsstelle gewährleistet, dass die vom Betreiber der Infrastruktur festgesetzten Entgelte dem Kapitel II entsprechen und nichtdiskriminierend sind. Verhandlungen zwischen Antragstellern und einem Betreiber der Infrastruktur über die Höhe von Wegeentgelten sind nur zulässig, sofern sie unter Aufsicht der Regulierungsstelle erfolgen. Die Regulierungsstelle hat einzugreifen, wenn bei den Verhandlungen ein Verstoß gegen die Bestimmungen dieser Richtlinie droht.

(4) Die Regulierungsstelle ist berechtigt, sachdienliche Auskünfte von dem Betreiber der Infrastruktur, Antragstellern und betroffenen Dritten in dem betreffenden Mitgliedstaat einzuholen, die unverzüglich zu erteilen sind.

(5) Die Regulierungsstelle hat über Beschwerden zu entscheiden und binnen zwei Monaten ab Erhalt aller Auskünfte Abhilfemaßnahmen zu treffen.

Ungeachtet des Absatzes 6 sind Entscheidungen der Regulierungsstelle für alle davon Betroffenen verbindlich.

Wird die Regulierungsstelle mit einer Beschwerde wegen der Verweigerung der Zuweisung von Fahrwegkapazität oder wegen der Bedingungen eines Angebots an Fahrwegkapazität befasst, entscheidet die Regulierungsstelle entweder, dass keine Änderung der Entscheidung des Betreibers der Infrastruktur erforderlich ist, oder schreibt eine Änderung dieser Entscheidung gemäß den Vorgaben der Regulierungsstelle vor.

(6) Die Mitgliedstaaten treffen die erforderlichen Maßnahmen, um die gerichtliche Nachprüfbarkeit von Entscheidungen der Regulierungsstelle zu gewährleisten.

II. Allgemeines Eisenbahngesetz a.F. (AEG)

§ 14b Aufgaben der Regulierungsbehörde

(1) Der Regulierungsbehörde obliegt die Aufgabe, die Einhaltung der Vorschriften des Eisenbahnrechts über den Zugang zur Eisenbahninfrastruktur zu überwachen, insbesondere hinsichtlich

1. der Erstellung des Netzfahrplans, dies gilt insbesondere für Entscheidungen über die Zuweisung von Zugtrassen für den Netzfahrplan einschließlich der Pflichtleistungen,

2. der sonstigen Entscheidungen über die Zuweisung von Zugtrassen einschließlich der Pflichtleistungen,

3. des Zugangs zu Serviceeinrichtungen einschließlich der damit verbundenen Leistungen,

4. der Benutzungsbedingungen, der Entgeltgrundsätze und der Entgelthöhen.

5. der Zugangsberechtigung im grenzüberschreitenden Personenverkehr

(2) Die Aufgaben und Zuständigkeiten der Kartellbehörden nach dem Gesetz gegen Wettbewerbsbeschränkungen bleiben unberührt. Die Regulierungsbehörde und die Eisenbahnaufsichtsbehörden sowie die Kartellbehörden und die nach dem Telekommunikationsgesetz und dem Energiewirtschaftsgesetz zuständigen Regulierungsbehörden teilen einander Informationen mit, die für die Erfüllung der jeweiligen Aufgaben von Bedeutung sein können. Insbesondere sollen sie sich gegenseitig über beabsichtigte Entscheidungen informieren, mit denen ein missbräuchliches oder

diskriminierendes Verhalten von Eisenbahninfrastrukturunternehmen untersagt werden soll. Sie sollen einander Gelegenheit zur Stellungnahme geben, bevor das Verfahren von der zuständigen Behörde abgeschlossen wird.

(3) Die Regulierungsbehörde und das Eisenbahn-Bundesamt sind verpflichtet, anderen Regulierungsstellen der Mitgliedstaaten der Europäischen Union Informationen über ihre Arbeit, ihre Entscheidungsgrundsätze und ihre Entscheidungspraxis zu übermitteln mit dem Ziel, zur Koordinierung der Entscheidungsgrundsätze in der gesamten Union beizutragen.

(4) Die Regulierungsbehörde erstellt für jede Fahrplanperiode einen Bericht über ihre Tätigkeit sowie über die Lage und Entwicklung auf ihrem Aufgabengebiet für die Bundesregierung. Die Bundesregierung leitet den Bericht der Regulierungsbehörde dem Deutschen Bundestag unverzüglich zu; sie kann dem Bericht eine Stellungnahme beifügen.

Die Mindesthöhe der Versicherungssumme beträgt insgesamt 20 Millionen Euro je Schadensereignis und muss für jede Versicherungsperiode mindestens zweimal zur Verfügung stehen.

§ 14f Nachträgliche Prüfung durch die Regulierungsbehörde

(1) Die Regulierungsbehörde kann von Amts wegen

1. Schienennetz-Benutzungsbedingungen und die Nutzungsbedingungen für Serviceeinrichtungen,

2. Regelungen über die Höhe oder Struktur der Wegeentgelte und sonstiger Entgelte

eines Eisenbahninfrastrukturunternehmens überprüfen. Die Regulierungsbehörde kann mit Wirkung für die Zukunft

1. das Eisenbahninfrastrukturunternehmen zur Änderung der Bedingungen nach Satz 1 Nr. 1 oder der Entgeltregelungen nach Satz 1 Nr. 2 nach ihren Maßgaben verpflichten oder

2. Bedingungen nach Satz 1 Nr. 1 oder Entgeltregelungen nach Satz 1 Nr. 2 für ungültig erklären,

soweit diese nicht den Vorschriften des Eisenbahnrechts über den Zugang zur Eisenbahninfrastruktur entsprechen.

(2) Kommt eine Vereinbarung über den Zugang nach § 14 Abs. 6 oder über einen Rahmenvertrag nach § 14a nicht zustande, können die Entscheidungen des Eisenbahninfrastrukturunternehmens durch die Regulierungsbehörde auf Antrag oder von Amts wegen überprüft werden. Antragsberechtigt sind die Zugangsberechtigten, deren Recht auf Zugang zur Eisenbahninfrastruktur beeinträchtigt sein kann. Der Antrag ist innerhalb der Frist zu stellen, in der das Angebot zum Abschluss von Vereinbarun-

gen nach Satz 1 angenommen werden kann. Überprüft werden können insbesondere

1. die Schienennetz-Benutzungsbedingungen und die Nutzungsbedingungen für Serviceeinrichtungen,
2. das Zuweisungsverfahren und dessen Ergebnis,
3. die Höhe oder Struktur der Wege- und sonstigen Entgelte.

Die Regulierungsbehörde hat die Beteiligten aufzufordern, innerhalb einer angemessenen Frist, die zwei Wochen nicht überschreiten darf, alle erforderlichen Auskünfte zu erteilen. Nach Ablauf dieser Frist hat die Regulierungsbehörde über den Antrag binnen zwei Monaten zu entscheiden.

(3) Beeinträchtigt im Fall des Absatzes 2 die Entscheidung eines Eisenbahninfrastrukturunternehmens das Recht des Antragstellers auf Zugang zur Eisenbahninfrastruktur,

1. verpflichtet die Regulierungsbehörde das Eisenbahninfrastrukturunternehmen zur Änderung der Entscheidung oder
2. legt die Regulierungsbehörde die Vertragsbedingungen fest, entscheidet über die Geltung des Vertrags und erklärt entgegenstehende Verträge für unwirksam.

III. Eisenbahninfrastruktur-Benutzungsverordnung (EIBV)

§ 21 Entgeltgrundsätze für Schienenwege

(1) Der Betreiber der Schienenwege hat seine Entgelte für die Pflichtleistungen so zu gestalten, dass sie durch leistungsabhängige Bestandteile den Eisenbahnverkehrsunternehmen und den Betreibern der Schienenwege Anreize zur Verringerung von Störungen und zur Erhöhung der Leistungsfähigkeit des Schienennetzes bieten. Die Grundsätze der leistungsabhängigen Entgeltregelung haben für das gesamte Schienennetz eines Betreibers der Schienenwege zu gelten.

(2) Das Wegeentgelt kann einen Entgeltbestandteil umfassen, der den Kosten umweltbezogener Auswirkungen des Zugbetriebs Rechnung trägt, wobei nach der Größenordnung der verursachten Auswirkungen zu differenzieren ist. Die Höhe des Gesamterlöses des Betreibers der Schienenwege darf dadurch nicht verändert werden.

(3) Das Wegeentgelt kann einen Entgeltbestandteil umfassen, der die Knappheit der Schienenwegkapazität auf einem bestimmbaren Schienenwegabschnitt in Zeiten der Überlastung widerspiegelt.

(4) Verursacht eine Verkehrsleistung gegenüber anderen Verkehrsleistungen erhöhte Kosten, dann dürfen diese Kosten nur für diese Verkehrsleistung berücksichtigt werden.

(5) Um unverhältnismäßig starke Schwankungen zu vermeiden, können die in den Absätzen 2 und 4 genannten Entgelte und das Entgelt für die Pflichtleistungen über angemessene Zeiträume gemittelt werden.

(6) Die Entgelte sind, soweit sich aus dieser Verordnung nichts anderes ergibt, gegenüber jedem Zugangsberechtigten in gleicher Weise zu berechnen. Sie sind bei nicht vertragsgemäßem Zustand des Schienenweges, der zugehörigen Steuerungs- und Sicherungssysteme sowie der zugehörigen Anlagen zur streckenbezogenen Versorgung mit Fahrstrom zu mindern.

(7) Die Entgelte der Betreiber der Schienenwege sind einen Monat vor dem Fristbeginn nach § 8 Abs. 1 Nr. 2 nach § 4 Abs. 1 zu veröffentlichen oder zuzusenden. Sie gelten für die gesamte neue Fahrplanperiode.

B. Geltendes Recht

I. Richtlinie 2012/34/EU

Artikel 56 Aufgaben der Regulierungsstelle

(1) Ist ein Antragsteller der Auffassung, ungerecht behandelt, diskriminiert oder auf andere Weise in seinen Rechten verletzt worden zu sein, so hat er unbeschadet des Artikels 46 Absatz 6 das Recht, die Regulierungsstelle zu befassen, und zwar insbesondere gegen Entscheidungen des Infrastrukturbetreibers oder gegebenenfalls des Eisenbahnunternehmens oder des Betreibers einer Serviceeinrichtung betreffend:

a) den Entwurf und die Endfassung der Schienennetz-Nutzungsbedingungen;

b) die darin festgelegten Kriterien;

c) das Zuweisungsverfahren und dessen Ergebnis;

d) die Entgeltregelung;

e) die Höhe oder Struktur der Wegeentgelte, die er zu zahlen hat oder hätte;

f) die Zugangsregelungen gemäß Artikel 10 bis 13;

g) den Zugang zu Leistungen gemäß Artikel 13 und die dafür erhobenen Entgelte.

(2) Unbeschadet der Befugnisse der nationalen Wettbewerbsbehörden für die Sicherstellung des Wettbewerbs in den Schienenverkehrsmärkten ist die Regulierungsstelle berechtigt, die Wettbewerbssituation in den Schienenverkehrsmärkten zu überwachen; sie prüft insbesondere von sich aus die in Absatz 1 Buchstaben a bis g genannten Punkte, um der Diskriminierung von Antragstellern vorzubeugen. Sie prüft insbesondere, ob die Schienennetz-Nutzungsbedingungen diskriminierende Bestimmungen enthalten oder den Infrastrukturbetreibern einen Ermessensspielraum geben, der die Diskriminierung von Antragstellern ermöglicht.

(3) [...]

(6) Die Regulierungsstelle gewährleistet, dass die vom Infrastrukturbetreiber festgesetzten Entgelte dem Kapitel IV Abschnitt 2 entsprechen und nichtdiskriminierend sind. Verhandlungen zwischen Antragstellern und einem Infrastrukturbetreiber über die Höhe von Wegeentgelten sind nur zulässig, sofern sie unter Aufsicht der Regulierungsstelle erfolgen. Die Regulierungsstelle hat einzugreifen, wenn bei den Verhandlungen ein Verstoß gegen die Bestimmungen dieses Kapitels droht.

(7) [...]

(9)　Binnen eines Monats ab Erhalt einer Beschwerde prüft die Regulierungsstelle die Beschwerde und fordert gegebenenfalls einschlägige Auskünfte an und leitet Gespräche mit allen Betroffenen ein. Innerhalb einer vorab bestimmten angemessenen Frist, in jedem Fall aber binnen sechs Wochen nach Erhalt aller sachdienlichen Informationen entscheidet sie über die betreffenden Beschwerden, trifft Abhilfemaßnahmen und setzt die Betroffenen über ihre begründete Entscheidung in Kenntnis. Unbeschadet der Zuständigkeiten der nationalen Wettbewerbsbehörden für die Sicherstellung des Wettbewerbs in den Schienenverkehrsmärkten entscheidet sie gegebenenfalls von sich aus über geeignete Maßnahmen zur Korrektur von Fällen der Diskriminierung von Antragstellern, Marktverzerrung und anderer unerwünschter Entwicklungen in diesen Märkten, insbesondere in Bezug auf Absatz 1 Buchstaben a bis g.

Entscheidungen der Regulierungsstelle sind für alle davon Betroffenen verbindlich und unterliegen keiner Kontrolle durch eine andere Verwaltungsinstanz. Die Regulierungsstelle muss ihre Entscheidungen durchsetzen können und gegebenenfalls geeignete Sanktionen, einschließlich Geldbußen, verhängen können.

Wird die Regulierungsstelle mit einer Beschwerde wegen der Verweigerung der Zuweisung von Fahrwegkapazität oder wegen der Bedingungen eines Angebots an Fahrwegkapazität befasst, entscheidet die Regulierungsstelle entweder, dass keine Änderung der Entscheidung des Infrastrukturbetreibers erforderlich ist, oder schreibt eine Änderung dieser Entscheidung gemäß den Vorgaben der Regulierungsstelle vor.

(10)　Die Mitgliedstaaten gewährleisten die gerichtliche Nachprüfbarkeit von Entscheidungen der Regulierungsstelle. Die Beschwerde kann nur dann aufschiebende Wirkung auf die Entscheidung der Regulierungsstelle haben, wenn die Entscheidung der Regulierungsstelle dem Beschwerdeführer unmittelbar irreversiblen oder offensichtlich unverhältnismäßigen Schaden zufügen kann. Diese Bestimmung lässt die etwaigen durch Verfassungsrecht übertragenen Befugnisse des mit der Beschwerde befassten Gerichts unberührt.

(11)　[...]

II. Eisenbahnregulierungsgesetz (ERegG)

§ 33 Ermittlung und Genehmigung der Entgelte in Ausnahmefällen
(1) Es bedürfen der Genehmigung:
1. Entgelte der Betreiber der Schienenwege, die von den Vorschriften zur Entgeltbildung für Schienenwege befreit sind und
2. Entgelte der Betreiber von Personenbahnhöfen.
Die jeweilige Genehmigung ist zu erteilen, wenn die Anforderungen des § 32 erfüllt sind. Für Betreiber der Schienenwege der Eisenbahnen des Bundes und für Personenbahnhöfe der Eisenbahnen des Bundes gilt abweichend von Satz 2 für Personenverkehrsdienste nach § 36 Absatz 2 Satz 2 Nummer 2 der § 37, soweit nicht § 37 Absatz 3 Abweichendes regelt.
(2) Andere als die genehmigten Entgelte dürfen nicht vereinbart werden. Ist in einem Vertrag eine Entgeltvereinbarung wegen Verstoßes gegen Satz 1 unwirksam, gilt das jeweils genehmigte Entgelt als vereinbart. Das genehmigte Entgelt gilt als billiges Entgelt im Sinne des § 315 des Bürgerlichen Gesetzbuches.

§ 45 Genehmigung der Entgelte und der Entgeltgrundsätze
(1) Die Entgelte eines Betreibers der Schienenwege für die Erbringung des Mindestzugangspakets sind einschließlich der Entgeltgrundsätze nach Anlage 3 Nummer 2 von der Regulierungsbehörde zu genehmigen. Die Genehmigung ist zu erteilen, soweit die Ermittlung der Entgelte den Anforderungen der §§ 24 bis 40 und 46 und die Entgeltgrundsätze den Vorgaben der Anlage 3 Nummer 2 entsprechen.
(2) Der Betreiber der Schienenwege darf für das Erbringen des Mindestzugangspakets keine anderen als die genehmigten Entgelte vereinbaren. Ist in einem Vertrag eine Entgeltvereinbarung wegen Verstoßes gegen Satz 1 unwirksam, gilt das jeweils genehmigte Entgelt als vereinbart. Das genehmigte Entgelt gilt als billiges Entgelt im Sinne des § 315 des Bürgerlichen Gesetzbuches.

§ 66 Die Regulierungsbehörde und ihre Aufgaben
(1) Ist ein Zugangsberechtigter der Auffassung, durch Entscheidungen eines Eisenbahninfrastrukturunternehmens diskriminiert oder auf andere Weise in seinen Rechten verletzt worden zu sein, so hat er unabhängig von § 52 Absatz 7 das Recht, die Regulierungsbehörde anzurufen.
(2) Ist ein Verband im Sinne des Satzes 2 der Auffassung, dass durch Entscheidungen eines Betreibers der Schienenwege oder eines Betreibers einer Serviceeinrichtung Rechte der Kunden im Personenverkehr oder im Güterverkehr nicht gewahrt werden, so hat er das Recht, bei der Regulie-

rungsbehörde eine Beschwerde einzureichen, auf die ihm innerhalb einer angemessenen Frist eine Antwort erteilt werden muss. [...]

(3) Kommt eine Vereinbarung über den Zugang oder über einen Rahmenvertrag nicht zustande, können die Entscheidungen des Eisenbahninfrastrukturunternehmens durch die Regulierungsbehörde auf Antrag des Zugangsberechtigten oder von Amts wegen überprüft werden. Der Antrag ist innerhalb der Frist zu stellen, in der das Angebot zum Abschluss von Vereinbarungen nach § 13 Absatz 1 Satz 2 oder § 54 Satz 3 angenommen werden kann.

(4) Überprüft werden können auf Antrag oder von Amts wegen insbesondere

1. der Entwurf und die Endfassung der Schienennetz-Nutzungsbedingungen,

2. der Entwurf und die Endfassung der Nutzungsbedingungen für Serviceeinrichtungen,

3. die darin festgelegten Kriterien,

4. das Zuweisungsverfahren und dessen Ergebnis,

5. die Entgeltregelung,

6. die Höhe oder Struktur der Wegeentgelte, die der Zugangsberechtigte zu zahlen hat oder hätte,

7. die Höhe und Struktur sonstiger Entgelte, die der Zugangsberechtigte zu zahlen hat oder hätte,

8. die Zugangsregelungen nach den §§ 10, 11 und 13,

9. Entscheidungen zum Verkehrsmanagement hinsichtlich möglicher Verstöße gegen das Eisenbahnregulierungsrecht,

10. Entscheidungen über die Art und Weise der Erneuerungen und von geplanten und ungeplanten Instandhaltungen hinsichtlich möglicher Verstöße gegen das Eisenbahnregulierungsrecht, wobei die jeweiligen Planungen von der Überprüfung mit umfasst sind; § 9 des Bundeseisenbahnverkehrsverwaltungsgesetzes bleibt unberührt; und

11. die Erfüllung der Anforderungen der §§ 8 bis 8d, einschließlich der Anforderungen in Hinsicht auf Konflikte zwischen den Interessen von Eisenbahnverkehrsunternehmen und Eisenbahninfrastrukturunternehmen.

§ 68 Entscheidungen der Regulierungsbehörde

(1) Binnen eines Monats ab Erhalt einer Beschwerde prüft die Regulierungsbehörde die Beschwerde. Dazu fordert sie von den Betroffenen die für die Entscheidung erforderlichen Auskünfte an und leitet Gespräche mit allen Betroffenen ein. Innerhalb einer vorab bestimmten angemessenen Frist, in jedem Fall aber binnen sechs Wochen nach Erhalt aller erforderlichen Informationen entscheidet sie über die Beschwerde, trifft Abhil-

femaßnahmen und setzt die Betroffenen von ihrer Entscheidung, die zu begründen ist, in Kenntnis. Unabhängig von den Zuständigkeiten der Kartellbehörden entscheidet sie von Amts wegen über geeignete Maßnahmen zur Verhütung von Diskriminierung und Marktverzerrung.

(2) Beeinträchtigt im Fall des § 66 Absatz 1 oder 3 die Entscheidung eines Eisenbahninfrastrukturunternehmens das Recht des Zugangsberechtigten auf Zugang zur Eisenbahninfrastruktur, so

1. verpflichtet die Regulierungsbehörde das Eisenbahninfrastrukturunternehmen zur Änderung der Entscheidung oder

2. entscheidet die Regulierungsbehörde über die Geltung des Vertrags oder des Entgeltes, erklärt entgegenstehende Verträge für unwirksam und setzt die Vertragsbedingungen oder Entgelte fest.

Die Entscheidung nach Satz 1 kann auch Schienennetz-Nutzungsbedingungen oder Nutzungsbedingungen für Serviceeinrichtungen betreffen.

(3) Die Regulierungsbehörde kann mit Wirkung für die Zukunft das Eisenbahninfrastrukturunternehmen zur Änderung der Regelungen im Sinne des § 66 Absatz 4 verpflichten oder diese Regelungen für ungültig erklären, soweit diese nicht mit den Vorschriften dieses Gesetzes in Einklang stehen.

(4) Widerspruch und Anfechtungsklage gegen Entscheidungen der Regulierungsbehörde haben keine aufschiebende Wirkung. In den Fällen, in denen die Regulierungsbehörde durch eine Beschlusskammer entscheidet, findet ein Vorverfahren nicht statt. Satz 2 gilt auch, soweit der Vorsitzende anstelle der Beschlusskammer entscheidet.

(5) Die Regulierungsbehörde veröffentlicht die nach § 68 getroffenen Entscheidungen in nicht personenbezogener Form. Sie kann daneben Informationen über die Durchführung von Verfahren in nicht personenbezogener Form veröffentlichen.

§ 76 Beteiligung der Regulierungsbehörde bei bürgerlichen Rechtsstreitigkeiten

Für bürgerliche Rechtsstreitigkeiten, die sich aus diesem Gesetz ergeben, gilt § 90 Absatz 1 und 2 des Gesetzes gegen Wettbewerbsbeschränkungen mit der Maßgabe entsprechend, dass an die Stelle des Bundeskartellamtes und seines Präsidenten oder seiner Präsidentin die Regulierungsbehörde und ihr Präsident oder ihre Präsidentin treten.

III. Bundeseisenbahnverkehrsverwaltungsgesetz (BEVVG)

§ 9 Zusammenarbeit zwischen Regulierungs-, Sicherheits-, Genehmigungs- und Kartellbehörden

[...] (3) Die Aufgaben und Zuständigkeiten der Kartellbehörden nach dem Gesetz gegen Wettbewerbsbeschränkungen bleiben unberührt. Die Regulierungsbehörde und die Eisenbahnaufsichtsbehörden sowie die Kartellbehörden und die nach dem Telekommunikationsgesetz und dem Energiewirtschaftsgesetz zuständigen Regulierungsbehörden teilen einander Informationen mit, die für die Erfüllung der jeweiligen Aufgaben von Bedeutung sein können. Insbesondere sollen sie sich gegenseitig über beabsichtigte Entscheidungen informieren, mit denen ein missbräuchliches oder diskriminierendes Verhalten von Eisenbahninfrastrukturunternehmen untersagt werden soll. Sie sollen einander Gelegenheit zur Stellungnahme geben, bevor das Verfahren von der zuständigen Behörde abgeschlossen wird.

The Tycoon's
Secret

Baby for the Billionaire
Book Four

Melody Anne

DEDICATION

This is a very long overdue dedication to my
best friend, Nikki. I love her so incredibly
much that I just assumed I'd already dedicated
a book to her! Nikki, you are honestly the
reason I am the person I am today. Had you
not come into my life when I was 12, I
would've chosen a much different path to go
down. Thank you for being there for me for
over 20 years. May we have another 60 or
more! I love you.

Books by Melody Anne

*The Billionaire Wins the Game
*The Billionaire's Dance
*The Billionaire Falls
*The Billionaire's Marriage Proposal
*Blackmailing the Billionaire
*Runaway Heiress
*The Billionaire's Final Stand

+The Tycoon's Revenge
+The Tycoon's Vacation
+The Tycoon's Proposal
+The Tycoon's Secret

-Midnight Fire – Rise of the Dark Angel – Book One
-Midnight Moon – Rise of the Dark Angel – Book Two
-Midnight Storm – Rise of the Dark Angel – Book Three

www.facebook.com/authormelodyanne
www.melodyanne.com
Twitter: @authmelodyanne

Coming Soon:

New Series:

+The Darkness Within: Book One

=Because of Honor: Book One: April 2013

ACKNOWLEDGMENTS

There aren't enough pages to acknowledge all the people who help me, inspire me and challenge me on a daily basis. I love my family, friends, the people who work for me, my fans, all of you. Each person holds a place in my heart and I wouldn't be able to do any of this without your continual support, love and encouragement. Thank you Jeff for the countless hours you put into the bookwork, Patsy for being willing to do anything and everything, Mom for being my biggest cheerleader, Phoenix and John for sharing in my joy and excitement, Isaiah, Jacob and Jasmine for giving me a lot of good material with your never-ending childhood joy, and of course, Nikki for the limitless hours you work to make sure my books are the best instead of second rate. And my fans, oh my, there are too many of you to name names this time, but you bring me joy beyond anything I ever imagined possible. Thank you for the pics that make me smile, the words of encouragement that make me work long hours, and the love you've shared with me. I love you all!! I couldn't do it without you.

Powerful, Loyal, Unforgettable
Follow the Titans
As they find true love
The Tycoon's Secret
Baby for the Billionaire Series
Book Four

Prologue

"Damien, you must always remember who you are!" his mother wheezed before she fell back against her pillows, the words interrupted by her severe cough filling the room.

"I will, Mom. I promise. You *have* to take your medicine now," Damien begged the frail woman.

"I'm dying, Damien. Those little pills can't help me any longer," she whispered, causing fear to cut through the heart of the thirteen year old boy.

"We gotta go to the hospital, Mom. Please," Damien begged.

"Not this time, son. Not this time. I'm tired, Damien. I just need rest. You have to promise me that you'll never forget who you are. They took everything from us. Everything! They killed your father, just as surely as if they would've walked up and stabbed him in the heart. If they wouldn't have stolen all he'd worked so hard for his entire life, he wouldn't have died the way he did. He wouldn't have left us all alone and broken, without a penny to our name."

"I know, Mom. I'll make them pay. I promise you, I will…" Damien trailed off, reaching deep inside for the courage to keep him from crying.

"Don't you shed tears, boy! You better not disgrace me in my dyin' moments. Do you hear me?" his mother scolded.

"Yes, ma'am. I'm sorry, Mom," Damien said, willing to say anything to make that censure leave her eyes.

He hated to see her in so much pain, knowing there was nothing he could do. She was mean, always verbally and physically abusive…, but she was his mom. She had the right to be mean because she'd had to endure a hard life, especially because of having him. He knew he was nothing but a burden to her, which was why he had to fulfill his promise.

"I'm going to sleep now, Damien. If I don't wake up this time, you never forget why I'm dyin' like this. You never forget it's *those* people, those rotten bastards who left us like this. If they wouldn't have taken everything, I'd be all better. I coulda afforded the medicine I needed to stay alive. You coulda went to a good school. You get them, Damien. You get them real good."

His mother's voice faded as she closed her eyes and drifted to sleep. Fifteen minutes later her breathing stopped.

Damien sat by her bed for another hour before finally standing up and walking from the room. One lone tear slipped from his dark green eyes. He didn't turn back around and look at her lifeless body - there was no reason to. He didn't even stop to gather any possessions from their meager apartment.

There was nothing worth taking. He'd slept on the floor from the time he was a baby. His clothes were tattered and the cupboards desolate. He'd never received a gift for any reason. There was literally nothing in the home to take.

It was *their* fault – all of it. His mom could've been a good mother, if only *they* hadn't ruined her. Some people were just greedy, out to get their hands on everything. Well, they'd pay. They'd pay if it was the last thing he did.

He walked from the house – vowing never to go back to such conditions again, though he'd never forget how much he'd suffered. He'd seek revenge on those who'd killed his mother, those who were supposed to be his family. He didn't care how long it took…

Four Years later

Damien strutted through the school yard, looking for a fight. None of the boys would look him in the face. They were used to the set of his shoulders, the gleam in his eyes, almost begging for a challenge. He was just waiting for one of them to look at him

5

wrong, or say the simplest remark to set him off – giving him an excuse to thoroughly waste them.

They'd lose – they were well aware of the speed with which Damien threw a punch, after witnessing plenty of his brawls in the past. His childhood had made him rage internally, and it was always at a low simmer, ready to ignite. The only reason he stayed in school was because he promised his mother. He had to finish school, had to succeed so he could seek revenge on those who'd killed both his parents.

"Shut–up, Skank!"

Damien turned to find a petite girl being pushed to the ground by a group of girls. Normally, he wouldn't get involved. He didn't hit girls, no matter how much fury reigned inside him. He turned to walk away as one of the gang grabbed the girl on the ground by her hair and yanked her head back, spitting in her face.

The small girl in clothing as tattered as his own was sobbing as another one of the older girls slapped her. Where in the hell were the teachers? He looked around, not seeing anyone doing anything to stop the bullying.

A third teenager in the group stepped forward and kicked the girl in her ribs and he'd seen enough. He strode over to them.

"You want to try that crap on me?" he asked, his voice thundering across the yard.

"Go away, white trash," one of the snobby girls snapped as she loosened her grasp to glare at him.

He smiled at her, a smile full of evil delight. Let her think he was crazy. She could go running home to mommy, sobbing about the guy who nearly took her life.

"Let's get out of her Stacy," one of the other girls said, nervously looking back and forth between him and her friend.

"I'd listen to your friend, *Stacy*," he paused, "before something really bad happens," he threatened. There was no mistaking the menace in his voice as he stepped closer to the main tormentor.

She stumbled backward, finally realizing her danger. Her glare disappeared, anger transforming into an expression of fear.

"I'm telling Mr. Sorenson," she threatened as she took another step back.

"Go ahead. As a matter-of-fact, I think I'll take this girl to his office now," Damien told her.

The pack of intimidators scampered off, he was sure to beat him to the principle. He didn't care what they had to say. It was obvious the girl on the ground had been the victim.

"Thank you," she wheezed as he bent down to see how badly she was hurt.

"I'm going to lift you up. You need to see the nurse," he said as he gently stretched his hand out and wiped the other girls disgusting spittle from her face. Her entire body was shaking.

"I'm fine," she told him on a trembling voice as she tried to sit up.

"Yeah, real fine," he said with sarcasm, but there was no heat behind his words. He felt nothing but sympathy for the young girl.

He carefully slid his hands beneath her legs and back and lifted her into his arms, barely able to detect her undernourished body against his own.

"What's your name?" she asked as she rested her head against his chest. He felt his cold heart heat up at the sound of her trusting voice.

"Damien."

"I'm Trinity. Thanks for saving me," she said before she passed out in his arms. He picked up his speed and rushed to the nurse's station, and she quickly called the ambulance.

From that day on, he and Trinity became inseparable. She was his best friend, his confidant, his family – his sister. She was the only person in the entire world keeping the demons at bay – making him remember to love instead of only hate.

She was also the only woman he trusted, even as the years passed. He used women, used them to satisfy *his* needs, but felt no guilt, as the type of women he dated were those who used him just as much, used his name, his power, and whatever it was they thought they could get from him.

Damien still never forgot where he came from – never forgot the promise he made to his mother. There were weeks, months, years even when it was pushed to the back of his mind. Only because of Trinity, because of his love for his friend. Revenge would happen, though – at any cost.

Chapter One
Fifteen Years Later

Sierra was exhausted.

Deeply, utterly, fall-on-her-face exhausted.

She also had a feeling of unmitigated accomplishment. The wedding was over. With zero regret, she tossed the slightly wilted Calla Lilies into the nearest garbage can, and then found a chair to rest in for a few minutes.

It had been a circus, but it was over. Her *incredibly* babied, and *very* spoiled little sister was married to the man of her dreams. She loved her sister, though she didn't know why, really. For the past twenty-three years, her father had dotted on Sandy, spoiled her, given her everything.

He hadn't been so kind to Sierra. She'd never forget when she was six years old, her sister only four. Their mother had died in an automobile crash. From that moment on, her life had been hell.

Her father told her almost daily that her mother was a cheating whore and that Sierra most likely wasn't even his kid. He'd also told her, he owned her and would make her pay for her mother's transgressions. The beatings had begun, only escalating through the years.

He was a smart man, respected in the business community. She feared him, knowing he could make her life so much worse than it was. She'd learned at a young age if she just suffered silently through the pain, he'd stop much faster. If she shouted out, he seemed to get an evil glee from it, and would go on and on.

She ran away once. A shiver passed through her body remembering the pain she'd gone through when he'd found her. She'd been bruised from head to toe, unable to leave her bed for two weeks. Her father had kept her at a cottage on the outskirts of town so the servants wouldn't get suspicious.

Though a couple had been brave enough not only to suspect, but ask her if she was okay, she learned quickly never to say anything. The sympathetic employees quickly disappeared. Soon, no one would help her, or look out for her. She learned silent suffering was the key to survival.

Sierra looked around the reception as she pulled herself out of her depressing memories. The event was still going strong, causing her to sigh. Her sister had departed a while ago, amid a sea of birdseed, and the crowd calling out advice. The moment the Limo pulled away, Sierra's fake smile had vanished.

Friends, from near and far, were taking advantage of the open bar, free food, and euphoria at being at the exclusive country club. It was all a joke. None of them cared one iota about Sandy. Sierra figured it didn't matter as her little sister didn't care about anyone but herself, anyway.

The one positive note to the entire charade was that at least Sierra wouldn't have to watch as Sandy acted like a brat, threw a fit, and then got her way. She'd learned quickly that if Sierra didn't do what she wanted, all she had to do was complain to her father, and he'd make Sierra into Sandy's servant.

Sandy was Mason's problem now, and Sierra hoped her father would let her leave now that Sandy had moved out. There was no reason to keep her locked up in his enormous mansion.

Sierra felt the slightest pang to her heart as Mason's name popped into her head. She slowly got to her feet, making her way up to her room. Thank goodness she was staying there that night. She didn't have the energy to drive home.

As she climbed in the elevator, her heart pounded while thinking about Mason. She thought she'd been in love with him, deeply, over-the-moon in love. She may have been, but it had obviously been one sided because the moment Sandy decided she wanted him, he'd followed her sister like the willing puppy he'd turned out to be.

His pathetic apology and explanation of not being able to control his heart hadn't helped Sierra's pride – not one little bit.

The wedding had taken place in only four months, and their father had seemed to think there was nothing amiss with Sandy suddenly marrying Sierra's boyfriend. When Sierra had made the slightest comment about it being wrong, her father had begun his lecture of how Sierra needed to keep her jealousy of her perfect sister to herself.

Sierra hadn't dared argue any further. If she honestly thought about it, she'd only wanted to be with Mason to get away from her father, anyway. Surprisingly, her dad had approved of her relationship with his faithful employee.

Sandy had demanded a perfect wedding with her flawless groom, and that's what she'd gotten – a glamorous event, attended by Hollywood actors, musicians, and the elite of the elite. People wanted to attend the wedding of one of the wealthiest men in the United States. They may be able to get something from him.

"It doesn't matter," Sierra said out loud, trying to convince herself. She needed to let the entire thing go. She was lucky to have found out what a creep Mason was so early in their relationship. It could've been worse. She could've married him, and then been humiliated when he left her for her sister.

Standing as her sister's maid of honor and holding her ridiculously gaudy bouquet of flowers while Mason swept Sandy into his arms, kissing her in front of everyone couldn't be humiliation enough for Sierra. Sandy also had to toss her bouquet straight into Sierra's hands during the reception.

Sierra had smiled as if she was thrilled, but she hadn't missed the snickers as people behind her made comments about her never using the flowers since she couldn't keep a man long enough to get him to walk her down the aisle. When she heard the woman add that at least she didn't have any other sister's to steal her man, Sierra was done.

Mason worked for her father, and marrying either Sierra or Sandy pretty much sealed the deal of him becoming the corporation's next CEO. He'd moved his way toward the top, and when he'd hit the mother-load by marrying the owner's daughter, he got it all. He would've settled for Sierra, but why settle when he could have Sandy, everyone's choice of the better of the two siblings.

Sierra finally made it to her room and swiped the key card across the reader, grateful when it registered on the first try. She stepped inside and tightly closed the door behind her. All she wanted was freedom, and maybe, just maybe, that's what she'd finally get. Besides, she didn't want to get married. Why place herself in a position where a man had control of her again. If she ever escaped her nightmare, she vowed to stay single the rest of her life.

She glanced at the clock, noting that it was just past midnight. Sandy and Mason were well on their way to Europe by now. Sierra felt more of a pang over her sister getting to visit one of the country's *she'd* always wanted to go to, than over the loss of Mason.

With a sigh, Sierra unzipped the uncomfortable dress, letting it fall to the ground in a sea of satin. She kicked it away from her, knowing she wouldn't take it from the hotel. She had no desire to wear it again. Let one of the maids find it. They'd appreciate the expensive dress more than she ever would.

Sierra didn't need any more reminders of her sister's wedding. She'd have plenty of daily reminders as she watched her happily married sister in the arms of her ex-boyfriend.

She took out the hundreds of pins from her up-do, a feeling of bliss overcoming her as the tight curtain of hair fell loosely around her shoulders. Her head ached, along with the soles of her feet.

She jumped into the shower and massaged her scalp, dreading the next day. Her father wanted to speak to her. She had no clue what it was about, but he'd been so formal, it couldn't be good.

Sierra managed to make her way back into the bedroom of her roomy suite, where she collapsed face-first onto the comfortable bed, and vowed not to get up until her body woke her. She knew the wrath of her father wasn't worth an extra hour or two of rest, but she just couldn't convince her physically and emotionally exhausted body of that.

Chapter Two
One week earlier

Damien set the papers down on his desk and sat back. He was perplexed – intrigued but perplexed.

When he'd received the phone call yesterday, he'd thought it was a joke. A father couldn't truly be serious – offering his child in exchange for money. Though, as Damien went through the files on Sierra Monroe, he was beginning to realize that her father, Douglas was more than serious.

The man was willing to trade his daughter for cash. Normally, Damien wouldn't give the scum of a man the time of day. His time was too valuable to waste, and he didn't make poor business decisions.

However, he was curious – a tremendously bad thing. What was in it for Sierra? Was she going along with her father? How far was she willing to go?

He looked at her photograph, picking it up from his desk for at least the twentieth time. She was attractive – more than attractive, for that matter.

Her long dark hair was pinned back in the photo, and her dark brown, almost black eyes, were solemn as if she had secrets she was trying to hide from the world.

Her nose had the slightest bend to it as if it was broken at one time, but had healed nicely, giving her face an almost softer look. Her beauty was rounded off by her high cheekbones, and the oval shape to her face.

He hadn't been intrigued in a long time over a woman, but Sierra Monroe had his undivided attention.

He'd placed a post a week ago, needing a new public relations representative. It was placed in extremely select listings as he didn't want, nor need, the general public to apply. He wanted only the best.

The call from Douglas Monroe hadn't been the call he'd been expecting. With irritation, he lifted his phone and dialed the man's direct line.

"Douglas Monroe."

"This is Damien Whitfield. I've thought about your offer, and I've decided to accept." Damien felt no need to offer anything else.

"That's great, Damien. Why don't you come by my home tomorrow and we can sign the papers," Douglas replied, excitement rushing over the line.

Damien was even more disgusted.

"It's Mr. Whitfield, and I have conditions," Damien warned, to which there was a long pause on the other end of the line.

"What would those be?" the man finally asked, not responding to the scolding of the man being too familiar with his name.

"Is your daughter aware of our...deal?"

"I've told her that it's time she gets a job. She's had it too easy for too long. It's time she stops living off of me and learns how to make it in the real world," Douglas said, evading the question.

She was a spoiled heiress, then. Damien should just let it go and move on, but for some reason he couldn't. Well, he had a couple reasons. One of which was the people Sierra knew, the other, well, the other he still hadn't figured out.

"Is she going to give me trouble?"

"Not at all, Mr. Whitfield. My daughter has been taught to behave," Douglas said with an evil laugh.

A shudder rippled down Damien's spine. He wasn't even in the room with Douglas, but the man oozed filth. People like him would eventually fail. That's why Damien was confident in his plans to finally keep his promise to his mother.

His supposed family was just like Douglas Monroe, full of greed and not afraid to walk on people to get what they wanted. They'd fail as well.

"Fine, I'll meet you at your place, but not until next week. My attorney will have the paperwork ready." Damien hung up the phone without saying anything further.

The less he talked to the slime ball, the more he'd be able to stomach making a deal with the devil.

Pushing those thoughts from his mind, he picked up the second stack of paperwork on his desk, this time a genuine smile popping out on his face. It was time. Finally, he had what he needed to start his takeover of the men who'd killed his parents.

It was long past time.

Damien's lips turned up in what would look like a smile to the rest of the world. It may have even been a smile – or at least as much of one as he was capable of giving. He watched Sierra wearily stumble away.

Since making the deal with her father, he'd studied up on her, making sure he wanted to hire the spoiled heiress. The more he learned, the more intrigued he became. He was suddenly impatient to close the deal.

He thought about going after her, but he wasn't an impulsive man, or at least with most people he wasn't. His lips softened as he thought of his one and only friend, Trinity. His only impulsive act, ever, had been to offer to marry her.

He would've, too, had she said *yes*. Luckily, Drew, the baby's father, had come back into her life, and not only wanted to do the right thing, but Drew was deeply in love with Trinity.

Damien didn't believe in happily-ever-after love, but it was hard to deny that Trinity and Drew were, indeed, in love. The way they looked at each other was almost disturbing.

He shook off thoughts of Trinity. He couldn't carry out his plans if he thought of his best friend. She'd *kill* him if she knew what he was up to. He'd never spoken of his past with anyone, not even Trinity. He hardened his resolve. He'd made a promise to his mother – a promise he intended to keep. He'd made that vow before Trinity found him so many years earlier, before she rescued him from the dark bitterness of his life.

Damien's eyes snapped back to Sierra as she walked away from the reception. She was just another piece of the puzzle to the grand design of his life, to the purpose he'd practically been made for. He could succeed without her, but why should he. He liked what he saw, and with such an appealing package up for grabs, he figured, *why not?*

She had a natural grace and beauty about her that could easily reel a man in. He wasn't worried about getting too attached. He wasn't interested in love. He'd been there, done that. He should've just listened to his mother, and never tried any road but the one that led to his parent's vindication.

His so-called *family* would pay. They'd pay big.

Sierra was almost meaningless – almost. She just happened to have a best friend who was a part of the family he was close to taking over. With her father so easily trading his daughter, who was he to refuse?

The meeting with her father hadn't been pleasant. The man was the lowest kind of scum, but Damien figured he was doing Sierra a favor getting her out of there, not that she seemed to be in a hurry, from everything he'd learned so far.

Damien's mind drifted as he thought about his conversation with Douglas Monroe:

"Thank you for meeting with me, Mr. Whitfield?" Douglas said, obviously pleased at having Damien in his office. The man was practically salivating as he waited for Damien to sign on the dotted line.

Damien was silent as he towered over the guy. He wasn't there to make friends with Douglas. He was there for a business transaction. Damien had done his research. He knew Douglas was in deep enough trouble that he needed the deal they were making.

Mr. Monroe still had the rest of the world fooled, planning a huge, over-the-top wedding for his daughter, living large in his twenty-thousand square foot mansion, driving his over-priced vehicles - but Damien knew Douglas was close to bankrupt. He'd made poor business choices, and in-turn, had lost billions of dollars.

The man was practically a slithering idiot at the opportunity to do business with Damien's corporation.

The longer Damien was silent, the more nervous Douglas became. Damien could practically taste the man's fear. He had to remind himself that his battle wasn't with Douglas Monroe. He didn't care if the man failed or succeeded in life, though Damien had a feeling Douglas would soon be losing everything.

With self-taught control, Damien pulled himself together. He wasn't there to make Douglas sweat. Damien was successful in what he did because of how well he read people. He saw weakness, and he immediately wanted to go for the jugular – close the deal. And he certainly saw weakness in Douglas.

Damien owned thousands of properties throughout the world, making only the finest of wines. He knew how to choose the land, pick the vines and staff the property to make wine in which royalty was on stand-by for.

Damien seemed to have the Midas touch, because every venture he invested in, every dollar he made, ended up tripling. He couldn't seem to lose when it came to financials, but it was never enough. None of it was.

Only retribution could soothe his troubled soul.

"To be honest, *Douglas*," he stressed the name, letting the man know that even though Douglas couldn't address Damien informally, Damien certainly would take the opportunity to do so to Douglas. It was a power play, letting his opponent know he was the weaker man. "I wasn't going to take you up on your offer, but then I did some research… It made me change my mind. I'm intrigued by why you'd basically sell your child."

Damien left the words as a statement, seeing if Douglas would fill in the blanks.

"You placed an ad. I just happen to have a solution. I'm looking for investors, so it seemed a mutually benefiting deal. I'm a very private man, though, and the terms of our agreement are to stay between us," Douglas said, showing a bit of the backbone that had made him billions of dollars.

"I'm private myself, Douglas."

Douglas gazed at him for a few silent moments. Damien could see the man was trying to decide if Damien was for real or not. Though Damien's passion was his vineyards, he was well-known throughout the world as a smart investor. It was common knowledge that he never invested in a losing company.

Damien knew he'd most likely lose every dime of money he sunk into Monroe enterprises but it didn't matter. This wasn't about making money, it was about payback, and Damien didn't care if he lost millions. It was inconsequential to him.

"Fine. It looks like we're both agreeable. Are you going to accept the offer?" Douglas finally asked, sitting back, trying to portray a man with confidence, who was slightly bored. He wasn't pulling it off.

"I'm willing to invest ten million into your project." He paused, letting his words sink in. "Only *if* your daughter is… cooperative."

Douglas waited for more. Damien said nothing else.

"How cooperative?" Douglas finally asked, his brow beading with sweat as he nervously waited for Damien's reply. It was obvious the man didn't think his daughter was worth ten million dollars. In reality, he was most likely right. The only woman Damien could think of worth that kind of money was already taken.

"Do you really want to know?" Damien mocked.

Damien was still standing, towering his six-foot-plus frame over the small man. He bent down, his knuckles grazing the desk. He knew intimidation was his best tactical maneuver.

"I can't make any guarantees about her attitude, but I'll make sure she works hard," Douglas said, perspiration starting to drip from his brow.

"I wouldn't be too concerned about her attitude. From everything I've learned about her, she seems to be quite…accommodating," Damien mocked.

He watched as Douglas blanched, but didn't back down. The man was truly selling his daughter, even with Damien leaving the impression that he wanted her for nothing more than a slave.

He wanted to turn and walk from the room, dismiss the entire deal, but the more he sunk into this twisted family, the more he desired to know about Sierra Monroe. He'd have his answers soon enough.

Damien's cold eyes showed none of the emotions raging through him as he pulled the pen from his breast pocket. He signed the paper before looking into the greedy eyes of his newest investee. It was the first time he'd signed a deal that made his stomach turn.

Chapter Three

Sierra awoke, stretching out her arms before daring to look at the clock next to her bed. With a quick glance, she saw it was only seven in the morning and she was a bit disappointed with herself. She knew she'd never be able to get back to sleep, but she'd so hoped she'd sleep until at least nine, maybe even ten.

With frustration running through her, she stumbled from the bed and made her way to the bathroom. The long, hot shower woke her in a refreshingly pleasant way, and she scrubbed the rest of the wedding stink from her body.

She took her time putting her hair up and applying make-up. She wanted to make her father wait on her for some reason. It was her small form of rebellion. She hated it when he yelled, hated it even more when he hit her, but she was trying to gain some small piece of independence.

He refused to let her move from his home, though she was twenty-five years old. He had no problem with his darling Sandy running all over the place, jumping from one man to the next, then finally marrying her sister's barely ex-boyfriend, but he had a problem with Sierra moving out on her own.

She hadn't understood why, especially since he hated her. When he finally explained that she was paying for what he believed were her mother's sins, she was horrified. She'd fought him, but in the end the battle hadn't been worth it. He was a powerful, domineering man, and she didn't have the strength or energy to fight. He'd broken her spirit long ago.

With Sandy now gone, though, so many possibilities loomed before her. Maybe he'd finally let her go and get her own place, actually start living her life.

She'd managed to stash money away through the years. It was enough to survive on her own long enough to get a job and start living. She had a college degree and did volunteer work, so it shouldn't be that difficult finding work. She just had to get away from her dad, get away with his permission so he wouldn't drag her back.

For two precious years she'd had freedom, a taste of what it would be like to be away from him. It wasn't two full years, as she'd had to return home during breaks, but it was still more than she'd ever hoped for at that point in her life.

She'd gone to community college after high school, still having to stay home, but at least getting to leave during the day. Then, for two years she'd gone to the University and stayed on campus – a rule of the prestigious campus she'd attended.

Her first semester, she'd been too afraid and shy to meet anyone, but after that, she met her new roommate, who refused to allow her to hide away. She smiled fondly thinking of Brianne. She'd been like a mini-tornado, arriving in their room, full of energy and enthusiasm.

She'd refused to let Sierra stay in their dorm room alone, dragging her out to eat, party, and play until all hours of the night. They'd become best friends. It hadn't taken long, as Brianne was one of those girls who refused to be told *no*.

After they graduated, Brianne had wanted to get a place together, saying her family was suffocating her and she needed her best friend as a roommate and buffer. Sierra had certainly known how she felt, though, she'd disagreed with Brianne. Sierra had found her family charming, full of life, and always kind.

Sierra had eagerly agreed to move in together, wanting to live with Brianne, to start a career and continue the life she'd started on the college campus. When she'd made the mistake of telling her father her plans, he'd cut her off of all money, blocked her from getting any jobs by informing potential employee's he'd either make sure funding was pulled, or telling them she was highly inadequate. Finally, he'd threatened all kinds of retribution if she didn't come home. She knew it was about power and control, but she also knew he was capable of following through on his threats.

Brianne had tried to stop her, saying she'd pay for the place until Sierra could get on her feet. In the end, Sierra had done what her father wanted. He was just too powerful to fight. She was afraid he'd carry through on his threats, like he'd done the time she'd run away. He'd been good to her for about a month after she came home, too preoccupied with business to even notice her much.

It didn't last, though.

Soon, he was back to himself, hitting her when he felt like it, blaming her for her mother's loose life, and her sister running around, and just for being not quite good enough to be his child.

She'd taken it – as she always had and always would. She didn't know how to fight him.

Sierra snapped out of the past, knowing she was taking too much time to leave the room. She was late. Though her brief moment of rebellion had felt good, the thought of her father's wrath was beginning to outweigh it. She picked up her purse and started moving toward the door of her hotel room. She was sad to leave her small paradise.

She reached the door when the phone rang.

Fear slithered slowly down her spine like a snake. Should she answer? If it was her dad and he found out she was still there, he was going to be furious. On the other hand, if she didn't answer and then wasn't home for the twenty minutes it would take her to drive there, he'd still be furious, knowing she'd ignored his call. She was damned if she did and damned if she didn't. He always seemed to know, though she didn't know how.

In her last effort to leave, she felt her feet moving in the wrong direction in a mad rush and she tentatively picked up the phone before it could go to voicemail.

"H…hello," she said, her voice tripping over the words.

"Sierra? Is that you? What's wrong?"

Sierra breathed a sigh of relief.

"How did you find me?" she teased, her body relaxing to almost jelly as she sat on the bed. She knew she'd be even later to see her father, but the sound of the familiar voice – one she missed so much, was a welcomed distraction and she couldn't bring herself to take a rain check on the conversation. Bree was the one person she'd risk the wrath of her father for.

"I have my ways," Bree replied with a laugh.

"Or, you have a husband who has connections."

"Well…that, too. But, hey, I can find you without him."

"Did you?"

There was a long, telling pause. "Well…"

"That's what I thought. Did you have him place tracking devices on me?"

"You told me where you were going to be for the brat's wedding, remember? It didn't take much to deduce you stayed at the hotel, and which room you were in," Brianne said with a laugh.

"I wish you would've been here," Sierra said, knowing the wedding would've been so much more bearable if her best friend was there.

"We both know your little sister would've had a cow, throwing a tantrum and causing a big scene. She hates me."

"She's just jealous of you. I stopped taking so much crap from her after we met. It didn't help matters when she came to the campus acting like her spoiled self and you threw a cake in her face."

"I admit that might have upset her a little bit but, dang it, she should've been appreciative. That was really good cake and I wasted it on her face," Brianne said with mock exasperation through the receiver.

"You're such a trouble maker," Sierra said fondly.

"I miss you. We need to have a day out. Do you think the warden will allow it?" Bree asked with hope.

"I don't know. He's summoned me, and I'm running really late. I'm not sure what kind of mood he'll be in when I get home." Sierra hated admitting how controlling her father was, but at least Bree never made her feel badly about it.

"You know, Sierra, my offer always stands. I'll not only break you out of that prison, but be there for you every step of the way. You're an adult and can have a good life."

Sierra wished she had the courage to take her friend up on her offer, but she didn't. Each day she grew stronger, though – maybe someday soon.

Bree didn't know about the physical abuse. She'd guessed about the mental censures, but no one knew about the bruising continually covering her body. She was too ashamed to admit it to anyone, even her best friend.

"Maybe I just never want to grow up," Sierra tried to joke, but it fell flat. They both knew she wanted out of there.

"I'm going to kidnap you, just so you know. I'll bring my brothers to run guard, and I'm taking you away. I miss my best friend."

"I'll make sure and see you this week, okay? Just give me a few days. I know my dad's going to be all emotional about his baby getting married and leaving," Sierra said, not able to keep the resentment from her tone.

"Okay, I'll give you a couple days, but if I haven't heard from you, just expect to hear helicopters landing on your roof. I'm sending my husband and brothers in, and we're breaking you out."

Knowing Bree would actually follow through on her threat was the scariest part of the conversation. Sierra would have to find a way to see Bree soon, because she didn't know what her father's reaction would be if Bree really did storm the house.

They talked a few more minutes before Bree reluctantly allowed Sierra to hang up the phone. With a heavy heart, she gathered her purse and walked from the room. It was going to be a long day. Her shoulders and neck unconsciously began to tense, preparing for the stress of the upcoming conversation with her father. All she could do now was hope that her father wouldn't be too angry...

Chapter Four

"Sir, another letter has come in."

Damien turned, only half-listening to the man who'd just walked in, speaking to Douglas. Sierra was late. Damien watched as her father nervously looked toward the door, then the clock. Damien didn't miss anything, and he could see the fury brewing in her father's eyes. It seemed he didn't like his daughter taking her sweet time getting there.

Damien didn't like waiting on the girl, either, but his irritation was pushed down as he watched Douglas grow more upset.

Women were notoriously late, and Damien didn't see a reason for the rage behind Douglas's eyes.

Interesting, he thought.

"What are you talking about?" Douglas snapped at his head of security. The guy was huge and Damien had no doubt he could drop Douglas in the blink of the eye. He must be very loyal to take that kind of tone from the weak little man.

"Another threat against your daughter, sir," the man said, not showing the slightest reaction to the criticism in his boss's voice.

Suddenly, Douglas became nervous, his eyes darting toward Damien before jerking back to his security man. It seemed Douglas didn't want Damien to know about the letter, which meant that Damien *really* wanted to know. He hadn't been interested, in the least, until Douglas wanted to keep it from him.

"Just put it away. I'll look later," Douglas snapped.

"Wait," Damien interrupted, both men's eyes turning in his direction as he strode over to them. "I want to see."

"It's got nothing to do with you," Douglas said, his face flushing.

"Considering it's a threat against my newest employee, I'd say it has a lot to do with me," Damien countered, not backing down.

The security man looked from his boss to Damien, and then back again. He obviously didn't know what to do. He didn't want to defy his boss, but Damien's confident demeanor was hard to ignore.

"Whatever!" Douglas snapped, turning away with a wave of his hand.

The obviously relieved security man handed the envelope to Damien before stepping back. Damien walked to the couch and sat down, pulling out the contents of the envelope. His stomach dropped at what he saw.

"How long?"

"How long, what?" Douglas snapped.

"How long have these been coming in?" Damien growled, his patience gone.

"Oh, who knows? Months? Years? I've lost count," he said while dismissively waving his hand again, as if it didn't matter in the least.

"Are you telling me that your daughter has been getting death threats, and you don't think that's worthy of your attention?" Damien asked, his voice deceptively soft, not alerting the man to the danger he was in.

"You know how it is when you're wealthy – people send all kinds of crap. It doesn't mean anything," Douglas replied, brushing the matter under the rug.

Damien looked again at the picture, a close up shot of Sierra. There were holes poked through the photo and fake blood smeared on the image with a message that read, "just a picture of what you'll look like when I'm finished with you."

"This isn't something to be taken lightly. She should have twenty-four hour supervision on her," Damien snapped.

"Well, it looks like you'll be handling that, now, doesn't it?" Douglas snapped back. The two men glared at each other for several strained moments.

"Apparently in the nick of time, too," Damien goaded, knowing his words would upset Douglas.

"I could call this whole thing off…" Douglas threatened, to which Damien just smiled. He knew a false threat when he heard one. Douglas was the one who'd called him. Damien really had nothing to lose, other than curiosity and some strange need to solve the puzzle of Sierra Monroe.

"Go ahead." Damien had zero concerns about calling the man's bluff.

Douglas glared at him for a moment longer, before he mumbled something and then resumed pacing across the room, once again looking to the door.

Damien returned to the sofa and sat quietly, his eyes blank as he thought about the situation. Maybe this deal was all more than he wanted to get involved in. Was one woman worth all the trouble? He had an agenda to follow through on, a tightly controlled schedule to meet. Having Sierra around would break the ice with her best friend, Brianne, which in turn would make it easier for him to get closer to Joseph and George Anderson, the men who'd killed his father, Neilson, when Damien was only a baby, but he could do that on his own.

At the thought of the men who'd destroyed his life before he'd even said his first words, rage shot through him. Any time he thought of those men, he remembered why he was so dead set on revenge. He'd lost the opportunity of a normal life, with two loving parents, because they'd stripped his father of his pride, and robbed his mother of every dime.

He'd come too far to change plans now. He was so close to exacting his retribution, and he couldn't start feeling sorry for Sierra. His father deserved retribution for what those lying thieves had done. Sierra was just another tool – and a minor curiosity – nothing more.

∞∞∞∞

Sierra stood outside her father's study and took a few steadying breaths. She was nervous and didn't want to open the door. She still had no clue why her dad wanted to see her, but his formal summons were never good.

With fear practically dripping from her, she slowly pushed the door open and stepped inside the dreadful room. So many horrible events had happened in there. It was the first place he'd backhanded her, causing her to fall to the floor and nearly pass out. She'd worn a bruise on her cheek for over a week.

He'd kept her from school, telling them she'd come down with a nasty flu and he'd make sure homework was done before she came back. He'd threatened even worse punishment if she were to ever tell anyone about the abuse.

She feared him – hated him – and yet, oddly, still loved him. She wanted to get away, but she didn't want terrible things to befall upon him. The odd emotions caused such confusion inside her.

She stepped through the doors, immediately feeling the heavy tension lingering in the room. Her heart pounded as she feared what that would mean for her. She was safe as long as people were in the room, but the second he sent them away...

Sierra felt the shiver from the top of her spine to the bottom of her toes. With stress mounted so high, he'd surely be taking out his aggression on her later. She had to fight back the tears threatening to fall in trepidation of her night ahead.

She didn't even flinch anymore when he raised his hand. She knew there was nothing she could do to stop it, so she tried to let her mind take her somewhere else. Sometimes the beatings weren't as bad as others.

As she glanced around at the familiar faces of her father's employees, her eyes stopped at the couch. She could see the profile of a man she didn't recognize. Maybe he was new, and not working out, and that's why the room seemed so suffocating.

Her father's security detail, consisting of three men in suits, kept glancing nervously at the stranger, which was even more odd. The guy oozed confidence as he sat back in what seemed a casual way.

From the cut of his expensive suit, to the custom made loafers on his feet, even to how his legs were crossed, he seemed like a man not to be messed with. Maybe her father had done a lot of business with him, and that's why he seemed to be the one in charge.

She hadn't even seen his face yet, and still, his intimidation penetrated her skin in an unwelcomed intrusion.

Curiosity began eating at her almost instantly as the need to see his face, to know who he was. She felt somehow like he was her enemy, which made no sense whatsoever. She didn't know him, so how could he be a threat? Another shudder passed through her. Maybe she should listen to her instincts and just run as fast as she could.

Her father would never allow her to do that.

Sierra took a few more steps into the room, finally gaining the notice of the other occupants. She saw the slight movement in the stranger's shoulders as he shifted his weight. Slowly rising to his feet, his every gesture seemingly planned – coordinated.

Though his movement seemed to convey that he wasn't in a hurry, somehow she knew he did nothing without thinking it through, planning ahead with precise calculation.

He turned around and before she could divert her eyes, their gazes locked together. From within her own head, she commanded herself to turn around, dismiss him with nothing more than a look, but she couldn't seem to break the connection.

His gaze held her rooted to the spot, locked tightly to his, his expression almost a command for her to bend to his will.

Nonsense! This is nonsense, her brain was shouting, trying to take control of her frozen limbs.

His lips turned up the slightest fraction of an inch, as he sent a cold, arrogant stare her way. Finally, the egotistical look managed to break her from his spell. While her stomach turned over, and her skin felt like it was on fire, she shifted, glancing at her father, who looked slightly ill.

"Why did you need me, Father? It looks like you're busy," she asked, growing angrier at the breathless weakness in her voice.

Her dad gazed at her for a moment with an odd look in his eyes, one she'd never seen before, almost a look of regret mixed with anger. He said nothing for several seconds, and her annoyance over the spell the stranger had seemed to cast, faded as fear quickly claimed the forefront of her emotions.

Her glance quickly moved from her father, returning to the stranger, and he gazed back at her with a mixture of self-conceit, and something she couldn't identify. His lips contained a smirk that seemed to say he owned the world and could do whatever he pleased. His green eyes held a lifetime worth of knowledge in their depths, and his attitude was that of a man twice his age. She really wanted to know who he was and why he was staring at her as if she were his property to do with as he pleased.

She ripped her gaze back from his mesmerizing eyes to look around the room. None of the other men would meet her gaze. Again, her stare focused back on her dad.

"Take a seat, Sierra," her father eventually commanded, his gaze turning from her. For the first time she could ever remember, he seemed unable to meet her eyes. What was going on?

"But…"

"Sit!" he commanded, his tone that of a man barely holding on to the edge of control. She knew better than to defy him. She quickly sat on the couch the stranger had just vacated. Her legs wouldn't have held her up much longer, anyway.

Before she had a chance to say anything further, she felt movement beside her. She turned her head to stare into the dangerous eyes of the dark haired stranger. Her breath was snatched from her lungs. He was sitting far too close to be appropriate.

She didn't know how close to the mark she truly was in fearing him.

Chapter Five

Damien watched the emotions flicker across Sierra's expression.

Fear.

Anxiety.

Apprehension.

She was afraid, he silently noted. The fear of her father was obvious, but there was more to her story. There was something just below the surface of all the other emotions.

He almost laughed aloud at the thought. He *was* paying money to find out more about Sierra Monroe. Her father was basically selling her to him. Damien was starting to think he was the one who'd gotten the bargain out of the deal. She was even more intriguing up close.

Damien waited for Douglas to introduce them, but the man was silent, so Damien took charge. He wasn't patient and wouldn't wait around wasting any of his valuable time.

"Damien Whitfield," he said with a slight nod.

"Sierra Monroe, though you seem to know that," she said with hesitation. It was obvious she was nervous, not used to being called in to her father's office when he had guests over.

"It's a pleasure to meet you, Ms. Monroe. I'm looking forward to getting...acquainted," Damien told her as he offered his hand. She looked at it with suspicion, but her father had taught her well, because even though it was obvious she didn't want to touch him, she accepted his hand, allowing his large fingers to engulf her delicate hand.

"What do you mean?" she asked, her gaze refusing to meet his. Damien noticed her father's silence as the two of them sat on the couch, almost in a world of their own. He ignored her question.

For all her father knew, Damien wanted Sierra for his own personal sex slave. Damien was disgusted that the man so willingly sold his daughter to the highest bidder. Almost disgusted enough to walk from the room.

Almost.

Not quite.

His eyes took in her petite form, the way her legs were pushed tightly together, how she was twisting her fingers in her lap. When her tongue quickly moistened her surprisingly plump pink lips, he felt a shimmer of desire awaken within him. Surprise filled him.

He narrowed his eyes. This wasn't about desire, and it was best if he remembered that. He got a new employee and an inside connection to the Anderson's. He was glad Douglas had called him. The timing had been impeccable.

With an iron-will that had made him overly successful, he ripped his gaze from her, his attention focusing once more on her father. He looked at the man, waiting for him to inform his daughter of their arrangement.

Damien knew he didn't live in the dark ages. Sierra could refuse to go with him, refuse to be his virtual slave, not that he was telling her that was her job title. He also somehow knew that she wouldn't defy her father. What had him most intrigued was whether her obedience came from loyalty, greed, or fear. He was determined to find out the answer.

With Sierra squirming uncomfortably beside him, he felt an odd stirring of protectiveness rise within him. *No!* He refused to feel any weakness toward the girl. She wasn't some innocent bystander who needed protection. He'd researched her well, and knew she was as good as any other at playing the games of the rich and famous.

He'd seen her on the arm of many influential people. Whether it was her choice, or her father's, she hadn't seemed unhappy to be traipsed around as nothing more than arm-candy for her different escorts.

"Sierra, Mr. Whitfield has offered you a very generous position with his company," Douglas eventually explained. Damien observed the man who showed no emotion as he spoke. He was stone cold as he talked to his daughter, as if she were nothing more than another business transaction.

Well, to be fair, that's what this was for Douglas Monroe – a business deal, where he got a significant sum of money, and Damien got a high-priced…employee.

"What? I…I don't understand…" Sierra stumbled over her words, her voice confused as she looked up, gazing at Damien with shock filled eyes.

"It's very simple. He's in need of a public relations representative, someone who's reliable, trustworthy and free to travel. He only advertised in the most exclusive of listings. He heard about the excellent job you've done with your charity work, and he'd like to hire you. I've accepted on your behalf. The position starts immediately. You should be honored that a man as influential as Damien Whitfield would even consider you for the position, much less hire you, especially with your lack of…experience. Positions like this don't come around often, and they're never just handed over."

Damien didn't like Douglas's underlining threat to his daughter. He was making it more than clear that she would take the job or face his wrath. The authority he used in his voice was unmistakable. Her complete cooperation was his unyielding expectation.

Even though Damien was getting what he wanted, the way Douglas spoke to his daughter infuriated him. He wanted Sierra to stand up for herself, tell her father to 'go to hell', anything other than sit on the couch, looking so defeated.

"Why me? I wasn't looking for work, yet," Sierra said.

"Of course you weren't," Douglas practically snarled as if Sierra were nothing more than a burden. Damien decided it was time to interrupt again.

"I always know what I want, Sierra. Your father contacted me and I've done the research, and decided you'd accommodate my needs perfectly. It's really quite simple." Damien was still as he waited for any kind of reaction from her.

"What if I refuse?" she asked with reserve, her shoulders slouching as she uttered the words.

"Then you'll disappoint me," Douglas said, menace pouring through his words.

Damien watched as a small shudder passed through her. What had her so afraid of her father? Was it a fear of being cut off from her trust? He wanted to believe that, but somehow he doubted his earlier beliefs that she was nothing but a trust-fund baby. It just didn't add up.

"What are the requirements?" This was asked with hesitancy as if she were afraid of the answer.

She should be.

Damien wanted to know how far she was willing to go to secure her funds. He knew what she was truly asking. She wanted to know if he *really* needed an employee, or if he was looking for a mistress.

Let her wonder, he thought.

He slowly lifted his hand and ran his fingers across her cheekbone, pushing fallen strands of her dark hair out of her eyes. Those expressive brown eyes flashed to his own, locking their gazes together as his thumb slid across her moist bottom lip. He pulled his hand back quickly, irritated at his sudden lack of control.

"Anything an assistant is asked to do," he said, his voice showing no emotion as he reined himself back in.

He watched in fascination as her eyes widened. There was fear behind her expressive depths. She was out of her element, looking confused, but he saw a spark of excitement there, too. He watched as she glanced to the ground, placing a mask on her face before she looked back up to her father.

His body hummed as he sat next to her, thought of the possibilities of all the hours they'd work together. He felt an attraction to her that seemed to be growing by the minute. It had been a while since his last arrangement with a woman. He knew better than to get involved with employees, however, Sierra wasn't going to work for him forever.

What would be the harm if they had an affair? He'd still get what he ultimately wanted, and after all, they were both consenting adults...

"I...um...don't think I'm qualified," she said, bringing him back to their conversation. It took him a moment to realize she was talking about the job, not about being his lover. Her tongue slipped out and moistened the corner of her lip, sending a surge of heat though him as his attraction to her took another leap.

"I'll be the judge of that. Personally, I think you're more than qualified," he said, managing to place that hint of steel into his tone that had made dignitaries shake.

His eyes roved across her face, then drifted down the column of her throat to the small opening at the top of her blouse. Her generous curves were heaving up and down as her breath quickened. Whether she was excited about the job, or him, he'd soon find out.

"Go pack a couple of bags while I speak with Mr. Whitfield. He has business in Australia so you'll be leaving straight away," Douglas said, dismissing her from the room as if the deal was done.

Damien tensed, waiting for her reaction. He knew he wasn't leaving that house without her. She was a mystery that had to be solved. His focus was shifting from revenge to desire, which he didn't like, but he knew she'd consume his thoughts if he were to walk away at that point. Once he set his mind on something, he had to see it through. It would become an obsession otherwise.

"I… I haven't decided if I'm taking the job," she protested.

"You'd be a fool not to," Douglas said scornfully. "We'll take care of all the small details. You can run along, now."

Damien's irritation with Douglas was at an all-time high and he was about to say something to him until Sierra slowly stood from the couch, lifted her head high, and walked from the room.

Her father had basically told her that her life was his to command, and she hadn't put up much of a protest at all. She'd almost blindly obeyed him.

Damien stood as he faced Douglas. It appeared all the negative information he'd heard about the man through the years had been accurate.

He hadn't liked, nor respected Douglas before their meeting. Now, he couldn't stand him. He was the worst kind of bottom-feeder. He was willing to sell his own daughter as if she were nothing more than a slave. Damien's respect for Sierra wasn't much higher – she was just as willing to sell herself. *How does someone get to such a point in their life?* he wondered.

There was a voice in the back of his mind countering his thoughts. It was impossible to deny the way she seemed utterly broken, as if her father had somehow bent her will to his command. The way she barely fought back, the slump in her shoulders, the defeated tone she used.

Was all of that fear of losing her home, incurring her father's wrath, or more? One thing Damien knew for sure was that there was a lot more to Sierra than the small glimpse he'd just seen of her. It shouldn't take him too long to unravel the mystery.

"Let's sign the papers," Damien said as he approached Douglas's desk. Damien's face was stoic, giving nothing away. Sitting through the meeting had wreaked havoc on the ghost of a Band-Aid covering his own childhood skeletons. His wounds were now fully exposed, feeling extremely raw. He wouldn't give Douglas even the most fleeting moment of his respect.

It wouldn't take long to figure out Sierra – when she wasn't in the presence of her father.

Damien had an iron-clad contract. If Sierra left his employment before three months was out, all his money would be pulled out of the investment with Monroe Enterprises. Douglas got a third up front, then the rest in three months. Still, if she left, even the initial third would be pulled. If Douglas didn't have the money to re-pay him, Damien would take it any way he could.

Douglas wasn't a stupid man. He'd see very clearly that the contract was impeccably solid. Damien hadn't made his billions by making mistakes.

He watched in disgust as the man signed on the bottom line.

∞∞∞∞

Sierra slumped down on her bed, proud she'd managed to walk from the room without shedding a tear. She didn't understand what had just happened.

As she looked around her room, the realization of her leaving slowly started sinking in. Some of her fear lifted. It was her way out. She was going away – with her father's blessings, which meant he wouldn't be chasing after her.

She didn't understand why he wanted her to go with Mr. Whitfield, and she was terrified of what their deal was really all about, but still... it was freedom.

She wouldn't have to stay in the empty mansion, fearing her father's next drunken rage. She may even be able to spend some time with Bree, get away, live a real life. Maybe this was the beginning of her true liberation.

With fear and uncertainty still coursing through her at her job expectations, as well as excitement to be leaving, Sierra stood and pulled out two suitcases. She started packing clothes, and certain items that actually meant something to her.

She picked up her picture album, the only one she had. She took a moment to open the cover, looking at the picture of her sitting on her mom's lap, their arms wrapped tightly around each other. Each time she looked at the photo she always wondered how differently her life would've turned out had her mother lived.

Would her mom have left her father, taken her daughters away so they could live normal lives? Would she and Sandy get along? Sierra somehow doubted it. If Douglas wouldn't let her leave, she couldn't see him allowing his wife to leave him. He was all about keeping up appearances, and that's exactly what he did, no matter the cost.

She flipped the pages and looked at a picture of her and Bree. She'd go see her soon even if only for a weekend. She shut the cover and carefully placed the album in her bag, then quickly gathered the rest of her belongings she wanted to take.

Sierra's expensive pieces of jewelry were of no interest to her. Douglas had purchased them for high class functions he forced her to attend. He didn't buy them as a reminder of his love for her, but because he had an image to maintain, and he certainly couldn't have his daughter show up to a fundraiser looking anything less than what their family image was. He'd worked hard to create such a facade.

She had few items, considering she was twenty-five years old. Her father didn't buy her gifts, and she wasn't much of a shopper. She had her clothes, her few sentimental keepsakes from her college days, and that was it. She didn't really consider anything else in the room hers.

With what she hoped was a final look at her bedroom, Sierra flicked the switch and bathed her prison in darkness before shutting the door. She pushed down both the fright and elation as she asked one of the servants to help her carry her bags down the stairs.

Chapter Six

Sierra stood next to the stretch limo, unsure of how she should say goodbye to her father. She had to bottle the excitement she was feeling at escaping him. He'd probably strangle her on the spot, if he knew the extent of her elation. She was unsettled about Mr. Whitfield's expectations, though and couldn't keep a bit of that from showing through her otherwise stony expression.

Still, she couldn't push away the thought that she was finally getting away from her father. She hoped and prayed she'd never have to step foot inside his house again.

"I'd like to speak to my daughter alone for a moment," Douglas said as the three of them stood beside the sleek car.

"Make it quick. I have a stop to make before the jet takes off," Damien said as he glanced at his watch. Sierra was blown away with how the man spoke to her dad. She'd never heard anyone act so disrespectful to Douglas Monroe. People normally did everything they could to impress him, practically bowing at his feet.

What surprised her even more was the fact that her father was allowing the insubordination. She almost wanted to hug Damien, she was so happy to see her father taken down a peg.

Before she could feel too smug, her father was gripping her arm tightly as he led her away from the limo. She didn't even cringe as pain shot from where his fingers dug in. The pressure was nothing compared to some of the past abuse he'd inflicted on her.

When they were far enough away that he felt confident in not being overheard, he stopped and turned his back to the limo. He obviously didn't want Damien to see the menace on his face.

"I don't know how long *Damien* will put up with you being his personal escort, but you'd better keep your damn mouth shut about what happens in this house. He's paying a lot more money than your worth for the privilege of your company. Do not disappoint me, or your life won't be worth living. Do you understand me?" he snarled, emphasizing Damien's name like it was a swear word.

Sierra felt bile rise in her throat. She knew her father was evil, how could she not? But, without saying the words, he was telling her she was nothing more than a slave to be traded. She knew he felt nothing but disdain for her, but she'd thought somewhere, maybe deep down inside, that he cared the tiniest bit.

She'd been wrong.

With brief words, he'd explained what was expected of her. She feared there wasn't a job at all. Maybe Damien had just bought her as his mistress. Could she go through with it if that was the case?

The reality was that she probably could. What made the entire matter worse was that she'd rather be this stranger's sex-toy than her father's whipping post. There weren't words to describe the misery coursing through her in that moment.

Only the angst of defying her father kept her standing before him with no expression. She knew better than to show weakness, or release the tears that so desperately wanted to fall. The cost was too great at showing him any emotion.

"I understand, Father. I won't disappoint you," she reluctantly responded. She knew she'd been taking too long to reply, because she saw the twinge in his jaw, her alert that he was losing control.

"Good. Don't forget it. Now, give me a hug to keep up the Monroe image," he commanded, his body stiff as if having to touch her disgusted him.

Obediently, she moved forward, keeping a few inches from touching him, as she carefully wrapped her arms around his shoulders and gave him an awkward hug. He lifted one hand and patted her back, before pushing her away.

To an observer it may have looked like a sad goodbye between a father and daughter, but only if they were far away. Up close, their faces would've given them away. His was filled with loathing, hers filled with resolve.

Sierra once again thought of her mother. How could the woman actually marry such a cruel man, and then make it even worse by having children with him? She'd never do that to a child of hers – not for all the comforts in the world. She didn't want to think her mother had married for money, but she didn't see any other reason anyone would choose to marry Douglas.

Without saying anything further, Douglas turned, knowing she'd follow him, and they walked silently back to the limo where Damien was casually leaning against the door.

"All set?" he asked, his eyes searching her face.

She looked down, unwilling to let the Master-of-Reading-People, read her.

"Of course," she quietly replied.

Damien gave a short shake of his head in a silent command as he glanced to his left. Sierra turned and noticed their driver turn around and head back to the front of the vehicle. Damien then opened the door and motioned for her to climb inside. Without saying anything else to her father, she stepped into the back, and waited for Damien to follow.

He joined her and pulled the door shut. As the car started to move, Sierra looked out the window, watching as her home – prison – started to fade from view.

The fear of Damien faded as pure elation filled her. For a few precious moments she forgot the man across from her and reveled in her liberation.

As she turned her head, a small smile playing on her lips, her eyes connected with the dark green depths of Damien's. Her smile faded as her earlier anxiety rose to the surface. She may be free from her father, but could she have possibly jumped into a fire much worse than the one she'd been in?

A shudder racked her body as his eyes darkened even more, his gaze holding her captive.

∞∞∞∞

With reluctance, Damien pulled his gaze away from Sierra's large, captive eyes. Everything about this woman seemed to rattle him to his very core. She was beautiful, sure, but so were a million other women in the world.

He figured it had to be the mystery surrounding her. He wanted to know the reasons she'd so willingly sacrificed herself. Who would so quickly submit to leaving into the unknown with a stranger? She was either that greedy, or that desperate.

If it was a matter of greed, he knew how to deal with that, but if it was the other... Well, he feared going there, as it brought up too many memories of his own past.

They rode in silence for several minutes as she looked out the window and he examined the set to her shoulders, the way she gazed at the passing scenery as if seeing it for the first time. When he felt the quiet had gone on for long enough, he moved to the small fridge and pulled out a bottle of sparkling water, pouring two glasses.

"Here," he said, holding the crystal out to her. She slowly turned around and looked at his hand as if it would bite her. He found himself wanting to smile, but held back.

He had left her with the impression she was to be basically nothing more than his beck-and-call girl. He understood her hesitancy in accepting anything from him.

"It's not poisoned. I can *almost* guarantee that," he added as he took a sip from his own glass.

"I didn't think it was," she quickly said, as if worried she'd offended him. She reached out and took the glass, bringing it to her lips and taking a small sip as if to please him.

He wanted her to please him – in many erotic ways. His aroused body throbbed as he started picturing a few of the things he'd like to do with her in the very large and private back seat.

Luckily the car ride to Trinity's home wasn't long, and soon the car stopped and Damien sat back while waiting for the driver to open his door. He saw the curiosity on Sierra's face, but he didn't bother explaining what was going on.

His door opened and he gracefully exited the car before holding out his hand to assist Sierra. She looked startled that he was having her come with him. They were at a home, not a business and she didn't see why he'd want her to join him.

"Where are we?" she tentatively asked.

"My friend's home. I promised to stop in before I left. We'll be away for at least two weeks and today is her daughter's birthday party."

"I can wait if you'd like…" she said as she looked at the large house before her.

"No." He gave her no further elaboration as he took her arm, then moved quickly toward the front door.

"Damien Whitfield, you're late," Trinity scolded as she came running down the stairs. "I thought you were going to miss out. Cindi's been asking for you for the past hour."

"I'm sorry, Trin. I got held up." His arms opened and she leapt into them. Seeing Trinity brought warmth to the cold shell around his heart, melting it quickly. She was the only person on the planet he'd drop everything for.

"You can quit pawing all over my wife at any time, now," Drew said as he stood in the doorway with little Joshua sitting on his hip.

"If she wasn't so dang delectable, I may be able to," Damien taunted him. Drew rolled his eyes as he looked over and noticed Sierra standing awkwardly next to the two of them.

"Hi. I'm Trinity, Damien's best friend, though you wouldn't know it since the man never comes to see me anymore. The handsome man up there is my husband, Drew, and he's holding our son, Joshua," Trinity said as she introduced herself and her family.

"I'm Sierra Monroe…uh, Mr. Whitfield's new employee," Sierra said, stumbling over her words a little. Sierra's nervousness could be felt by everyone. Damien felt a bit of guilt over not explaining where they were going.

"Mr. Whitfield. Ha! That's amusing. Don't worry about formalities here. It's a four-year-olds birthday party," Trinity said as she took Sierra's arm in hers and started leading her up the large entrance stairs.

Damien followed behind, not too sure he liked his new employee getting cozy with his best friend. He didn't want his business and personal life to mix. He certainly didn't want his plans for revenge to come anywhere near Trinity. For one thing, she'd throttle him, for another, she'd talk him out of it. He wouldn't be able to stand the conflicting emotions of trying to do the right thing for his deceased mother, and trying not to hurt Trinity.

"Come on Damien. Let's get a drink while the ladies finish setting things up. Don't worry, you're not the last arrival," Drew assured him.

Damien watched as Trinity led Sierra to the kitchen. He shouldn't have brought her to the party. He should've just had the limo drop her at the jet and made her wait on him. He hadn't realized how uncomfortable it would make him to have her alone with Trinity. He should've known she'd try and befriend Sierra. That's just how Trinity was. She instantly liked everyone, and unless they did something to not deserve her trust, she gave everyone the benefit of the doubt.

He accepted a glass of wine from Drew and downed half the glass. He had to refocus and get his head back in the game. He wouldn't let unwanted emotions get in his way.

The Andersons had to pay for what they'd done.

"How's business, Damien?" Derek, Drew's cousin, asked.

"It's been good. I'm heading over to one of my vineyards in Australia right after the party. The land next to my largest property just came up for sale. The man knows I want it so he's trying to charge twice what it's worth. He'll be singing a different tune by the time I leave."

"I have no doubt he will," Ryan piped in with a laugh. Damien figured he'd better tone down his voice. His emotions were a bit out of control.

"I have to say I'm glad you're best friends with my wife, and not a mortal enemy. You tend to get quite the predator's gleam in your eye when you're talking about something you want," Drew said with a laugh.

Drew's cousins both nodded their heads in agreement while joining in the laughter. Damien looked around the room, realizing how uptight he was acting. He forced himself to smile while relaxing his shoulders. He could let down his guard for a couple hours, being among men he trusted.

"I don't know about the rest of you, but I'm starving, and if I'm not mistaken it smells like Jasmine's in the kitchen cooking up something delicious," Damien said as his eyes darted toward the door.

"You'd be correct. Let's drive them crazy until they cave and give us an appetizer," Derek said with a gleam in his eye.

The men walked from the den, letting the incredible aroma filling their nostrils lead the way. When Jasmine cooked, the entire neighborhood opened their windows just to get a sniff.

"Smells delicious, Honey. I could smell it all the way in the den," Derek said as he wrapped his arms around his petite wife.

"Are you trying to sneak some food by shamelessly flattering me?" she asked as she turned and kissed him on the chin.

"Of course not. I just couldn't seem to resist touching you," he quickly replied as his hands moved down her back and quickly swatted her butt.

Damien shifted on his feet, the moment feeling awkward as he watched the two of them flirt.

"I thought this was a children's party, not a swinger's festival," Damien said, trying to break up the intimate scene.

"Damien," Trinity scolded him, but there was a smile across her lips.

"Fine, you boys can have a snack, but you have to either go back to the den or out by the pool," Nicole jumped in. "Seriously, Jasmine, behave. You're making me want to drag my husband to the nearest bedroom."

"I'm okay with that," Ryan quickly said with a predatory gleam in his eyes.

"Don't you dare touch me, Ryan Titan. If you do, the kids will never get their cake," Nicole said as she darted around the kitchen island.

"Fine, we'll go," Derek said with reluctance as he pulled away from his flushed wife.

"See you soon," Trinity called as she blew a kiss to Drew.

Before the men walked outside, Damien looked toward Sierra who was refusing to meet his gaze. Surprise filled him as shimmers of desire shot down his stomach. He found himself wanting to grab her chin and force her gaze to meet his. A need to taste her lips, experience her unique flavor was almost overwhelming. He found he liked the confusion of the foreign desire.

For a man who was known for his impeccable control, it was a unique feeling to experience the uncharacteristic emotions overpowering him.

"I could use a beer," Damien said as Drew prodded him in the arm. He followed Trinity's husband and the other men as they stepped outside into the cool evening air.

"You know where to get them," Drew replied. Damien headed straight for the outdoor fridge and grabbed a bottle of dark liquid, quickly unscrewing the top and taking a long swallow. The icy drink felt good going down, internally turning down his escalating temperature.

"So, are you going to tell us about the sexy new employee?" Ryan asked with a laugh.

"Nope," Damien quickly replied as he took another long swallow.

"Hmm, interesting," Drew said with a smirk.

"Nothing interesting at all," Damien replied with a glare.

"Yeah, I know that look. It seems Sierra may be more than just a new employee," Ryan taunted.

"Not at all. There's just nothing to tell. I've actually only met her today."

"Come on, Damien. Sparks are sizzling between the two of you. You may have just met her, but that's not stopping your mind from stripping her naked in my kitchen," Drew said with a knowing smile.

"Mind your own damn business, Drew," he snapped.

"All right. I'm done," Drew told him while holding his hands up in surrender.

"I think I'm going to take a swim and cool off," Derek interrupted as he moved to the pool house. To Damien, the thought of swimming until exhaustion overrode his hormones sounded like the perfect solution, so he walked in the direction of the pool with Derek.

∞∞∞∞

"Spill the gossip, Sierra. How long have you known Damien? I'm not trying to hurt your feelings if it's been a while, but usually he tells me everything and he hasn't mentioned having such a gorgeous employer," Trinity said as soon as the guys were out of earshot.

Sierra instantly turned red, hating how she was so easily embarrassed. Other than Bree, she didn't have girlfriends to talk to, so she was on unfamiliar territory with the whole gossip thing.

"I was just hired today," she finally answered.

"Today? And you're already going to Australia with him. Mmm, that's a long jet ride. A lot can happen," Jasmine said with an exaggerated wink. Sierra flushed even more.

"It's not like that," Sierra quickly replied, hoping they'd drop it.

"No way. I saw him watching you. His body was tense, and his eyes were practically stripping you where you stood," Trinity said with a giggle.

"Mmm, agreed. We didn't even need to turn the oven on to boil the water," Nicole added.

Sierra didn't want to say how close to right they may actually be. He may have hired her for nothing but a call-girl. He'd be disappointed if that's what he was after.

"Honestly, I swear it's not like that," Sierra said, but as the women laughed, she couldn't help but smile with them. Her fear was quickly evaporating in light of Damien's choice of friends. He couldn't be too terrible of a man if he associated with such good people.

"You do think he's hot, right?" Trinity asked, her gaze boring into Sierra, not allowing her to lie.

"I *am* human. It's pretty hard not to notice he's a bit better looking than the average guy. Then again, all your husbands are on an equally sizzling scale, so I think it may just be that this house has some incredibly good lighting," Sierra said with a giggle.

"Ah, great come-back. No, it's certainly not the light. Those men are definitely drool-worthy. Seriously, though, they have hearts of gold – each one of them," Trinity said, her eyes softening as she talked about the men she loved.

"I'm sure they do," Sierra replied, a bit envious at the connection these women shared with not only their husbands, but each other, as well.

"Okay, we promise not to grill you anymore tonight, but only *if* you swear to tell us if anything does occur on that lengthy flight," Jasmine said as she pulled a tray of sizzling meat from the oven.

"Deal," Sierra promised, feeling confident there wouldn't be anything to tell.

Chapter Seven

"What exactly am I supposed to be doing for you?" Sierra asked as they buckled their seatbelts and prepared for take-off. She wasn't a fan of flying and hoped he'd at least speak to her, take her mind off the fact that soon they'd be flying over the ocean for the next fifteen or so hours.

She'd been in awe of his private jet, which had luxuriously soft carpet, a comfortable seating area, two bedrooms, full-sized bathroom, and a kitchen. Her father had a company jet, but it paled in comparison to Damien's. She felt like she'd stepped into a whole other world.

"My corporation has various arms to it – investments in multi-billion dollar properties throughout the world, exports to and from many countries, and most importantly, wine. My vineyards are my passion. I take pride in creating a superior product. The most elite wine connoisseurs are on waiting lists for my best products. I have various P.R. Reps, but only one who travels with me as I close deals. The rest are stationed in different countries and do what needs to be done year round."

"That didn't answer my question. What is *my* job?" Sierra said with some frustration.

"Your job is to do whatever I need you to do," he said, his gaze connecting with hers. A shiver ran down her spine at the look in his eye.

"I'm exhausted. My world has been flipped upside down. This morning I woke up after a long and grueling week, only to be told I've been hired for a position I didn't apply for. I'm not complaining, I'd just like to know what that position is, exactly. Do I type up papers, file documents, take notes? What are my daily tasks?"

"Yes to all of the above, along with a lot of research. I'll go over more of what I need you to do when we land. My week has also been exhausting and I have a lot to get done on our trip. Taking the time to find a new employee is always frustrating, but I don't trust anyone else to hire certain positions, especially the placements where the employee will spend a lot of time with me. You'll have access to a lot of personal data, and I take that seriously. After take-off, why don't you go try and get some sleep. I have work to do and don't have time to visit," Damien said, dismissing her.

Sierra felt her temper flare. She was sick of men telling her what to do, expecting her to bend to their will. She was sick of being a punching doll, whether mentally or physically. Fine. If he didn't want to explain her duties, then she'd just enjoy the ride and explore the island of Australia. It didn't really matter to her one way or the other. At least she was away from her father.

Once the captain cleared them to remove their seat-belts, Sierra got up and walked down the plush hallway to the smaller of the two rooms. Inside was a double bed with the blankets turned back, inviting her to lie down.

She opened a door and found a small bathroom, which even included a shower. She made use of the facilities, then laid down, not expecting to catch any sleep.

Sierra woke up, slowly rising to a sitting position. She rubbed her eyes before glancing at the clock, shocked when she noted the time. She'd slept for ten hours straight. How had she managed that? She couldn't remember ever sleeping that long. Maybe it was because of their high elevation, or possibly the stress of the last few weeks catching up with her, but whatever it was, she felt better than she had in a long time.

She climbed out of bed, taking a minute to stretch her stiff muscles. After once again using the small, but nice bathroom, she made her way back out to the front of the jet.

Sierra stood in the dim light of the aircraft as she entered the main cabin area. Damien was in the same seat she'd left him in, but his head was leaned back against the soft back, his eyes closed as he gently breathed in and out.

She took a moment to glance over his softer features. He really was quite handsome, even more so without his eyes shooting sparks at her. He had a five-o-clock shadow shading his jaw, and the top two buttons were undone on his shirt, showing just a hint of the toned flesh beneath the stark white fabric.

She found herself wanting to reach out and run her finger across the opening, see if his skin felt as silky as it looked. Her eyes traveled down his body, the strong, wide shoulders, defined arms stretching the fabric of his shirt. She moved lower, past the flatness of his stomach to where his shirt was still tucked into his custom fitted slacks. He'd removed his belt, and like his shirt, the top button of his pants was undone. Her eyes were drawn to the button-hole, her fingers almost itching to reach out and tug on his zipper.

With a shake of her head, she pulled her gaze back up, and collided with his now open eyes.

"Have a good look? Would you like me to stand, maybe remove some clothes?" he mocked her sleepily, causing her face to turn scarlet. She *had* been ogling him, though, and deserved his snide remark.

"I just…uh, well, I thought I saw a bug," she said, trying to come up with a reasonable explanation of why she was looking at the juncture of his thighs.

"A bug?"

He could've been a gentleman and just let it go, but she was quickly learning that Damien Whitfield was the furthest thing from a gentleman.

"Yes, a bug," she said with more conviction. It may be a stupid lie, but it was hers, and she was going to own it.

"Take a seat. I'll have Amber bring out a menu," he said as he stood. She was rooted to the spot when he reached his arms above his head and stretched, his hands touching the ceiling of the jet, his shirt pulling tautly against his torso.

The man should be on magazine covers, not sitting behind a desk.

"Is there another bug…Sierra?" he whispered as he stepped closer.

It took a second for his words to compute in her brain. She didn't bother replying, just quickly scurried away and plopped down in a chair as far from his as possible.

It didn't help her nerves when she heard him chuckling as he walked away to his private bedroom.

The rest of the flight went surprisingly fast. Damien ate dinner with her, or at least she was assuming it was dinner. Her body was already turned upside down with traveling through so many different time zones. After their meal of delicious food, and ridiculously polite small-talk, he went back to work and she watched a couple movies.

She wouldn't have minded helping him, but she didn't want to start the whole "job" discussion again. That could wait until they were on solid ground.

As they began their descent, Sierra's eyes were glued to the window. She looked out, beaming with joy that it was daylight and the sky was clear. She had a perfect view of the famous Sydney Harbor. It was all she could do to stop herself from clapping with excitement. She didn't want her new boss to think her too much of a child.

They landed safely, allowing Sierra to breathe a huge sigh of relief, and before she knew it, they were stepping off the jet. A warm breeze blowing against her skin was a welcome and surprising relief. It was the beginning of December, freezing back home, but here it was warm, sunny, and just about perfect.

She hadn't thought about the season's being reversed. She was itching to explore the area, but she'd wait and take cues from Damien. She didn't know if they were going to immediately get to work or not.

"This way," Damien said, placing his hand on the small of her back, leading her to an awaiting limo. The man sure liked his long cars. She found it humorous, but managed to somehow keep her laughter to herself.

They quickly traveled from the airport and she drank in as much of the bustling city as she could through the tinted windows of the large car. Too soon they were pulling up to a stunning hotel.

"Where are we?" she asked with awe. The seemingly endless building was stunning.

Her father was a wealthy man, wealthier than most, but she hadn't traveled the world with him, hadn't gotten to experience the same privileges her sister had. It was a real treat to visit Australia and stay in such a luxurious hotel.

"This is the Park Hyatt," he answered her matter-of-factly. He seemed slightly bored. Sierra couldn't imagine ever getting to a point in her life where coming to such a beautiful place would seem boring to her.

A doorman was instantly at their car, holding the door open for them. Sierra took his hand as she stepped from the limo, her eyes wide as she looked up at the impressive entrance to the five-star-hotel.

Damien joined her, then placing his hand on her back again, guided her inside. She looked around the incredible lobby, as she followed beside him. She didn't hear his conversation with the staff, but soon they were riding in an elevator, and walking down a beautifully decorated hallway.

The bellman assisting them slid his card through the key card slot in their door and they walked inside a massive suite with floor to ceiling windows seemingly everywhere. She walked over to them and looked down at a perfect view of the famous opera house. Maybe she'd be able to attend a show. Oh, how she hoped so!

The room was spacious, with work areas, a kitchen, bar, luxury bathrooms, even a baby grand piano. She didn't understand the need for such a large room for just the two of them, but she wasn't going to complain.

Within minutes of arriving, Damien told her to order what she'd like for food, and then he disappeared into the office, shutting the door behind him. She stood there, feeling out of sorts.

Not knowing what else to do, Sierra ordered room service, then settled in on one of the comfortable couches to watch the huge screen television. She fell asleep not long after picking at her meal and setting it aside.

Chapter Eight

Sierra looked at the outside of the tall building and felt her stomach drop. What was she doing? She should just turn around and go back to their hotel suite. She had no business being there.

She was tired of sitting in the interminable room. She loved the suite, especially the deep tub in the bathroom, and twenty-four hour room service. The room was stunning, beyond luxurious, and she'd taken advantage of just about every spa service the hotel offered, but still, she wanted to explore, not stay indoors.

Damien had been gone constantly, telling her to wait for him, that he'd have work for her soon, but a week had passed and it was getting ridiculous. She was going to confront the man. He either needed to give her some work, let her act like a tourist, or else let her fly back home to the states.

There was no way she wanted to go back to her father's empty home. The longer she was away, the more sure she was of that fact. She wanted to go and visit Bree, maybe even take her best friend up on her offer of a place to stay until she got on her feet.

The longer Sierra was around Damien, the more sure she was that his P.R. position was nothing more than a smoke screen. At least she was sure he didn't want her as his mistress as he hadn't made a single advance toward her since they'd arrived. She felt an odd pang at the thought.

No, she urged herself. She didn't want to be any man's plaything. But still, Damien was just so virile, it was hard for her not to want to run her hands along his incredible form. Only a blind woman could miss his flawless body, but loss of sight wouldn't be enough to keep lust away in his presence.

No, even the sound of his voice, rich, deep and so dang masculine could melt a girl, turning her into a puddle at his feet. She was in trouble and she certainly didn't want to feel that way. She'd felt too many negative emotions her entire life. She felt like it was her time to grow, live – really experience life to the fullest. She'd been a prisoner her entire life, and now she looked at her future in a whole different way. It was a feeling of true liberation, unlike anything else, and it was far overdue for her to spread her wings and fly.

With a lot of finagling, and bribery, Sierra had finally managed to figure out where Damien was on this particular day. She was now standing in front of the building he was inside and she found herself terrified of walking in the huge double doors and confronting him.

Dang it, though, if he wasn't going to have her doing a job, then he should at least have the decency to let her fly home. If he didn't say anything, her father wouldn't even know she was back in the States, and that would give her more time to build up her courage, find the will to stop fearing him.

Damien was at some sort of guy spa or gym. Heck, she didn't know, but it had been like pulling teeth to get the information out of the hotel staff. Finally, one of the desk operators had taken pity on her and disclosed his location.

He'd warned her it wouldn't be easy to get in and see Damien. He'd also made her promise not to tell where she'd gotten the information. Every time she called Damien, it went immediately to voicemail, so she was out of options. It was either this or, well, she didn't really have an 'or' in mind.

She looked at the security cameras lined up along the roof eaves, and the solid glass doors in front of her. She was waiting for the national guard to come storming out and haul her away, somehow knowing she didn't belong there, even though technically, she did have a lot of her own money.

The money didn't do her any good, though, when she wasn't allowed to touch it. Maybe she should've dressed a bit better, at least. She'd just thrown on a pair of old jeans and a sweatshirt. She hadn't seen the point in wearing business attire. She hadn't been doing any business.

With a final breath of courage she approached the doors and stepped inside. Her intake of air was quickly let out as she glanced around the ostentatious spa. There were several well-outfitted men sauntering the premises, a couple of them glancing in her direction as they moved about, but what really caught her attention were the furnishings.

A beautiful fountain sat centered in the lobby with cushioned benches surrounding it. The floor was done in a marble tile, patterned with small animals throughout it. Huge plants were strategically placed, making a person feel as if they'd just walked into an exclusive hotel.

Though she'd been raised in a life of wealth, her father hadn't let her go anywhere he didn't specifically plan out. While most of the kids she'd gone to school with had been going to spas from the time they could barely walk, she was lucky to have a person come to the house to trim her hair.

Her father had told her when she was young that it was because he was protecting her, but the older she became, the more she realized it was really to protect *himself.* The more he kept her home, the more control he had over her, and the less likely she was to spill his secrets.

She'd only been allowed in the public eye with dates he'd set up, and she'd only been allowed out when he deemed it necessary. As she looked around the room, anger burned inside her over what she'd missed out on.

No wonder the girls from school had glowed after a spa weekend. It was the ultimate in opulence. Her week of indulgence had shown her she deserved to have a few luxuries in life. She'd gone through enough that she shouldn't feel the least guilt over taking a day each month to pamper herself.

Sierra shook off her melancholy thoughts, and reminded herself to focus. If she could go back home and visit Bree, she'd have the elbowroom she needed. Bree loved a day at the spa. Sierra now wished she'd actually gone with her friend when she'd had the chance. She'd wasted her small time of free rein when she'd been in college, her fear of her father carrying too much weight, even from a distance.

Sierra glanced at the front desk where immaculately dressed men and women stood watching her approach. One of the women managed to actually tilt her nose in the air while still looking down it at Sierra. She didn't care what the snobby woman thought. She was comfortable with what she was wearing, even if the bleached blonde didn't approve.

"Are you lost?" one of the fake-and-bake guys asked her when she stood there gaping at them. *If Ken and Barbie were to come to life, this is what they'd look like*, she thought in fascination.

"No, actually. My boss is here and I need to speak with him," Sierra said, happy with the confidence echoing in her tone. She didn't feel all that confident, but she was used to faking her emotions to create her desired effect.

"Sorry, darling. We have a 'do not disturb' policy that's strictly in effect. If your boss wanted to see you, then he'd have left you with a number. Even employers need time to themselves," one of the girls said, as if Sierra were nothing more than an annoyance in her otherwise perfect day.

"Thank you for visiting our spa. Now, please exit the way you came in. Have a wonderful day," Mr. Ken doll said before turning his back and continuing his conversation with another employee.

Sierra felt like steam was coming out of her ears. She was normally calm, almost submissive, but she'd had enough. Her dad walked all over her, her sister treated her like she was there to serve her, Damien acted like she didn't exist, and now real life Barbie dolls were dismissing her. She was done.

Squaring her shoulders, Sierra stepped closer to the desk and slapped her hand down on the polished surface, making one of the girls jump. The four employees standing there slowly turned with eyes of astonishment, as if no one ever challenged them behind the desk.

"Look. I'm tired, not thrilled about having to be here, and getting more irritated by the minute. Why don't you stop acting like there's a stick shoved up your ass, and make yourself useful by doing your job. I need to speak with Damien Whitfield immediately. It's urgent," Sierra said, taking time to look each person in the eye.

She felt a stirring of pride as she watched the shock enter their faces at the authority in her tone. For being a door-mouse for too many years, she was sure making up for lost time. She had to fight back the smile wanting to break free at the surge of adrenaline rushing through her.

Barbie doll number two was the first to break eye contact as she took a step back, then whispered something to one of the guys, who then turned slightly toward her so they could have a quiet discussion.

"Could you tell us what this is about?" the guy asked when they were finished.

"It's none of your business, but I will tell you *this*. Mr. Whitfield doesn't like to be kept waiting."

Sierra really hoped Damien didn't tell them to throw her out on her butt, making her look like a complete fool. If he did, she was done, fear of her father, or no fear. She was tired of being humiliated. It had to stop at some point.

"Fine, I'll go speak to Mr. Whitfield personally, and tell him he has a… guest out front. Please go sit over there," Barbie number one finally said before pointing at benches off in the corner, out of view of the front doors.

Sierra fought back a smile as she turned and walked to the benches. *So this is what it feels like to win a small victory*, she thought. They obviously couldn't have someone looking so raggedy out in the public view. What would their rich clients think about that?

Sierra took a seat and picked up one of the magazines lying on the table. She started flipping through pages, glancing at the latest fashions. She'd never really cared, not even being allowed to pick out the majority of her clothes. Her father had felt he was far more qualified to choose for her.

Sierra hadn't really thought to argue with him about it until later in life, then she'd been too afraid. Her sister had never had the same issues with their dad. He'd spoiled Sandy, giving her whatever she wanted.

She'd been one of the girls going to the spas with girlfriends, and getting new clothes practically every other month. She'd been daddy's little girl, while Sierra had been daddy's whipping post. The more she thought about it, the angrier she became.

How dare he do that to her! With growing confidence and rage, a shiver of alarm still traveled down her spine. What if she was sent back to him? What if her dad somehow was able to hide her away? She couldn't let that happen. She wouldn't. She'd rather die.

She remembered the day he told her why he wouldn't let her leave, why she had to pay him back for her mother's sins. It had been a dark and terrible day.

Apparently, her mother had been extremely unhappy during their marriage, telling Douglas she was going to leave him. She found out a few weeks later she was pregnant. Instead of being elated of her pregnancy, he'd been jealous, claiming she must've had an affair. They fought about her, her mother swearing she'd been faithful, and Douglas insisting she'd cheated.

It hadn't helped that Sierra looked like her mother, while a few years later Sandy had been almost a twin of their father. It seemed Sandy's birth confirmed his suspicions that Sierra wasn't his. He'd been humiliated; not wanting anyone to know his wife would dare cheat on him.

Her father had felt it almost a duty to sleep with as many women as possible, throwing it in their mother's face. He'd told her she could leave, but he'd never allow her to take the girls with her. She'd vowed to the end that Sierra was his child, but Sierra figured death had been a welcome relief out of the hell her mother's life had become.

With how much her father hated her, Sierra figured he'd be happy to have her leave, but instead of pushing her out, it had become his life's obsession to make her pay for what he deemed as her mother's infidelity, so instead of kicking her out of his home, he'd refused to let her leave - refused until Damien Whitfield had shown up.

Now that Sierra had a glimpse of freedom, there was no going back. She refused to allow Douglas Monroe any further power over her. With new resolve, she waited for Damien. It was time to let him know she wasn't going to take being anyone's whipping post ever again. She refused to allow the man to try and bring her down with his cold stares, and ridiculous requests.

Sierra heard a movement and turned to find Damien standing before her. Her mouth gaped open in shock. He was wearing a low slung towel wrapped around his waist, water dripping down his rock solid chest and six-pack abs. She couldn't even manage to bring her eyes past his incredible athletic build to see the expression on his face.

She was sure the man was irritated about obviously being interrupted, and she knew she should meet his gaze, but instead she continued to stare with utter reverence and awe at the work of art before her.

She heard him clear his throat, and it was just what her brain needed to become un-frozen. Quickly closing her mouth, she drew her eyes up the additional eight or so inches to meet his eyes. She was right, he wasn't happy.

"Is something wrong? An employee told me you were demanding to see me, refusing to leave," Damien said as his eyes looked over her. "You don't seem unwell," he finished accusingly.

Sierra frantically searched for her voice, coming up with nothing. Damien Whitfield was extremely attractive on a normal day, but with water dripping off him, and his hair tousled, he was downright devastating. She felt instant desire heating her stomach, the sensation foreign, but not altogether unwelcome. She curled her toes, trying to pull herself together.

Before this moment, Sierra really had thought she may be broken from all the years of abuse. She'd never felt desire toward a man, not even her ex-boyfriend, never wanted to reach up and run her tongue down a guy's glistening chest, like all her college friends would brag of doing. She found herself wanting to taste his hardened nipples, test them, see if they were salty or sweet. Sweat broke out on her forehead and she still hadn't said a word, stretching the awkward silence beyond the point of no return.

"Sierra!"

"What? You don't have to shout," she finally whispered, her voice sounding far too husky, even to her own ears.

"Obviously I *do* need to shout, as it seems you've lost the ability to speak. From what Kendra was saying, you were speaking just fine earlier," he snapped.

"Oh," she replied, forgetting why she'd even come to the spa.

"Look, Sierra. I don't have time to stand here and play guessing games. You can either tell me what you need, or I can turn around and head back in. I work hard, and when I get five minutes to work-out, I like to do so uninterrupted. That's already been ruined for the day, so I'd at least like to get back to my swim."

"I want to leave," she said, her voice a bit stronger.

"Then leave. I didn't ask you to come here," he said in exasperation as if the matter was settled.

"I didn't ask to be here," Sierra snapped, jumping to her feet and pushing her fingernail into his chest to make a point. "I'm sitting around all day and night, doing nothing but twiddling my thumbs while you're out having the time of your life. Fine. I really don't care what the heck you do, but I do care about my time, and it's being wasted in that hotel. I want to go home, now," she demanded.

Damien's eyes narrowed to dangerous slits, and Sierra felt a moment of dread. His hand moved and she fought the flinch, proud of herself for her control when she did nothing but stand strong, holding her ground, looking him in the eye.

He finished lifting his hand, running it through his wet strands and she breathed an internal sigh of relief as her stomach loosened from the knot it had instantly tied itself into.

"Follow me," he commanded as he started to move toward one of the 'oh so exclusive' doors.

Sierra couldn't stop herself from smirking at Barbies one and two as she followed Damien inside the exclusive spa.

"I think it would've been easier to get to you at Fort Knox," Sierra muttered after they passed through to the other side of the gym.

"There's a reason it's hard to get in here. The members don't want to be interrupted. Maybe you should've considered that before being so rude and rushing down here."

Sierra ignored his comment as she looked around the place. He led her to a small fruit bar. She'd heard her sister talking about the amazing shakes they made from all fresh ingredients. Suddenly she realized she hadn't eaten anything since early morning, and she felt her stomach begin to growl as she smelled something delicious in the air.

She glanced up, hoping to spot the juice bar, when her eyes landed on his back. She lost her breath as her heart pounded. She didn't think it possible, but he was even sexier from behind. His wide shoulders looked strong, sure, able to hold a woman against a wall as he slowly pressed his body against her...

The thought sent a shiver of delight through her. Since he couldn't see her ogling him, she let her eyes drift down his tapered waist, the muscles of his back flexing as he moved his arms, his body in perfect symmetry as he practically glided across the floor.

She so badly wanted to move closer, wrap her arms around his waist, run her fingers along all that tanned expanse of skin. What he was doing to her was unbelievable. He walked with confidence, but also with grace and agility. She'd bet her inaccessible trust fund, he made love the same way, confident, strong, in-control, and with a smooth technique guaranteed to send a woman over the edge.

She'd heard every story out there during her college days. Some of her roommates would come back complaining their boyfriend had finished in two minutes, only to leave her unsatisfied and in a hurry to get home so she could finish on her own.

It was the other stories, the ones where the girls were still well-sated as they practically floated into the dorm rooms, their eyes dreamy, their faces glowing. Those stories had awakened her curiosity and made her possibly consider the thought of having sex someday. With her ever-growing attraction toward Damien, she was thinking she'd prefer trying it real soon.

Sierra moved her eyes over the stark white towel that was gripping his perfectly proportioned hips, hugging the curve of his solid butt. Her fingers itched to reach out and slowly slide over him, to see if he was as solid as he looked. She continued her gaze onto his muscular calves, appreciating the way they flexed with each step.

They arrived at the juice bar, and Sierra quickly looked away, not wanting him to catch her gaping at him. She felt her face heat, but hoped the dimmer light of the bar would cover up her embarrassment.

The small area was chic, but with a sense of comfort, too, as tables were artfully arranged to give members privacy. Damien led her to a corner booth and motioned for her to sit.

"Are you thirsty?"

"Yes, and starving."

He raised a brow in question at her answer. Maybe she'd spoken out of turn, but how was she expected to concentrate on her words if she was focused on her stomach.

"Do you want anything in particular?" he asked, his tone slightly annoyed. In a moment of surprise, Sierra realized she really didn't care. She was just excited to have found the assertive woman she always wanted to be, but never could find within.

"It doesn't matter, really. Anything solid to eat, and if they have a banana-strawberry smoothie, that would be excellent."

"I'll check," he answered stiffly before turning around and walking to the counter.

Sierra sat back and looked around, watching as different members approached the bar and made their orders. A few of the girls, wearing work-out clothes that could barely be considered legal, made sure to stand extra close to Damien while ordering. Sierra watched while they fluttered their eyes at him.

She was shocked by the tiniest spark of jealousy that flared inside her. She'd never felt the emotion before. She had no reason to feel that way. He wasn't her boyfriend; she didn't even know him, much less like him.

It had to be the different time zone affecting her. She was still off kilter. After she ate something, she'd get back to feeling normal. She sat back and waited for Damien to return, taking a few minutes alone to try and clear her head.

When he turned back toward her and his gaze caught hers, she knew she was in trouble. Her heart rate increased, and from his predatory expression, he could smell her desire like a lion smells its next kill.

This wasn't good. Not one little bit.

Chapter Nine

Damien had been avoiding Sierra most of the week, and then she had the gall to hunt him down. He was tired, irritable and frustrated.

All week he'd been behaving as if he were a teenager out with a date for the first time. He would walk into their large suite, and instantly smell her perfume. She was always in bed by the time he got in, and he made sure he was gone before she woke, but he could still *feel* her there, know she was only a door away from him.

It was playing hell with his senses, and he hadn't slept more than a couple hours each night since they'd arrived. His plan was supposed to be simple, easy. It was anything but.

He had a feeling nothing was going to be easy as far as Sierra was concerned. He made his way back to their table and set the tray down, watching with amusement as she picked up the drink and took a deep swallow.

His amusement quickly fled when she groaned, the sound sending a sharp pain straight to his groin. Was she doing it on purpose? Did he simply need to take her back to their room and relieve the ache for both of them?

"This is great! Thanks," she said with a huge smile, her entire face lighting up. She set the drink down and grabbed ahold of the sandwich. She took a bite, and once again groaned, further hardening his previous reaction.

He shifted uncomfortably in his seat, grateful for the towel covering him.

"Whenever you're ready," he said, his tone thick.

"One sec," she mumbled around her bite. She finished chewing and took another deep swallow of the shake. "This really is great. I didn't realize how hungry I was."

"Anything else I can do for you?" he mocked dryly.

His bad attitude bounced right off her. She finished half her sandwich before coming up for air. While she was eating, he grabbed his gym bag and slipped a shirt over his head and a pair of athletic pants on under his towel. His shorts were still wet, but he was tired of the women slowing as they passed his table. He didn't have time for it. Besides, Sierra had all his attention at Present.

"Okay, I don't know what the whole deal is with you insisting on hiring me, but I'm obviously not qualified for the position as you haven't had me do a single thing. I wouldn't normally complain about a trip to Australia, but considering I haven't gotten to do or see anything, it's not much different than being back home. Why don't you just let me fly home while you finish up here? I can go stay with my best friend for a few days, or a week, and then when you return to the states, you can decide if you still want to employ me."

Damien instantly tensed. On one hand what she was suggesting was perfect. She'd go running to Brianne Anderson, where he could then come and get her. He'd show up at the door, and they'd never be the wiser that they were allowing the enemy free access of their home.

On the other hand, he found himself not wanting her to leave. He didn't understand why. She was right, he'd done nothing but avoid her all week. It was true that he was busy, but he could have brought her to the office with him so she could at least begin learning how to do her job.

He figured after a week, his strange pull toward her would be gone, if not extremely dim. He was wrong, each day only made him seem to desire her more.

"That doesn't work for me," he heard himself saying.

"Why not?"

"I hired you for a job. I need you to stay here."

"What the heck is my job, then - to keep anyone from breaking into your hotel suite? If that's the case, I'm telling you, the security at that hotel is excellent. Your clothes will be just fine with or without me there."

"There's no need to be a smart ass, Sierra," he said in a tone of steel. She didn't even flinch.

"I don't know what way to *be* because you haven't given me the time of day since we landed. All I have is a short job description. Some people may love getting paid for nothing, but I'm not one of them. I'm bored and don't see any point in being here when I kept myself busy enough doing volunteer work before your job offer," she said, not backing down.

He was impressed.

"I've already told you. Your job is to assist me..." he said, making sure to pause just long enough to make her wonder.

She glared at him, reading his message loud and clear.

"I have no idea what's going on between you and my father, but I'm a human being, Mr. Whitfield. I deserve to be treated with dignity and respect, and if you want me to work for you, then you should at least give me tasks to complete.

Damien sat back, liking the fire in her eyes and the way she almost growled his name. There were images in his mind of many things he'd like her to do for him, none of them appropriate, none of them having anything to do with *public* relations.

His body tightened more as he took in her flushed cheeks and the rapid movement of her chest as her breathing sped up in her agitation. With all her pent up passion and anger, she had be incredible in the bedroom.

They could use those emotions for much better uses than fighting.

"Fine. You want to work. We'll start tonight," he said in a whisper, his throat suddenly dry.

His tone did the trick. She leaned back, her eyes widening as she looked at him warily. Good. She needed to be wary of him. He was hanging on by a thread and it wasn't going to take much to push him over the cliff – let all rationale fly out the window.

"What exactly do you have in mind?" she asked as she picked up her cup, her fingers slightly shaking. He ignored her question as his mind drifted.

Nothing she could do at that moment was going to lessen the desire coursing through him. He wanted her and now that he had that on his mind, he was fixated on it. He was picturing her lying beneath him, a moan of pleasure escaping her lips as he slowly sank himself deep inside her slick folds.

He could practically taste the softness of her lips; feel the tightness of her body gripping him. He wanted out of the spa and back in their room.

It wouldn't change anything if they slept together. His plan wouldn't be altered. He'd just feel a lot more satisfied, and be able to focus. *Yes*, he reasoned with himself, taking her to bed was the smart thing to do. He'd rid himself of the mystery of her.

It was really quite brilliant of him. He saw the hunger in her eyes, the longing in their depths. He noticed how she kept glancing at his chest, the way her tongue would nervously moisten her soft pink lips.

She was hungry – for far more than just food. They were consenting adults and there was just no use in them suffering, when they could both so easily relieve each other's pain.

Yes, he relaxed as he made up his mind. His previous thought of getting his workout was long forgotten as his eyes focused on her. Once he made a decision, he didn't go back on it. Sierra Monroe would be his – soon.

"Wait here, I need to change. These clothes are already damp from my wet shorts," Damien curtly spoke, before he quickly got up and left.

Chapter Ten

"You drive. I have some work I need to finish," Damien said as he tossed her the keys.

Sierra thought about protesting since he was arrogant enough to demand she drive for him instead of politely asking her.

She looked at the shiny red convertible and her eyes widened in excitement. The site of the car encouraged her to suck up her pride and climb inside the driver's door. She'd never driven such a fun car before.

She turned the key and the motor purred to life in the sleek mustang. She knew the car was actually a cheaper rental for him, but to her it was a fine piece of machinery.

She threw the gear shift into drive and quickly pulled out of the spa parking lot. She couldn't help the laughter that spilled out as the wind whipped through her hair. What a fun time she could have exploring the island if only he'd let her borrow the car while he was at his endless meetings. She wouldn't be so anxious to leave if she got to play a little.

With a frown, Sierra slowed for a red light, almost pouting as she had to stop her acceleration.

"Can we take a drive around the island before going back to the hotel?" she asked. She hated to beg, but she was willing to do it to feel the exhilaration of fresh air blowing through her hair.

"I have a lot of work to do," he told her in an annoyed tone.

"Can I drop you off then and go explore for a while?" she asked, trying to sound pleasant, but thinking it wasn't coming across that way by the glare he sent her.

"It's not safe for you to be out driving in unfamiliar territory," he answered in a final tone of voice.

"I'm sick to death of your chauvinistic pig attitude. I get it from my father, his permanent bodyguards, the few men I've dated, everyone! Just because I'm a woman doesn't mean I'm incapable of making a decision or keeping myself safe," Sierra snapped as she turned to glare at him.

Damien looked at her in astonishment for a moment before his lips slowly spread upward in a grin.

"You think I'm a pig?"

"Yes."

"Just because I believe a man is stronger than a woman, more capable of taking care of himself in dangerous situations?"

"That's exactly why," she answered as she rolled her eyes. He was nothing more than a typical male, thinking he was the protector of the universe. Why did men either have to beat their women into submission, or else think they had to always save them? Why wasn't there a middle ground?

She thought of her best friend, Bree. Her husband, Chad, had tried the he-man stuff on her, but she'd quickly put him in his place, and he'd actually listened to her. Sierra liked Chad. He was kind, yet she had no doubt that if it came down to it, he'd fight to the death for those he loved. Sierra also knew he'd never even think about hitting his wife, or any woman, for that matter.

As Damien continued gazing at her, she wanted to stay angry, but he was so dang adorable with his amused expression. She should be even more infuriated with him that he thought so little of her, but it was hard to stay angry while looking at his chiseled jaw, and very kissable mouth, which was still grinning at her.

Her thighs quivered as she glanced at her own reflection in his dark sunglasses, suddenly wanting to know what was going through his mind.

Dang it! She didn't want his confident sexuality to throw her equilibrium off balance. She needed to stay focused around him.

"I think you just hate women, look down on them, believing they're an inferior race," Sierra said when the silence stretched on too long.

He pulled his shades down so she was finally looking into those deep green depths, leaving her no doubt of the desire behind their stare. His eyes dropped down her body, causing her nipples to tighten in response, before they came back up and met her widened gaze.

"I love everything about women... every...single....thing," he said slowly. His lips spread even more as his stare kept her rooted to the tan leather seat.

A horn blared behind her, alerting Sierra that the light had changed. Thanking her lucky stars for the interruption, she managed to tear her eyes from his. She looked forward as she placed the car back into drive and slowly accelerated. She was too shaken up to drive fast.

She forgot all about her desire to tour the island. She needed to get as far from Damien as she possibly could, before she pulled the car over and jumped into his lap.

After they drove in silence for about five minutes, her irritation was back, replacing some of the all-consuming desire still bubbling its way to the surface.

"You know, I don't need a babysitter. I've managed to survive this long without getting kidnapped, raped, or joining a cult. I don't need you on top of me."

"Oh, Sierra, I think that's exactly what you need," he quickly responded with a wicked grin.

Sierra felt her face flame, berating herself for not using a different choice of wording. The man was throwing her hormones off the charts. She slammed her foot down on the accelerator, trying to outrun the raging desire he ignited within her.

"I'm right next to you, Sierra. Speeding up won't get you away from me. I have a feeling you don't actually want to get away. I think you're just as worked up as I am, and can't get back to that hotel fast enough. Don't worry; I'll quench the burn..." Damien uttered, his mouth only inches from her ear.

She swerved unintentionally, causing him to sit up and send another glare her way.

"Slow down," he commanded.

"Are you worried? Think messing with me while I'm controlling a vehicle at sixty miles an hour is a bit unwise? You'd probably be correct," she taunted.

"Do you want to play games, Sierra," he asked, his hot tone sliding across her skin.

"No," she quickly answered, knowing she could never keep up with him in any kind of game he chose to play. Still, her heart was thundering, a huge part of her wanted to take that answer back. She wanted to be that girl who could look seductively at him while she flirted with her eyes, and asked, *what game do you have in mind?*

Sadly, that just wasn't going to happen. They'd get back to the hotel, and she'd go directly to her room and he'd go to his, then tomorrow, he'd be gone, and their routine would be the exact same.

Suddenly, she didn't want that, not even a little bit. She'd interrupted his day earlier to voice her desire to go home, and he was going to dang well give it to her. She couldn't play games with him, she knew that, but she could at least get some peace.

She'd obtain freedom from her father, and distance from Damien. It was a win-win.

He said nothing further as she drove the last couple of miles to the hotel. He also didn't do any work on the computer as his gaze was boring into her the entire drive, her head stiffly facing forward, her eyes on the road.

As tense as she was, she was pretty sure her body would be sore the next day. It was better strength training than three hours in the gym.

When she approached the valet and waited for them to take her keys, she finally looked over at the tense expression on Damien's face. His profile was to her, thankfully, allowing her to see the perfection of his sculpted chin, the slightly arrogant straight line of his nose, and the fullness of his lips – lips that looked entirely too inviting.

She found herself wondering what they would feel like to kiss. His lips were perfection as were all his features, but his beautifully sculpted lips were full and she could imagine how soft they'd be against her own – how his mouth would open to her and explore her tongue. What else could he do with that tongue…? She quickly snapped out of her short lived revelry, reminding herself how egotistical he was.

She could see why he commanded large crowds of people, how he always got his way. He was easily the most arrogant man she'd ever met, and that was saying a lot, considering she'd grown up with a dictator father.

Where her father inspired fear, though, Damien inspired… almost unnamable emotions. Fear was there, sure, but not fear of him hurting her, more like a fear of him transforming her. She tried telling herself she didn't want to enter into an affair with him, and she had no illusions about it being nothing more than an affair, but each time she spoke the words in her own head, her body rejected them.

She'd yet to feel what most women her age experience. She'd yet to have a man sink deep inside her, making her body come undone.

For years she'd listened to her sister speak of the different men who panted at her doorstep. Sandy had told her, in explicit detail, what it felt like to have a man worship her body. Sierra had been repulsed at first by her sister's casual attitude about sex, but for the last few years, that repulsion had turned into slight jealousy.

Sierra just wanted to feel anything other than insecurity, fear or anxiety. She wanted to experience deep, all-consuming passion.

She glanced at the hotel employee as he opened her door, her thoughts interrupted. She may want to feel desire, but she'd never act on it. She was too well trained to ever let herself go like that.

Almost desolately, she thanked the man taking the keys, and silently followed Damien inside the luxurious lobby of their hotel.

When they entered the elevator, some of her earlier irritation returned, and she resolved to finish their show-down. She was bound and determined to get back to the States and spend quality time with her best friend.

She wasn't taking *no* for an answer.

The Tycoon's Secret

Chapter Eleven

Damien and Sierra entered their suite and he immediately moved toward the small kitchen area, flicking on the coffee pot. It was already set up, so all he had to do was push a button to get the dark liquid brewing.

His cell phone rang as he was turning over one of the cups. He looked down, sighing before hitting a button and speaking into the small device. He paced away from her, she assumed, for privacy.

Sierra figured she had time. It looked like he was in for the evening, so she could surely convince him the best course of action was for him to stay and finish his business, and for her to head home.

"I have to go out," Damien said, startling Sierra with the irritation in his voice.

"What? We have to talk," she said, not even trying to hide the annoyance in her voice.

"A friend's in town who I haven't seen in a while."

Sierra looked at him in surprise, noting a tiny bit of jealousy trying to creep inside her. It didn't matter if he went out every night of the week so long as she wasn't stuck in the dang hotel room.

She sent him a glare, irritated even more by the insolent way he was leaning against the counter. It seemed he really didn't care about her opinion, like his time was the only thing of value.

She was bound and determined to get her say, even if she had to pin him down to do it.

Damien grabbed his coffee cup then moved out of the kitchen area, leaving Sierra no choice but to either stand there with her mouth gaping, or run after him. She was getting tired of chasing him.

He stepped into his large hotel bedroom and she paused in the doorway, her stomach once again tightening. It felt wrong to follow him in there, like she'd be crossing a taboo line – inviting something she truly wasn't ready to give.

"We can talk later, Sierra. I need to shower and change," Damien said as he began removing his shirt.

Sierra was grateful his impressive back was to her, because her eyes drank in the sight of all that golden flesh, his muscles tightening with the upward movement of pulling the shirt over his head. His arms flexed, making those strange sensations start emerging in her core. She forgot how to speak, suddenly feeling paralyzed – completely rooted to the spot.

His hands reached down to his pants, the sound of his zipper falling echoing in the otherwise silent room. Sierra really hoped her quickened breathing wasn't as loud as she thought it was, because she could feel herself panting as she drank him in.

As her eyes studied his body, she suddenly realized she was now looking at his stomach, not his toned back. Her eyes quickly darted up, colliding with Damien's.

His mouth twisted in the most seductive smile she'd ever seen a man use before, and she felt her knee's shake. With momentous effort, she tore her gaze away from his, took a few shaky steps to his bed and plopped down on the end of it. She felt like she'd just run a marathon, the way her breathing was ragged, sweat was beading on her brow, and her stomach was churning.

Without saying anything, he moved his long, elegant fingers to the top of his hips and gripped the fabric of his trousers, then slowly started sliding the pants down, taking his underwear with him.

When she realized he had zero qualms about stripping naked in front of her, she managed to rip her gaze away, taking a sudden and fascinated interest in his bedside lamp.

"Enjoying the view, Sierra?" he asked, his voice cascading over her like a cool waterfall on a hot day. She felt her face heat with embarrassment; mortified he found her awkwardness with the situation so shocking.

She really wished she could just turn, look at him from head to toe with a dismissive glance, and come up with a great retort.

While she was still trying to think of a witty response, she heard the shower start, and she quickly looked over to the spot he'd been a moment before. She turned and saw the bathroom door open, and steam starting to softly drift through it.

She was running out of time.

If he thought she'd go away because she was embarrassed or nervous, then he had another thing coming. For the first time in her life, she wanted something badly enough to not worry about the consequences of asking for it.

So what if he was naked in there, probably using those strong fingers to rub soap across that incredibly hard chest, then slowly moving downward... *Stop!* she commanded as she pulled her thoughts from the shower stall.

It didn't matter what he was doing in there. She needed to speak with him, and she was safe for the moment from having to see all that flesh, so she'd just talk to him while she at least had him trapped in one place.

∞∞∞∞

Damien stepped under the pulsing shower while his body reacted, knowing Sierra was just a few feet away. He nearly groaned as all the blood rushed to his lower half, and he hardened in a painful way.

With a curse, he turned the temperature dial to cold and shivered uncontrollably as he quickly washed himself, his teeth chattering.

His plans of taking Sierra to bed were destroyed when he got a call from his very distant girlfriend, begging him to have dinner with her. He hadn't seen her in a month, was planning on ending their casual relationship, but owed Shelby the courtesy of doing so in person.

She was in the wine business, which was how they'd met. Her father owned a track of land next to his and Shelby did a lot of the sales for her father's large business. They'd been trying to go into business with Damien, but he'd quickly decided it wasn't to his benefit. He had, however, hit it off with Shelby and had been seeing her for a year, though neither of them were often in the same location at the same time.

Being with Sierra, he'd completely forgotten about the woman, showing him he was making the right choice in ending Shelby's hopes of them having a future together.

He couldn't sleep with Sierra, in good conscious, while leaving Shelby dangling. All of that meant he'd have to deal with an aroused body and a lot of frustration, for at least one more night.

Damien was confused about Sierra's obvious embarrassment at him undressing. He'd seen pictures of men parading her around town, read articles about her one-night date status. She was known to go out with a man for one night, and then leave him high and dry in the morning.

She should've been a whole lot more comfortable in his bedroom, if the rumors were true. They had to be true, because the alternative meant he was dealing with an innocent woman. That couldn't be the case – it would make what he was doing too wrong.

"I spoke with my best friend earlier today. She wants me to visit with her. I'm doing nothing here, and I see no point in staying. I don't know if you have some power play thing going on with my dad, or if you really do need an employee, but it's obvious you don't need me right now. I'd like to go ahead and take a flight out of here tomorrow if one's available," Sierra said, speaking loudly to be heard over the sound of the shower spray.

Damien ground his teeth together, irritated that she was still harping on that subject. He figured the discussion was over as he'd already said he didn't want her to leave.

Stubborn woman.

He turned the blast of cold water off, his body sufficiently numb. Before stepping from behind the curtain he grabbed a towel and swiftly dried himself before wrapping it around his waist. At least the cold had temporarily done its job, and his body was somewhat back under control. He couldn't guarantee how long it would stay that way. One look at her gazing at his chest again, and he'd turn solid in a heartbeat.

He stepped up to the sink, not bothering to get dressed. He could see her shoulder, as she leaned against the doorjamb, her head turned away as if looking at him would burn her eyes.

"No." He grabbed his toothbrush and started brushing his teeth.

"What do you mean, *no*? I'm a grown adult. You can't just tell me *no* and think that's the end of the discussion," she huffed, her body turning as she stood in the doorway, hands on her hips, glaring at him.

He faced her, his hand still moving the toothbrush in his mouth as he lifted his brows. Then, to really irk her, he winked. He saw the flush start in her neck as her mouth gaped open in shock at his boldness. He turned away and spit in the sink.

It was better if she was mad. Let her stomp off and throw a tantrum, because honor, or not, he was a full-blooded man, and her standing there with her breasts heaving, and her eyes on fire was working him up all over again.

What he really wanted to do was forget about his night and simply throw Sierra on his bed, which happened to be only a short distance behind her. He felt himself rising underneath his towel and cursed as he bent down and took some water in his mouth to rinse.

"Don't you dare ignore me, Damien Whitfield. I'm trying to talk to you!"

Damien slowly turned, surprised at her tone. She was getting fully worked-up. Heck, one kiss, just one. Was that really so bad? He took a menacing step forward, feeling adrenaline rush through him. She quickly took a retreating step back.

He was in charge – he was hungry – he really wanted to prove how easily he could have that tone of voice of hers changing. Within minutes, he could have her begging him for more, not yelling at him from a doorway.

He stopped only inches from her, taking delight at the desire he saw in her eyes.

"Is this better, Sierra? Do you want my full attention," he whispered, his hand stroking the bone just below her neck, running his fingers across the top of her blouse. Her nipples instantly responded to his light touch, poking through the thin material of her bra and shirt, causing him a whole lot of new pain in his groin. He barely managed to hold in the groan.

"Well, uh, this is a bit too close..." she started saying when she finally gave up and closed her lips. He brought his hand up and traced her mouth, wanting just one taste. The way she was looking at him was making him come undone. One taste would be enough...

∞∞∞∞

Sierra felt her heart thundering in her ears. He was going to kiss her. She could feel it. Her mind screamed for her to kick him, yell, do anything but stand there like a statue. She should be turning tail and running.

Her body was telling her something entirely different. Her feet refused to retreat any further, and her nipples were pressing painfully against the cotton of her bra. Her core, oh her core, was on fire as sensations rocketed inside.

Her eyes glanced down, taking in his masculine chest, only inches away. She found herself wanting to lean forward and trail her tongue across his dark nipple. She wondered if he'd like the sensation.

How would he feel? Was he as solid as he looked, or was he velvety with a steel undercarriage? She suddenly wanted to know the answers more than she wanted to leave. She was caving to her body's desires.

Damien leaned down, his head getting closer, and she wanted to shout *yes, please, yes,* but no sound could escape her closed throat. Why fight it? It was useless. She wanted him.

Suddenly, Damien's phone was ringing again, causing him to pause with only an inch between their lips.

Ignore it, she silently begged, wanting to reach her limp hands out and tug him the rest of the way to her.

He quickly leaned back, the moment lost. She wanted to sob in despair. Why couldn't she have gotten just one kiss first? She wasn't asking for much; just a simple kiss, well, and maybe also to run her hands across the smooth skin of his impressively bare chest.

Sierra watched Damien speak a few curt words into his phone before he moved to the large dresser. She didn't turn her head when he grabbed a pair of incredibly sexy black underwear and pushed his feet inside the openings, then moved them up his muscular thighs. His hands disappeared underneath the towel for a moment, and she found herself hoping it would fall.

It didn't.

He kept his back to her as he grabbed a pair of fitted slacks and quickly tugged them on, only releasing the towel when his sculpted ass was covered. He hadn't been so modest when they'd first come into the room and she'd been too embarrassed to look. When she *did* want him to show her his full package, he refused her. She couldn't win.

At least the view of his back was enough to keep her heart accelerated.

Damien walked over to the small closet and grabbed his surprisingly bright blue dress shirt and slipped it on, further covering up her view. She managed to turn her head away and take in a couple of deep breaths.

Sierra didn't even know who the heck she was anymore.

"I have to leave. We'll finish…this…later," he said as he turned back around and faced her.

She started to regain a bit of her sanity the more clothing he put on, though she had to admit he looked *just about* as good dressed as undressed. When he grabbed a tie and slung it around his neck, then began working it into a knot, her stomach clenched again. Okay, he looked *just* as good dressed as he did naked.

Tension was practically a living entity in his suddenly very small bedroom. They weren't going to have any decent conversation in there. She should've known better than that. What woman follows a man into his room to tell him she's leaving?

In her defense, it wasn't like they were a couple. They were a supposed employer and employee, not that she'd done anything so far to earn the title of employee.

"Did you hear what I said?" he demanded as he paused to shoot her another glare.

"What? No," she said with hesitation.

"It's not that difficult, Sierra. All you do is nod your pretty little head and say, *yes sir*," he mocked. Sierra's desire fizzled at his words - the mocking, arrogant, pig. After the enduring years of abuse from

109

her father, she was surprised she wasn't cowering in the corner, but instead of feeling terror of standing up to Damien, she felt excitement.

She was through with being a victim.

Sierra stomped over to him, not even noticing the look of shock on his face. She poked her finger into his chest, hoping her nail was biting into his skin, marring the perfect surface.

"Don't you ever speak to me like that again. Dogs and cats will be singing romantic ballads together before I bow down to you. I'm through letting men walk on me. You can run off to your little date. That's just fine. But I *will* be waiting when you get back and we *will* finish this," she said, her voice coming out in a mixture of a growling shout.

With slow movements, Damien reached his hand upward and cupped her wrist in his unyielding fingers. He took a step forward, leaving her no choice but to fall back, or else land on her butt.

He took a few more steps, making her stumble in retreat. She was thinking maybe it had been a bad idea to poke him so hard.

As he stopped, the look in his eyes melted her from the inside out. There was a look of anger in there, sure, but desire was burning out of control just beyond it.

"Yes, Sierra, we most certainly will finish this when I get back," he whispered, his head moving down so the words were spoken against the sensitive skin of her ear.

He released her hand and she tumbled backward, landing in a heap on his bed. His stare froze her to the spot, the heat instantly rising to combustible temperatures with nothing but the look in his eyes.

One second he looked ready to pounce on top of her... then the next... he was gone.

Sierra heard the hotel room door shut, and she didn't bother trying to move. Her body was so overheated, she was sure she'd melted his mattress.

She laid there for an incredibly long time, desire churning inside her, his scent surrounding her in the most pleasant ways. Eventually, she gained the energy to get off his bed. She figured she had a few hours to pull herself together before he came back.

She'd use the time wisely. With a groan of frustration, she went in her own bathroom and ran the bath. First step to relaxing was a nice and hot, scented bubble bath. Second, was to purge Damien from her head, her body, and her life. This game he was playing was getting too personal. It was time for game over.

Chapter Twelve

Damien rode the elevator back to the top floor. On one hand he hoped Sierra had gone to bed, giving both of them a chance to cool off, think first before they did something impulsive. On the other hand, he wanted her awake, standing by the front door while holding out a glass of wine and a seductive come-hither expression on her face.

Shelby hadn't been happy about being dumped, not even a little. The first ten minutes of their date had consisted of him telling her why it wasn't ever going to work. The next hour had been torture listening to her rant about what a jerk he was.

If he hadn't been feeling so guilty about his ever-growing desire for Sierra he would've never allowed Shelby to vent that long. He would've coolly gotten to his feet and walked out the door. After an hour that's exactly what he'd done.

She was too embarrassed over public displays to chase him down and slap him in the middle of the restaurant, but he had a feeling she wasn't through. The look of utter disbelief in her eyes as he stood up had convinced him of that.

He opened the suite door, noting the place was dark except for a dim lamp glowing in the corner of the room. He decided not to flick the switch.

He headed over to the wet-bar and poured himself a glass of wine, the smooth taste of chardonnay easing down his throat.

When he turned around, his heartbeat skipped before starting again, only to go immediately into overdrive.

Sierra was walking from her room, looking toward the floor, wearing only a small silk nightie with a matching robe loosely tied around her slender waist. Her hair was damp, telling him she'd just gotten out of the bath. Her scent was drifting toward him, a combination of vanilla and spice, the same smell that had been haunting him all week.

The soft looking satin was caressing her thighs about halfway between her knees and her core, perfectly modest, and yet unbelievably sexy at the same time. He had an instant need to slide his hands up her smooth legs, see if she wore anything beneath the shimmering satin.

Damien slowly set his drink down. He could only be pushed so much in one night before he broke. He'd reached that breaking point.

The sound of his drink clinking on the glass table alerted Sierra to his presence in the room. She looked up; her expression fearful for a moment until she noticed it was him, then she relaxed before once again tensing.

"I wasn't expecting you back for hours," she said as she stood by silently.

"You and I had unfinished business I needed to get back for," he said, immediately going into hunting mode. He had her in his sites and this time he wasn't letting her escape.

"Uh… I'm actually really tired, now. I…uh, think it would be better if we finished our talk in the morning. There's really no hurry," she slowly said as her eyes shifted to his steadily moving feet.

"No. You told me earlier how important it was to have this discussion, so let's…talk," he uttered, his voice calm, quiet, and predatory.

His eyes roved her sleek curves. Her breasts were obviously braless, softly swaying underneath the delicate satin of her gown, her legs defined, toned and incredibly appealing as the gown slid against them.

She was a walking vision, freshly bathed with nothing altering her appearance. No make-up covered her natural beauty; no bands pulled her thick mane of dark hair back in a severe bun. She looked innocent, appealing and ready for him to take her.

"Look, I understand your hesitancy in letting me leave. You hired me for a job. I agreed to do it. I just don't get the job, as I've done nothing so far. I think we can work this out like reasonable, mature adults. I can go to the States for a few days, and then begin work. No harm done," she said hopefully as she continued to retreat.

She was speaking quickly, obviously becoming more nervous with each calculated move he made in her direction.

His excitement grew. He'd never force a woman to have sex with him – there was no need for that. If she was fearful or disgusted by his advances, he'd easily walk away – but no, that wasn't what she was expressing at all.

Each step he took closer to her, caused her breath to hitch, her eyes to widen. Her body was just as on fire as his, her gown hiding nothing from his view. He saw the way her nipples beaded underneath the revealing fabric. She wanted him as much as he wanted her.

He lifted his hands as he slowly and carefully began undoing his tie, his eyes never leaving hers. He deliberately ran the expensive silk through his fingers as he undid the knot, then left the ends hanging down the front of his shirt.

Her eyes moved from his to the base of his throat where his fingers were starting to undo the buttons of his shirt, deliberately, one by one. He watched as she swallowed, her lips then parting as her breaths began coming out in shallow pants.

"I'm sorry I've neglected you this week, Sierra. I'll make sure to not do that again. From this second on, I'll give you plenty of...*work*... to do," he crooned, his lips turning up in a satisfied grin. Oh yes, he could think of many, many ways Sierra could work on him.

He was starting to forget all about revenge as he began focusing solely on pleasure. Before he had a chance to worry about that thought, Sierra spoke again.

"That's really great. We'll definitely come up with a game plan tomorrow. Night, Damien," she whispered as she reached her room. She pushed her hand against the door, trying to shut it in his face. He slid his foot out, stopping it from closing.

"We aren't done speaking, Sierra, not by a long shot," he said as he easily pushed the door back open, steadily hunting her as she looked around the room for an escape route.

"I'm really tired, Damien," she said as she covered her mouth and imitated an impressively fake yawn.

"You don't look tired, Sierra. You look hungry, in need, wanting…" he countered as he reached his last button. "I can help with all of that."

She stopped at his words, her chest heaving as he seduced her with nothing more than a few sentences. He stepped up to her, his shirt falling to the ground before he reached out his arms and placed both hands on either side of the small indent of her waist.

She craned her neck back, her wide eyes meeting his desire filled depths. He was holding back by not immediately capturing her lips. He knew he could make her submit with nothing more than one kiss, but he wanted her to ask.

He needed her to quiver with desire for him, beg him to take her. He had to have her – but he had to have her shaking with need.

"What do you want, Sierra? What do you need?"

He pulled against her body, bringing her soft curves into contact with his heated skin. A soft moan escaped his throat at the pleasure of feeling her pressed up against him for the first time.

She was about ten inches shorter than him, her breasts rubbing against the lower part of his chest, her hot core just out of reach.

He moved his hands lower, slid them over the slick satin of her gown, his fingers skimming the round curve of her butt, as he pulled her even more tightly against him.

Sierra's breathing quickened while in his arms, but she didn't say anything, her head falling forward so he could no longer see her eyes. She didn't try to pull away, but she hadn't reached for him yet.

It wasn't good enough.

He slowly backed her up, his leg sliding between her sweet thighs with each small step they took, as if they were slowly dancing in the dim room.

"As soon as you admit you want this, want me, I'm going to take your mouth, slide my tongue inside your lush lips, then taste your sweetness. After I have you begging me for air, I'll move down the column of your throat, find every sensitive point in your body, before I cup your soft breasts in my hands and devour them with my mouth," he whispered, his tongue sliding out and caressing the edge of her earlobe.

His already throbbing arousal jumped when she groaned from deep within her throat.

He reached up and gripped her hair, slowly pulling her face back from his chest so he could look into her half-opened, desire-filled eyes.

"Tell me you want me, Sierra. Say you want me to make you scream," he commanded, his lips lightly brushing hers as he spoke, getting just the barest of her taste on him, making him regret his power game.

She shook her head a very minuscule amount as her lips opened in invitation. She wanted him, she just didn't want to say the words.

He needed her to admit it out loud. He wouldn't allow her to come back with regrets or accusations later.

"I'm going to take you tonight, Sierra. I'm going to pleasure you over and over again, make your body burn for hours, make you come so long, you'll beg for it to stop. When you think you can't take any more, I'm going to start all over again, rekindle the burning embers inside you. You'll cry my name all night long. All of this will start as soon as you say a few simple words," he promised.

She again was silent. He smiled. He wouldn't enjoy this so much if she submitted too easily. If he wanted a submissive woman, he could've taken his ex home, or any number of the women in the downstairs lounge.

No.

He wanted Sierra, her fire, her spunk, the yearning desire dancing off of her. Just the feel of her in his arms was both a relief and a burning sensation. The touch of his sold arousal against the soft smoothness of her stomach was pleasurable in a way he couldn't ever remember feeling before.

With the slightest touch of her small fingers wrapping around his stiff erection, he'd be done. She had no clue how much power she held at that moment. Heaven help him if she figured it out.

He took a step back, triumph racing through him at the look of lust-filled panic in her face. He didn't retreat far, just enough to begin undoing his pants. He watched her body quiver as he quickly unhooked his belt, then slid his pants and underwear down in one smooth motion, his thick shaft standing up on his body.

Without pausing, he reached into the pocket of his discarded pants and pulled out a foil wrapper, setting it aside. He didn't want to lose his mind later and forget to use protection once she was calling out his name.

Her eyes moved down his now completely naked torso and widened at the sight of his erection. Her look made him throb, need burning through him. He watched as her small fingers clenched at her sides, as if she was fighting the desire to reach out and touch him.

He wanted those fingers clenched around his most sensitive body part, wanted it more than he'd ever wanted anything. He needed the pleasure her grip would bring him.

"Do you like what you see? A few words and the hunger burning through you will be sated...repeatedly," he promised as he moved up to her again, his body twisting so his arousal was touching her hip, close to where her hand was clenched.

She moaned again as his naked body came in contact with her, the satin robe not much of a barrier between them. The feel of the slick material against his naked body was exquisite. He shifted his body, gently rubbing against her, and it was his turn to moan.

"Yes," she finally whispered – the word barely audible over the pounding in his ears.

"More, Sierra, I need more," he growled, his hunger making him grow impatient.

He moved his hands back around her, his fingers swiftly moving to the bottom of her nightgown, lifting it upward, sliding along her silky smooth thighs.

A shudder racked through her, the movement echoing in him, as well. Her highly aroused state was beginning to make him shake with longing. He was only seconds from devouring her, spreading her milky thighs apart so he could plunge deep inside, ride her luscious body hard, and make her shatter into a million pieces of pleasure.

She'd be his then – his to pleasure until neither of them could walk. Each time she cried out in ecstasy, he'd fall with her, relieve the almost constant pain inside him since their long jet ride together.

"Take me, Damien, please," she cried, anger and desire fighting for dominance in her voice. Her hand reached out and gripped him, her fingers tightening around his arousal, causing moisture to escape its head as her thumb rubbed across the sensitive tip.

"Oh, I'm too far gone for you to do that," he groaned, trying to pull from her tight grasp. She gripped tighter, rubbing her thumb across his peak again, causing more moisture to spill, then using it to lubricate her hand, sliding it quickly up and down his erection.

"Enough," he cried before gripping her butt in his hands. When he felt that she indeed wasn't wearing panties, a guttural cry escaped his throat. He lifted her, thrilled when her legs automatically wrapped around his waist.

With her face lined up with his, he bent forward, his lips taking hers in an urgent kiss. Her hands wrapped around his shoulders, her fingers tangling in his hair, pulling him closer to her as she tilted her head to allow him better access. He tasted her lips, consumed her mouth as he pushed his hips forward, feeling the slick heat of her smooth core resting against his hard staff.

He moved back and forth, his erection easily sliding along the outside of her heat, her moisture coating him, heating him, sending him over the edge of sanity.

"You're so wet, so hot," he groaned as he pulled back from her mouth, taking in a breath of needed air.

"Take me, Damien. I'm wet for you. I need you. Please. I need you to end the ache," she begged.

Her words stripped him of the last of his control. He lost all sanity as he felt her heat drip onto his shaft, naturally lubricating him.

He sheathed himself, then stepped toward the wall, pushing her back against it, anchoring her body in place. He held tightly to her hips as he brought his body back, poising the head of his thick shaft at her entrance. He leaned back, her hands still gripping his shoulders, her head thrown back against the wall with her mouth open and her eyes closed.

The sight of her smooth, wet opening nearly made him explode before he could slide inside her. With slow precision, he positioned himself at her entrance, circling the head of his erection against her lubricated opening and then finally started sliding inside.

"So unbelievably hot," he groaned as her heat enveloped him.

"Yes, more," she demanded, trying to buck her hips forward.

"Yes," he cried as he moved his hand back to her hip and surged forward, his desire causing him to thrust hard.

Sierra's eyes snapped open, her body immediately tensing as she cried out – not in pleasure. He felt the tight resistance of her body as his iron hardness plunged through her innocence.

"You're a virgin?" he gasped, his mind barely able to grasp the reality of what he'd just done.

"No," she lied as her face grimaced and she moved her hips, trying to accommodate his girth.

He was too large to have taken her like that for the first time. He should've worked the area, eased into her, taken his time. He shouldn't even be doing what he was doing. He'd only been with one virgin before and he'd been eighteen and stupid.

This was different. She was twenty-five, far too old and experienced to have never had sex.

"Why? How?" he uttered, his body throbbing with the need for release, but his horror at the situation refusing to let him move.

"Finish. Please. I need…it hurts…" she cried, frustration, pain and confusion mingled in her voice.

"Of course it hurts. I'm too big. I shouldn't –" he started to say as he began pulling out of her.

"No!" she cried in panic. "No. My body. It hurts. It's burning. Please, please don't leave me like this," she finished, her voice breaking as her eyes started to fill with tears. "Please."

She moved her hips again as she tried to find her release.

Still almost senseless with his burning desire, he couldn't resist her pleas, though he knew he should. He knew the right thing would be to pull from her and stop. *It's too late, anyway. You've already taken her innocence,* his body taunted.

He pulled her tightly against him and moved away from the wall, taking gentle steps across the room, back to the bed. He wasn't making love to her for the first time against a wall. He'd make sure her first time was perfect, and pleasurable.

He sat down on the bed, their bodies still flush, then he moved them both backward until he was on his back with her sitting on top of him. She looked down at him with confusion.

"You set the pace, Sierra. I don't want to hurt you," he uttered, the words passing through his clenched teeth. It was taking everything in him not to grip her tight, thrust hard inside her and relieve the pressure making him feel like he was going to explode.

"I...I don't know what to do," she uttered, her face flushing.

He reached his hand up and caressed her warm skin, his eyes gentling as he looked into her frightened eyes.

"Just do what feels good to you. Slide up and down me, listen to your body. When the pressure builds, move faster. Your desire will lead you."

She looked deeply into his eyes, hers filled with trust as she tentatively began moving. She flexed her hips, adjusted her knees, then moved off his body a couple inches before dropping back down.

She did this a few more times, her tight heat gripping him as her expression turned from insecurity to wonder. She shifted, allowing her to move further up and down his shaft, her body almost releasing him before she pushed back down, taking him fully inside her again.

He wasn't going to make it through her exploration. He felt like he'd pass out from the intensity of the pleasure. From the eroticism of watching her feel new sensations, and the tight grip of her body, he was doing everything in his power to keep from exploding.

Her face brightened with pleasure at the feelings surging inside her. He could practically read the emotions flickering through her eyes.

She began moving faster – up and then quickly down – over and over. As she became more confident, she started moving in a steady pace, pulling almost all the way out, and sometimes only a few inches.

He felt the pressure building, felt his orgasm reaching higher and higher, just barely able to hold it back as she searched for her release.

She leaned back, her hands resting on his thighs, unknowingly exposing her incredible breasts, flat stomach, and pink core to his view. The sight of her wet folds moving up and down his throbbing staff was too much.

She was stunning.

Sweat glistened on her body as she exerted herself, her breasts bounced with each thrust, and her pleasure center was wide-open for him to see.

Reaching his hand forward, his fingers quickly found her swollen womanhood. She cried out as he began circling the sensitive skin, coordinating his movements with each of her thrusts.

She moved faster, her body taking over, knowing what she needed.

"Yes, yes, yes," she called with each rotation. He sped his fingers up, knowing her release was rising.

"Oh!" she screamed in pleasure, her head thrown back as she pushed down hard against his body, her tight core flexing, squeezing his staff in wave after wave of contractions. He continued circling her flesh with one hand while he gripped her hip with his other.

He moved his hips up, taking over the movements as he thrust deep inside of her a few more times, making her cry out as he prolonged her orgasm. Her cries of pleasure led him to his own. He rose up into her, buried himself as deep as he could, and then exploded.

His body released, monumental tremors overtaking him as his erection pumped over and over again, his shaft releasing inside her.

By the time he stopped pumping, the last of her tremors settled. With a sigh of pleasure, she collapsed against him, obviously drained of every last ounce of energy.

Damien knew they should discuss what had just happened, knew they had to talk, but he couldn't even open his eyes, much less speak.

With the very last ounce of energy he possessed, he pulled out of her, then grabbed the edge of the blanket and pulled it over them. She was already asleep before he even covered their bodies. He soon followed her.

Chapter Thirteen

"You have one week."

"What?" Sierra mumbled as she woke up and stretched her sore muscles. She felt aches in places she didn't know possible to feel pain. She'd lost track of the number of times Damien had woken her during the night with his hands sliding over her body.

They made love once more in the night, though after that he'd continued to use his hands and mouth to do things to her she hadn't known were possible.

A shudder racked her as she remembered her last orgasm. She'd literally blacked out afterward. The man knew his way around the female anatomy.

"I called the board and told them everything's on hold for one week so I can take you exploring," Damien said.

Sierra looked at him in awe. Was this the same man she'd arrived on the jet with? He was actually smiling at her. She'd never seen him looking so carefree and happy.

"You called who?" she asked, her brain still foggy from lack of sleep. She glanced at the clock, noticing it was almost ten. She never slept that late. Of course, she hadn't slept much at all last night, so it didn't really count.

"I called my board of directors, here. I told them to put everything on hold – that something important came up."

"Really?" She grinned, starting to feel excitement. "Really. Now, I have a hot bath ready for you to ease your aches, and room service will be here in forty minutes. I told them to send up double of whatever they've been sending all week."

At the thought of feeling so completely taken care of, Sierra couldn't help but pull his head close to her, kissing him good-morning. His arms quickly wrapped around her as he deepened the kiss. She forgot all about the bath and food.

"No," he said with a chuckle as he untangled them and jumped from the bed. She was disappointed to see he was already dressed.

"We could stay in bed a while longer," she offered shyly.

"You're going to be the death of me, woman," he groaned as he took another step back.

Sierra felt instantly self-conscious. Maybe she'd been horrible at sex and he was taking her on a tour of the island to avoid sleeping with her again. Her good mood instantly vanished.

"Hey," he said as he quickly bent down and lifted her naked body into his arms. "What's with the face?"

"I...guess it wasn't that great for you," she mumbled, feeling her face flush – her humiliation was complete.

"Are you kidding me? It was fantastic!" he exclaimed, his eyes rounding in shock.

"Then...uh...why don't you..." she trailed off, too embarrassed to finish the sentence.

"Oh, I want to, I really, really want to, but the reality is that last night was your first time, Sierra. You're sorer than you realize which is why I drew a bath for you. I had some special salts sent up to help with the soreness. You'll feel it soon, believe me," he said as he started walking to the bathroom.

They entered the steam filled room and he carefully lowered her into the almost scalding tub.

"Too hot," she screeched, trying to scamper back out.

"Give it a minute and you'll adjust. The heat will work on your sore muscles. When we get back tonight, we'll take a bath together and I'll rub the aches out of you," he said, his eyes dilating.

She was still unsure if he was humoring her or not, but he did seem to be uncomfortable. As if he could read her mind, he reached out and grabbed her hand, quickly placing it on the stiffness straining against his pants.

"You turn me on so much that this is killing me not to take you. You're something to behold, surrounded in bubbles, your breasts skimming the water's surface...It's going to cause me to have a stroke," he growled before giving her back her hand.

Sierra felt elation fill her as she took in his pinched features. She felt a surge of power unlike anything she'd ever felt before. Testing her newfound boldness she pushed her breasts up, exposing them to his view.

His gaze snapped to her curves bobbing on top of the water before finally moving back to her face. She smiled at him in what she hoped was a seductive manner.

He glared for a moment before turning around and practically running from the room. Sierra felt so good, laughter spilled out as she lay back in the comfortable tub and let the heat start working her sore muscles.

When she started washing her body, she realized he was right. As she came in contact with the sensitive area between her thighs, she grimaced. It was incredibly tender down there. She gritted her teeth and finished washing, then climbed out and found the fluffy white robe hanging behind the door.

She wrapped it around her before brushing her teeth and putting her hair up in a bun. She placed a minimal amount of makeup on, and went to find Damien. Her day was starting out great.

She found him in the dining area, a table with covered dishes already waiting.

"Sit down. We have a lot of ground to cover today, so you'll want to fill yourself," Damien said as soon as she entered the room.

"Where are we going?"

She sat and he lifted the lid, exposing the French toast and extra crispy bacon she loved. She picked up a piece and started nibbling as she waited for him to speak.

"It's a surprise."

She'd never been surprised before and found herself even more excited. She hurriedly ate her meal so she could get dressed and leave the room. It was large and beautiful, but after a week, the enormous space felt claustrophobic.

Sierra was surprised when the bellhop came to start packing their luggage. Where were they going?

"We have a short flight so we can do this right. Make sure you have your swim suit," Damien told her, but he wouldn't say anything further.

As they made their way downstairs Sierra was giddy with excitement. She couldn't imagine what they'd possibly be doing, but she'd wanted to go swimming since she'd arrived, and not just in the hotel pool.

They got into the car and drove straight to the airport where they boarded the jet. She sat back, her eyes glued to the windows as the jet took off and climbed into the air. Before long they began making their decent.

"First stop is Cairns," Damien said as the removed their seatbelts.

"Isn't this where the Great Barrier Reef is?" Sierra asked, wishing she had her dozens of pamphlets she'd collected back at the hotel.

"Yes, and that's our first stop. I've hired a boat. We're going to tour the reef, then do some snorkeling."

Sierra wanted to reach over and kiss him she was so happy, but she held back, not sure if he'd welcome that or not. She wasn't letting doubts ruin her day, though.

They arrived at a large boat, and one of the crew members handed them each a glass of wine as the boat set out. Another of the staff started speaking and Sierra was mesmerized. She loved the rich deep timber of his accent, and to make it even better, he was a humorous and knowledgeable guide.

"The Great Barrier Reef is the world's largest coral reef system, and the biggest single structure made up entirely by living organisms. It's composed of over twenty-nine-hundred individual reefs, and nine-hundred islands. The total area is over a hundred-and-thirty thousand square miles. Several years back the cable news network named it as one of the Seven Natural Wonders of the World."

"I'm actually seeing one of the Seven Wonders of the World?" Sierra asked, elated at the thought.

"I can take you to see them all," Damien said, his eyes intense as he looked at her. Sierra smiled, knowing it wasn't a promise, but that he was caught up in the heat of the moment. Still, the thought of traveling the world excited her.

"I've never gotten to travel. My father didn't see it as necessary, so I plan on making up for lost time. This is amazing."

"You haven't traveled anywhere?" he asked, his voice radiating disbelief.

"No. I've never left the country," she said, understanding his shock. Bree had been around the world and back a few times, and Sierra had been stuck at home. Come to think of it, she had no clue how Damien had managed to secure her visa so quickly for her trip to Australia. Before she had time to ask him about it, the guide continued speaking.

"The reef is protected by the Great Barrier Reef Marine Park. There are a limited amount of people allowed on it, so it's protected from human consumption. Only a small amount of tourism and fishing is allowed. Recent studies have shown that the reef has already lost more than half its coral cover and we're trying to prevent more disaster to this natural wonder."

"Is there a possibility of it being completely destroyed?" Sierra asked.

"I guess the best answer to that would be, anything's possible," the man said. It was outlandish for Sierra to imagine something so incredible being destroyed.

"If you both want to go downstairs now, you can view the reef from our protected observatory."

Sierra didn't need any more prompting than that. She followed the man down a set of stairs, and then stopped, causing Damien to bump into her. It was amazing. There were seats lined up, and she had a clear view of the underwater reefs. Sea animals were swimming past, the colors of the reef, the animals, the plants – all of it was remarkable.

She sat down with Damien quickly joining her and just took it all in. They chatted as the boat slowly toured the area and Sierra was sure this was the best day she'd ever experienced. When the guide came down and told them they were stopping, she wanted to refuse to leave.

"Don't worry, there's plenty more," Damien reassured her. She reluctantly got up and followed him up top.

"Are we leaving already?"

"No, we're going snorkeling," he said with a smile.

Sierra didn't hold back this time as she threw her arms around him and gave him a kiss. It took him only half a second to return it with enthusiasm. The guide, loudly clearing his throat, was the only thing that stopped Sierra from dragging Damien back downstairs to make love below the surface of the water. She put that on her to-do list.

They spent the rest of the beautiful afternoon swimming in the warm water, Sierra seeing marine life she didn't even know existed. By the time Damien took her back to the hotel, she was barely able to stand on her feet, but the exhaustion was well worth it.

"Are you ready for your bath?"

Sierra turned, her weariness evaporating at the hungry look in his eyes. She couldn't believe she'd waited so many years to experience love-making. Her body hummed with anticipation of what was to come.

"More than ready," she answered. After spending the entire day flirting with him, sneaking kisses when they came up for air, and having him touch her body in every intimate spot, she had no worries.

She pulled her shirt over her head, encouraged by the fire lighting in his eyes. She started backing up toward the bathroom as she reached her arms behind her back and unhooked her bra, letting it hang on a moment as his eyes devoured her nearly naked breasts.

When she let it drop to the floor, Damien quickly stepped forward and pulled her into his arms, his lips capturing hers in a kiss of hunger. Her nipples ached as her breasts pressed boldly against the material of his polo shirt.

"I've wanted you all day. How do you feel?" he asked as his lips trailed down her jaw.

"I feel like I need you inside me," she said, shocked by her brashness. One night of love-making and she was turning into a nympho. She'd much rather be that than the locked up prude she'd been for the first twenty-five years of her life.

Damien lifted her and carried her the rest of the way to the bathroom. He set her down long enough to start the tub, then finished undressing her, his hands sliding along each inch of skin he exposed.

By the time he stripped and set a row of three condoms on the side of the tub, Sierra was practically dripping wet without having set foot in the tub.

They didn't climb out until the water was almost cold.

Chapter Fourteen

Damien lay there and watched the sunlight sneak through the mostly closed blinds. It was too early for Sierra to wake considering they hadn't fallen asleep until the early hours of the morning for the second day in a row.

He couldn't seem to take his eyes off her. She was stunning, and he found himself enjoying their time together. The need to let her tour the island had started out of guilt for taking her virginity, especially so roughly, but as he'd spent the day with her, his guilt had ended and he found himself enjoying her company.

She had such childlike wonder over everything she saw, causing him to see it for the first time through her eyes. He'd had this image in his mind of her, and she was smashing that visual to pieces. She wasn't at all who he'd expected her to be.

She mumbled something and he stilled his hand that was brushing a piece of her hair from her eyes. She turned, her arms stretching out as if seeking something, then she settled back down into the pillows with a frown marring her features, before finally she relaxed and her deep breathing started again.

Was she reaching for him? He found himself hoping she was. With reluctance, he rose from the bed and took a hot shower. He was used to strenuous activity as he made sure to get some form of exercise in daily, so he wasn't dealing with the soreness that Sierra was, but the steaming water still felt good washing the last of his sleep away.

He spent a couple hours getting work done, and confirming reservations before he ordered room service then went in to wake her.

Their second day had to start a little earlier to get everything in. Sierra didn't fight him at all when he woke her. She jumped from bed and rushed to the bathroom to begin getting ready. He couldn't resist joining her in the shower, causing them to be a little bit late.

"We have to leave now or we'll miss our train," Damien said with a laugh as Sierra kissed him again, both of them standing in the bedroom with nothing but towels on.

"Oh, a train!" she exclaimed as her arms fell from his shoulders and she rushed to the closet to grab her clothes.

He didn't know whether to be happy she was listening or upset that she was choosing a train over him. He decided to go with being happy.

"We're going to tour the Kuranda Rainforest, and stop in the village."

"I don't remember seeing that pamphlet. It sounds fun," Sierra said, her voice muffled by the shirt she was pulling over her head.

Damien took a moment to appreciate the slightly tanned skin of her stomach as she struggled to pull her shirt down. Amazingly, he felt himself growing hard as his eyes traveled up and took in the ripe mounds of her breasts before she got the shirt to cooperate and his view was blocked.

"Don't look at me like that or we'll never get out of here," Sierra begged him. His eyes lifted and he was surprised to see the desire shining in her eyes. It seemed neither of them could get enough of the other.

"I'm trying not to hurt you, Sierra. You may like sex, but I'm going to do some damage if we don't take breaks. Your body has to have time to heal," he warned, his voice deep with desire.

"Then we'd better leave," she purred.

Damien took a menacing step toward her and she giggled before grabbing her pants and running from the room. He took a step after her before stopping himself. If he pursued her, it would end with them on the bed, or a table, for all he cared. He had to remind himself of her inexperience.

He quickly dressed, happy when he found her in the living room holding her purse and waiting. He had to get her out of the room.

As they stepped into the hall and made their way to the elevator, he reached down and took her hand. He'd never before felt the need to hold a woman's hand, but suddenly he had to touch her, had to feel her warm skin against his own. He swore he heard a sigh from her as his fingers tightened around her palm, but she didn't say anything. He tried acting like it was no big deal, though his emotions toward her were growing – making it a very big deal.

They boarded the train and went deep into the heart of the tropical rainforest of Kuranda.

"I just can't believe something so beautiful exists. It almost looks untouched," Sierra said as they looked out the large windows. Various animals were playing in the trees, and the scenery was stunning.

The train stopped in the village and they had a nice meal with the other tourists, Sierra instantly making new friends. Damien just sat back and watched as she conversed with various people.

He did find himself constantly reaching for her – his hand either gripping hers, or resting against the small of her back, sometimes brushing the hair from her shoulders, or resting on her thigh. She'd turn often and smile at him, making his stomach tighten with desire and…more.

He was having a good time with her, not thinking about the work being left undone, revenge, or his mother. He was simply enjoying a few moments of uninterrupted time with a beautiful woman. He was discovering he liked her – really liked her. She was the first woman he'd enjoyed being around since college when he'd fallen in love, or what he'd thought was love.

It had turned out to be simply infatuation and the relationship had never had a chance. He'd already been through so much in his life that the experience had turned him off of the happily-ever-after kind of love. He wasn't falling in love with Sierra, just infatuated, he assured himself.

Marriage was about what two people could give each other, not about love and devotion, anyway. He tuned out the negative thoughts and just let himself feel good without guilt. He pushed his mother's voice from his head.

After lunch they took a ride on the skyrail, soaring over the tops of the trees, getting a magnificent view of the Barron Falls and Red Peak. Each new sight had Sierra grabbing for him while she animatedly pointed. He looked out the windows, seeing the beauty all around him.

He honestly couldn't remember the last time he'd slowed down enough to simply enjoy himself. He decided it was going to become a priority. He'd have to get Trinity and Drew to join him in Australia. Damien had a feeling it was going to become a favorite place for him.

The sun was starting to set when they arrived back at the train terminal. Sierra looked disappointed the day was over, but he had to keep them on schedule or he'd never get to show her everything he planned.

They got in the rental car and drove to the airport. "Where are we going?" Sierra asked, almost in a panic.

"Don't worry, we're just heading to our next stop," he reassured her as he helped her from the vehicle.

"What about our luggage?"

"I had it packed and delivered while we were gone."

"Don't you worry they may take some items?" she asked.

"Not at all. I've stayed at that hotel many times. The owner is a personal friend of mine," Damien said with a smile.

"That's good enough for me."

They boarded the jet and made the short ride to Alice Springs, which was at the very heart of the Australian Outback.

Sierra stepped into their new hotel room, excited to see where they'd be staying this night. It was opulent, of course, but as she walked in, her eyes instantly filled with tears. On the living room table sat a huge bouquet of roses with a card attached. She slowly walked over and lifted the envelope with her name on it.

Damien watched, fascinated by the eager anticipation as she slowly opened the envelope. He moved so he could see her expression as she read the card.

"Really?" she asked with excitement.

"Go look," he told her.

Sierra bolted from the room and entered the bedroom. Lying on the bed was a stunning green dress with beads attached, making it almost seem alive as the fabric moved. He'd called Trinity and asked her to have one delivered. She hadn't disappointed.

"It's stunning," Sierra gasped as she ran her hand over the material. His curiosity was peaked.

"I did my research on you, Sierra, before you ever got this job. You've worn many beautiful gowns, but you look like you've never seen one before," he said, not really a question, but he knew she'd understand he was looking for an answer.

"My father always picked my clothes for every function I attended, though he didn't do it to please me, but because he had an image to maintain," she said, her voice catching as several tears trailed slowly down her face.

"Talk to me about it," he commanded.

"I can't."

"Yes, you can. What's going on between you and your father?"

"It's better left alone. Besides, the card says you're taking me to dinner and dancing," she said, her tears fading away as she looked at him hopefully.

How could he resist.

"Yes. I'm sorry it's all so rushed, but you only have an hour to get ready. I'm trying to fit as much as possible into this trip. I have to get back to work in just a few more days," he apologized.

"I'm getting far more than I thought I would. You won't hear any complaints from me," she told him as she gently set the dress back down on the bed and went to the bathroom where all her toiletries were already laid out.

He heard the shower start so he went and made coffee while he waited for his turn. He didn't dare join her.

Once Sierra finished, he snuck in behind her and jumped in for one of his own, then the two of them shared the bathroom as they prepared for the night ahead.

Damien's eyes met Sierra's in the mirror, his face masked by shaving cream, her hand up to her eyelashes as she applied mascara. It hit him how domestic the situation was, and it felt like he received a kick in the gut. Things were moving too quickly. He found himself scared for the first time since he was a child.

He took her on the town that night, holding back from her, but not enough for her to notice. When they returned to the room, he made love to her again, his movements frantic as he tried to prove to himself it was only sex, but as her lips captured his, he was lost, not able to get enough of her taste, feel, or smell. He was falling fast for the girl who wasn't supposed to mean anything to him.

Chapter Fifteen

"Oh my gosh, I can't believe how far it flies away and still manages to make it back," Sierra exclaimed as she watched the boomerang sail far into the sky and then make an arch and return to the man throwing it. "Can I try?"

"Of course," he said as he offered her the small piece of wood.

Sierra threw it as hard as she could, watching it soar a short distance before making an arch. Several people ducked as it almost collided with them on its return trip.

"It takes time to master the right technique in throwing it," the man told her with a smile. Sierra threw the boomerang several more times, not even coming close to the elegance with which the guide portrayed.

She then listened to stories of the Aboriginal people, and how they'd settled the land. She was fascinated by the history of the beautiful island, wishing they could stay in the remote village for days, or even weeks, instead of only one short afternoon.

"We have to go. I have a surprise," Damien said when she missed her target for the hundredth time.

"Just once more?" she pleaded.

"Okay," he conceded.

She threw it, straining on her tiptoes as it made its arch back toward the can she had sitting out. When the boomerang hit the can, she stood stunned before suddenly jumping in the air and clapping her hands with energetic accomplishment.

"I did it!" she cried as she hugged the guide and then Damien. She was amazed at how proud she was at finally hitting her target.

"Great job," Damien said with humor in his tone. She tried to settle down, realizing she wasn't acting in the least like an adult. She didn't care - what she'd just done was difficult to do and she was reveling in her victory.

"Come with me," Damien said as he held out his hand. She took it without question, as she'd been doing over the last several days, and followed him around a corner where several large balloons were filling up the land.

"What's this?" she asked.

"I'm taking you for a ride," he replied as he led her over to a hot air balloon. Her eyes widened as she looked at the contraption with suspicion. She wasn't all that sure she wanted to go high in the air in a giant balloon.

"Are you sure it's safe?" She knew the tone of her voice implied she didn't have a lot of confidence in it, but she didn't care. It wasn't on her to-do list, to plummet to her death when a bird struck the balloon at their highest point in the air.

"It's perfectly safe, Sierra. People do this all the time. Quit being a chicken. I'm trying to be romantic here," he said with an indulgent grin.

Those words did it for her. She could handle her fear of death for a little bit of romance. She did fear her heart would never be the same again after the spur-of-the-moment vacation. It was worth the pain for a week of bliss, though.

They lifted into the air as the sun started fading from the sky, and her breath was taken by the beauty of it all. It was such a contrast, the brilliant colors arcing across the sky, while the almost desolate land gleamed below them.

"Champagne?" the guide offered. She took the glass without much thought and took a sip. She didn't really care for the taste, but the bubbles tickled her nose, and she liked the feel of the cool glass in one hand, and Damien's warm grip in her other.

She took a moment to glance at Damien, leaning against the side of the balloon as he gazed at the glorious sunset. With the setting sun behind him, casting its beautiful colors across his features, he looked mysterious and masculine.

He turned his head and their eyes caught, a sparkle in his, beginning devotion in hers. She fell for him a bit more with each new adventure he took her on. She was fearful of what that meant for her future.

"You look stunning," Damien said as he moved next to her and took the glass from her shaking fingers.

"I was just thinking the same thing about you," Sierra replied.

"Mmm, do you care to elaborate?" he asked with a wiggle of his brows.

"Does someone need their ego stroked a bit?"

"My ego, among other things," he said as he moved his head to nuzzle her throat and his hands rubbed along her lower back, his fingers moving along her spine. Sierra felt the kiss on her neck all the way to her toes.

"Damien, we're not alone," she whispered in embarrassment, but couldn't find the will to push him away.

"He's busy, not paying the least attention to us. I have to kiss you, or I may not make it back to the ground," he said before running his lips up her jaw, trailing kisses the entire way before taking her lips in a slow, sweet kiss.

She melted on the spot. The moment was everything she'd ever dreamed of, but never thought she'd get. She wouldn't survive his week of undivided attention if he decided to go back to the cold business man she'd met the first day, once the week was over.

Damien was still kissing her as they began their descent. Sierra missed the rest of the sunset, missed the ground reaching up to meet them, missed half of the ride, but she didn't care. Being in Damien's arms was far better than anything else she could see or do.

The ride ended with them safely on the ground, and Sierra followed Damien to their car. She leaned her head against him in the backseat, glad he'd chosen to have a driver this time. She fell asleep before they reached the hotel.

The next few days flew by in a whirl of activities. Damien took her to Melbourne, and they strolled through the diverse neighborhoods. She was charmed by the nineteenth century architecture, the use of trams, and the beautiful park - she even got to watch the Fairy Penguin Parade. Each night the tiny Fairy Penguins of Phillip Island waddled up from the water, looking like they were on parade. After a hard day of fishing they returned home each night to feed their babies. She was entranced by the entire event.

At a cabin where they stayed, she'd gotten up in the middle of the night and found a couple turtles crawling from the ground and making their way toward the sea. Damien joined her on the porch as she watched in fascination as the tiny creatures scurried along the sand and dove into the water. The wonders of nature appealed to her more than all the expensive excursions.

Her favorite part of the trip was when he took her to his vineyard. It had been stunning, and she'd stood back and watched as his staff greeted him, everyone from the lead manager to the pickers came out to say hello. She strolled with him through the miles of vines as he pointed out different grapes and then gave her a tour of where the fine bottles of expensive alcohol was made.

She sampled a few too many glasses and by the end of that day, she'd become unsteady on her feet. She realized why he was so successful, though - the taste of it was amazing.

They arrived back in Sydney on the sixth day. She was a little sad to be back where she knew he'd soon return to work. He took her on a tour of the world famous opera house, and to an exquisite five-star restaurant, but she felt the change in him as soon as they landed in Sydney.

He was still a gentleman, opening doors for her, making love to her each night, and giving her his attention, but he stopped holding her hand, stopped caressing the small of her back, and started pulling away.

Her vacation was amazing, but she felt her heart expanding, her emotions getting too involved. She decided she needed some time away from him so she could think. Sierra had to figure out what exactly she was doing with him, with her father, with the rest of her life.

It was time to visit Bree. She knew Damien would be mad, and that was the last thing she wanted to evoke in him, especially after all his generosity, but she had to do something for herself. Sorting out her feelings and life plans was impossible to do with Damien around. He was just such a distraction. She needed this, and it was her turn to take care of herself and do what was best for her.

Chapter Sixteen

Damien awoke and stretched, feeling good. The week had been a whirlwind of activities, but he'd found himself having some long overdue fun. He tried telling himself it was nothing more than fun, but as he'd spent every hour of every day with Sierra, he'd found himself needing to be with her. He'd forced himself to tone it down a little, but he couldn't pull fully away.

At least not yet, he couldn't.

He didn't know how the two of them were surviving on so little sleep. They hadn't yet made it through an entire night without waking at least once to make love again. Twice last night, he'd woken with an urgent need to take her. The first time, she'd been just as hungry, and they'd come together quickly, a tangle of arms and legs. The second time had been more leisurely, both of them quickly falling back asleep.

Damien reached out, hungry once more just thinking about sinking into Sierra's tight heat. He came up empty and was immediately irritated. She never woke before him, not once since they'd started sleeping together. The sheets below his hand were cold, telling him she'd been up for a while.

His irritation turned to anticipation as he grinned and quickly threw off the bedspread. If he was really lucky, he'd catch her in the shower. He didn't bother putting on his clothes as he strode to the bathroom. Empty.

He wasn't concerned as he walked back to their bedroom. He was about to move to the living room when his brain clicked and he made his way back to the bathroom. He'd thought something was odd when he walked in but had been so focused on finding Sierra that he hadn't put it together.

He looked at the counter and noticed none of her belongings were there - no toothbrush, hair accessories, or little vials of makeup that she always had out. If it weren't for his few items, it would look as if the bathroom wasn't being used at all.

The first alarm sounded in his head. He rushed back into their room and opened the closet, feeling his gut clench when he found all her clothes gone.

Anger flared in Damien's stomach as he flung a robe around himself and walked back out to the living area of the hotel suite. He was about to pick up the phone when he found a note next to it.

When he hesitated before picking it up, fury spread through him.

Damien Whitfield didn't hesitate – ever.

He swiped the piece of paper up, wrinkling the page in his haste as his narrowed eyes scanned her words.

Damien,

> *Please don't be upset. I really need some time to think. The last week with you has been almost magical, and I truly enjoyed myself, but I had to get out of there for a while. I'm going to my friend's house, back in the States. I'm taking an early flight and should be airborne by the time you read this. You can get ahold of me at the email listed on the bottom of the note and let me know when you get back to the States if you'd still like for me to work for you. I need time to think. I know our little affair was a lot of fun and that's something you're used to, but as you know, I'm not. I just need to process all of this. Please don't be too upset. I think it's best if we take some time apart and then if you still want me to work for you, we can discuss that. I think it best if we stay professional, though. The sex was pleasant, but I don't think it wise to continue the affair. Please don't be angry.*

Sincerely,
Sierra

Pleasant? Pleasant! Damien wadded the paper in his hand, tossing it across the room. He reached for the phone again, planning on calling his pilot to prepare his jet, before he remembered there was no way he could leave – not for a couple days, at least.

When he realized how angry he was, he forcibly made himself calm down. He wasn't letting a woman get under his skin – especially a woman who meant nothing more to him than a means to an end. Once he got what he wanted from her, she'd be history.

He cringed at the callous thought, but firmed his shoulders and marched back to his room, where he went straight for the bathroom and a hot shower. He had business that day. He'd deal with Sierra later, and make sure she regretted her impulsive flight home.

∞∞∞∞

"I can't believe you're really here," Bree exclaimed as she engulfed Sierra in a hug. "Please tell me you're not leaving for at least a year," she added, only half-kidding.

"I've missed you, Bree," Sierra answered with a grin. She didn't know how much time she had and she certainly didn't want to waste it. Right at that moment though, she was exhausted. It had been an incredibly long flight in coach. She had jet lag, stress from not knowing how Damien was going to react, and fear of her father finding out and hunting her down.

She tried reminding herself that her father couldn't touch her. She was an adult and didn't have to ever go back there again if she didn't want to, but no matter how much she reassured herself, years of abuse and fear didn't disappear overnight.

"I love you to death and want to do nothing but talk and talk, but I can see you're barely keeping your eyes open. Let's get you out of this airport and to my house where you can sleep for twenty-hours. Once you do that, we'll spend the next twenty doing nothing but catching up," Bree said as she grabbed the small carry-on-bag Sierra was barely holding on to.

"I think you've read my mind," Sierra told her friend with gratitude in her voice.

"Chad is waiting out front with the car. He had to circle around because I absolutely didn't want to walk five miles just to park," Bree exaggerated.

"I'm grateful for that, too."

"I knew you would be," Bree said as she placed her arm through Sierra's and quickly led her through the maze of the Sea-Tac airport. They arrived at luggage, and thankfully didn't have to wait too long for Sierra's bags. Even better was the fact that both her bags had made it safely. At least she wouldn't have to deal with the nightmare of any lost luggage claims.

As they walked outside, Sierra smiled at the familiar rain soaked street. The area was loud with cars quickly pulling up to the curb to pick up passengers, and the smell of exhaust was prominent, but it was still home.

They weren't waiting long when Chad approached in a large SUV. He parked at the loading and unloading curb, and hopped out, quickly giving Sierra a hug before taking the bags and placing them in back.

"It's so good to see you again, Sierra. Bree's been pacing the house for what seems like months waiting for you to visit," Chad said, making Sierra sigh. Bree's husband was drop-you-to-your-knees gorgeous, and had a voice that could melt butter.

"If I would've realized I'd get to be in your company, I may have arrived sooner," Sierra teased him, then laughed when he actually blushed.

"Sierra, you're terrible. You know you're making my husband think all kinds of terrible thoughts about our college days, now. He's dying to know if we did actually have pillow fights in tight camisoles and panties," Bree said with a huge grin.

"I'd never picture any woman but you, baby," Chad quickly recovered as he kissed his wife with the passion of a newlywed, though they'd been married for several years.

"You're a very wise man, Chad," Sierra said as he held open the back door for her.

"I get things right on occasion."

Sierra peaked in the window noticing the baby wasn't there.

"Where's Mathew?"

"He's at the house with his Uncle Max at the moment," Bree said. "Max brings over Ariel and the two of them play. They're really cute together."

"You're so lucky to have such great siblings, Bree. I've always envied that about you."

"I do love them all, even when their nothing but a pain in my butt," Bree admitted.

Chad held open Bree's door, then jogged around to the driver's side and slid in. Before long, he was weaving through traffic and the gentle motion of the car had Sierra falling asleep.

"Wake up, we're home."

Sierra slowly pulled herself from the dream she'd been having, the very erotic dream, starring none other than Damien Whitfield. It was a good thing she was half-way around the world from him, because her body hadn't yet taken the hint she wasn't enlisting in an affair with the man.

"Already?" Sierra grumbled, wanting nothing more than to fall back to sleep.

"Yes, already. Let's just get you inside where you can crash for the rest of the day. We'll spend all day tomorrow catching up," Bree promised.

"That sounds heavenly," Sierra said as she slowly extracted herself from the rig and stumbled into Bree's large home.

She barely made it up the stairs and to the bedroom before falling face first into the comfortable bed.

Chapter Seventeen

When Damien was in Seattle, he normally had a driver for his travels. He preferred to maximize as much time as possible to work and found driving a waste of his time. However, with his confrontation looming with Sierra, he found he preferred to have as few witnesses as possible.

His gut was churning in anticipation. He was on his way to Bree Anderson's home. Sierra didn't know yet that he was about to arrive. He hadn't bothered with speaking to her on her email as she'd suggested.

No. He wanted to see her face, know what thoughts were going on inside her head. He hadn't spoken to her in almost two weeks, unable to leave Australia before now.

He'd been back for two days, forcing himself to wait before going to her. He didn't want jet lag to be a hindrance when they had their confrontation.

Two weeks had done nothing to cure his desire for her. He wanted her now more than ever before, knowing he'd take the first possible moment to ravage her lips. Just the thought of tasting her again had him hardening uncomfortably in his pants. Fury and passion intensified inside him, each feeling trying to topple the other.

He'd made the deal with her father, giving the man large sums of money in exchange for her being his employee. It had obviously turned into more than an employer – employee relationship, which made him even angrier. He'd never had a woman walk out on him before. He didn't like it one little bit. When he finally got her alone – well, he wasn't sure he could be responsible for his actions.

The longer he drove, the more he warred with himself, but he came to the conclusion that his seemingly insatiable lust for her was just getting started. What began as nothing more than a business arrangement had quickly fallen off course.

He didn't know how to deal with it. But Damien Whitfield always knew how to deal with things. This wasn't a welcomed confusion.

He approached the gate guarding Bree's home, a smile forming on his lips. It seemed his cousin was a cautious woman. If only she knew who she was about to invite inside her protected space.

Old anger and hurt buzzed inside him like a swarm of angry bees, fighting for a stronghold on his tightly reined-in emotions. The Anderson's had caused his father's death, thrown his mother out in the middle of the night, and wanted nothing to do with him. His mother was dead because of them, because she couldn't afford decent medical care.

It was unacceptable.

He pressed the button, watching as the camera focused on him. He did his best to keep his mask of emotions in place.

"How may I help you?" a voice asked over the speaker.

"Damien Whitfield. I'm here to see Sierra." He didn't elaborate.

"One moment, Sir."

Less than a minute passed before the gates started opening. To Damien's surprise, he found his hand slightly shaking as he placed the vehicle into drive. He glared at the offending fingers, clenching them once – inserting his will over his body. When he opened his fist, the fingers were steady.

With a satisfied look in his eye he began his journey down the long winding driveway. Nerves tried to eat away at him as reality set in that he'd be standing next to one of his blood relative, and have to act polite, as if he didn't give a hoot who she was.

His pre-occupation with seeing Sierra helped control his emotions toward his *so called* family.

He pulled up to the house and stepped from the car when several large men filed through the doorway. Damien had to smile as they lined themselves up on the enormous porch. He was sure to most people the sight would be intimidating. Damien only looked on in anticipation. He could use a good brawl to work out some of his aggression.

He cursed himself for continuing with his vendetta against the Anderson's. Becoming a multibillionaire on his own, without their help, should've been good enough to satisfy his mother's wishes... but it wasn't.

She'd made him promise to make them pay. He just had to remember they'd killed both his parents. They may not have done it with their own two hands, but they'd done it by their greed and selfishness.

"Afternoon," one of the men said as Damien walked with confidence up the stone stairs.

"Hello. What's with the welcoming committee?" Damien asked, noting the surprised look on the man's face before he managed to mask his expression. It looked like the muscle-bound gorillas hadn't expected him to be so forward.

"Just coming out to say, hi," the man said as he took another step in Damien's direction, making sure to show him he wasn't intimidated in the least. *Of course, he's not intimidated, he's surrounded by his body-builder friends,* Damien thought snidely.

"I'm looking for Sierra," he said as he sized up each man.

"Why don't we chat first? I'm Chad Redington and this is my place. These are my brothers-in-law and various family members," Chad said, not moving an inch. Damien tensed. He didn't like being blocked.

"I'm Damien Whitfield, as you already know. Now that introductions are over with, maybe I can see my employee." Damien didn't need to know who the men were. He recognized them from the research he'd done for years on the Anderson men, but he was silent as Chad continued.

"Introductions have just begun, Mr. Whitfield. You haven't been formally introduced to the rest of the guys. This is Lucas Anderson, my wife's cousin, and next to him is Trenton Anderson, her brother. The two in the middle are Max and Austin, also my wife's brothers. We're all a bit protective of who comes around," Chad said, not once breaking his even, smooth tone. To an outsider, it may sound like he was having a pleasant chat, but Damien had zero doubt he was warning Damien that if he was there to cause trouble, he may as well turn around. Damien wondered how much Sierra had said.

After that thought hit, he finally realized he was standing there with half the Anderson family. This was what his end goal was, to get in a room with them without being seemingly eager to do so, learn what made them tick, find out their weaknesses.

He was so far gone on his obsession with Sierra, he'd thought of nothing but getting through them and to her. What was wrong with him?

"Chatting sounds like a good idea," Damien finally said, ignoring the small voice inside him that just wanted to find Sierra.

"Good. Let's go to my den," Chad said, looking pleased it wasn't going to turn into a brawl on his front steps. Damien would bet money that Chad's wife would ream him out if that ended up happening. If she was like Trinity, in the least, and most women were the same in the sense that they didn't want their men fighting. It was almost worth it to start the battle.

Damien was confident in his strength, but he wasn't stupid. He was too outnumbered to have a chance of winning a physical battle with all the men surrounding him.

Chad walked in the door while the other men parted to let him through. He walked ahead, his eyes connecting with each man, showing he wasn't about to cower. The group was silent as they went down a wide hallway, then through a set of double doors into a warm den.

Damien looked around the room, surprised by the number of framed photographs on the walls. Most men liked trophies in their private man-caves, but it seemed pictures were Chad's trophies.

He strolled over to a wall filled with images. Damien realized he recognized most of the people in them, those who were currently in the room with him, and those not present. There were only a few he couldn't recall ever seeing.

Damien had done a lot of research through the years on the Anderson's and could spot them from a mile away. To avoid making a fool of himself, he stopped just before reaching for one of the framed pictures.

It was of his Uncles, George and Joseph, surrounded by what seemed their entire family. Smiles abounded in the group filled with adults and hordes of children of all different ages and sizes.

It looked to the outside world like a beautiful family, but Damien knew what truly ran through their veins. He wouldn't be surprised if they bled black tar. Greed changed a person.

No one said a word as he silently gazed at his family, at a picture he rightfully should've been in, had they not cast his mother aside so coldly. When he realized he'd taken longer than he should have, and also that he shouldn't have any interest in family pictures of strangers, he turned around, making sure to compose his features.

"What would you like to drink?"

Chad knew it was a test, but he wasn't there to please them or worry about what they thought. He knew his liquor but he didn't like whiskey or rum. He was a wine man, and only when the occasion struck him. But he didn't want them to know anything about him, so he decided to request a beer.

"I'll take a bud if you have one," he answered. Chad looked surprised for a minute, but recovered quickly before going to a fridge that blended into the wall, looking like just another panel.

Damien had something similar in his own place. As he looked around the room, he noticed that he and Chad had a lot of the same tastes.

"Here you go. Have a seat."

"I'm fine standing," Damien told him, not wanting to give that advantage to the men.

"Suit yourself. How did you meet Sierra?"

Damien could appreciate a guy who didn't beat around the bush, coming straight to the point. It was how he did business, as well. He did have to be careful with his answers, though. He didn't need the Anderson men to know who he really was. He'd been careful through the years not to run into them while he did business. He wanted to meet them when he was ready for it, and not a moment before. He had to be in complete control.

"I'm doing business with her father. I wanted her to work for me." Damien's best option was to keep his answers as short and to the point as possible. He also needed to sneak in a few of his own questions.

"Why?" Lucas asked.

"Why, what?" Damien responded.

"You're a smart guy, Damien. You don't mind if I call you by your first name, do you? I get real tired of formality, especially in my cousin's house." When Damien nodded his assent begrudgingly, Lucas continued. "Why would you be doing business with Monroe? It's well-known he's losing his shirt right now for some incredibly poor choices. There may even be criminal charges filed on him soon, ranging from tax fraud, to downright bad business practices. The guy has more sexual harassment complaints on him than anyone I know."

"I have my reasons and they're my own business," Damien said, his tone clearly making it known the topic wasn't up for discussion.

"You having Sierra work for you, especially when she doesn't even understand why, makes it our business," Chad said, stepping closer to Damien with his eyes narrowing.

"Look Chad, I don't mind having a little chat with you and the in-laws in which you felt the need to bring out in force today, but I won't discuss my business practices," Damien said, not backing down a single inch.

He thought he saw a small flash of respect in Chad's eyes, but the man quickly masked the emotion.

"Look *Damien*, first of all, we were having a family gathering. I had no idea you were showing up on my front porch, so I didn't know I needed reinforcement, unless there's something else to this situation. Secondly, if you hurt Sierra, then my wife is going to be furious and demand your balls on a silver platter. I'm trying to avoid all that by finding out exactly what your intentions are. Sierra... well, she's not like the rest of her family. She's a great gal, who's had some hard knocks in life. I don't want to see her get any more of them."

"Duly noted," Damien snapped. Then, with a sigh, he decided to give them something, though he said it through gritted teeth. "I like her, okay?"

The men stared at him for several moments, as if they were assessing him, seeing if he were speaking the truth. The reality was that he liked her more than he should. He had no business feeling anything for her. She should be nothing more than a tool, another pawn in his game of revenge. That was long out the window, though. He wanted to see her. He was still angry she'd managed to get away from him so easily. He'd make sure it didn't happen again. He'd make sure she knew better than to run from him.

"Well then, I guess we can all relax," Chad said as he smiled. Damien didn't like the knowing look on the man's face – not one little bit.

Chapter Eighteen

"Let's go out back," Trenton said as he grabbed his own bottle of beer and moved toward the den's door.

Damien didn't hesitate. He followed behind his cousin, and then realized he hadn't asked one single question of any of the Andersons. How was he supposed to get information if he wasn't even thinking about interrogation? The only person he seemed to want to interrogate was Sierra. He vowed to himself he'd just make sure she was really there, then he'd focus on his "family."

As they neared the back of the house, delicious aroma's started drifting through the room, reminding Damien he hadn't eaten in twenty-four hours. He'd been in too much of a hurry to get back home, and exhaustion had pulled him under on the long jet ride. Then, stress had prevented him from eating much once he arrived at his house and waited to see Sierra. His stomach rumbled loudly at the smells surrounding him.

"The girl's all cooking together has that effect on me, too," Austin said as he patted Damien on the back. The friendly gesture threw him for a moment.

If these men were anyone else besides the sons of the men who'd killed his father, he might find himself enjoying their company, actually wanting to be around them. He pulled away, sending a "don't touch" signal for Austin and the rest of the men. Damien missed the look Austin sent the other men in the room. His signal had been read loud and clear.

"You picked a good day to show up. The weather's good, and we're getting ready to barbecue in a few minutes. Bree and the rest of the girls have been making side dishes for a couple hours. They wouldn't let us sneak into anything either, so I'm starving," Max said as he picked up his pace and passed the rest of them.

"Hey, hold up," Trenton said as he raced his brother into the kitchen.

Damien heard the laughter before they turned the corner. He found Max and Austin both with their arms wrapped around who Damien assumed were their wives.

"Not a chance are you taking off with any of this. It would be gone before we got our steaks grilled, then you'd be too full to finish the best part," one of the women was saying.

"Ah, just a little bite, Cassie?" Max pled, looking kind of comical as the huge guy was practically on bended knee in front of his wife.

"Okay," she sighed with an adoring look on her face. She picked up a fork and let him taste her dish. He didn't disappoint her when he sighed dramatically before lifting her from the ground and spinning her in a circle.

"Oh," she cried, her face going white. Max's face turned practically the same shade when he realized he'd hurt her.

"I'm sorry –" he said when he was cut off.

"It's okay," she said before pushing against him to get free and then running down the hallway. He waited a stunned second before following her. Damien stood, confused.

"It's okay. Cassie's in her first trimester of pregnancy, and it looks like she just got motion sickness. I'm Jennifer. How are you?" the woman who was previously in Trenton's arms asked before walking over to Damien.

"I'm fine. Have you seen Sierra?" he asked as he automatically took her hand.

"She'll be right back. She's just changing Maya for me," Jennifer replied.

Damien could feel her the minute Sierra stepped in the room. He didn't know how, but one second he was standing next to Chad as the group of people chatted around him. The next minute, his body tensed and he found himself wanting to look over his shoulder. With great self-control, he managed not to.

He then heard soft footsteps on the tile floor, finally allowing himself to turn.

Sierra walked in, holding a delicate infant in her arms, the sight making his throat close. Her cheeks were flushed and a glorious smile filled her face as she looked mesmerizingly down at the small bundle in her arms.

"Thank you, Jennifer. She's so incredible," Sierra said before her head finally came up. Her expression froze when she spotted Damien standing amongst her friends.

"Hello, Sierra," he softly said, grateful he'd regained his voice. Without even trying, seduction rolled through his words.

He found himself relaxing just seeing her again, noticing the way her eyes drank him in. *She* may not realize she was hooked on him, but everyone else in the room could feel it, notwithstanding Damien. Confidence rolled through him at the knowledge.

He also found he liked the sight of her with a baby in her arms, how natural she looked. He couldn't stop the picture forming in his mind of it being their child. Before he had a chance to chastise himself, he was walking toward her, his movements slow and sure.

He wanted her with an intensity that didn't make sense, but he wasn't taking the time to analyze it. His anger was still warring with his desire and he didn't know if he wanted to kiss her more or strangle her. Maybe a bit of both, but desire won out.

Without saying anything, he gently pulled her into his arms, being careful so he wouldn't crush the small baby between them. Without hesitation his head descended capturing her lips in a kiss.

His tongue glided enticingly across her gaped bottom lip, before he gently bit down on the soft pink flesh. He drank in her soft sigh before releasing her as he took a retreating step.

"You shouldn't have left," he whispered for her ears only and her eyes widened.

He watched the emotions flicker across her face as she realized the anger behind his desire. She was starting to realize he wasn't as calm as he was portraying.

"I...uh, well, I..." she stuttered, having a difficult time with her words.

"Exactly," he said with a satisfied grin on his face. He found his anger simmering down, placed on the back burners as he held her. He'd missed her, more than he'd even be willing to admit even to himself.

"Well Sierra, I think you've been holding out on us," Bree said with a laugh. "You've just made me want to drag my husband off for some alone time," she added with a wink, causing a becoming shade of red to infuse Sierra's cheeks.

Damien turned and gave Bree a smile before looking back at Sierra who looked quite shaken. He was a bit concerned for the baby in her arms, at the shell-shocked expression in Sierra's eyes. He gently took hold of the infant before she dropped her.

Damien felt warmth spread through his chest as he looked down into the soft grey eyes of the innocent face looking back at him. She was just so small. He found himself unable to look away, taken in completely by her sweet little features.

"I can take her so you two can have some time to talk," Jennifer said as she walked up and held out her arms.

With reluctance, Damien handed over the baby, bemused at his desire to continue snuggling the little one.

"You seem like a natural," Jennifer said as she smiled at him.

He'd held his best friend's children and found himself always happy to do so, but something was shifting in him, some desire to have his own – something he'd never really thought he'd want. He told himself it was just a desire to make sure his name lived on – make sure his parents lived through him, and then their grandchildren.

When he'd thought Trinity would be alone in raising the baby she carried, he'd offered to marry her, and would've been the best dad possible for her child, but he hadn't wanted to be a father at that time, he'd just wanted to do the right thing for his best friend.

Now he found himself wanting a child, wanting to ensure his life wasn't for nothing, that he'd somehow continue living, even after he was gone. He tried shaking off the thoughts, but they were planted in his head, and weren't going away. He shook of the disturbing images as he focused once again on Sierra.

"Let's take a walk," he said, putting his arm around her back. He finally realized she hadn't said one word to him. He wanted to know what was going through her mind. He also needed to make sure she never ran from him again – not without facing his wrath.

Silently, she allowed him to pull her from the room. He led her out the back door and looked around. He wasn't sure where they were. He just started walking further from the house.

"What the heck was that?" Sierra finally asked, gaining her voice. Good. He liked her with some fire.

"What?" he asked, wanting her to have to spell it out.

"The kiss. Now, they're all thinking we're...we're...well, that we're a couple," she spluttered, confusion and anxiety heavy in her tone.

"Aren't we a couple, Sierra? Before you ran away, I seem to recall one heck of a week in bed together," he said, his voice low, making her have to step closer to hear him.

"We're not a couple, Damien. I work for you, though who knows what I'm supposed to be doing. Our week together was, well, I don't know what it was, but it's not continuing. I just got out of one prison, and I refuse to step into another," she said as she started pacing.

Damien froze as he looked at her. She didn't reveal much about herself, was very secretive of her life, so her little slip gave him a small piece of insight into her past. She considered her life at home a prison. That was interesting.

"I want you, Sierra. I am so hard for you right at this moment that I'm having a difficult time thinking of anything else, which is lucky for you, because I've been alternating between wanting to ring your neck, and wanting to slam you against a wall and screw you until you never even consider walking out again. I want to take you in my arms, press you against that

172

tree and ravage your body until you're begging for mercy. Do you really think we can go back to a normal employee, employer relationship?" Damien whispered.

∞∞∞∞

Sierra gaped at Damien, her heart thundering in her ears. She couldn't believe what he was saying to her. His lips were turned up in a confident smile, his eyes burning into hers, and his body tense.

Her eyes traveled down his flat stomach and stopped on the bulge in his trousers, confirming his words. She gulped before her eyes jerked back up to his.

His smile grew even wider at what must be a surprised expression on her face.

What was she supposed to say to a comment like that?

What killed her most was how badly she wanted him, too. She wanted him to take the choice away from her, to lift her in his arms and take her against the tree, exactly how he'd said. She didn't want the time to think about it, didn't want to make the right choice and deny him, and herself.

"I...uh, don't think that's a good idea," she said a bit breathlessly, with reluctance. Her lips were still tingling from the kiss in the kitchen, her body continuing to burn with unfulfilled desire. Why was she saying no to him?

Because she knew it was the right thing to do.

She had just escaped her overbearing father. It wouldn't do her any good to get into an unstable relationship with a man who made her father look weak. She'd never survive it. If Damien were to control her, abuse her like the man who was supposed to be her protector already did, she'd never survive. She didn't know how she'd survived all the years with her dad, as it was.

"Why isn't it a good idea, Sierra? We obviously burn for each other. We explode when our bodies connect. Why not explore it, enjoy one another? We're going to be together for a long time, so it will happen no matter how much you try and deny it. You can't fight this thing between us. You can't fight me and win. I always win, Sierra – always!"

It was terrifying how much she wanted to fold. She understood what he was saying, found herself wanting to cave to him. Why fight it? It was inevitable. She knew they'd sleep together again, as surely as she knew she'd take another breath of air.

Her shoulders firmed as she glared at him. *No*! She didn't know that. She was done with men controlling her, taking away her free will.

"You know what, Damien? I think you've been handed things so often in your life that everything has been easy for you. You just assume all outcomes will be in your favor. Well, not this time. I'm not going to lie and say I hated the sex, but I most certainly can live without it. It was good, sure, but not the end-all everyone's always talking about. Why don't you do us both a favor and stop playing whatever game this is your playing and just get out of here," Sierra told him, adding a smirk to the end of her small speech for added affect.

When she saw the fire ignite in his eyes, she thought she may have pushed it a bit too far. He took a menacing step toward her, and panic flared.

With a surge of adrenaline rushing through her, Sierra decided not to wait for his response. She turned and started running back to the house. When she was less than twenty feet from the back steps, an arm snaked around her middle, slamming her into the rock solid wall of Damien.

"Oh, Sierra, you were very smart to run, very smart indeed after making a comment like that," he whispered, his hot breath slithering down her neck.

He flipped her around so she was looking into his flaring eyes, his expression determined. Suddenly, he was lifting her in his arms as he strode around the house.

Before she thought to cry out, he was tossing her in his car and then they were driving down the pavement. She looked back at the house with longing as it faded into the distance. What had she just done?

Chapter Nineteen

The silence was stifling as Damien pulled out of Bree's driveway. He had to get her alone. He felt like if he didn't get her into his bed again, he'd explode.

He didn't need her. He'd proven that. He could easily insert himself into the lives of the Anderson's without suspicion. Heck, there was a fundraiser event coming up shortly he'd be attending with them. He'd already made contact, so he could drop Sierra off at home, and then drive away. No harm done.

Except, he knew that wasn't true.

Even the thought of leaving her with that man who called himself her father caused an ache in Damien's chest. He couldn't do it.

He tried telling himself it was because she still had a job to do for him, but he knew better. It was so much more than a job, just as it had been from the moment he'd laid eyes on her - started studying her, decided she'd be perfect for what he wanted.

If only he could figure out exactly what it was that he wanted her for.

"I can't believe you would do that. Bree is going to hunt you down and –"

"And what, Sierra? You play hot and cold, do things however you like, want everything your way. Well, this is the real world, and its time you learn that actions have consequences. If you push me, I'm going to push back," Damien thundered as he made a sharp right turn.

"Where are you taking me? I demand you return me at once!"

"Not going to happen."

"Stop this car right now or I swear I'll jump out of it," she threatened as she reached for the door handle.

Damien's emotions were sliding on a thin sheet of ice. He could already feel it begin to crack beneath him. His anger was consuming, but his need was overwhelming. He saw a sign for a park, and swerved into the parking lot, needing to pull over before he ended up crashing the vehicle.

Damien turned in his seat, looking over Sierra, her flushed cheeks, heaving chest and rage filled eyes. His arousal jumped at how badly he wanted to pull her onto his lap. He had to end the torture, had to sink inside her – now.

"Why keep fighting me, Sierra. You want this just as badly. I'm not forcing you. I'm not demanding anything you don't want to give, so why don't you stop playing games and tell me what you want?" he said, his voice dropping an octave.

∞∞∞∞

Sierra felt his words all the way to her core. She did want him, desired him in a way that had to be unnatural. She just couldn't think when he spoke to her like that, used that tone of voice.

"You have to stop, Damien. This is wrong."

"Why, Sierra? Are you afraid of the passion between us? I've thought of little else but you for the past two weeks, because each day that I wake up, I smell your scent and it sends desire coursing through me. I come in at the end of the night, wanting to find you waiting for me, hungry, aching with need. If you want to play games, that's fine by me – I'll play all the games you want." His tone was melting her. She was falling quick.

"I don't want to play games. I...I need air," Sierra told him as his hand moved to the handle.

"Where are you going?" he demanded, all seduction leaving his tone.

"Wherever I feel like," Sierra snapped. Exhilaration filled her as she realized he was the first man she'd ever so openly defied.

"You're not leaving. We haven't finished this," he said, his voice oddly calm, though the anger fueled his words.

"You can't stop me."

"Sierra, I swear if you run off –" He suddenly stopped as if trying to compose himself.

Sierra felt a twinge of alarm at the implied threat of his command. Old habits die hard. If she'd ever argued like this with her father, he would've beaten her to a pulp. She knew Damien wouldn't hit her – she didn't know how she knew, but she just did.

Sierra didn't give him a chance to finish the rest of his statement. She opened the door and jumped from the car. Not taking any chances, she started running toward the trailhead straight ahead.

For a few brief moments she thought she'd actually achieved her goal – that she'd gotten away. At least she did until she heard footsteps quickly approaching from behind only seconds before Damien's hand snagged her around the waist and lifted her in the air.

She thought about crying out, but she didn't have a chance. Within seconds she was cradled against his chest and his mouth descended.

She didn't even have time to take a breath of air before his mouth sucked all protests away. He kissed her long and hard, his tongue quickly slipping inside her mouth and tangling with hers. She felt the movement from Damien's footsteps, knowing he was going somewhere but she was lost in the moment and couldn't focus on anything else but being in his arms again.

"You make me burn. One minute I want to throttle you, and then the next I want to make you submit to me. Just remember, Sierra, I love a good chase. You can run from me anytime you want, because I'll always catch you. Lucky for you, the punishment will be mutually satisfying," Damien said with a wicked gleam in his eye before he set her down and gripped her blouse.

Her cotton shirt went flying behind her seconds before she felt the clasp of her bra unhook inviting the cool evening air to touch her exposed nipples.

She looked around in panic, afraid someone was going to walk by at any moment. She realized they were in the middle of the brush and she was sitting on a large fallen tree. As the sun started dropping in the sky, vibrant colors casting shadows across Damien's now naked chest, desire consumed her.

She should refuse him, not allow him to cart her off into the woods and ravish her body. As his face descended and his mouth grasped her nipple, all thoughts of fleeing evaporated. She groaned as he sucked her sensitive tip into his mouth and washed it with his tongue.

"Yes, this is what I need," he cried as he lifted his head and moved to her other breast. He sucked her nipple deep inside his mouth before lightly clamping his teeth down, causing a surge of wetness to soak her panties.

"Please, just take me, Damien," she begged as her thighs opened, her body instinctively knowing what she needed.

His hands drifted to her pants, and he quickly undid them, stripping her naked in seconds before laying her down on the moss covered log. The coolness of the moss felt incredible as her body went up in flames.

He quickly stripped his own clothes, his erection standing proudly in front of her. With no thought but a need to taste him, Sierra reached out and gripped his silken rod.

Before he could protest, she wrapped her lips around him, tasting the salty desire on the solid tip of his shaft.

Damien groaned as he reached down and pushed her legs apart as he skimmed his fingers across her swollen folds. She cried out around the fullness of his arousal. He knew how to make her lose her mind with nothing more than a few brushes of his hand.

Within a minute, Sierra exploded, her mouth clamping tightly around his solid shaft, her body a trembling mess as she shattered repeatedly. He pulled from her before she could hurt him and she gasped as she pled for mercy.

"No more," she begged, the pleasure so intense it almost hurt.

"Oh, Sierra, there's plenty more," he growled as he stood, lifting her easily in his arms. He set her on a higher log, perfectly aligning her heat with his swollen manhood.

"Yes, I want you in me," she said as he pushed against her. This is what she needed. His hands ran up her sides, his fingers skimming her quivering flesh as he rubbed his arousal against the outside of her heat, making her want to scream.

"Now, Damien. Take me now," she commanded him as she gripped his head and pulled him closer to her. She was through playing. She wanted his body buried in hers.

"I thought you said no more, Sierra," he taunted as he kissed the corner of her mouth, his tongue moistening her dry lips.

"No, I want more. Please, Damien. Please give me more," she begged. She didn't care. She needed him.

At her pleas, he stopped taunting her and with a smooth, strong push, he buried himself deep inside her heat, nearly lifting her from the log with the power of his thrust.

"Yes, like that. More," she panted as he pulled out and quickly pushed back inside.

"You're so hot, Sierra, so hot and tight. I can barely think when I'm buried inside you. I want nothing more than to pound against you so hard you won't be able to move for a week," he panted as his movement quickened.

"Yes, do it hard, Damien," she encouraged.

He groaned as his hands gripped her hips roughly and he began thrusting his hips quickly in and out of her wet heat. She felt the build-up of another orgasm, welcomed the pressure starting in her stomach and radiating outward.

Her body tensed as his steel penetrated her, moving in and out in lightening quick movements, touching her to the very depths of her womanhood. She felt her body gripping him tighter, felt his smooth rod filling every available inch of space inside her.

With a hard thrust that rocked her entire body, Sierra shattered around him, her body coming undone as the pleasure peaked and she gripped him in convulsions, causing him to cry out as he slammed against her a few more times before he finally stilled.

His head came down and rested on her shoulder as he slowly started regaining control of his breathing.

He looked up, the last of the evening light barely illuminating his face. She was speechless as she gazed into his emerald eyes, which were radiating pleasure.

"Please feel free to run from me anytime you want," he said as his lips turned up into a cocky grin.

Sierra was dumbfounded for a moment until she realized it would be pretty hard to pull of indignation considering he was still firmly locked inside of her and she was naked in his arms. She could either get upset, or decide to let it go.

"You weren't half bad," she mocked him.

His brows furrowed as he looked at her. She could tell he was trying to decide if she was taunting him, or if she really felt that way.

"Not half bad? Well, I guess I'll just have to do it better this time," he said with a smile before his mouth descended on hers.

By the time they found their clothes in the dark and made their way to the car, Sierra was practically frozen and could barely walk, but it was certainly the most exciting trip she'd ever had to a park.

Chapter Twenty

"Look, Damien, you've proven that I want you. You've shown me a world of emotions and sensations I never even imagined existed before meeting you," Sierra started.

"Why do I get the feeling there's a *but* coming up?" he asked, his tone wary.

" – But…" Sierra paused, "This isn't a good idea. Yes, the sex is great, but I'm in no way capable of having a cheap affair followed by you discarding me like yesterday's trash."

"You think pretty little of me, obviously," he stated, his tone turning cold.

"It's not that I think little of you, it's that I know how men like you work."

The truth of what she said – his original intentions – stung as if she'd slapped him across the face. Had he not let his heart become involved, he certainly would've discarded her without a second thought.

The reality was that he *had* let his heart complicate the matter. He enjoyed her company…her laughter…her femininity. Her words stung, causing him to disguise the pain with the coldest chagrin. Damien Whitfield was never denied.

They were silent for the rest of the drive to his house. Sierra looked weary as she followed him inside his home.

He walked to his study with her slowly trailing behind. His first stop was his liquor cabinet. He needed to soothe his wounded ego. After a shot of whiskey, which he hated, he could feel the effects numbing the ache in his chest.

"What would you like to drink?" He said, turning to her.

"I'm fine," she answered as she nervously licked her lips.

He poured her a glass of red wine and walked over, handing her the glass. She lifted it to her lips and automatically took a sip.

"This is ridiculous, Damien. The silent treatment isn't helping. You said you wanted to talk about the work issue, then let's talk about it. I don't want to talk about the sex thing anymore."

"You work for me. What else is there to understand," he said as he crowded her personal space. She backed up and sat down in one of his chairs.

"I don't know what my job is. It's still unclear as to why you even hired me," she said as she stepped back. "You're my assistant. Your job is to do whatever I need you to do," he reminded her.

"Well, if the job is to just sit around day in and out, I'd rather resign," she said, her gaze meeting his for the first time since the park.

"I have plenty of 'hands on' things you can do, Sierra," he said with a growl in his voice. He slowly started approaching her again.

He watched as she finished her glass and nervously swallowed. He reached her chair and leaned down, his hands gripping the wood arms on either side of her.

"I'm not used to this kind of life, Damien. To tell you the truth, you frighten me," she whispered, her breath hitching as he leaned closer to her.

"You're a smart woman, Sierra. You should be afraid. I want a lot from you, a lot more than I originally planned," he said with a wicked smile.

∞∞∞∞

Panic washed through Sierra in waves. What if he tried taking more than she was capable of giving? What did she have to give, anyway? She had nothing – nothing that would appeal to a man like Damien. He may be amused by her for a short time, but then what? What happened when she was half in love with him, and he was done playing? She wasn't afraid of him physically abusing her like her father did, but she had a feeling that Damien could do far more damage to her heart in a short amount of time, with nothing more than his words, than anything her father had ever done to her body, with his fists.

She couldn't think when he was so close to her, his hot breath softly caressing her face, his scent filling her nostrils, his body so temptingly near. She fought the desire to reach out and touch him, run her fingers along his solid chest, trail her hand down his stomach, feel the bulge she knew was present in his pants.

"Is this only a game?" she finally asked.

He tensed as he shot up straight and began removing his jacket. The muscles in his shoulders rippled beneath the thin linen shirt he was wearing. The man exuded agitation, causing a pang to tear through her chest. It seemed he *was* playing a game. Until that moment, she didn't realize how badly she'd wanted him to tell her she meant something – anything other than a cheap lay. She quickly stood from the chair, needing to pace to help sort out the annoying stir within her.

"What game are you playing, Damien? Is it a power struggle with my father? Did he wrong you in some way? Is the whole point to humiliate me? If that's the case and you're seeking revenge on my dad by hurting me, it won't work. He could care less if you hurt me. You would've been much better off going for my sister," she said with bitterness.

Damien stilled and turned to look at her, as if assessing if her words were true or not. She held her head high while she looked back. Let him think what he wanted. She was too tired of men using her to care much at that point.

"I want revenge!"

Sierra was stunned by the passion in his tone as the words barreled out of him. She couldn't imagine what her father had done to cause him so much anguish and hatred, though she wasn't surprised.

Douglas Monroe took what he wanted, when he wanted it, and anyone who happened to be in his way got run over.

"I want what was robbed from me, from my mother. I want revenge and I won't stop until I have it."

Sierra looked at the myriad of emotions flashing in Damien's eyes, the rest of his face like stone. She didn't understand what he was saying. What was taken from him? What did she have to do with it? What had her father done now?

The silence was suffocating in its intensity. She had to make him see that he'd get nothing by going through her.

"My father hates me, Damien. You won't get anything out of him by using me. I don't know how to make you understand that," Sierra said, the admission puncturing a hole straight through her. To utter the words aloud was humiliating. It wasn't a secret that Douglas despised her. Sure, he put on airs when they were out, but he didn't try very hard to mask his disdain for his eldest child.

"This has nothing to do with your father, Sierra," he said as he took a determined step in her direction.

Confusion ran rampant through her mind. She'd never met Damien Whitfield before that moment in her father's study, so she couldn't see what she could've possibly done to wrong him – or worse – hurt him.

"I never even knew you in the past, Damien. I couldn't have possibly done anything to cause you to seek revenge against me."

Sierra took several retreating steps as he continued his deliberate approach. It didn't matter how long it took him, because in the end he *would* pounce and come out victorious.

"It's not you, either," he said, his lips turning up in a sardonic smile.

"Then, who? I don't want to play your games, Damien. I demand you stop this!"

At her words, he actually complied. Sierra was surprised enough she stopped her retreat and stared at him as he threw his head back and laughed. What the heck? Had he lost his mind? Was she going to end up on the front page of all the tabloids? She could see it now, Unwanted Heiress killed by crazy Tycoon. She was sure they'd find her body mutilated, and then manage to get a shot of her father presenting a tear.

The thought of her father crying for the camera angered her more than the thought of Damien going crazy and killing her.

Damien began his accent, pinning her to the back of the couch, her legs trapped against the high backed piece of furniture, his arms caging her in.

Desire flooded through her, causing her breath to deepen and her tongue to drift out and moisten her lips. His eyes narrowed in on the movement before slowly lifting upward and connecting with her gaze.

"I will get vengeance, Sierra, revenge against your best friend and all her relatives. You see, you were my ticket in because of who you knew. When your father called, I wanted nothing to do with him. I know the kind of man he is, but when I found out who you associated with, I figured it was my lucky day. I want them comfortable around me, thinking they're safe and sound. They may have no trouble sleeping at night, but I know the truth about the Anderson's. I know who they really are," he said, his mouth only an inch from her own.

What?? Sierra's mind raced trying to make quick sense of Damien's words. She couldn't understand why he'd want to hurt Bree or any of her family? They were some of the best people she knew.

"I...I don't understand."

"It's really quite simple, Sierra. Joseph and George Anderson swooped in and stole everything from my father – the corporation he helped his father build, the money he was left, everything! He was with my mother at the time, and she was pregnant with me. A few months after she had me, he died. She believes he took his own life, though that wasn't proven. Every last dime was ripped away from her. To make matters worse, she found out she was pregnant again. She knew she couldn't feed two children, so she left the hospital without my sister. To this day I haven't been able to find her.

"My mother died in a filthy apartment after leading an impossibly hard life. I swore to her I'd seek revenge, and I will. You were just a convenient step at getting Joseph and George's children to trust me. Once they do, I can get to their fathers, and they'll pay – they'll pay for what they put my mother through, for the loss of my sister, for the hell I endured as a child."

Damien took a breath, not backing up even the slightest as he pushed his words out through his teeth.

No. He didn't have the facts right. She knew Joseph and George. They would never be that cold-hearted.

"They would've helped your mom if she asked," Sierra said, regretting her words instantly when she saw the fire flare in his eyes.

"She went to them. She begged for their help, and they shut the door in her face, saying they wanted nothing to do with her or her bastard son," he seethed.

"That can't be true. I won't believe it," Sierra said, her own anger rising at his ill will of this family she loved.

"Believe it. The world isn't all fairy tales and pixie dust, Sierra. You need to grow up and face reality. You've signed on to help me, and if you go back on your word, I'll return you to your father and you can face his wrath," Damien threatened.

Sierra would face a thousand lashes from her father to save her friend. Even though she in no way wanted to return to the horrible man, being away from him for a few weeks had strengthened her in many ways. She still feared him, knew he'd come through on his threats and kill her if he so deemed, but for some reason, the longer she was away, the more she realized what a weak man her father truly was.

If he wanted her dead, she'd already be gone. No, death wasn't what Douglas wanted for her, he wanted her miserable. Once she stopped giving him the power over her, the thrill would be gone and he'd stop. If not, she'd rather die than live with him again.

Her mind whirled as she tried to figure out why Damien felt so hostile toward the Anderson's. If she rushed to Bree and told her everything, she wouldn't learn the rest of Damien's plan. She needed more information, what his next move would be. If he really knew these people who he thought had wronged him, he'd realized how mistaken he was. The Anderson's were truly good.

"What's the matter, Sierra? Will daddy cut you off of your colossal allowance if you displease him? He assured me you'd do whatever I want. Well, the cards are on the table – how much is your integrity worth?" he mocked.

Sierra narrowed her instantly rage filled eyes. Let him think what he wanted. She'd rather he thought she was a greedy socialite than him knowing the reality of the years of abuse she'd suffered, of how long she'd been nothing more than a weak, pathetic, beaten-down child. She'd never get the image of her father's hand rising high in the air, only to slam down on her innocent flesh, out of her head.

Maybe it was the years she'd taken care of her sister, or the countless times she'd needed rescuing and no one came, but she felt a desire to fix Damien. She had to mend the fences between him and his family. She was clueless on how she was going to do it and she had a feeling she'd despise Damien by the time it was all over, but maybe their family would be healed, and her best friend safe.

She couldn't seem to get words past her throat to either confirm or deny his accusations, but by the smile on his lips, he already knew what she'd say.

"I knew the thought of losing all that precious money would make you more cooperative. You're no better than those greedy bastards who couldn't bother to help a widow and her infant child," he snarled before his hand came up, causing her to visually flinch, though he only gripped the back of her head.

The heat of his breath brushed across her lips sending flames shooting to her core.

Sierra was repulsed at the renewed desire burning inside her. She hated him in that moment, but yet her body still yearned for his touch. She wished she could pull away, but her body wouldn't obey her mind.

His thumb traced her cheek, softly wiping a single anger filled tear making its way down her face. He brushed over her lip just as her tongue rushed out to moisten it again, the taste of salt from her tear instantly filling her mouth. His eyes dilated as she brought her tongue back inside.

"I'm not going to be used, Damien. You just said I'm nothing but a convenient step to you, yet you want me to turn over and forget all of that," Sierra said, trying to keep a clear head.

"I said that's how it started, Sierra. It's more, much more now. I can't resist you. I need you – need you more than anything else in this world right now. I...I can't explain what you're doing to me. You chase it all away."

Sierra was falling fast. She knew they were most likely just words, but they were having a strong impact on her.

"You're crowding me, Damien. I need air," Sierra said, trying with every last reserve to gain back a semblance of her sanity.

"I could be a whole lot closer, darling." Bitterness was radiating off of him in waves, and she was torn in half, trying to find the man she'd spent a week with in Australia inside this man who was so angry. She could see him masking the anger in sexual remarks and innuendos, and she didn't know how to deal with it.

As if to prove his point, he leaned in, his hips pushing against hers, leaving her with no doubt that their argument hadn't dimmed his desire. The feel of his solid erection pressing into her stomach created an instant response within Sierra.

"Point taken, you can ease back," she said, but the breathless quality of her tone bellied her words. It was obvious to both of them that she wanted him – needed him – was hungry like a wild animal. Her pheromones were practically screaming out to take her.

Without another word, he closed the gap and took her mouth in a fit of rage, passion, frustration, and something more. It was the something more that had her moaning as her arms wrapped around his neck.

Chapter Twenty-One

Damien pulled back as he tried to regain control over his body. He was frustrated. He'd just told her everything of his past, something he'd never shared. He was angry at his mother, his relatives, the pain he'd gone through. He didn't know any other way to reign in the pain other than by taking control. He had to get control, needed it more than he needed air. He had to push away the vulnerability.

As he pushed her, he noticed the flush to her skin, that her eyes were dilated. She wanted him and he had to take her, had to push away the past.

As he focused on desire, he was able to push the ill feelings away, forget about the Anderson's and revenge. Everything in him pushed him to move forward, claim her as his own and ease the pain inside.

With reckless abandonment, he swooped down and captured her lips, holding nothing back as his tongue filled her mouth, taking immediate advantage of her gaped lips to dip inside, taste her softness, ease his desire.

The flames of his desire stoked out of control, soon reaching the point of no return. His right hand gripped the back of her head, holding her tightly against him, though she gave no effort of struggling, nor a sign of even wanting to.

His other hand moved from the couch, wrapping around her hip, his fingers caressing the tight plumpness of her curvy ass, pulling her tighter against his throbbing erection, making his intentions extremely clear.

Her hands were wrapped around his shoulders, tugging him closer to her, her mouth opened wide, inviting him inside. His movements became frantic as his need for her couldn't get any greater. He couldn't wait. He needed to bury himself within her. Even though he'd already taken her only a few hours earlier, he'd dreamed of her for two weeks, his body aching, day and night. Sierra's responses mirrored his insatiable hunger.

With a groan from deep within, he tried to ease back, his mouth biting the skin on her neck and then sucking softly to soothe the intensity, ravishing each part of her. Damien's heart accelerated at the soft moan escaping her swollen lips. Her arms clung to him, refusing his attempt to try to slow their eagerness. She wouldn't allow him to stop. At this point, he couldn't stop. He *had* to finish.

The sensations of her fingers boldly moving through his hair, parting the strands as her nails dug into his scalp, was driving him insane. He licked the pulse on her neck, felt the strong beat against his tongue as he inhaled her scent of vanilla and spice, something he'd forever associate with her.

An almost primal growl escaped his throat as he continued moving downward, his lips tasting the slight vee between her breasts. He leaned back far enough to undo her shirt. When he saw the many buttons, he knew he'd never have the patience to undo them all.

"I'll replace this," he said, his voice ragged, barely recognizable.

He quickly gripped each side of her blouse, and with the smallest effort, her shirt ripped open, the tinkling sound of buttons filled the air as they ricocheted off the table and walls. Her eyes widened in sheer craving.

If anything, the aggressive ripping of her shirt seemed to send her to another level of desire. She reached for him, trying to draw his head back to hers, but he wanted to kiss her exposed breasts, barely concealed by the lacey peach bra.

He moved his head to her peaked nipple, jutting through the fabric, begging for his attention. With his mouth opened wide, he took her nipple into his mouth – bra and all – sucking it deep, her nipple on the other side of the lace.

"Yes, more!" Sierra cried out, her hands changing direction and gripping the back of his head, pulling his face into her ample breasts.

Her words fueled him on. He sucked harder on her swollen peak, wetting the delicate fabric of her bra, showing him the dark outline of her dusky pink nipples.

His hands trailed up her back, quickly unhooking the latch of her bra. He wanted to taste her skin. He lifted his head only long enough to toss the delicate garment across the room, then his head descended again, this time, to her other breast, immediately devouring it.

Her whimpers of delight and need intensified his already maxed out desire, giving him the strength to satisfy her before plunging forward and taking care of his own needs.

With an ardent touch, his hand moved downward, skillfully unclasping her pants, and pulling them to the floor. As much as he wanted to behold the exquisite display of Sierra's body in her satin panties, he wanted her naked and wet beneath him even more.

In one swift movement, he slipped off her panties, leaving her bare, vulnerable and glorious before him. His firm staff was dripping its clear fluid in anticipation, no longer able to keep it at bay. His hand paused before gliding smoothly against her silky skin, worshipping the beauty of her incredible body – soft and supple, yet firm and tight all at once. She was perfect in every single way, perfectly made for him to make love to – over, and over, and over... a perfect fit.

He dropped to his knees in front of her. Before she could utter a single protest, he kissed the top of her thigh, his tongue swirling across the quivering flesh.

"Damien…" she moaned and took a sharp inhale of breath, her legs trembling, barely holding her up.

He lifted her, setting her on the back of the couch, leaving her to balance herself as he quickly spread her thighs, her hot pink core perfectly positioned for him.

His mouth again descended, this time for an intimate kiss right at the heart of her. With a guttural growl of possession, he opened his mouth, licking with his tongue up the folds of her most sacred area. She cried out, encouraging him to continue. Damien noticed her soft skin change underneath his hands, with goose bumps surfacing everywhere, and he quickly glanced at her face, relishing in her expression of ecstasy.

Her incredible smell, taste, and heat – it was all too much. He ran his tongue across her hot pink folds, following them to the soft hood of her womanhood where he sucked her swollen pink pearl into his mouth.

With a cry of pain and pleasure, he felt Sierra shatter around him. Her body shook as wave after wave of pleasure filled her and released, again and again. With new tenderness, he sucked her flesh in and out of his mouth, drawing each cry from her, as he reveled in pleasing her.

When the last of her shudders died down, he rose on unsteady legs. He quickly discarded his clothes and protected himself, then looked into her half-closed eyes. She appeared sated, and half-awake.

He'd fix that.

With a quick movement, he pulled her from the couch and pressed his mouth back against hers.

"No, you were just kissing me…" He cut her off. She was protesting him kissing her so intimately, then kissing her lips. Tough. The thought was sending him over the edge of sanity.

"You need to taste how sexy you are. It's all I can do to not lose it–"

Her struggles ceased, and he felt her body coming back to life as his hands tugged against her hips, pulling her tightly against his manhood.

He reached down between them, inserting his fingers inside her, feeling the renewed moistness in her core, the heat practically scorching him.

She was ready, and he couldn't wait any longer.

He kissed her once more before pulling back and turning her around. He pushed his throbbing erection against the softness of her ass as his hand ran up her flat stomach, then gripped her soft breasts. Taking her hard nipples between his thumb and finger, he gently twisted them, tugging on the pink flesh.

"I need you," she cried as he leaned forward and gently nipped the skin on her neck.

"Yes, now," he agreed as he stepped forward, pushing her body over the back of the couch so her lush behind was sticking up in the air for him. With his knees, he spread her legs apart, exposing her hot pink core to him, enough to make him let it all go at just the sight.

He took a moment to fully appreciate the beauty before him, the milky white skin, with splotches of red where his mouth had tasted her, the incredible curves in every place that was meant to turn a man on. She was exquisite – and she was his.

With no more ability to wait, he guided his throbbing erection to her opening, watching as the head slid inside her, the angle of her body allowing him to see it disappear in her heat.

"Yes, more!" she demanded eagerly.

He gave her what she asked for.

With speed, he thrust all the way inside her opening, wrapping his arms fully around her, his fingers caressing her stomach, hips, breasts, and neck as he thrust his hips forward, again and again.

He lost track of who's moans were filling the air – his, hers – he didn't know. He just knew the pleasure was unending, the feel of her gripping his rod was unbelievable. He could make love to her all night long.

When he felt her start to shake around him, his movement accelerated. He knew she was close, her body getting wetter, her walls tightening around him, making movement more difficult.

With a cry of pleasure, she started shaking, her heat gripping him repeatedly as he continued pumping inside her. He thrust faster, harder, drawing out her pleasure, her cries of ecstasy going on and on. When he finally shot his release, all energy left his body at the same time, leaving him completely drained, unable to stand.

He continued pumping inside her, her pulses drawing out every last ounce of his own pleasure, gripping him, squeezing him dry.

With a final thrust, he released the last of his orgasm, then slumped against her, pushing her body into the hard back of the couch.

It didn't take long for her to squirm beneath him. Too tired to fight with her any further that night, he lifted her in his arms, and moved to the front of the couch. Relief flooded him, when she relinquished herself and allowed him to set her down.

He'd think about what he was doing later. Right then, he wanted to enjoy the extreme pleasure his body felt, and just relax, with Sierra laying right next to him. Both fell asleep, still buzzing from the incredibly intimate coupling.

Chapter Twenty-Two

Sierra was trapped. She couldn't move and panic filled her as she cringed. What was her father going to do now? She hadn't done anything. She could handle the pain if she knew it was coming, but when it came out of the blue, she wasn't prepared.

She began struggling, trying to get away. She knew it wouldn't do any good, but she had to try. She couldn't just give up and take the beating. She didn't deserve it – she'd been good. She did everything he asked of her.

"Sierra, stop. Ouch! What the hell?"

The deep voice sent her panic over the edge as she kicked her trapped legs, moved her shoulders, struggled to free herself.

"Please, I haven't done anything. Please, no more. It hurts. I can't…" Sierra sobbed, knowing her punishment would be worse, but in her sleepy delirium she couldn't stop herself. She just didn't want to be hurt.

She sobbed as her body grew weaker. She couldn't get away. He'd really hurt her now. She shouldn't have struggled.

"Sierra, wake up, you have to wake up. It's me – Damien."

Sierra tried to open her eyes, tried to rise from the nightmare, but panic was still clogging her, still keeping her under its spell. She was still trapped.

"Please..." she begged in one final attempt.

"Sierra, it's me," the voice said. It didn't fit, it was too gentle, too caring. That couldn't be her father. Hazily, Sierra pulled herself from her half-sleeping state and cracked her eyes open.

Damien was warily watching her, the lamp beside his bed casting a glow across his face, showing the concern radiating from his eyes.

"Are you okay?"

"I'm fine," she automatically replied with tightness in her voice.

"My groin begs to differ. You have one hell of a good knee," he said with a slight grimace. It took Sierra a moment to figure out what he was saying, and then it dawned on her.

"I'm so sorry," she gasped.

He was leaning over her, supporting his weight on his elbow, the blanket ridding low on his hip. When she looked down and noticed her chest fully exposed to his view, she quickly reached for the blanket, trying to tug it from underneath their bodies.

Damien gave her breasts a leisurely look before shifting and allowing her to pull the blanket clear up to her chin. She didn't know how she'd ended up in his bed. The last thing she recalled was lying down on the couch with a cup of hot chocolate and a movie playing.

"I carried you upstairs. You fell asleep before the opening credits even started," he said. It was unnerving how he always seemed to guess what she was thinking.

After they'd finished having sex, they'd fallen asleep on the couch, only for him to wake her a couple hours later with a second round, even better than the first. When she'd gotten up and tried to grab her clothes, Damien had scooped her into his arms, saying he liked her naked.

He'd then re-deposited her on the couch with a blanket, before going to the kitchen to make her hot cocoa. She'd been so comfortable she hadn't put up too much protest.

"I need to get some water," she told him, hoping he'd be a gentleman and turn away.

"I'll get it for you," he offered as he started to move.

"I need to use the bathroom, too," she said, her face immediately turning red.

"Need me to carry you?"

"No!" She felt her face go from red to burgundy. He started laughing, then flipped over on his back. As she tugged one of the blankets the rest of the way loose, her eyes glanced down and she couldn't help but notice the impressive tent his body was making of the sheet barely covering him.

Her eyes shot back to his face and his satisfied expression. How could he even think about sex after the extreme rounds they'd had not long ago.

"Don't take too long," he said with lazy indulgence.

She scooted from the bed and made a beeline for the bathroom, stopping at the sink and splashing cold water on her face to wash away the last of the terror still making her heart pound. She must have been tangled up between Damien and the blankets.

"You're okay," she promised herself in the mirror. Her heart finally slowed down as she took a long drink of cool water and gave herself a few moments to talk herself down.

She emerged from the bathroom, not sure what she should do next. She didn't think it a wise idea to climb back into Damien's bed, letting him think she was planning on jumping full on into the affair.

Her mind mocked her. She hadn't refused him yet, so what was the difference. She glanced to the bed and let out a relieved breath when she noticed he wasn't there anymore. She could sneak from the room and find a guest bedroom. With the size of his house he had to have at least three or four of them.

"I brought a snack and wine," Damien said as she reached the door only to run into him. "Where are you going?" he finished as his eyes narrowed.

"I…well…" she stumbled, feeling frustrated with herself. Just say it! "I'm going to another room," she finished stubbornly.

"No." He didn't elaborate as he placed his hand on her back and led her to his bed. She glared at him when he gave her a soft push and she landed on the bed on her behind.

"You can't just tell me no like I'm two, Damien," she said with exasperation.

"Then don't act like you're two," he said as if he was making perfect sense.

"I told you last night I don't want to jump into an affair."

"It's a bit too late for that, Sierra. Try this, it's my favorite," he offered as if they weren't having an important discussion.

"Fine, I'll try the wine if you tell me more about your vendetta," she compromised.

"You first. What were you dreaming about?" Sierra hesitated, but knew he'd keep on pushing.

"It wasn't a dream. I just…when I woke up, I couldn't…um…move, and it scared me, that's all," she said half-truthfully.

"That was more than panic over being trapped. What are you hiding, Sierra?"

"Nothing. That's what happened," she stubbornly answered.

"I don't believe you," he persisted.

"I felt like I was trapped. I panicked, end of story. Now, it's your turn to talk," she said as she sent a glare his way, letting him know she wasn't giving him anything else.

His eyes narrowed as he stared her down. A small shiver passed through her. The man really knew how to intimidate with nothing but his eyes. She firmed her resolve, though, desperate to hold onto her newfound will-power.

"What do you want to know?" he finally asked as he sat next to her and grabbed a cracker and a slice of cheese.

"Everything."

"That's a little vague, Sierra."

"You're avoiding the subject, Damien. You expect me to turn on my best friend, the only person who's always been good to me, and you're not willing to give me any details. I hate to tell you this, but you must not have any friends if you think I'd do that," she said, refusing to break their eye contact.

Instead of anger, he gave a sheepish smile. The almost unguarded expression on his face sent her heart into overdrive. Wow, he was stunning when he didn't look so angry.

"Actually, Trinity is my best friend and she'd have my hide if she knew anything about this. She's amazing."

Sierra felt the tiniest twinge of jealousy, but then she remembered that Trinity was a happily married woman. Her husband was incredibly gorgeous, too, and seemed like a nice guy. Sierra had been far too nervous on their short visit to really pay much attention, but the little she'd seen of the couple, had made it seem they were in love.

"Trinity seems like a smart woman," she said after a long pause.

"She is."

"Are you done stalling? Why do you hate the Anderson's?"

"It goes back to before I was born. My father was twenty-five years older than my mom. I know, it's a lot of years, and I wouldn't even think about dating a woman half my age, but they fell in love, according to my mom. He pursued her, and she fell hard for him. He was charming, wealthy, and promised her the moon. About the time they met, my grandfather passed away and there was a huge race for the company. It should've gone to my dad. His brother, Milton had zero interest in the corporation, and my dad had been working there for years," Damien started.

Sierra was fascinated by the intense look on his face. She still didn't understand what any of this had to do with the Anderson's, though.

"Joseph and George are twins, the only sons of Milton, my father's nephews. When my grandfather died, they both rushed home to get their greedy hands on what my father had worked so hard for. The board of directors chose Joseph to run the corporation and my father was left with nothing. His own dad didn't leave him a dime in the will. The corporation was all he had. The old man left what he had to charity's, saying the boys needed to build their own wealth, that they'd appreciate it better in the long run. Well, Milton didn't have to build his own wealth. He had a nice little ranch that his father bankrolled for him, while my father had nothing, because he'd been sure he'd take over the Anderson Corporation."

Damien's eyes narrowed as he told a story Sierra was sure he'd heard a thousand times. Sierra knew there was no way it could be true. Even a young Joseph couldn't be monster. There had to be more to the story and she was determined to find out what it was.

"Were you able to verify if all of this is true?" she asked, afraid of his reaction, but still having to ask it.

"Of course I verified. I found the old newspaper articles. There was a fight for the CEO position. In the earlier papers, apparently Joseph was playing it cool, because they said he didn't seem interested in taking over his grandfather's reign. Apparently, he'd already amassed a huge fortune. However, greedy people always want more, and Joseph was no exception."

"How do you know it was about greed? What if he wanted to run the business his grandfather put so many years into?"

"If that was the case, why did he leave in the first place? Why wouldn't he have stayed and learned how to run the business like my father had?" Damien asked with bitterness.

"Don't you think the best way to get answers to those questions is to ask Joseph?"

"Why? So he can tell me lies? The story doesn't end there. My father was so upset about his losses that he quickly went downhill, started drinking himself to death. One night he drank too much and lost control of his car. He was dead before the paramedics arrived."

"Oh, Damien, I'm so sorry," she said, sincere sadness draping her words.

"I was only a few months old at the time, and later my mother found out she was pregnant with my sister. She went to the Anderson's for help. Even though begging from anyone was against everything she believed in, she did it for my sake – mine and my sister's. She showed up at their door, and they laughed at her, told her they didn't believe her story, that they were glad my father was dead, and then they shut it in her face. She had to leave my sister in the hospital's care, and my mother lived a rough life from that moment on," he said, pain evident for the mother he'd lost at too young of an age.

Sierra could relate to how he felt. She missed her mom every day. She always imagined how differently her life would've turned out had her mom been there. She may have actually been a normal child. She'd never believe the things her father said about her. She hoped her mother was far happier wherever she was, and the only thing that kept Sierra from falling apart was knowing she'd someday see her again.

Sierra set down her empty glass of wine, surprised she drank the entire amount. It really had been good. She then wrapped her arms around Damien, not able to give him the cold shoulder when he was obviously fighting such a ferocious internal battle.

"I'm fine," he said, not letting his walls down, but he didn't push her away. She took that as a good sign.

"What do you plan to do?" This time he didn't try and pretend he didn't know what she was taking about.

"I've already started. The Anderson's have a lot of different divisions to their vast empire. I've been working for years to take away the one thing that matters to them – their income. They have several shipping yards throughout the world, so I'm building my own shipping company. I'll supply the same products at a lower cost, taking away their business. If they have a mall in a city, I'll build a larger, better one with lower rents. Every market they're invested in, I'll come behind and undercut them. In the process, it will most likely break me, too, but I don't care. I've lived with nothing before, and I can live that way again."

"I think you're making a mistake. I know them, Damien. They aren't anything like my father. They're good people. If you'd just talk to them –"

"No! You have no idea what you're talking about," he interrupted.

Sierra didn't know what else to say. Her heart was broken at his internal turmoil and she felt like she was being torn in half between him and her loyalties to Bree and the Anderson's. She knew without a doubt that she was falling for him, and she also knew they had no chance of a future together. He was too angry, too set on revenge, and the people he wanted to hurt were the people she loved most in the world.

With a lump in her throat, Sierra lay back down. She didn't feel like fighting with him anymore that night. She knew if she tried to get up, he'd just drag her back. Hopefully, if she just turned over and went to sleep, he'd leave her alone, let her have time to think.

She was grateful when the light went out and she felt him shift behind her. His arm wrapped around her waist and pulled her tightly against his body.

"I have to do this," he said, almost a plea in his voice.

"No, Damien, you don't. What you should do is learn the truth," she said, her own voice sounding defeated.

It seemed she was destined to go from one battle zone to the next. Sierra was grateful when she felt herself beginning to drift to sleep. She'd start fresh the next day.

Chapter Twenty-Three

Sierra watched Damien walk into the room and her mouth literally fell open. He was beyond simply stunning, he was one-hundred-percent mouthwatering in his custom made tux which fit him to perfection.

She couldn't take her eyes off the man as he stopped and chatted with various people as he made his way across the large ballroom floor.

They were at a fundraiser for the Red Cross, raising funds to help the military troops during the upcoming season. On one hand she was thrilled to be there, loving fundraisers, and how much money could be raised in a single night. The money that meant little to nothing to the wealthy donors, fed soldiers, supplied their families while they were away, and for the unfortunate many, buried them properly.

A sense of dread filled her, though, because she knew her father would be in attendance. She hadn't wanted to come alone, but Damien had been called away at the last minute to one of his local factories, so he'd sent her ahead.

She smiled when she thought about the day before. She didn't know how it had happened, but she'd been living with him for about a month, ever since that first night in his home. He'd changed. He hadn't brought up his vendetta against the Anderson's. The way he spoke to her, the many simple things he did, like bringing her flowers when they were apart and always opening doors for her, was securing him tightly into her heart.

As she gazed at him, she knew she was in love – hopelessly, infectiously in love with him. She could tell he was starting to feel the same way about her. She did her job each day and then made love to him each night.

For the past month, Damien had put Sierra to work. Literally. She'd complained he wasn't giving her a job – well, now she was almost as busy as him. She was more than pleased when she discovered she was actually quite good at being his P.R. Rep.

She handled clients, organized meetings, and typed endless amounts of letters. One thing she discovered about Damien was that he was generous to a fault. He donated far more than what would look good for him on taxes. He personally handled most of the donations, never refusing anyone who called.

Some of the clients received smaller donations, one or two thousand dollars. Some of the amounts he gave were staggering, in the seven figure range. She found the man she'd met who'd been seeking revenge, and the man she was falling in love with were two completely different people.

They'd traveled a few more times to various places, none as far away as Australia, but still beautiful locations. He had a stunning vineyard in California. She didn't understand why he chose to live in Seattle when he could live in Napa Valley, where it was warmer, gorgeous, and he already had a home waiting for him on the edge of his ten-thousand acre estate.

She'd enjoyed their three night stay there, strolling through the rows of grapes, talking with the workers, and drinking too much wine.

She'd found she was quite limber when she had a couple of glasses of wine in her. Damien had seemed to enjoy that immensely. Her smile grew at the fond memory.

"Don't you look mighty happy."

Sierra froze at the all too familiar sarcastic voice of her father. She'd been so focused on Damien, she hadn't even noticed the man who'd terrorized her nearly her entire life, approaching. She concentrated on putting on her mask before turning to him.

"Hello, Father," she said formally.

"I'm surprised you remember who I am since I haven't heard from you once. I've tried getting in contact but your old number is turned off and Damien's security is tighter than mine. Come with me," he commanded as he tightly gripped her arm and dragged her through one of the many terrace doors to a dimly lit patio. He moved to the edge, ensuring more privacy.

The evening was almost bitterly cold, with a light drizzle filling the air. The small area had a roof but it didn't offer much protection. Sierra could tell her father felt the place allowed him privacy, as no one else would be foolish enough to venture to one of the balconies without a heater.

"I shouldn't be gone long, Dad, I'm working tonight," Sierra said as she pushed down the ever present fear of being in her father's presence. She was angry that he was able to invoke the emotion after being away from him for months. She'd felt she had made such great progress on her new independence, too.

"You'll stay as long as I want you to. Have you forgotten who I am! Just because you have a new man in your life doesn't mean jack to me. I can yank you back to my house anytime I feel like it," he snarled as his fingers tightened around her arm.

Years of abuse welled up inside her, until she was boiling. She was sick of his threats, sick of his abuse. She was done. She'd much rather he carried out his threat and killed her than for her to ever live under his roof again. Damien had told her about the deal he'd made. She'd been sickened that her father had basically sold her, but she was also grateful for it. The time away from him, her growth as a woman, and falling in love with Damien had all added up to her no longer being that cowering little girl in the corner.

"No, Douglas, I haven't forgotten anything. The many years of your fist smashing into my face, the threats, the accusations, the slander against my mother, all of it is still fresh in my mind! Do you want to know something, though? I really don't care whether you want to know or not, because I'm going to tell you. I've had enough. I'm not afraid of you anymore. You can't control me. After this little meeting, I never want to speak to you again. You're a miserable man who compensates for short-comings by threatening and harming others. You treat your employees like crap, and what you've done to me is criminal. Release my arm this minute or I'll –"

"You'll what, Sierra!" he interrupted her before lifting his hand and slapping her so hard across the face she became dizzy. She shook her head, trying to clear it, planning on fighting him back for the first time ever. She didn't care if she lost. She'd get a few good kicks in, at least.

Before she could react, though, he was thrown back from her. Her head finally cleared and she looked down, seeing her father lying on the cold floor with blood oozing from his nose as he released a stream of swear words.

She looked up and saw Damien gazing at her, his eyes flashing with fury. He lifted his hand and she flinched, not knowing why, he'd never done anything to harm her – but that look in his eyes was frightening.

"I'm so sorry, Sierra. He should've never been allowed to do that," he whispered as his hand gently caressed her cheek. His fingers shook as they held her face, his eyes still stormed, but his tone was gentle, pained.

"It's not your fault," she whispered as the first tear fell.

"I should've put the puzzle together by now. I knew something was wrong, that your life wasn't what I'd first assumed, but I never thought he was abusing you. I should have figured it out because my mom did the same to me. I, above anyone, should've seen the signs. It's just a part of my life I've blocked out."

His confession shocked her. Even though she'd grown up with an abusive parent, she had a hard time comprehending how anyone who was supposed to be your biggest protector could instead be your worst nightmare. A parent's hands were supposed to be strong, caring, and lift you up, not strike you down and inspire fear.

Douglas had his handkerchief in hand as he attempted to wipe up the blood still oozing from his nose. He was making feeble attempts at standing. She was so focused on Damien she barely noticed her pathetic father.

"Oh, Damien, I'm sorry you went through that," Sierra said as she wrapped her arms around him. How could he want to avenge a parent who'd hurt him so badly.

"I'll make you pay for this, Whitfield, just you wait," Douglas spluttered as he finally managed to rise to his feet.

"You'll leave this porch, and then continue out the front doors. If I ever see you come anywhere near Sierra again, I'll bankrupt what little you have left and make sure you spend the rest of your life on the streets. You've already proven you're an untrustworthy business partner; it wouldn't even take more than a phone call. Make the choice, Monroe," Damien said, never letting go of his grip on Sierra.

Her father looked at her in shock, then back at Damien before he scurried off like the rat he was. Sierra wanted to fall to her knees, thanking Damien. She had a feeling that her father was truly out of her life for good.

"Thank you," she offered as her sobs began. She couldn't say anything more than that.

Damien held her, brushing the back of her head with his hand, making gentle hushing sounds. Sierra couldn't believe what had just happened and that Damien had come to her rescue. All her life she'd wished for someone to deliver her. It was almost too much of a fairytale to believe. As her sobs subsided, Damien led her back inside, straight to a private restroom where he washed away her tears. Her cheek was red with a slight bruise beginning to form. Out of old habits, she always carried thick cover up to mask her father's abuse. She grabbed the compact and applied it, and only upon close inspection would a person see the results of her father's hand.

"Do you want to go home?" he asked.

"No. I want to forget all about Douglas Monroe and just focus on the fundraiser.

With that, Damien gave her a gentle kiss and led her back to the ballroom where the party was in full-swing. A couple hours passed and Sierra forgot about her worries and started enjoying herself.

Damien disappeared with a group of men who wanted to discuss business, promising he'd come back soon. Sierra wandered around, looking at the items up for auction. She found a beautiful sculpture and decided to bid.

"Are you seriously going to outbid me, Sierra Monroe!"

Sierra finished filling out the bidding paperwork, then turned with a huge smile on her face.

"Every chance I get," she responded before she leaned forward and gave her best friend a hug.

"Well, I was buying it for you anyway. The second I saw the figurine, it reminded me of our weekend in Canada. That was when I knew we'd be friends the rest of our lives. When you abandoned me on the dance floor with three guys trying to get down my pants –"

"I was drunk, and I've apologized a million times," Sierra said with a laugh.

"Okay, I guess I can forgive you, but really, that weekend was one of the most fun times I've ever had. I honestly did know I wanted to be friends forever after that trip," Bree said.

"Bree, I have to talk to you," Sierra told her as her eyes welled. She'd put it off because she didn't want to betray either of them, but if Damien did actually follow through on his threats, and Bree was harmed, Sierra could never forgive herself.

Sierra also knew that once the Anderson's found out that Damien was their lost relative, they'd embrace him with open arms. He needed them – he just had to realize that. The first step was talking to Bree.

"What is it? You've turned as white as a ghost. Let's go sit down," Bree said as she took charge, like she always did. Their friendship had worked on so many levels because Bree had been the only person, until Damien, capable of bringing Sierra out of her shell, allowing her to have fun without guilt.

Bree led her to a quiet den and before Sierra could lose her nerve she told her the whole story of how Damien was her relative and what he thought had happened, and what he planned to do.

"I love him, Bree, *really* love him, and I don't want to betray him, but I could never betray you, either, because I love you. I've been so torn over this whole situation or I would've come to you sooner," Sierra said. She was so afraid Bree would be disappointed in her.

"Hey, stop that! You've done nothing wrong. Don't feel guilt over it. I can't believe Damien is Neilson's son. Seriously. Not very long ago, remember me telling you about my Aunt Katherine telling us the story of how she and Joseph met. She also told us about Neilson. Damien's got it all wrong. His mother wasn't rejected. She showed up on the front porch, yes, and Aunt Katherine was there all alone. She invited her in, fed her, and gave her a bed. The next morning when she went to find her, she was gone. They searched for years, until they finally had to accept she didn't want to be found," Bree said.

"I don't know if he'll believe you, Bree."

"We'll make him believe – he's family." Right there was why Sierra loved Bree so much. She didn't focus on the fact that Damien wanted to destroy them, take away everything they had. She focused on the happiness of finding a lost relative she never thought she'd find. "I have to tell my dad. Come on," Bree said with excitement as she pulled Sierra to her feet and the two of them rushed from the room.

Chapter Twenty-Four

Damien's eyes scanned the crowd for the twentieth time in twenty minutes. He hadn't seen Sierra since she'd been looking over the auction items, and he was getting ready to seek her out. He knew he didn't have to be with her twenty-four-seven, but he was concerned her father may have snuck back in. There was strong security present, but still, he felt better having her in his site.

He excused himself from the conversation, then turned around to find Joseph and George Anderson approaching. Years of hatred brewed instantly to life as he eyed the men walking so casually toward him.

This is what you want, he reminded himself as they neared. *You want them to feel safe around you.* In reality, he'd nearly forgotten all about his vendetta against them during the last few months. Something inside him was shifting the longer he was with Sierra. She was so full of life, and filled his days with laughter and his nights with unbelievable passion. She was changing him, though he wasn't sure he wanted to change.

"Hello, Damien," Joseph said as the two men stopped in front of him. Damien was surprised for a moment that Joseph was acting so casual with him. Normally, people speaking for the first time had the courtesy to use last names.

"Joseph," Damien replied, his voice coming out a little too cold.

"We're very happy to meet you. Would you like to come with us – there's something we'd like to discuss that I think would be much better done in private," Joseph said.

Damien's mind whirled as he wondered if they'd somehow found out about his plans. He'd been very careful. He didn't want them knowing until it was too late for them to do anything about it. He felt confident as he nodded his head and followed the men through the crowd.

He was a little annoyed at how people seemed to part for both of them as if they were royalty. If the men and women in the room knew who they truly were, they wouldn't act with such deference to them. They didn't deserve it.

Joseph stepped into a private office with George on his heels, and Damien, taking a deep breath, followed. He stopped in the doorway when he saw the other occupants. His eyes narrowed when they connected with Sierra.

As he looked at the faces around him, Joseph, George, Lucas, Trenton, Bree, Sierra, and a couple people he didn't recognize, his stomach turned.

She'd told them. Sierra had betrayed him. His heart felt like it was shattering inside him. He'd felt like she was special, like she truly cared about him. The evidence was clear. Her loyalties were with his enemies.

"I can see by your face that you're upset, Damien, but to my brother and I, this is a happy day. We've searched for you for years, tried countless times to find you. Your mother came to my Katherine with you wrapped in a blanket, resting in her arms. She was only there one night, and in the morning she was gone. We were unable to track you down," Joseph said.

Damien looked at him incredulously. The man was a hell of an actor; Damien would have to give him that. Lies! It was all lies. His mother had told him the truth. They'd killed his father and then thrown out a woman in need. Only monsters did that.

"That's a great story, Joseph, but we both know it's nothing but fabrication. I've always been right here. If you'd truly wanted to find me, you would have. With your limitless fortune and resources, nothing you want can be out of reach. My mother told me the truth. By the look in Bree's face, over there, it looks like Ms. Monroe has already told her everything, so I don't really see a need for this farce of a reunion to continue," Damien said as he glanced for a brief moment at Sierra.

What little color she had left in her face washed away and her expression fell, but he hardened himself against her. She'd betrayed him – he had no use for her anymore.

"Damien, please, I have proof. Your mother left a toy at our home. Katherine saved it. It has the initials D.W. on it, but we didn't know what that stood for. Your father married her under a fake name, giving you a false identity. We had no idea how to find you, what your mother's name was, let alone yours. The only clue we had was the toy," Joseph said.

Damien shifted on his feet. The man made so much sense – but no, he was lying. He had to be lying. There was no way his mother carried that much bitterness around inside her unless her story was true. He couldn't' believe Joseph's story because then it made his mother into a monster.

"I'm done here," Damien said, his emotions churning. He had to get out of the room. He turned on his heel and started walking away. He needed some air.

"Damien, wait!" Damien paused in the hallway as he slowly turned, his face giving nothing away.

"What do you want?" he asked Sierra, his voice cold enough to freeze the hall.

"I…I'm sorry. I was trying to do what was right. I know you're upset right now, but if you'd just listen, you'll see they really are good peo –"

"Stop. I don't care. I don't want to have anything to do with them. I already know who they are and they're the type to take and take until there's nothing left to take any more. I thought I knew who you were. I was wrong. You're fired. Notify my secretary of your address and I'll have your belongings delivered."

"But...Damien," she gasped, tears spilling over as he gave her one last look. He didn't give her a chance to finish whatever she was going to say. He simply turned and walked away.

Chapter Twenty-Five

"Why do people choose to do this over and over again? I don't understand how they can bare it," Sierra said, her voice quiet, her body almost numb. She hadn't seen Damien in two weeks. The first week she'd cried so often, her face had looked like a white Oompa Loompa from *Charlie and the Chocolate Factory*.

Finally, the tears had stopped and a deep sense of numbness had set in, thankfully. She didn't smile, didn't cry, she just sort of existed.

"I promise it will get better. I know this answer sucks, but just give it some time. He'll come around, you'll see. You know what, though, if he stays away then he just doesn't deserve you because he's a fool. Don't give up on love. People fall in love over and over because we're meant to be with someone, meant to have a happily-ever-after. We aren't solitary creatures. We need a companion, someone to care for us. You will have that, either with Damien or another very lucky guy. Whoever wins you has won the lottery," Bree said.

"You have to say that, Bree. Thanks anyway, though. I need to get out for a while. I've stayed in here feeling sorry for myself for long enough. I'm through with love forever, but I do need to get a life. I have job hunting to do."

"You can take as long as you want. I love having you stay with me. I've been trying to get you to do it forever. Before you start working full-time again, we've got to have some play time, please?" Bree begged, a smile on her face.

Sierra could see Bree was trying her hardest to act positive, but she knew her best friend, and knew she was worried. She needed to quit stressing Bree out. She had enough on her plate with her son Mathew and her ever-growing family.

"I'll be fine, Bree, and I'll spend as much time with you as possible, but I really want to work. I miss Damien, but I miss my job, too. I enjoyed working for him. I hope to find something similar to that. I'll just make sure my boss is ugly and old. There's no way I'm working for a hot guy again," Sierra vowed.

"They're not that easy to hide from. I *so* wasn't looking for love when my brothers decided I needed a personal bodyguard, but I'm thankful every night I lay down beside him. Don't give up – love is worth the pain you have to go through sometimes to reach your happy ending."

"I truly envy you right now, not enough to hate you, just enough to steal your husband," Sierra joked.

"You don't even know how those words are music to my ears. I'd loan him to you, but then I'd have to kill you, and I love you too much to do that," Bree gave right back.

"All right, I guess I won't flirt shamelessly with him. I can't promise not to gaze at his incredible chest when we're all swimming, though."

"Deal," Bree said as she laughed. "Don't worry, I'd be doing the same if the situation were reversed. When Chad comes in from a long run, and his chest is gleaming, I become an animal. I don't think I'll ever get enough of that man!"

"Okay, Bree, Damien introduced me to the most earth-shattering, phenomenal feelings in the world, and then took it away. I *so* don't want to hear about your amazing sex life," Sierra said, but she smiled to take the sting from her words.

"You started it," Bree pouted. "How about we go shopping? That will get you out of the house."

"That sounds perfect. I have a quick errand I have to run first, so why don't I do that and then pick you up here in one hour?" Sierra asked.

"That's great. It'll give me enough time to shower and change. Mathew decided it would be funny to spill his breakfast all over mommy instead of eating any of it," Bree replied pointing at the dried milk on her shirt.

"I wondered what that awful smell was…" Sierra joked.

Bree left to get ready and Sierra walked downstairs, climbed in the borrowed car, and started driving to her father's home. There was one employee still working there, a maid, who Sierra had befriended. The girl had begged Sierra to get away, threatening to turn her father in, but Sierra had finally managed to convince her that he'd just make her go away and Sierra would lose her friend if that happened, so Mara had agreed to keep silent.

Sierra realized she'd left her ornaments behind. It was a tradition for her mother to buy the girls a new Christmas ornament each year, and Sierra had to have them. Mara had told her that her father was away for the entire day in business meetings, so Sierra should be safe to run in and out. She knew if she asked her dad for them, he'd just destroy the irreplaceable treasures. She couldn't let that happen.

Mara opened the gate for her and Sierra parked up front. She wanted to get in and out as quickly as possible, not taking any chances of running into her father.

"Sierra, I've missed you," Mara said as she flew down the steps.

"I've missed you, too. As a matter-of-fact, Bree told me she's looking for a new maid. Hers got pregnant and is moving in two weeks. The position comes with room and board," Sierra told her.

"Really?"

"Yes."

Mara gave her another hug, obviously excited to get away from Douglas Monroe.

"Let's hurry and find your treasures so you can leave here. I don't want to take any chances on your father returning early," Mara said as she looked around.

"I agree. Go finish cleaning so you don't get in trouble. I'll tell Bree you want the job. You can leave here in two short weeks. I can't wait to visit with you again."

"You're right. I'm already behind schedule. I'll see you soon, my friend." Mara quickly left and Sierra made her way to the stairs. The decorations were in the attic.

When she reached the top of the landing, terror momentarily paralyzed her.

"You do realize I have all the calls made to and from here monitored, don't you?" Her father was standing before her.

Panic filled her as fight or flight kicked in. She didn't know which direction to run, she just knew she had to get away. The stairs – that would be her quickest escape route. She turned and took a step when she felt his foot in the small of her back.

She desperately tried to regain her balance, but it was a losing battle. With horror flashing through her, Sierra went flying down the stairs. She felt a shooting pain in her leg before everything went dark.

∞∞∞∞

Damien took a drink of coffee as he prepared his briefcase. He was utterly exhausted, not having slept more than a couple hours a night since he'd broken it off with Sierra.

He missed her.

Refusing to cave into even himself, he guzzled the rest of the hot liquid and grabbed his keys. She was the one in the wrong, not him. She'd betrayed him.

He opened his front door, barely catching himself from stumbling backward.

"You miserable, rotten bastard!"

"What the hell." Bree poked him hard in the chest, her short but sharp fingernail almost tearing through his shirt.

"Sierra is lying in the hospital right now, black and blue, three broken bones, and a partial concussion all because of you!" Bree yelled as she poked him again.

It took several seconds for her words to compute in Damien's brain. Sierra was at the hospital? He needed information. In his worry, he forgot Bree was the enemy.

"What happened? My fault? How? Why? Is she going to be okay?"

"No, she's not. She'll never be okay again because you've ripped her heart out into a million pieces and then stomped on those just to make sure there was no chance of her healing," Bree snarled.

"Did she try to kill herself?" Damien asked in horror, all color leaving his face at the thought.

"Of course not, you moron! Sierra would never do something like that. What I meant was that her father nearly killed her, but that doesn't compare to the devastation you've put her through. She has to want to get better in order to survive; otherwise the slightest infection can sneak up on her and take her life. Right now, she's so miserable because she's in love with you and you tossed her aside like yesterday's news, so she's not trying hard enough. She doesn't feel like she has anything to live for anymore…"

Bree choked on her final words as tears welled in her eyes. Damien was horrified. Was Sierra really in love with him? She couldn't be, because she never would've betrayed him if she was.

"Where is she?"

"You don't need to go there and upset her all over again. I swear if you hurt her again, you'll have to deal with me!" Bree threatened.

Damien looked at the petite girl before him, not standing more than a couple inches over five feet, weighing less than half of him, and he realized she actually thought she could harm him. The thought was so absurd it made him smile, which was apparently the wrong move on his part. He jumped when the heel of her shoe slammed down on his foot.

"Damn!" he shouted as his toe began to throb. She knew how to aim those things. He glared down at her.

"Do *not* laugh at me, Damien Whitfield. You may think that me and my family are horrible people, but we love each other more than you could ever comprehend. I consider Sierra my family, and I swear I can take you out if you so much as make one more of her tears fall," she roared.

Damien almost staggered again as the realization hit him that he liked her, he actually liked this woman he'd thought of as his enemy for so many years. He fought the warm feelings building inside toward her, but he couldn't stop it.

"Let's go," he said, his voice gruff.

"What?" It was Bree's turn to be confused.

"You obviously aren't going to tell me where she's located, so you'll just have to drive me there," he commanded as he locked his door and swiftly walked down the stone steps. He eyed her small convertible with suspicion as he glanced at the open roof and the grey sky.

Oh well, nothing like living on the edge, he thought as he maneuvered his large body into the small passenger seat. He suddenly had sympathy for sardines.

"I didn't invite you in my car," she said as she eyed him with suspicion.

"Well, too bad. You'll just have to deal with it because I'm going to see Sierra." He crossed his arms as he waited for her to make her decision.

With a roll of her eyes she finally climbed in, then gave him an evil smile before she threw the car into gear and pealed out of his driveway.

Damien grabbed the door handle, thinking he may have been a bit too rash in his decision to ride with the woman. She was obviously insane. He tried to yell for her to slow down, but as their speed picked up and she wove around traffic on the busy Seattle freeway, his words were carried away by the self-made wind.

He said a prayer for the first time in his life.

They arrived at the hospital and Damien really hoped his legs would hold him up. He hadn't been that frightened since he was a young boy. As he touched solid ground again, he looked over at Bree with her ridiculous Cheshire grin. His respect went up another notch, dang it.

"Just remember, Whitfield, you've been warned," were her parting words before she preceded him into the hospital.

Damien had no trouble keeping up with her as she moved through the hallways of the vast hospital. She stopped in front of a closed door, sent him a final warning with her eyes, then slowly turned the knob and walked inside.

Damien was stunned silent by the sight of Sierra. There were wires coming from seemingly everywhere, and a machine next to her with consistent monitoring beeps coming from it. Her face. Her poor face. Her right eye was bruised and swollen, and a scrape ran across her chin. The rest of her body was covered, but he almost didn't want to know what it looked like.

"Her leg was broken, and she has two cracked ribs. The leg happened on the stairs. To the paramedics who came, it looked like the bruise on her side indicated someone had kicked her – hard."

"I'm going to kill him," Damien said, his voice quiet, but deadly truth lying behind his words.

"Not something a man who doesn't care would do," Bree taunted him.

He glared at her before moving to Sierra's bed. It was his fault. He knew Douglas was a horrible man and he was under no disillusions that parents were always perfect. Though his mother had beaten him regularly, it was never to this severity. Looking at Sierra, he thought he'd had it pretty good.

Before he knew what he was doing, he lifted his hand and gently brushed her hair back. Her eyes fluttered as they slowly came open.

She looked at him with a sweet smile as if they were waking up on any ordinary day.

"Morning," she mumbled, then flinched as she tried to move.

"Don't move," he warned.

Her eyes widened as she slightly shook her head, then looked around. Damien felt his heart clench as he watched the sweet smile disappear as reality set in. She looked back to him, and he saw her trying to mask her emotions, too weak to pull it off.

"What are you doing here?" she asked with a little hoarseness in her voice, while looking past him at Bree.

"Bree picked me up," he said. He didn't know what he was doing there.

"You hate her, though," she rasped in confusion.

"Thanks, Sierra," Bree mockingly said, but with humor.

"Yeah, well, she's kind of stubborn," he answered with a sheepish grin. "She has a hell of a stomp, too."

Sierra looked between the two of them in shock as they both smiled. He couldn't explain it to her because he couldn't explain it to himself.

"He shouldn't mock me when I'm being serious," Bree countered.

"Yes, I'll be sure not to do that next time."

"Next time?" Sierra asked with hope. Damien looked at her, surprise radiating from him. She was lying in a hospital bed with broken bones, her body bruised, her future uncertain, and what she was most concerned about was his relationship with Bree.

He turned to Bree and looked at her with new eyes. Could his mother have lied to him? How could a monster inspire such loyalty, such love? He thought back to everything he'd found on the Anderson's. All of it contradicted what his mother had said, but he didn't want to believe that.

He couldn't.

"Sierra, are you feeling any better?" Joseph asked as he walked in the room with a giant bouquet of flowers, balloons and a stuffed animal.

"Yes, Joseph, much better, thank you. You really shouldn't have gotten me this room, though. I was fine in the other one," Sierra answered softly.

"Of course we weren't leaving you in that room. I'm so sorry your father would dare do this to you. If he wasn't already in jail, I'd go give him an ass kicking right now," George said as he bent down and kissed her forehead. "I have a couple friends on that force, maybe they can sneak me in," he added with hope.

"No you won't George Anderson, and before you even think it, neither will any of the boys. You won't stoop to that man's level by getting in a brawl. He won't ever come near Sierra again. Now, quit talking about him or you're going to upset Sierra," Esther, George's wife, said as she walked in behind him.

George's shoulders slumped as if he was really disappointed he didn't get to go give a whooping to the man.

"Thank you, George. Your concern means the world to me," Sierra said as a tear fell. George bent down and tenderly hugged her before stepping away, giving Esther a turn.

Damien turned to Bree and mouthed, *it wasn't me*, while pointing at his eye and implying the fresh tear from Sierra. He enjoyed the way Bree's eyes opened in surprise at the joke. He was starting to realize Bree just may take him down if he made her best friend cry again. The love and affection was overwhelming in the room and though it was a foreign family sensation, Damien loved being a part of it.

"Damien, I brought this with me. It's yours so you should have it back," Joseph said as he stepped beside him and placed a small toy in his hand. When he looked down and noticed the faded D.W carved in the bottom of the wooden rocking horse, he felt a lump form in his throat.

"I'm not ready," he said, his voice a bit gravely.

"Take all the time you need. All we ask is that you give us a chance," Joseph said, respecting Damien's need for space.

"I need to think. You focus on getting better, Sierra. I need you better. I'm so sorry I was such a jerk. I've really missed you…," Damien said as he reached down and reassuringly squeezed her hand. She nodded as her eyes grew watery, but no tears fell, thankfully.

He wanted to lean down and kiss her, but it was too much right then. Without saying anything more, he gripped the small rocking horse in his hand and walked from the room.

Chapter Twenty-Six

"I'm sorry, Mom, but you let me down. You lied to me my entire life, preventing me from having a family who loves me, and you almost cost me everything. You did cost me years – many years of happiness. You used your hands as punishment, you cut me down, and still, I loved you. I tried my best to honor you. What I've come to realize in the last three months is that you didn't deserve my honor or respect. I won't come back here again. What you did to me was unforgiveable. I hope you've found happiness wherever you are, I truly do, but I'm done with your burdens."

Damien stood over his mother's grave, a solitary flower in his hand. He'd come to say goodbye. For the last three months, he'd slowly gotten to know the men he'd vowed to harm, the cousins he'd thought were so evil. He found them the opposite of everything he'd ever believed. They were kind and caring, and he actually had a lot in common with them when he let go of the bitterness.

His mother had been wrong. He'd never know why she'd made up the lies she did, never understand how she could deliberately try to damage her son so deeply, but he had to let it go. There was nothing he could do about the past. He did, though, have control of his future.

A pang hit his heart as he thought of his future. He'd tried speaking with Sierra a couple weeks after she'd gotten out of the hospital, but she'd told him he needed time to bond with his new family – he needed time to heal.

He missed her. In a few short months, she'd shown him so much more than he ever thought he deserved. Her passion for life, her unguarded love, when in all rights she should've been even more bitter than he was. She had a natural light about her that drew people in, and he wasn't immune. He wanted so much to be with her.

With new resolve, he turned, determined to make her listen to reason. They were meant to be together. As he looked up, his mouth lifted in a sad smile.

"I thought you could use a shoulder to lean on."

"More than you know," he said as he fought back his emotions.

Trinity wrapped him in a hug and he leaned on his best friend, grateful she was there.

"I figured you'd be here. You always visit on her birthday, though I'm glad you finally realize she doesn't deserve it. I'm sorry, Damien, I'm so sorry for what you went through. I'm sorry she was such a bitter, cruel woman. I'm so impressed with the man you've turned into. That's all because of you, because of what's in your heart. You've chosen to be a good man even though you have every right to hate the world," Trinity said as she cried in his arms.

Damien smiled as he attempted to comfort Trinity. He thought it amusing she was so bad at staying strong. Her greatest appeal, in his opinion, was how she had the softest heart of anyone he knew.

"What would I do without you in my life, Trinity?"

"You'd fall to pieces. Speaking of which, I should ring your neck. I can't believe your harebrained scheme, and what you were planning on doing. The only thing saving you right now is that you realized you were being a fool," she said as she pulled back to give him a watery glare.

"I knew all along how stupid I was being, which is why I didn't share my plans. I didn't want to face you – you're the epitome of goodness. I'm starting to love them, Trinity. Joseph is so full of life, his voice could wake the dead. George is just as stubborn and willful as his brother, but he's quieter, more the comforter. My cousins, wow, I don't even know where to start with them. I have to say I truly enjoy Bree. She's hell on wheels and so loyal. You should've seen her when she was protecting Sierra." Damien smiled with affection.

"I know the Anderson's a little as my husband and his brothers do business with them on various jobs, but I'm looking forward to getting to know them a lot more now that they're your family."

"You know, you'll always be my family, right? I wouldn't have made it this far in life had I not met you. I'm so glad I have you."

"I feel the same way, Damien. We'll stick together no matter what," Trinity said as she instantly forgave him for being a fool.

"I need to see Sierra," he told her as she wrapped her arm in his and they began walking back to their cars.

"Yes you do, but don't be an idiot. Tell her you love her, buy her a million roses, and beg her on bended knee for forgiveness. Don't just demand she submit to your will," Trinity warned.

"Ah, you really know how to wound my pride. I don't crawl, Trin," he said with a pucker between his brows.

"Then you don't love her enough, Damien," Trinity said, stopping to look him in the eye.

Damien thought about her words. He did love Sierra – even enough to crawl. The realization was staggering as he stood rooted to the spot with Trinity giving him time to sort out his emotions.

"She'll be at the Anderson's party tonight," she said.

"I guess I'd better go and get ready for a dance then," he said as a smile took over his face. He wasn't willing to take no for an answer this time, even if he did have to ignore Trinity's advice and carry Sierra from the room over his shoulder. That thought actually excited him.

"Should I be worried? You two always seem to have your arms around each other," Drew said as he stepped out of the car he'd been in while waiting for his wife.

"Of course you should be worried. I had her first," Damien goaded Drew before bending and kissing Trinity on the cheek.

"Now you realize I'm going to have to defend my honor and challenge you to a duel," Drew told him.

"Anytime, anywhere, Titan," Damien said before the two men laughed.

"If you brawny men are finished, there's a party tonight we all have to get ready for," Trinity said as she let go of Damien and walked over to her husband.

Damien watched the two of them drive off before he got in his own car. The wheels in his head slowly started turning as he made plans for the evening.

∞∞∞∞

Sierra stepped inside the Anderson mansion, nervous as she looked around the familiar ballroom. She'd been inside Joseph and Katherine's home a few times with Bree, but she knew Damien would be at the party, and she didn't think she was ready to see him yet.

Even though it had been three months, and six days since their last brief moment together in the hospital, her heart still hadn't healed. She received regular updates from Bree and was very happy Damien was getting to know his relatives. She truly wished him a happy life. He deserved it after everything he'd been through.

A small part of her insisted she deserved happiness, as well, but she pushed that down. She'd someday find her own path. She just had to find the will to get over Damien and move on with her life.

"You're late. I thought I was going to have to drag you here, Sierra," Bree said with exasperation.

"I'm only a half hour late, and that's actually on time for one of your Uncle's parties, because it takes him two hours to greet everyone before anything actually begins," Sierra replied with a smile.

"You are certainly correct," Bree said as she led Sierra into the room.

There had to be a couple hundred people there, all dressed to perfection. Sierra was wearing a new dress she felt confident in. She was working for a small marketing company, making a great salary, and had spent the entire afternoon shopping for the perfect dress. She tried to convince herself she was doing it solely for her own pleasure and not because she knew Damien would be in attendance.

She'd told herself repeatedly that she'd be polite if they ran into each other, offer him well-wishes, then confidently sashay in the opposite direction. She didn't want him thinking she was pining over him after three months.

The music started and couples began filling the enormous dance floor. Sierra's stomach tightened as her gaze roamed the room. There was no sign of Damien anywhere. She told herself that was a good thing.

"Would you care to dance?" a gentleman asked as he approached.

"That would be lovely," she responded as she followed him to the center of the dance floor. One dance let into several others as she was asked by different strangers, and a few acquaintances she recognized from other functions.

When the song, *You Are So Beautiful*, came on and a man asked her to dance, she paused as her throat clogged with tears. It was the first song she'd danced to with Damien when she'd been slowly falling in love with him. He'd glided across the floor with her, her feet barely touching the ground as his hands caressed her back.

She couldn't accept the man's invitation; the song was much too personal for her. Before she had a chance to reply, he was interrupted.

"She's already taken for this dance."

Sierra looked up into Damien's intense face, his features so familiar, so stunningly handsome. He was wearing his tux, looking even better than she remembered. Her breath hitched as her body reacted. She felt herself wanting to fall into his arms.

Without giving her a chance to refuse him, he pulled her into his arms and started moving in a slow circle, his hands positioned on her hips, his fingers caressing the sensitive dent of her back. Goosebumps appeared on her skin as his breath whispered across her face and he looked into her eyes, his own filled with intensity. The room faded away until it became just the two of them, the sound of the music guiding them along.

When he started singing the words of the song while still looking deep in her eyes, her knees nearly buckled. She'd done so well at convincing herself she was healing, and in the matter of a few moments, she was falling over a cliff – ready to crash in a heap she'd never be able to stand up from.

The song ended and the room grew quiet as Joseph walked to the stage and stood gazing out at the crowd with a microphone in his hand. He spotted Damien and smiled.

"As you all know, we have much to celebrate with the spring of a new year upon us. My long lost nephew has been found, and we're so pleased to have him as a part of our family. He's been in Seattle the whole time, but circumstances kept us from each other. Because of a beautiful young woman in the crowd, we connected and have spent the last few months getting to know each other. It's been a joy and filled this old heart of mine with overwhelming happiness. Whenever I think my life can't possibly get any greater than it already has, our family is blessed with even more," Joseph said.

Sierra felt tears sting her eyes as she listened to the joy and pride in Joseph's voice.

"I'll be back," Damien whispered before he released her and moved toward the stage.

Sierra decided not to stick around. She couldn't bear any more that night and still have any of her heart left intact. Before she was able to make a retreat she was caged in. She looked up to find Damien's best friend, Trinity on one side of her, and Bree on the other.

"I need to use the restroom," Sierra told them in a desperate attempt at escape.

"It can wait," the two women said in unison before they looked at each other and giggled. Damien approached the stage with confidence and gave Joseph a hug before he turned to the crowd. His eyes scanned the room before settling on Sierra.

"I've made many mistakes in life. I don't regret them, because they've shaped me into the man I am now, however, I wish I wouldn't have been such a fool for so many years. My best friend gave me some beautiful advice, of which I took some, and ignored the rest," he said as he sent a wink toward Trinity.

"It gets better," Trinity whispered to Sierra who looked at her with confusion. What was she talking about?

"You see, I've done many foolish things in my life, held grudges that weren't warranted, sought revenge that wasn't called for, and the most ludicrous of all, let the woman I love escape." Damien's gaze connected with hers and she looked back with uncertainty and…hope.

He wouldn't be so cruel to say those things about another woman, so maybe…" she was afraid to even think the thoughts.

The room started to stir as people shifted. Sierra was so focused on Damien she didn't notice the men and women coming toward her. She was suddenly lifted into the air and placed in a chair which was then picked up, as the group of men carried her to Damien.

"I've only loved one other person my entire life, and she saved me when I was a child. I've only ever been in love once, and you saved me as a man. Please forgive my foolishness, my faults, and my insensitivities. I can't live in a world where you're not by my side – I'm just a shell of a man without you in my life."

Sierra's convoy placed her on the stage and she was quickly pulled into Damien's arms. Tears streamed down her cheeks as she looked into his eyes, the truth of his words shining from him.

"Damien –"

"Wait, there's more," he said as he placed his finger over her mouth.

There was a collective gasp as dozens of people stepped forward, each with a bucket filled with different colored rose petals. They filled the stage with the fragrant pieces, creating a romantic bed of color.

"Take a seat," he told her before he helped her sit, and then walked off the stage. The crowd parted and there was a stage in the center of the room with a microphone and guitar.

Sierra looked at the men standing along the back of the stage, it was all the Anderson and Titan men, dressed to the nines, looking amazing as they gazed back at her and winked.

Damien joined them, then picked up the guitar. She watched in awe as music started drifting through the room and he stepped up to the microphone and began singing, *I Won't Give Up by Jason Mraz.*

When he sang the lyrics speaking of sunrises and never giving up on their love, tears began streaming down her face. When the men behind him joined in on the chorus, some of their voices off-key, some singing beautifully, she was sobbing.

At the end of the song, he set the guitar down and walked to her, pulling a small box from his pocket as he knelt on the bed of rose petals.

"I won't ever give up on our love again. You are my sun, moon, and stars. You're everything to me. I don't want to live a life without you beside me.

Please, marry me, Sierra, take away my worst regret and let me show you what you mean to me every day for the rest of our lives and beyond."

There was no doubt what her answer would be. She'd never imagined loving someone so greatly, never thought a man would love her so much. His hands trembled in front of her as he held out the opened velvet box with a simple solitaire surrounded by beautiful diamonds on either side.

"Yes, Damien, oh yes," she whispered, and he slipped the ring on her finger, a perfect fit.
Sierra didn't notice the applause from the crowd, or the tears in her new family's eyes. She noticed nothing but the love in Damien's beautiful face…and it was all for her.

Epilogue
One Year later

"You realize this wedding killed my uncle a little bit, don't you?" Bree said as she stood next to Sierra.

"Yes, I know, but it's what I wanted. I think it turned out perfectly. I did give him free reign on the reception, which I'm thinking wasn't the wisest idea. I figured I'd be safe seeing as we're on a secluded island. I should've known better."

"Yes, you should have. He has zero qualms about flying five-hundred people here. You're lucky it was only a hundred. I have to say I'm very happy they're all gone and it gets to just be family now. Has Damien told you where you're going for your honeymoon, yet?"

"Yes, he's taking me back to where it all began. We fly out tomorrow for Australia."

"Yea, now that you know, I can tell you that Chad and I are joining you there in a week, along with my brothers, and cousins. Trinity and her family are coming, too," Bree said with enthusiasm.

"Bree, I don't know how I ever got so lucky as to have met you, but thank you for being in my life. I will love you forever," Sierra said, getting choked up for the hundredth time that day.

"I love you, too."

"Girl time is over. I've got dibs on my wife," Damien said as he wrapped his arms around her.

"Mmm, claim away," she told him as she reached up and kissed him. Neither of them noticed Bree slipping away.

"Thank you for inviting Bree and the rest of the family to join us."

"I knew it would make you happy. I promised you I would bring you nothing but joy the rest of our lives, and I intend to keep that promise," he said before bending to kiss her again.

"How do you feel about children?"

"I've already told you I'll have a dozen if you'll let me get away with it," he said before nuzzling her neck.

"Why don't we start with just one for now," she said with a laugh.

"Sounds good to me. Let's get started right now," he said as he scooped her into his arms and started heading toward their secluded cabin which Katherine and Esther had stocked up for them.

"I expect you to make love to me all night long, but there's no need to create a child. I'm four weeks along," she told him, waiting for it to sink in. When her words registered, Damien's face grinned with pleasure as he looked into her eyes.

"I love you, Sierra Whitfield, and I will the rest of my life. Thank you for giving me a second chance, and not giving up on me. Thank you for carrying my child. Let's go start our lives together," he said quietly.

"Damien, my life started the day you walked into my father's office."

Damien carried her inside and showed her many times over how much he loved her. He kept his promise to make her happy and continued expressing his love for many years to come.

ABOUT THE AUTHOR

Melody Anne is the author of the popular series, Billionaire Bachelors, and Baby for the Billionaire. She also has a Young Adult Series in high demand; Midnight Fire and Midnight Moon - Rise of the Dark Angel with a third book in the works called Midnight Storm.

As an aspiring author, she wrote for years, then became published in 2011. Holding a Bachelor's Degree in business, she loves to write about strong, powerful, businessmen and the corporate world.

When Melody isn't writing, she cultivates strong bonds with her family and relatives and enjoys time spent with them as well as her friends, and beloved pets. A country girl at heart, she loves the small town and strong community she lives in and is involved in many community projects.

See Melody's Website at: www.melodyanne.com. She makes it a point to respond to all her fans. You can also join her on facebook at: www.facebook.com/authormelodyanne, or at twitter: @authmelodyanne.

She looks forward to hearing from you and thanks you for your continued interest in her stories.

Printed in Great Britain
by Amazon.co.uk, Ltd.,
Marston Gate.